Texts in Philosophy
Volume 3

Monsters and Philosophy

Volume 1
Knowledge and Belief
Jaakko Hintikka

Volume 2
Probability and Inference: Essays in Honour of Henry E. Kyburg
Bill Harper and Greg Wheeler, eds

Volume 3
Monsters and Philosophy
Charles T. Wolfe, ed.

Texts in Philosophy Series Editors
Vincent F. Hendricks   vincent@ruc.dk
John Symons   jsymons@utep.edu

Monsters
and
Philosophy

edited by

Charles T. Wolfe

© Individual author and College Publications 2005. All rights reserved.

ISBN 1-904987-30-3
Published by College Publications
Scientific Directors: Dov Gabbay, Vincent F. Hendricks and John Symons
Managing Director: Jane Spurr
Department of Computer Science
King's College London
Strand, London WC2R 2LS, UK

http://www.collegepublications.co.uk

Cover design by Richard Fraser, www.avalonarts.co.uk

The original image used on the cover is from Ulisse Aldrovandi's *Monstrorum Historia* (Bologna, 1642), printed with the permission of the Bibliothèque Interuniversitaire de Médecine, Paris.

Printed by Lightning Source, Milton Keynes, UK

All rights reserved. No part of this publication may be reproduced, stored in a retrieval system or transmitted, in any form, or by any means, electronic, mechanical, photocopying, recording or otherwise, without prior permission, in writing, from the publisher.

CONTENTS

List of Contributors — iii

Acknowledgments — vii

List of Abbreviations — ix

Introduction — xi
Charles T. Wolfe

The Riddle of the Sphinx: Aristotle, Penelope, and Empedocles — 1
Johannes Fritsche

Science as a Cure for Fear: The Status of Monsters in Lucretius — 21
Morgan Meis

Nature and its Monsters During the Renaissance: Montaigne and Vanini — 37
Tristan Dagron

Conjoined Twins and the Limits of our Reason — 61
Annie Bitbol-Hespériès

Degeneration and Hybridism in the Early Modern Species Debate: Towards the Philosophical Roots of the Creation-Evolution Controversy — 109
Justin E. H. Smith

Leibniz on the Unicorn and Various other Curiosities — 131
Roger Ariew

The Creativity of God and the Order of Nature: 153
Anatomizing Monsters in the Early Eighteenth Century
Anita Guerrini

The Status of Anomalies in the Philosophy of Diderot 169
Annie Ibrahim

The Materialist Denial of Monsters 187
Charles T. Wolfe

Cerebral Assymetry, Monstrosities and Hegel. 205
On the Situation of the Life Sciences in 1800
Michael Hagner

The Lady Knight of the Perilous Place 217
Elfriede Jelinek

Monster: More than a Word... From Portent to Anomaly, 231
the Extraordinary Career of Monsters
Beate Ochsner

Index 281

List of Contributors

IN ALPHABETICAL ORDER

Roger Ariew is Professor and Chair, Department of Philosophy, University of South Florida. He is the author of *Descartes and the Last Scholastics* (Ithaca: Cornell University Press, 1999) and co-author of *Historical Dictionary of Descartes and Cartesian Philosophy* (Lanham: Scarecrow Press, 2003); he has recently published editions and translations of Descartes, *Philosophical Essays and Correspondence* (Indianapolis: Hackett, 2000), Leibniz and Clarke, *Correspondence* (Indianapolis: Hackett, 2000), Montaigne, *Apology for Raymond Sebond* (Indianapolis: Hackett, 2003), and Pascal, *Pensées* (Indianapolis: Hackett, 2005). His present research concerns Cartesian philosophy in the second half of the seventeenth century.

Annie Bitbol-Hespériès is the author of *Le principe de vie chez Descartes* (Paris: Vrin, 1990) and produced the critical edition of Descartes' *Le Monde* including the treatise on man (*L'Homme*) (Paris: Seuil, 1996). She recently prepared a large multimedia exhibition, "Les Monstres à la Renaissance et à l'âge classique," for the Bibliothèque Interuniversitaire de Médecine in Paris.

Tristan Dagron is Chargé de Recherches at the Centre National de la Recherche Scientifique (Lyon). He is the author of *Unité de l'être et dialectique : l'idée de philosophie naturelle chez Giordano Bruno* (Paris: Vrin, 1999), and co-edited (with Hélène Védrine) *Mondes, formes et société selon Giordano Bruno* (Paris: Vrin, 2003). He recently produced the critical editions with French translations of John Toland's *Letters to Serena* (*Lettres à Serena et autres textes* [Paris: Honoré Champion, 2004]) and *Christianity Not Mysterious* (*Le christianisme sans mystères* [Paris: Honoré Champion, 2005]).

Johannes Fritsche teaches philosophy in the Institut für Philosophie, Wissenschaftstheorie, Wissenschafts- und Technikgeschichte of the Technisches Universität Berlin. He is the author of *Methode und Beweisziel im ersten Buch der Physikvorlesung des Aristoteles* (Frankfurt: Anton Hain, 1986) and *Historical Destiny and National Socialism in Heidegger's Being and Time* (Berkeley: University of California Press, 1999), as well as many essays on Greek and contemporary philosophy.

Anita Guerrini is a Professor in the Departments of History and Environmental Studies at the University of California, Santa Barbara. Her books include *Natural History and the New World* (American Philosophical Society, 1986) and *Experimenting with Humans and Animals: From Galen to Animal Rights* (Baltimore: Johns Hopkins, 2003), and she is the author of many essays on anatomy, natural history and physiology in the eighteenth century.

Michael Hagner holds a Chair in Science Studies at the Swiss Federal Institute of Technology, Zürich. He is the author of *Homo cerebralis. Der Wandel vom Seelenorgan zum Gehirn* (Frankfurt: Insel, 2000) and *Geniale Gehirne. Zur Geschichte der Elitegehirnforschung* (Göttingen: Wallstein, 2004), among other books, and has edited collections such as *Der falsche Körper. Beiträge zu einer Geschichte der Monstrositäten* (Göttingen: Wallstein, 1995), *Ansichten der Wissenschaftsgeschichte* (Frankfurt: Fischer, 2001), and most recently *Einstein on the Beach. Der Physiker als Phänomen* (Frankfurt: Fischer, 2005).

Annie Ibrahim is Professeur agrégé de philosophie at the Lycée Chaptal in Paris as well as Directeur de Programme at the Collège International de Philosophie. She published *Le vocabulaire de Diderot* (Paris: Ellipses, 2002) as well as many essays in the field of seventeenth and eighteenth-century philosophy of the life sciences and metaphysics, focusing primarily on Diderot, with more recent studies on Buffon, Maupertuis, Epicureanism, Leibniz, and Descartes. She recently edited the collection entitled *Diderot et la question de la forme* (Paris: PUF, 1999) and *Qu'est-ce qu'un monstre?* (Paris: PUF, 2005).

Elfriede Jelinek is a novelist, playwright and essayist in Vienna. Among her works available in English are: *Lust, Women as Lovers, The Piano Teacher* (all published by Serpent's Tail Press); the latter work was recently adapted for cinema by Michaël Haneke. Recent dramatic works include the series "Der Tod und das Mädchen" and the political play "Bambiland" (2003). Jelinek received the Nobel Prize for Literature in 2004.

Morgan Meis is an Instructor in Greek and Latin at the Graduate Faculty, New School for Social Research, Senior Consulting Editor of the *Graduate Faculty Philosophy Journal*, and founder of the Flux Factory in Queens, New York, where he co-edits the *Old Town Review*.

Beate Ochsner is Assistant Professor in the Department of Romance Literature of the Universität Mannheim. Her PhD thesis dealt with the 19th-century French author Charles Nodier (*Charles Nodier. Digressionen* [Heidelberg: Winter, 1998]). Her Habilitationsschrift, *DeMONSTRAtion. On the representation of monsters and the monstrous in literature, photography and film* (München: Synchron, forthcoming) examined particular media representations of the monster in 19th-century French literature (Hugo, Huysmans) and photography (Charcot, Virchow), as well as in Tod Browning's film "Freaks." Her research interests concern literature in Romance languages (e.g. *Jarry: Le Monstre 1900* [Aachen: Shaker, 2002]), and media theory, in which she worked on the phenomenon of the cinematic serial killer, the theory of intermediality (*Intermediale. Kommunikative Konstellationen zwischen Medien*, Tübingen, 2001), the relation between medium and memory (*Medium und Gedächtnis*, Frankfurt, 2004), and different aspects of Italian cinema.

Justin E. H. Smith is Assistant Professor of Philosophy at Concordia University in Montréal. He is the editor of *The Problem of Animal Generation in Early Modern Philosophy* (Cambridge: Cambridge University Press, 2005), and has published numerous articles on Leibniz and his contemporaries. He is currently at work on a book on the problem of biological species in late 17th-century natural philosophy.

Charles T. Wolfe is Research Fellow at the Center for Philosophy and History of Science at Boston University. He edited *The Renewal of Materialism* (*Graduate Faculty Philosophy Journal* 22:1, 2000), and (with Ubaldo Fadini & Antonio Negri), *Desiderio del Mostro. Dal Circo al Laboratorio alla Politica* (Rome: Manifestolibri, 2001), and has published several articles on eighteenth-century materialism and the life sciences, as well as the identity theory of brain and mind, and concepts of organism; his next project is editing a special issue of *Science in Context* on medical vitalism and materialism. He is also an editor of the Paris-based journal *Multitudes*.

Acknowledgements

The original idea of assembling a collection of essays on monsters was suggested to me by Morgan Meis, in response to my earlier enthusiasm for the topic.[1] But the collection would never have come together, after fits and starts, if it were not for the support of John Symons. My thanks also goes to the translators, Stacey Dagron, Lynn Niizawa, Justin E.H. Smith (together with Michael Seifried), and Nicolas de Warren; to Alexandre Métraux for his inspiration over the years; to Badr El Fekkak and Fabrice Stroun for their advice; to Jérôme Massard for his brilliant visual contribution, and to Annie Bitbol-Hespériès for her assistance in obtaining the cover illustration, for which the Bibliothèque Interuniversitaire de Médecine at the University of Paris V-René Descartes graciously gave permission. Brill Academic Publishers (Leiden) also kindly allowed the reprinting of Roger Ariew's essay. Jane Spurr at King's College helped a great deal with the difficult, unseen stages of producing this book. In addition, I gratefully acknowledge the assistance I received from the Center for Philosophy and History of Science at Boston University.

Lastly, but most significantly in personal terms, I thank Suzanne Wolfe-Martin and Gal Kober for all their affection and support, and hope that some of it is reflected in these monsters.

---

[1] For instance, in my "Matérialisme et monstres," *Chimères* 31 (Paris, 1997).

List of Abbreviations

George-Louis-Leclerc de Buffon, *Histoire naturelle, générale et particulière*, 15 vols. (Paris: Imprimerie Royale, 1749-1767) (*HN*)

René Descartes, *Œuvres*, eds. C. Adam & P. Tannery, 11 vols. (Paris: Vrin, 1964-1974) (AT)

_____ *Philosophical Writings*, eds. J. Cottingham, R. Stoothoff & D. Murdoch, 3 vols. (Cambridge: Cambridge University Press, 1985-1991) (CSM)

Denis Diderot, *Œuvres complètes*, eds. H. Dieckmann, J. Proust & J. Varloot (Paris: Hermann, 1975-) (DPV)

_____ *Œuvres*, ed. L. Versini, vol. 1: *Philosophie* (Paris: R. Laffont, coll. "Bouquins," 1994) (V)

_____ *Correspondance*, ed. G. Roth (Paris: Éditions de Minuit, 1955-1961) (*Corr.*) *Encyclopédie de Diderot et d'Alembert*, 35 vols. (Paris: Briasson, 1751-1780; reprint, Stuttgart/Bad Cannstatt: Frommann-Holzboog, 1966) (quoted by article title in small capitals); *Supplément à l'Encyclopédie*, 4 vols. (Amsterdam: M.-M. Rey, 1777) (*Suppl.*)

Gottfried Wilhelm Leibniz, *Die philosophischen Schriften*, ed. G.J. Gerhardt (Berlin, 1875-1890; reprint, Hildesheim: G. Olms, 1978) (G)

John Locke, *An Essay Concerning Human Understanding* (1690, 5th ed. 1701), ed. P. Nidditch (Oxford: Oxford University Press, 1975) (quoted directly by book, chapter and paragraph number)

Nicolas Malebranche, *Œuvres complètes*, ed. G. Rodis-Lewis (Paris: Vrin, 1962) (quoted as OC followed by volume and page number)

Introduction
CHARLES T. WOLFE

> The old world is dying away, and the new world struggles to come forth: now is the time of monsters.
> – attributed to Antonio Gramsci.[1]

Why should philosophy be concerned with monsters? If this term referred solely to mythical figures such as griffins, gorgons or chimeras, that is, creatures of our imagination, they would be the object of philosophical inquiries into the faculties of the mind and their productions, and by extension, the demarcation between reason, madness and myth. But if we actually open a work of early modern philosophy[2] – by Michel de Montaigne, Francis Bacon, Nicolas Malebranche, John Locke or Gottfried Wilhelm Leibniz, to name a few – without a predetermined sense of what we are looking for (such as the usual, mildly anachronistic topics: the theory of ideas, the status of experiments, or perhaps the defense of a 'position' on substance, causality and the like), we will be struck by the presence of a different kind of monster: hairy men, "Changelings," "Drills,"[3] conjoined twins or even children bearing on their faces the marks of objects their mothers had coveted.

At the heart of early modern metaphysics, as already (but differently) in Aristotle, we find a concern with Nature 'missing its target' and producing non-viable forms, a concern in which metaphysical considerations of genus, form and essence, necessity and accident collide with emerging

---

[1] This quotation is often found in French versions of Gramsci; the *Quaderni del carcere*, ed. V. Gerratana (Torino: Einaudi, 1975), III, § 34, do not speak of "monsters" but of "the most varied morbid phenomena."

[2] Katharine Park and Lorraine Daston, in their *Wonders and the Order of Nature* (New York: Zone Books, 1998), describe just such an experience as graduate students in a philosophy course: monsters seemed to loom larger than other, 'classical' contents of their reading assignments.

[3] Changelings and drills abound in Locke's *Essay Concerning Human Understanding*, ed. P. Nidditch (Oxford: Oxford University Press, 1975), particularly book III, chapter vi, "Of the Names of Substances," and book IV, chapter iv, "Of the Reality of Knowledge."

biological science, producing what one might call an 'ontology of the biological world'. Are these anomalies a threat to order itself? "Where do anomalies end and monstrosities begin?"[4] In order to answer this question, philosophy has to enter into the fray of debates on form, species, and the mechanisms of generation themselves. As Jean Céard pointed out in his study of monsters in the Renaissance,[5] most classic treatises on generation in that period devoted a chapter to monsters.[6] This may be because accidents in the course of generation, such as the development of the embryo, call into question basic intuitions about organic life as a source of order.[7] Indeed, such accidents challenge the idea of Nature as something regular and law-like – as a source of order, a cosmos. As the young Darwin put it, "If all forms freely crossed, nature would be a chaos."[8] But of course, inasmuch as these anomalies seem to cross species boundaries, from the wolf-man to the monk-calf (*Munchkalb*), they also threaten our sense of what it is to be *human*, as appears in this remark by the sixteenth-century traveler and essayist Pierre Boaistuau:

> I remember that St. Augustine, in his book *The City of God*, makes mention of sundry monsters or strange forms, found in deserts or elsewhere, whereupon grew a question, whether they were descended of the first man Adam, or had a reasonable soul or not...[9]

Since our judgment about what constitutes a "strange form" or an extreme case of hairiness or deformity is of course dependent on our perception, there has been a long tradition of approaching the problem of monsters from the viewpoint of 'philosophical anthropology', focusing on our perception

---

[4]Louis Guinard, *Précis de tératologie: anomalies et monstruosités chez l'homme et chez les animaux* (Paris: J.-B. Baillière, 1893), p. 5.

[5]Céard, *La nature et les prodiges: l'insolite au XVIe siècle en France* (1977; 2nd edition, Geneva: Droz / Paris: Champion, 1996).

[6]Chapter 5 (out of 6) of Jacob Rueff's *De conceptu et generatione hominis* (1554) is devoted to all forms of 'teratogenic' development of the embryo; Ambroise Paré's famous *Des monstres et des prodiges* is actually the sequel of an earlier work, *De la génération de l'homme* (they occupy books 25 and 24, respectively, of his *Œuvres* [Paris: Brion, 1628]).

[7]Georges Canguilhem, "La monstruosité et le monstrueux," in *La connaissance de la vie* (Paris: Vrin, 2nd revised edition, 1992), p. 171.

[8]Charles Darwin, "1842 Sketch. On Selection under Domestication, Natural Selection, and Organic Beings in the Wild State," in *On Evolution*, eds. T.F. Glick & D. Kohn (Indianapolis: Hackett, 1996), p. 94.

[9]Boaistuau, *Certaine secrete wonders of nature : containing a description of sundry strange things, seming monstrous in our eyes and iudgement, bicause we are not priuie to the reasons of them : gathered out of diuers learned authors as well Greeke as Latine, sacred as prophane*, trans. E. Fenton (London: H. Bynneman, 1569), p. 111v.

of normality and abnormality, and usually revealing that it is constructed (socially, historically, culturally) or structured according to polarities (symbolic, psychoanalytic, etc.). This approach can be said to have its first 'patient' in Aristotle, who infamously declared that even a child who does not resemble its parents is already a kind of monster, closely followed by 'woman' as 'the monster of man'.[10] It informs many of the interesting works on monsters that have appeared in recent years.[11] But the approach taken here is neither a study of myth, or of perception, nor even of 'moral monstrosity', despite the relevance the latter might have to philosophical inquiry. This will become clearer if I specify how this project came to be. It did not begin with the contemplation of gargoyles on the façade of a cathedral, a painting such as Hieronymus Bosch's "Garden of Earthly Delights," or a disturbing anatomical collection like Peter the Great's Kunstkammer, his chamber of curiosities in St. Petersburg. Rather, it began with an interest in materialist thought in the French Enlightenment, and the realization that this episode, particularly Diderot's masterpiece, *D'Alembert's Dream* (c. 1769), was permeated with monsters, in its drive to 'apprehend' the emerging biological sciences – a drive which had a pronounced polemical and radical dimension.[12]

Rather than just being 'naturalized' away, monsters seemed to be stubbornly present in this philosophical episode, whether as transitional figures on the way to a 'positive science' of teratology – as in Fontenelle's comment that monsters, which were hitherto regarded as "games of nature" (*lusus naturæ*), must now be considered as part and parcel of 'serious Nature' with its rules and regularities[13] – or as a more metaphysical challenge of the sort glimpsed by Darwin, and flaunted by Lucretius and his Enlightenment avatar, Diderot:

But since Substance is One, why are Forms so various?[14]

---

[10] Aristotle, *Generation of Animals* IV.3, 767 b; see Johannes Fritsche's essay "The Riddle of the Sphinx" in this volume.
[11] Notably Claude-Claire Kappler's *Monstres, démons et merveilles à la fin du Moyen Age* (Paris: Payot, 2nd edition, 1999).
[12] The work of Alexandre Métraux and Annie Ibrahim, and discussions I have been privileged to have with them, strengthened this realization.
[13] Fontenelle, *Histoire de l'Académie des Sciences de Paris* (1703), p. 28.
[14] Gustave Flaubert, *La tentation de saint Antoine*, ch, 7, in *Œuvres complètes*, vol. 4 (Paris: Louis Conard, 1910), p. 187. This passage is discussed with a different emphasis in the opening chapter of David Williams' *Deformed Discourse. The Monster in Medieval Thought* (Toronto: McGill-Queens University Press, 1999).

Most of the essays in this volume focus on the answers that have been given to this question, in different ways, with

- the reaffirmation of norms over and against the apparent multiplicity and anarchic production of forms (Johannes Fritsche on Aristotle, Michael Hagner on nineteenth-century biological science in Germany);

- the recognition that our judgments about normality and order might turn out to be hollow (Tristan Dagron on the Renaissance destruction of the Augustinian worldview, Justin E.H. Smith on early modern species debates, Annie Ibrahim and myself on radical Enlightenment thought);

- the emphasis on the inextricability of anatomical and metaphysical questions (Annie Bitbol-Hespériès' discussion of the rich conceptual 'network' within which debates on conjoined twins took place at the Académie Royale des Sciences, Roger Ariew on Leibniz's inclusion of various oddities in his scientific project, Anita Guerrini on scientific analyses of monsters in learned societies in the mid-eighteenth century), or lastly,

- the concern with our own identity as beings in perpetual conflict with monsters (Morgan Meis on Lucretius, and Elfriede Jelinek on the "Alien" film series and beyond).

In addition, Beate Ochsner provides a more synoptic view, with her reconstruction of the 'word-history' of 'monster', which is also a conceptual investigation.

Considering the centrality of some of the figures discussed – Aristotle, Augustine, Montaigne, Locke, Leibniz and Diderot cannot be dismissed as cataloguers of anatomical wonders, like Gesner, Paré or Liceti – it may not be unreasonable to hope that the pairing of 'monsters' and 'philosophy' might shed new light on the history of the latter, no longer understood as a solitary, *a priori* enterprise, but as a more collective, more *engagé* contribution to the enterprise of deciphering the secrets of Nature.

The Riddle of the Sphinx: Aristotle, Penelope, and Empedocles

JOHANNES FRITSCHE

ABSTRACT. Aristotle develops his theory on monsters at the end of his biological writings. I examine his epistemological and ontological assumptions in order to relate Aristotle's biology to the Greek 'life-world', and discuss in that context his relation to some pre-Socratic philosophers, notably Empedocles. I argue that Aristotle's theory of monsters amounts to the ontologization and absolutification of the Greek conviction of his time, that it was the fabricating and tool- and slave-using animal that had cleansed the world of monsters. In closing, I relate the issue to two Christian dogmas.

Aristotle develops his theory on monsters at the end of his biological writings. To spell out its presuppositions I present, to the degree necessary, (1) some of his epistemological and ontological assumptions, (2) his theory of principles in the *Physics*, (3) the basics of his biological research, and (4) his own distinction between his ontology and biology on one side and assumptions of pre-Socratic philosophers on the other. Thereafter, I (5) relate Aristotle's biology to the Greek life-world, so to speak, (6) return to the issue of Aristotle and pre-Socratic philosophers and discuss for that purpose (7) Empedocles and (8) some similarities and differences between Hesiod, Empedocles, and Aristotle. (9) In sum, Aristotle's theory on monsters is, as it were, the ontologization and absolutification of the conviction of the Greek societies at his time that it was the fabricating and tool- and slave-using animal that had cleansed the world of monsters. Finally, I (10) relate the issue to two Christian dogmas.

1

At the beginning of Book II of his *Posterior Analytics* — the authoritative text, in Western philosophy, on the notion of science until the beginning of modernity two thousand years later — Aristotle maintains that every piece of knowledge we seek is of either of four types. For instance, we seek whether or not the sun is eclipsed; if we find out, or know from the start, that it is, we seek the cause of this fact. Or, we seek if a goat-stag or a god is or is not, and if we know that the thing in question exists, we seek what it is; that is, we ask for its definition, for an account of its essence (*Post. Anal.* II.1, 89 b 21-35). In types 1 and 2, one is dealing with possible states of things of whose existence one is sure while, in types 3 and 4, the very existence of things with possible states is at stake.

It has often been pointed out that the different projects of many of the early Greek philosophers had one thing in common, namely, to develop a notion of nature according to which the natural phenomena can be explained through natural laws. Whatever natural laws are and whichever natural laws one assumes to hold — they exclude the gods as agents in nature. Animals such as goat-stags belonged to all the myths with gods that "the many" believed in. Thus, it is not by chance that the question of existence and gods and goat-stags as examples occur in Aristotle's typology of questions. Emerging philosophy and science forced one to reflect on one's notions and recognize that very precious ones did not signify anything, or that they signified something rather different from what one had thought. Zeus did not exist; alternatively, he was the law of condensation and rarefaction that brought about the world and held it together, or he was the unmoved mover. This was the first and dramatic display of the basic 'nihilism' of philosophy and science that, later on, became known as Ockham's razor: less is more; seek for the explanation with the minimal amount of entities, or kinds of entities, as explanatory ones and cut out the others!

But so far humans have indeed assumed the existence of goat-stags and gods. Are humans systematically hallucinating animals? Are they subject to a blind mechanism of imagination that encloses them in a horizon of notions and ideas that have little or nothing in common with reality? Or, are their sense organs such that they always give a false or imaginary idea of reality? In which way does it matter whether the ideas humans have about reality are false or not? In the *Theaetetus* and the *Sophist*, Plato gave the answer for the Platonism and Aristotelianism to come, and it was a relief for a naïve and realistic common-sense perspective. Our inborn or empirically acquired ideas of things are not false. It is only our capacity, and need, of combining different ideas in sentences that can bring about falsehood and non-being. There are no goat-stags. However, there are goats and stags, and the monstrosity of the goat-stag results from combining the features of different things in one and the same thing. In other words, no matter how strange one's mental universe looks, there is reality in it, and one can find this reality.

In the history of Western philosophy, the basic statement about reality itself as well as an efficient broom to cleanse one's mind on one's way to reality has been the law of non-contradiction, namely, that nothing is at the same time and regarding the same aspect a as well as non-a. Plato has formulated this law (*Republic* 436 b), and Aristotle tried in a long series of arguments to show its validity (*Metaphysics* IV.3-6, 1005 a 19-1011 b 22). This law allows one to reject as false and impossible entire theories and things such as square circles and triangles with four angles. However, does the notion of an animal with the head of a goat and the body of a stag include a logical contradiction? Is it logically impossible that there ever was, is, or will be such thing? In fact, many interpreters say that, according to Aristotle's *Posterior Analytics*, science aims at analytic statements. As will become clear in what follows, I side with those for whom, in the natural sciences at least, Aristotle is talking about, not a logical, but a functional necessity that ties a feature — say, the upright posture of humans — to the definition, or essence, of the respective beings, in this case of humans. This functional necessity follows from his theory of principles of natural and artificial bodies, which he has developed, on the most general level, in *Physics* I-IV.

2

After introductory remarks and a critique of Parmenides and Melissus (*Phys.* I.1-3), he examines theories of other philosophers to conclude that each change involves either two or three principles (I.4-6). According to his own theory (I.7), in every kind of change there is something — the underlying subject or matter — that is present at the beginning, throughout, and after the end of the change; in cases of the coming into existence of things, for instance the wood and the stones as the matter of a house, and in cases of the change of already existing things — the so called accidental changes — for instance the table which was red but is now green. Thus, in a change the underlying subject acquires a shape, a form, that it did not have at the beginning of the change. While in some kinds of accidental changes the state of the matter at the beginning of a change — for instance, the red color — is a being and a form in itself, in others and in every coming into existence of a plant or an animal it is not, but rather nothing but the absence of the form that will be present at the end of the change. Before being assembled as a house, the pieces of wood and stone that lie around on the construction site are not informed by a being and a form that would disappear with the arrival of the form house. Similarly, according to Aristotle female menstruation is the matter of the coming into existence of an animal, and the form in this matter at the end of the coming into existence is brought about through the male seed (*On Generation of Animals* I.2, 716 a 2ff., I.17ff., 721 b 30ff., II.1ff., 731 b 18ff.). Before being inseminated, female menstruation of, say, a female human is not characterized by a form, say pig-ness, that is repelled by the form human-being brought about through the male seed.[1]

Thus, change is the acquisition (or, in corruption, loss) of a form by an underlying subject. Every change requires a cause, something that initiates it, often called the efficient cause. In *Physics* II, Aristotle rules out all the answers given by other philosophers and maintains that a change in which something acquires the form x can have as its efficient cause only a different individual in which there is the same form x. It is the famous formula that man procreates man (II.7, 198 a 26f.). If a specimen of female menstruation acquires the form human-being, this change can have been initiated only by an individual in which the form human-being was already present, the male parent. Similarly, if pieces of wood and stone acquire the form of this bridge, there must be an individual in which this form is already present, the architect, with the plan of the bridge in his head, who directs the workers who, in turn, move the wood and the stones such that, after some time, there is this bridge.[2]

As has often been noted and already many of Aristotle's examples in his *Physics* and his biological works show, his theory of principles is formulated from the viewpoint of craftsmanship, or handicraft-production.[3] Every craftsman has an idea, or form, of the product that he wants to produce, and he needs some material on which to work and in which to realize

---

[1] In other words, there are only two (and not three) principles involved in the genesis of an animal (see Johannes Fritsche, *Methode und Beweisziel im ersten Buch der "Physikvorlesung" des Aristoteles* [Frankfurt am Main: Hain, 1986], pp. 93ff.). Teaching under the shadow of the Counter-Reformation and the religious wars Mastrius and Bellutus found a comparison that, in a way, nicely illustrates what is at stake in the question of the number of principles: the two opposed forms are like two armies that fight over one and the same city as the underlying subject; if, however, there is the underlying subject and just one form, it is as though in kind of a pre-stabilized harmony the army holding the city moves out without any fight when the other army approaches the city and moves in (B. Mastrius de Meldula and B. Bellutus, *Cursus philosophiae ad mentem Scoti integer II [Physica]* [Venice, 1678], p. 152 D).

[2] On the definition of nature in *Physics* II.1 and the entire Book II see Johannes Fritsche, *Methode und Beweisziel*, pp. 71ff., and *idem*, *Nature, Science, Logic, and Politics in Aristotle and the Western Tradition* (in preparation).

[3] As is known, this issue was particularly important to Heidegger. For the young Heidegger, the Heidegger of the analysis of existentials, Plato and Aristotle's approach to the phenomena from the viewpoint of what he labeled productive comportment of Dasein toward beings had utopian qualities. For the later Heidegger, the Heidegger of the history of Being, however, this productive comportment and the domination of *logos* was the beginning of metaphysics (though still different from modern technology). On the basic assumptions of his interpretations of Plato and Aristotle before and after this turn (which is not the famous and for many Heideggerians crucial *Kehre* [turn]) see Johannes Fritsche, "With Plato into the Kairos before the Kehre: On Heidegger's different Interpretations of Plato," in Catalin Partenie & Tom Rockmore, eds., *Heidegger and Plato: Toward Dialogue* (Evanston: Northwestern University Press, 2005).

the idea. At the end of Book II of the *Physics*, Aristotle has reached the point where he can analyze change from the viewpoint of the main player, so to speak, namely, from the viewpoint of the form that temporally preexists — as the idea in the head of the craftsman or as the form of the male parent — its realization in some matter. An idea or form can be defined without reference to any matter, but can fully exist only as realized in some matter.

For instance, one wants something that enables one to be in an upright position without standing on one's legs, that is, something to sit on, commonly called a chair. One cannot sit on the idea, form, or definition of chair but has to build a physical thing in which this form is realized, something that is a chair as it can be used as something that enables one to be in an upright position without standing on one's legs. Therefore, one will think about how many different physical parts this physical thing has to have, and how these parts have to be arranged in relation to each other, in order for the whole thing to be a chair. In the next step, one will think about what kinds of materials one has to use for the different parts and will, in a standard example in medieval texts, not try to produce the blade of a saw out of glass. In this way, none of the physical parts of the resulting physical thing and no specimen of its matter are part of the definition of the form, but each of them is functionally necessary inasmuch as it realizes one or the other of the different functions and sub-functions that have to be realized in order for the whole thing to be functional and to be, for instance, a chair. Correspondingly, when one sees a humanly produced thing, one can reconstruct the form that the producer wanted to realize. In the spirit of Ockham's razor, the product is the better the less superfluous parts it has. If one sees, say, a chair with unusual parts, one will infer that the craftsman was either not very competent or wanted to realize some additional special purpose.

3

This functionalism constitutes Aristotle's biology. The form, the soul, uses the different parts of the body and the entire body as its *organa* (tools) of its existence and activities (*On Soul* II.4, 415 b 18f.). To some degree, every animal also uses entities in its environment as such tools, and human souls do so extensively. As Aristotle observes, humans use everything for the sake of themselves (*Physics* II.2, 194 a 33-36). Of all the bodily organs it is in the first place the hand that allows soul to do so for the hand uses other things as tools and thus is the tool of all tools (*On Soul* III.8, 432 a 1f.). This functionalism makes biology as one single science of many different kinds of animals possible inasmuch as it enables the scientist to think in terms of analogies and make the *metabasis eis allo genos* (the step into a different genus), from humans to other land animals, and from them to water- and air animals. The Aristotelian scientist checks every animal or plant with a list of functions that have to be fulfilled by bodily organs in order for a form to be alive and active. The list of these functions — nourishment (including reproduction), locomotion, perception, and, regarding humans, thinking — he has laid out, in general, in *On Soul* and specified in *Parts of Animals* and also *History of Animals*. For instance, no sublunary animal and no plant can survive without nourishment. One cannot acquire and process nourishment without an organ to take in food to begin with. Thus, every animal and plant has to have such an organ, which is normally labeled "head." In one's empirical research one discovers that plants take in food through the part that is commonly called roots. Thus, Aristotle can quite self-evidently say that plants have their heads in the earth (*Parts of Animals* IV.10, 686 b 34-687 a 1). Since roots and heads (of horses, etc.) fulfill the same function, roots are to plants as heads are to horses or human beings; roots and heads are one by analogy, and to be one by analogy is the most universal way of being one (*Met.* V.6, 1016 b 31-1017 a 3, XII.4-5, 1070 a 31-1071 b 2). Or, all animals perform locomotion, and one might call the organ necessary for locomotion "leg" as human beings have always already called the respective parts of land animals that way. In one's empirical research one discovers that birds perform locomotion by means of their wings, and fishes by means of their fins. Thus, fins, wings, and legs are all legs and analogically one as their relations to the respective animals are the same, namely, to be the organ by means of which the animal performs locomotion.

From the specific way in which a function is realized in a given animal and from the way the different parts are related to each other one can infer the form that is realized in that animal, and starting from that form one can deduce these specific parts as those parts that a body has to have in order for that form to be properly realized and active in a body.[4] Aristotle presup-

---

[4]It was a commonplace among the late antique and medieval commentators that the method of science developed in *Posterior Analytics* consists of three steps, namely, the way from the phenomena to their principles, the investigation of these principles, and finally the way from the principles back to the phenomena; in other words, that Aristotle is talking in the first place about a method of research. In the 1960's, however, Jonathan Barnes and others began to maintain that Aristotle was talking about a method of the systematic presentation of results of research, as in contrast to a method of research itself, and in 1993 Barnes said that this thesis had become "widely accepted" (Aristotle, *Posterior Analytics*, trans. J. Barnes, 2nd edition [Oxford: Clarendon Press, 1993], p. XVIII). In his *Analysis and Science in Aristotle* (Albany: State University of New York Press, 1997), Patrick H. Byrne reestablished in a brilliant way the thesis of the old commentators. See also the papers of Balme, Lennox, Pellegrin, Bolton, and Gotthelf in Allan Gotthelf & James G. Lennox, eds., *Philosophical Issues in Aristotle's Biology* (Cambridge: Cambridge University Press, 1987) and Wolfgang Detel in Aristoteles, *Analytica Posteriora*, 1. Halbband (Berlin: Akademie Verlag, 1993), pp. 285ff., 289ff.

poses that nature in its design of different bodies for different forms intends to act economically in the sense of Ockham's razor. While he acknowledges that, sometimes, one could have wished that a given part could have done its job with less matter or activity than actually invested, one never has the impression that such occurrences make him doubt the presupposition that, by and large, nature is very successful in its intention.[5] According to Aristotle's *Metaphysics* I.2 (982 b 11-983 a 23), to be horrified, frightened, or disturbed, by the phenomena stands at the beginning of philosophy, and philosophy does away with that emotional state by discovering the causes of the phenomena and showing that the phenomena cannot but be the way they are. An Aristotelian biologist has to be as careful as any other human in his dealings with, say, tigers or possibly poisonous mushrooms. However, he need not fear to be horrified by any animal he might encounter. For he presupposes that every possible animal operates on the same principles that he knows from all the animals he is familiar with and from humans in the first place. If to be a monster includes being irrational or to operate on a rationality that is different from the one according to which we function, and with which we are familiar, there are no monsters in the Aristotelian world. If, one fine day, someone should discover goat-stags, one can be sure that, given their form and life-style and the environment they live in, they operate reasonably and economically. However, Aristotle argues that there have never been goat-stags.[6] In addition, at no point in his writings does one get the impression that Aristotle takes into account the possibility that relatively few species of animals take over and ruin the other ones and the environment. The visible cosmos is hierarchically ordered – with the heavenly bodies at the top, followed by the humans who use everything else as means — but despite, or precisely because, of this hierarchy it functions as an equilibrium.

4

Different forms require differently formed bodily parts. According to Aristotle, in order to be properly realized and active the form human-being requires that there are, so to speak, sub-species of it. Aristotle uses his functionalist and hierarchical interpretation of biological organisms also in his interpretation of human politics. There are — by nature (*Politics* I.5-7, 1254 a 17-1255 b 40) — freemen and slaves. The slave is an ensouled

---

[5]The last two sentences are a rather general and vague formulation of the problem Aristotle discusses in the short passage at *Parts of Animals* I.1, 640 a 33-b 1; see Allan Gotthelf, "First Principles in Aristotle's *Parts of Animals*," in Gotthelf & Lennox, eds., *Philosophical Issues in Aristotle's Biology*, pp. 189ff.

[6]See below, n. 10.

property and tool of the lord (I.4, 1253 b 27-32), "a tool that directs other tools" (I.4, 1253 b 32f.) or

> an ensouled bodily part of the lord that [in contrast to the lord's other bodily parts as well as in contrast to other tools — like hammer, saw, etc. – each of which works only in spatial contact with the user of the tool who moves and directs it, J.F.] can work even in spatial separation from the lord. (I.6, 1255 b 11f.)

The lord does not need to work, to move himself, for he commands the slaves who, moved by the Lord's word, move themselves and take over the *ponos*, the pain of work, and the Lord can even delegate the work of planning and supervision to someone else. Aristotle's theory of form and matter allows him — against Plato's notion of soul as self moving motion — to envision and argue that soul, being the mover of the movements of the body, is itself not moved (*Physics* VIII.5, 256 a 4ff.; *On Soul* I.3-4, 405 b 31-409 a 30).

Aristotle explains the parts of animals in terms of the functions they fulfill in *Parts of Animals*, at the end of which one finds an excellent summary of his entire biology. Anaxagoras is not right in maintaining that humans are intelligent because they have hands; rather, it is the other way around, for humans have hands because they are the most intelligent beings (*Parts of Animals* IV.10, 687 a 5ff.), and nature gives to every form the necessary and appropriate bodily organs:

> The most intelligent animal should make good use of the greatest number of tools. Now, the hand is not to be regarded as one tool but as many for it is, as it were, a tool for further tools. Thus, nature has given the tool with the widest range of uses, the hand, to the animal with the capability for acquiring the greatest number of crafts. (687 a 18-23)

Some say man is the worst equipped of all animals because man is barefoot and has no cloth and no weapon (687 a 23ff.). However, as Aristotle argues, while every other animal has a definite set of organs each of which serves a definite purpose, and none of which it can change or take off, man can choose among many different weapons each of which he can take on and off as he likes (687 a 26ff.). For the hand can be used as a talon, a claw, a horn, a spear, a sword, or any other weapon or tool for it can seize and hold them all (687 b 2ff.) as Aristotle shows in an analysis of the mechanics of the hand (687 b 6ff.).

5

When Odysseus's wife, Penelope, refers to the ships with which her son has set off to search for Odysseus as "horses of the sea" (*Odyssey* IV, l.

708), she practices the same thinking in terms of analogies of functions that constitutes Aristotle's biology. For it is self-evident to her that horses with their legs, and ships moved by slaves using oars, fulfill the same function, namely, to be the self-moving legs with which one can perform locomotion without using one's own legs. In addition, she also recognizes the functional analogy between oars and water on one side and legs and earthy ground on the other. For by means of the oars the slaves use the water as a resistant surface analogically in the same way in which horses by means of their legs use the earthy ground.[7] In these cases the hands of the lord, the hands of the slaves, and the legs of the horses act, in different ways, as legs since the hands and mouth of the lord command and use animals that use their organs, their hands and legs, to perform locomotion at the will of the lord. More specifically, in order to function as tool of locomotion the leg has to have a part — relatively broad, rather even and firm but often at the same time also somewhat flexible — that immediately touches and pushes the resistant surface as do the paddles of oars, the hooves of horses or, in general terms, feet. In Greek, "slave" was *doulos* but also *andrapodon*,[8] a mixture of "man," "foot," and "ground," man as foot or foot of a man, so to speak. The hand can, of course, also act as leg and foot by using a wooden stick as cane or without any tool, as when one is swimming or when babies are crawling on their legs and hands, or Aristotle himself, with Phyllis, the mistress of Alexander the Great, riding on his back. In the respective sculpture in the Robert Lehman Wing of the Metropolitan Museum in New York City, Phyllis has placed one of her hands right on the exit of Aristotle's system of nourishment and thus strongly alludes to a further usage of the hand, namely, as the male sex organ, and Aristotle and his beard look like Muslims do in Western images of the time. Thus, the statuette seems to draw on the ideology of the crusades and the association of Aristotle with his Arab interpreters through whom he had become known in Western Europe, and it is less likely that the artist, or the commissioner, wanted to make a

---

[7]When an organic body moves one of its parts, there must be a part at rest, as for instance the elbow when the forearm, or the shoulder when the entire arm is moved (Aristotle, *On the Movement of Animals* I.1, 698 a 14-b 7). Similarly, if the entire body is to be moved there has to be something outside of it that is at rest and immobile. For nothing could walk, swim, or fly if the ground, the water, or the air did not offer sufficient resistance (I.2, 698 b 8-699 a 11). In his treatment of space, Aristotle says that space should be immobile (*Physics* IV.4, 212 a 19) without elaborating this notion. Interpreters usually assume that Aristotle means immobile space in the sense of an immobile spatial framework of reference for the identification of motions. In my view, Aristotle means the immobility developed in *On the Motion of Animals* (see Johannes Fritsche, "Space and Seafaring in Aristotle (*Physics* IV.4, 5)," to be published soon).

[8]See, e.g., Aristotle's *Metaphysics* XII.10, 1075 a 21 (where he thinks of slaves even in his contemplation of the gods in and above the heavenly spheres).

comment, as an eternalized profane gesture, on Aristotle's theory of slavery. In any case, as the example of Penelope shows, the rationality of Aristotle's biology is in no way peculiar to him but is the rationality of the societies in which he lived. This is also confirmed by another prominent myth in which the Greek societies celebrated their achievements.

At the gate of Thebes, a female human with the body of a lion and with wings, the so-called Sphinx, posed to every passer-by a riddle: "There is two-footed on the earth and four-footed that with the one voice and three-footed. It changes its shape as the only one of all that moves on the earth, creeping, or above in the air and down in the sea. When it walks leaned on the most feet, the strength of its limbs is most feeble" (Sophocles, *Oedipus Tyrannus*, Hypothesis). The Sphinx devoured everyone who could not solve the riddle and killed herself when, finally, Oedipus presented the right answer. The major point of my paper has, I am certain, become clear by now and is not in need of further elaboration: it was the Aristotelian scientist and, by implication, every Greek housewife; or, for "the Greeks" it was the fabricating and tool- and slave-using animal that has domesticated nature and cleansed the world of the monsters. Also, in terms of Ockham's razor, the red thread with which I led the Minotaur of the readers' curiosity and patience was, I am confident, by and large philosophical and scientific and even would have been that way without the short survey at the beginning. In the following sections, I briefly compare Aristotle, Empedocles, and Greek mythology with each other, and all of them with two articles of Christian faith.

6

Since the becoming present of an essential form x in an individual presupposes the temporal pre-existence of x in a different individual, Aristotle infers from his notion of causality that the different essential forms, the different biological species, have always existed, and he seems to assume that they also will always exist.[9] Medieval philosophers summarized Aristotle's notion of causality in the formula that every cause assimilates its effect to itself. As the finished house displays the features thought of in the

---

[9] In my view, regarding essential forms Aristotle is — or wants to be, as it were — a realist (that is, he assumes the existence of common forms each of which has existed and exists in many different individuals as, for instance, the form human-being has existed in the past in many different individuals and does so right now). However, even if he is a nominalist (and assumes that there are no common forms but only individual ones, and that the forms of, say, Socrates and Aristotle are just, as Ockham put it, "very, very, very similar to each other"), the major points of my paper — the differences between Aristotle, Hesiod, and many pre-Socratic philosophers regarding the axiom of causality, the status of organic and craftsmanship functionalism, and theory of monsters — remain valid.

blueprint in the head of the architect, the blueprint and the architect have assimilated, via the workers, the wood and the stones to the blueprint, and something analogous holds of the form in the male parent, the male parent himself, his seed, and female menstruation.

The faithful and exact realization of the blueprint is what matters to a technician qua technician, and every difference between the original plan and the result is an aberration. Some plans determine only some, others more or even all of the features of the product. According to Aristotle's theory of procreation the form in the male parent intends to produce not just a human being or a male human being but an exact reduplication — a twin, so to speak — of the father, and it is in principle capable of doing so. This criterion marks as monsters not only, as it were, old-fashioned monsters such as the Sphinx but half of the population of animals existing at every moment, and even many more:

> For even he who does not resemble his parents is already in a certain sense a monster (*teras*). For in monsters nature has in a certain way deviated from the genus. The first occurrence of such deviation is that a female is produced and not a male. Still, this is a natural necessity, for the genus of animals divided into males and females must be kept in existence. (*On Generation of Animals* IV.3, 767 b 5ff.)

Probably, the phrase "in a certain sense" does not indicate that the offspring is a monster only in a loose sense of the notion, but that it is a monster in the strict sense Aristotle himself introduces, and that he uses this strict sense even though it follows from it that the process of natural reproduction even requires the constant production of monsters in this strict sense. While difference, in one way or the other, is certainly a necessary condition of monstrosity, in Aristotle, due to his notion of causality, it is its sufficient condition.[10]

---

[10] For Aristotle's theory of resemblance between parents and offspring and his theory of monsters see *On Generation of Animals* IV.1-4, 763 b 20-773 a 32. In brief, the seed of a male, say, human being transmits into female menstruation moving forces that contain all the characters of animal, human being, and the individual father. These (hot) moving forces concoct (the cold) female menstruation (in which the characters of the female parent reside), and the better they manage to do so the more similar to the father the offspring is. Obviously, in about 50 percent of all cases the resistance of female menstruation against being concocted is so strong that a female human being results. It happens only very rarely that the resistance is that large that the offspring begins not even to resemble a human being. It is these borderline-cases, so to speak, that make people, reducing vague similarities to clear-cut ideas, speak of a human with the head of an ox or a calf with a child's head. According to Aristotle, such mixtures of different kinds of animals have never existed and will never exist. Thus, he continues that none

of the borderline-cases are what they are alleged to be but only resemblances in order to conclude: "It is impossible that such a monster — namely, one animal within an animal of a different species — [as in contrast to another type of monster, namely, animals with extra feet or extra heads, J.F.] comes into existence; this fact is shown by the widely different gestation-periods of man, sheep, dog, and ox, for none of these animals can possibly be formed except in its own proper period" (769 b 22-26).

Thus the sex of the offspring and the degree of its resemblance to the father depend on whether, and to which degree, the heat of the moving forces or the coldness of female menstruation prevails. Each "wants" to assimilate, or subdue, the other to itself, and the male, or form, is the cause of continuity and identity whereas the female, or matter, the cause of difference and monstrosity. For, on one side of the spectrum stands a twin of the father, on the other, however, animals that begin not even to resemble human beings. Aristotle calls male and female here and elsewhere opposites (*enantia*), and in *Physics* I.4-6 he maintains that most natural philosophers assume as principles of change an underlying subject and two opposites. In his own theory of only two principles he breaks with this motif of two opposites (see above, n. 1). Here, at the end of his natural philosophy, he reintegrates it as he often tries to minimize differences between himself and other philosophers. However, the motif of two opposites has become instrumental to the continuation and reproduction of pre-given identity, the identity of the form, as in the overwhelming majority of cases a form, say human-being, takes over the city — female menstruation or the offspring — anyway no matter whether heat or coldness has prevailed, and in order for the form to continue to exist it is even necessary that often the forces of coldness win through and render the city female (see Johannes Fritsche, *Methode und Beweisziel*, pp. 158ff.).

Aristotle's final definition of monstrosity is that it is "a sort of lameness/mutilation/deformity (*anapêria*)" (769 b 30) caused by an insufficient concoction of the respective matter. This definition is obviously thought from the perspective of the imperative of maintaining and reproducing the pre-given identity, the form, and from that point of view even a slight variation, or difference, is indeed already a monstrosity. His criterion of monstrosity is obviously also at work in his determination of noble birth (*eugeneia*) in his dialogue *On Noble Birth* of which only three fragments, though obviously the decisive ones, have survived. On the significance of this dialogue for Aristotle overall and for a theory of epochs see Johannes Fritsche, "Genus and *to ti hen einai* (Essence) in Aristotle and Socrates," *Graduate Faculty Philosophy Journal* 19:2-20:1 (1997), pp. 163-202.

The fact that, for Aristotle, the impossibility of monsters is a physical one, and probably also the rigidity of his thinking on the issue is shown by the exceptions that he acknowledges. According to his standards, the procreation of a rather benign creature — namely, the mule as the offspring of a horse and an ass — is against nature, and probably fulfills his description of monsters, as horses and asses are of different species (*Metaphysics* VII.8, 1033 b 33-1034 a 2; see *History of Animals* VI.23, 577 b 5ff.). Aristotle acknowledges that dogs and wolves or, in general, animals of different species, if their size is much the same and their periods of gestation of equal length, copulate and produce offspring, and that, with the exception of mules, such offspring can procreate as well (*Generation of Animals* II.7, 746 a 29ff.). However, according to him this happens only in few animals, and he shows no interest in the career of such offspring. Apparently, these phenomena don't trigger in him any doubt about his anti-evolutionist biology based on the motif of the human being procreating a human being. All those who, with reference to passages such as 577 b 5ff. and 746 a 29ff. or the remarks on spontaneous generation, maintain that Aristotle's biology and philosophy is compatible with evolutionist theories, if not itself one of theirs, ignore, it seems to me, that, as in contrast to

In his history of philosophy in *Metaphysics* I, Aristotle maintains that the natural philosophers before him were ignorant of forms and their activities as causes (I.7, 988 a 34ff., I.8, 988 b 28f.). In other words, since they don't operate on Aristotle's notion of causality they — implicitly or explicitly, intentionally or against their intentions — assume that something can come into existence without that, as according to Aristotle's notion of causality, it already pre-exists its own coming into existence; or, they assume that something essentially new can emerge. As this is the decisive difference Aristotle appropriately makes it his main point in his summary of his entire biology in the passage, quoted above, on Anaxagoras and the hand: it is not the case that, say, intelligence, after its non-existence for a long time, came into existence out of causes without intelligence. Rather, intelligence has always already existed as a feature of the form human-being, the form human-being has always already existed, and nature has always already given individual human beings hands.

7

Empedocles was obviously well versed in the logic of functional analogies between parts of animals of different kinds.[11] However, the relation between this functionalism of organs and the principles of things is very different from Aristotle. In Aristotle, the functionalism is a further aspect of the motif of the pre-existence of what comes into existence: if a bodily part is an organ, that is, if it serves, as most or all the bodily parts do, as a means to an end, it has always already been pre-designed for that purpose and has always already come into existence for the sake of it. In other words, nature, or an essential form, as the first cause of the coming into existence of an animal has always already acted in a teleological manner (*Physics* II.7-9), and all the different essential forms constantly repeat themselves without ever having come into existence.

According to Empedocles, there are the four roots, fire, air, water, and earth, and the unifying and dividing agents, love and strife. Everything

---

a modern law of nature, mythical and analogical thinking as in Ancient Greece and in Aristotle is "generous" enough to easily allow for exceptions.

[11] See fragments B 79, 82, 83. Kirk and Raven say, "Aristotle not only praised but systematically exploited the most striking feature of Empedocles' biology, his perception of homologous functions in apparently dissimilar parts of very different sorts of living being" (G.S. Kirk, J.E. Raven and M. Schofield, *The Presocratic Philosophers*, 2nd ed. [Cambridge: Cambridge University Press, 1999], p. 306). It is probably more a matter of a cultural know-how, which, of course, was cultivated and systematized by some individuals more than by others. The young Heidegger, in his lectures of the 1920s and early 1930s, tried to show that Aristotle (and Plato) in the first place explicated everyday knowledge and know-how. For this motif in the current Aristotle literature see in particular Wolfgang Wieland, G.E.L. Owen, and Martha C. Nussbaum.

else comes into existence and ceases to exist in the mixtures of the four roots and the dissolution of these mixtures under the influence of love and strife (Fragments B 17, 26, 35). In the unceasing moves back and forth between the extremes of complete separation and complete unification of the roots the extent of the mixtures of the roots and the level of their complexity increase and decrease, and phases of different complexity follow each other. Regarding animals, Empedocles distinguishes between four levels and phases. There emerge what, from the viewpoint of the animals as we know them, are separate limbs not joined together; such limbs combine so that many different creatures come into existence, among them man-faced ox and ox-headed men; thirdly, creatures more internally unified and more as we know them, but not yet differentiated into the two sexes; fourthly, animals as we know them, and which reproduce sexually (Fragments A 72, B 57ff.).[12]

In Fragment B 23, Empedocles compares the processes of mixture with painting. There are only a few basic colors, but through their mixtures in specific ratios all the different shapes and colors of images of humans and many other things come about. In other words, the causes don't assimilate something to themselves but things emerge that were not yet present as features of their causes. For, quite obviously, the analogy with painting is not meant to include a painter operating like an Aristotelian craftsman. Rather, the processes of mixture are not guided by any teleological design, and their results occur by chance. However, while some of these results cannot function, and do not survive, in the environment they happen to be in, others do so, and it is as though the parts of the latter had been designed for that purpose (Fragment B 61). Thus, as in contrast to Aristotle, in Empedocles the sphere of functioning organs is the incidental by-product of processes that are not teleological ones, and whose causes do not already possess the characters of their effects.

8

There is no original myth of the deeds and events that *Epoche machen*, establish a new epoch. Every myth already stands on the other side and is anachronistic regarding the past it narrates; it is always already part of a chain of myths in which the narrative is transformed according to the needs, means, norms, imagination, and struggles of the time. Probably, if something like the Sphinx had ever existed, she did not kill herself out

---

[12] On the different interpretations of where to locate the phases of the emergence of animals in the different phases of the cosmological process see Daniel Graham, "Empedocles and Anaxagoras: Responses to Parmenides," in A.A. Long, ed., *Early Greek Philosophy* (Cambridge: Cambridge University Press, 1999), pp. 159-180, here pp. 160ff.

of anger or shame about a defeat in a competition of wit and intelligence, and she did not look quite the way she was described. Did Empedocles really believe in the past existence of the creatures he took over from the mythological stories, or did he talk that way, as some maintain, as a means to introduce the notion of a kind of Darwinian evolution of species? Probably, in light of his Eleatism[13] the latter, at any rate, was not the case. Still,

---

[13] See on this topic Patricia Curd, *The Legacy of Parmenides: Eleatic Monism and Later Presocratic Thought* (Princeton: Princeton University Press, 1998), 155ff., and Daniel Graham, "Empedocles and Anaxagoras: Responses to Parmenides." Parmenides of Elea is the "founding father" of Eleatism. What-is is, in the first place, uniform and unchanging. According to Plato and Aristotle, Parmenides maintained that there was only one entity, Being, and nothing else; that this entity was a what-is; and that therefore there was absolutely no change. For the history of interpretation see Patricia Curd, *The Legacy of Parmenides*, pp. 3ff. passim, and Daniel Graham, "Empedocles and Anaxagoras: Responses to Parmenides," pp. 165ff. According to both of them, Parmenides was a pluralist, and he did not deny the reality of change; rather, he laid out the criteria that something had to meet to qualify as a metaphysically basic entity or as an explanatory principle of the world of change. In what follows, I mean by "Eleatism" and degrees of Eleatism the theoretical establishment of unchanging things (as in contrast to laws) and the maximization of their impact in the world. Regarding Empedocles see Fragments B 9ff. Probably, the rule of thumb would be that the higher the degree of Eleatism, the less leeway there is for monsters. Still, one could use this rule at most after, so to speak, successfully quantifying different forms of Eleatism. Atomist theory has some degree of Eleatism, and Anaxagoras' theory might even have a very high one. Still, in both theories the possibility of monstrosities is very high inasmuch as the present world is just one among many other possible or actual, past or present, ones, which makes the theories "unbearable" for both mythological thinking and Aristotle.

As long as changelessness of the/a what-is is the decisive issue, Parmenides has always been "the first metaphysician" (Graham, *op. cit.*, p. 168). There has been a non-metaphysical and, so to speak, "German" Parmenides. In 1933, using Heidegger's notion of *alêtheia* Kurt Riezler (*Parmenides* [Frankfurt: V. Klostermann, 1934, 2nd ed. 1970]) interpreted Being in Parmenides as a no-thing that holds together the opposites. For the Heidegger of the history of Being, for whom Plato and Aristotle had become the beginning of metaphysics (see above, n. 3), Parmenides was, along with Heraclitus, the paradigmatic pre-Socratic and non-metaphysical "thinker." When, in *An Introduction to Metaphysics* (New Haven: Yale University Press, 1959), a lecture course from summer 1935, he presented Parmenides for the first time that way, he most probably had got the idea of such an interpretation from Riezler. Nonetheless, to make Parmenides fit his own agenda at the time — namely, the promotion of the National Socialist revolution — he gave the main aspect of Riezler's interpretation a thorough twist, which he removed already in his Parmenides interpretation of 1942/3 (see Johannes Fritsche, "Heidegger in the *Kairos* of 'The Occident'," *Graduate Faculty Philosophy Journal* 21:2 [1999], pp. 10ff.). Reiner Schürmann develops Riezler's interpretation from the viewpoint of the later Heidegger's notion of *Gelassenheit* (releasement) in his *Broken Hegemonies* (Bloomington: Indiana University Press, 2003), pp. 51-135 [French original 1996]; a short version in Schürmann, "Tragic Differing: The Law of the One and the Law of Contraries in Parmenides," *Graduate Faculty Philosophy Journal* 13:1 (1988), pp. 3-20. Neither the "German" nor the "metaphysical" Parmenides can be found in Klaus Heinrich's comparison of Parmenides and Jonah in the Old Testament (Klaus Heinrich, "Parmenides und Jonas," in his *Parmenides und Jona. Vier Studien über das Verhältnis*

he assumed different phases of the cosmos with different kinds of beings whereas Aristotle did not do so.

In his *Theogony*, Hesiod combines the many myths with a narrative of the emergence of different generations of gods and the struggles between these generations — the revolutions of the state of the world and society — in which several monstrous creatures, children of the old gods, are relegated to the margins of the cosmos (*Theogony*, ll. 667ff., 820ff.; see also the proverb on Libya, Aristotle, *Generation of Animals* II.7, 746 b 7ff.). The entire narrative begins with, and terminates in, the praise of the latest state, the cosmos of Zeus. This state and its norms, as one can also see in Hesiod's *Works and Days*, must not be revolutionized but rather faithfully transmitted to each following generation. In other words, history — the establishment of a new epoch, a new state of affairs — happened several times in the past, but from now on it must not happen again. In addition, it is humans that make history, but they present their revolutionary actions as faithful and obedient imitations and repetitions of actions of the gods who in a mythical past have established the current state.[14] Relegation of revolutions to the past and revolution as imitation of past deeds of the gods — these two aspects constitute the framework within which the Greek myths take place. One finds it even in Aeschylus's adaptation of the myths of the Atrides in his *Oresteia*, but the cosmogonies of the pre-Socratic natural philosophers break with it inasmuch as their narratives don't terminate in a normative state that must be faithfully preserved and transmitted to the next generation. Aristotle, on the other hand, is even more mythical than the myths themselves inasmuch as he cuts out the narratives of the revolutions and, so to speak, sempiternalizes the normative states, the different biological species, that have to be faithfully transmitted into the future. In other words, while in Empedocles "monster" is a descriptive term, in Aristotle it signifies a deviation from a norm, and, as in contrast to Empedocles, the "principle of reality" that decides over being or not-being — namely, the functionalism of the working organism — has always already been built into the animal itself.

9

For Hesiod, monsters are the reminders of the old gods and their threatening productivity, which has been subdued and domesticated by Zeus. For Empedocles, monsters are creatures "along the way" of the productivity,

---

von Philosophie und Mythologie [Frankfurt: Suhrkamp, 1966], pp. 61-128).

[14]See Jacques Derrida ("Declarations of Independence," *New Political Science* 15:7 [1986], pp. 7-15) on modern republican revolutionaries. In the most abstract terms, it is what Hegel has analyzed as *Voraussetzen* (G.W.F. Hegel, *Wissenschaft der Logik: Zweiter Teil*, ed. G. Lasson [Hamburg: Meiner, 1969], pp. 15f. and often).

not guided by ends and reason, of the principles; creatures that just did not make it, in the long run, under the "principle of reality" — the logic of organic functions, the new, anonymous Zeus, as it were — in an environment that came about in the same way as the creatures within it. Probably, for Empedocles those mythical stories are indications of that past phase of the world with animals different from the ones we know from experience. Aristotle, however, explains the existence of notions such as "Sphinx" or "goat-stag" through the capacity of combining in speech ideas that belong to different entities. For, he describes such monsters, or summarizes their characterizations in myths and the talk of "the many," as an "animal in an animal of a different species" (*Generation of Animals* IV.3, 769 b 22f.) and denies them the physical possibility of existence.[15]

For Aristotle, there have never been the monsters of the Greek myths or a phase of the cosmos, different from the current one, with different animals. Rather, the cosmos has always been as it is today, and the species in the past have been the same as the current ones. In a way, women, but all males as well, are monsters. However, this monstrosity is necessary for the continuation of the species. The monster has become the slave of the species, so to speak, the temporary foot that is replaced by other such feet. Inasmuch as Aristotle maintains that this constant re-realization of the different species according to the always already inbuilt logic of organic functionality is, and has always already been, the logic of reality, he regards this logic as an ontology (and not as a transcendental, quasi-transcendental, or pragmatic scheme of how humans perceive and conceptualize reality).[16] In addition, inasmuch as he maintains that this logic of craftsmanship and of the functionalism of tools has always already been the only one that governs the realm of natural things, he makes it absolute; declares it to be the only god with no other gods, or monsters, besides, behind, or above it — at least, not within the realm of corruptible bodies.[17]

---

[15] See above, n. 10.

[16] In my view, Aristotle's *Physics* I and II develop an ontology (see Johannes Fritsche, *Methode und Beweisziel*, pp. 67ff.); an ontology that is presupposed in his theory of demonstration (see my *Nature, Science, Logic, and Politics in Aristotle and the Western Tradition* [in preparation]).

[17] In other words, it was certainly also a matter of recognition of hubris that, after Aristotle and Theophrastus, Aristotle's biological research program "seems to have fallen mostly on deaf ears" (James G. Lennox, "The Disappearance of Aristotle's Biology: A Hellenistic Mystery," in his *Aristotle's Philosophy of Biology: Studies in the Origins of Life Science* [Cambridge: Cambridge University Press, 2001], p. 114) (before it was taken up by the Christian Albertus Magnus, the teacher of Thomas Aquinas [*ibid.*, p. 123f.]), as Lennox puts it not without some regret even though or precisely because he, of course, recognizes Aristotle's strong claims (*ibid.*, pp. 111ff., 123f.).

Aristotle's theory of the weather in *On the Heavens* II and in his *Meteorologica* and his theology in *Physics* VIII, *On the Heavens* I, II, and *Metaphysics* XII provide his physics

10

Animals in animals of different species and animals with extra heads or arms[18] — the Greek myths also talk about monstrous or gracious metamorphoses from an animal into a plant, a stone, or a different animal. Probably, Empedocles' Eleatism does not allow for such changes, and Aristotle even explicitly excludes them (*Phys.* I.5, 188 a 31ff.). Still, those stories have an aspect — display a seminal Eleatism, so to speak — that many philosophers have happily picked up. Zeus and the other gods remained the same when they took on different bodily shapes, and Odysseus' companions quite literally did not loose their understanding (*nous*) when they were transformed into pigs and back into humans (Odyssey X, 1. 240). Similarly, Empedocles (e.g., Fragment B 117) and other philosophers, sharpening or reifying the difference between body and soul, assumed the transmigration of souls. While all those for whom soul is something bodily might regard, with or without irony, such composites as instances of the description of monsters in Aristotle and the Greek myths, Aristotle himself would not do so inasmuch as, for him, a soul is not a body, but the essential form of a body. Still, there is not that much of a difference between a composite of a body of one single species, including its proper essential form, and a different essential form and a composite of two bodies of different species with each body having its respective essential form. There are no entities with two different natures.[19]

Greek philosophers, through thinking and purification, liberated and deified themselves by themselves, and they deemed ridiculous or monstrous the notion of a god that becomes human, suffers, and dies. Also in early Christianity, it was controversial whether Jesus Christ's nature was human, divine, or both. The formula that was supposed to put an end to those controversies, the *Symbolum Chalcedonense* from 451 A.D., determines that Jesus Christ is "of one single kind/unique in two natures (*monogenê en duo phusesin/unigenitum, in duabus naturis*)," as these two natures are united in one person and subsistence, and yet, despite this unification in one person, they and their properties are in no way modified, changed or fused.[20] In

---

and natural sciences with a stable embracing frame, and the visible gods — the heavenly bodies — and the unmoved mover are the intensification and climax of the Eleatism of the main players — or gods (*Parts of Animals* I, 645 a 17-23) — down here on earth, the biological species.

[18] See above, n. 10.

[19] If Aristotle is a realist (see above, n. 9), each common essential form — say, human-being – is in many different individuals. Still, human-being would be the only essential form in each human being, and each individual human body would be functionally appropriate to it.

[20] H. Denzinger & A. Schönmetz, eds., *Enchiridion symbolorum, definitionum et declarationum de rebus fidei et morum* (Freiburg: Herder, 1976), p. 108. Thus, Jesus Christ's nature is neither purely human nor purely divine, and also regarding the union of his

addition, later on it became dogma that, after the consecration, the bread and wine did not signify, but had become — via transubstantiation, the utmost opposite of any Eleatism — the body and blood of Jesus Christ.

By Aristotelian and Greek standards, Jesus Christ is a monster, and the Eucharist host a similar relapse into mythological ways of thinking. Still, even if they meet the "Greek" description of monsters, their context differs from the contexts of monsters in Hesiod and in Aristotle, and therefore also their significance differs. For "the Greeks," a monster is a matter of the outer nature and the confluence of its dubious, dangerous, irrational, or just natural powers. The humans — as Antisthenes[21] put it, certainly "in the spirit" of many Greek philosophers — have to liberate themselves from these powers by building a city-wall between them and outer nature to keep the latter outside, and within this wall they have to built another one in order to cleanse the rational part of their souls from the influence of the other parts. In this way can they liberate soul from its double-headedness and establish it in its essential purity.

In Christianity, nature and the divine are not only clearly separated from each other, but nature has become fully objectified as the craftsman-product of an omnipotent and benevolent God. In this sense, there is, in principle, even less space for monsters than in an Aristotelian world. Thus, the intersection of two different natures in one and the same body does not point down into Hades, so to speak, into an abyss of dubious powers or to the caprices of frivolous gods, but upward to the one God. In addition, it points to the inner, the human nature with its drama of fall and corruption to promise a redemption that the individual human cannot achieve by himself or herself. While, for "the Greeks," the intersection of two different natures is a threat to the purity of soul against which the soul has to close itself, for "the Christians" it shows soul's distance from its pure state, provides the most compelling image of soul's proper directedness toward God, and heals soul and the will from the corruption that the will has brought about itself by turning away from God. In other words, while Aristotle's description of a monster certainly applies to Jesus Christ, his final definition of monstrosity — "a sort of lameness / mutilation / deformity (*anapêria*)" (*Generation of Animals* IV.3, 769 b 30)[22] — definitely does not do so.

---

divine nature and his human nature the Catholic faith keeps, as Thomas Aquinas puts it, the middle road between two extremes inasmuch as the union according to person and subsistence is neither an accidental union nor an essential union and blending of the two natures (*Summa Theologiae* III, qu. 2, art. 6, resp.). Similarly, a goat-stag would be a union in one person, or individual, of (parts of) two different bodies and natures, a union that leaves (all the parts of) both bodies and natures unmodified and unblended.

[21] Diogenes Laertius, *Lives of Eminent Philosophers*, VI.12, 13.

[22] See above, n. 10.

Science as a Cure for Fear: The Status of Monsters in Lucretius

MORGAN MEIS

ABSTRACT. In this essay I examine Lucretius' poem *De Rerum Natura* in the light of its its materialism and contribution to natural science, which reveals itself to be at the service of ethics and a philosophical therapy, and not the other way around. Through some reference to Hans Blumenberg and Martha Nussbaum, it is argued that Lucretius' Epicurean philosophy expels the threat of monsters from its system by trying to erase the role of the passions almost completely from human affairs. This was seen by Epicureans like Lucretius as a more effective way to cure human fears than that offered by myth or previous philosophies. The challenge for early modern philosophy, which was attracted to the materialism of Epicureanism but not to its taming of human *curiositas*, was to re-naturalize the passions. Another way to look at this re-naturalizing of the passions is that it took monsters out of human consciousness, as Lucretius saw it, and put them back into the world again.

It was impossible for someone ignorant about the nature of the universe but still suspicious about the subjects of myth to dissolve his feelings of fear about the most important matters. So it was impossible to receive unmixed pleasures without knowing natural science. — Epicurus.[1]

Epicurus was a man who disliked fear. In response to fear, he cultivated a refuge and a garden and began a project in rationalist natural science more ambitious than anything yet proposed. To conquer fear, he decided that he had to explain it all. His doctrine that everything is ultimately just atoms and void was the result of these labors. He built on the previous thought of Democritus and Leucippus and others, but he produced something new, and much bigger, and with an ethical twist that made Epicureanism a major,

---

[1]Epicurus, Maxim XII in *Hellenistic Philosophy: Introductory Readings*, trans. B. Inwood & L.P. Gerson (Indianapolis: Hackett, 1988), pp. 26–27.

continuous school of thought for five hundred years or so and with historical rebirths and resonances that continue today. In the Letter to Herodotus, handed down to us by Diogenes Laertius, he argues that:

> In addition to all these points in general, one must also conceive that the worst disturbance occurs in human souls because of the opinion that these things [the heavenly phenomenon] are blessed and indestructible and that they have wishes and undertake actions and exert causality in a manner inconsistent with those attributes, and because of the external expectation and suspicion that something dreadful [might happen] such as the myths tell about, or even because they fear that very lack of sense-perception which occurs in death, as though it were relevant to them, and because they are not in this state as a result of their opinions but because of some irrational condition; hence, not setting a limit on their dread, they suffer a disturbance equal to or even greater than what they would suffer if they actually held these opinions. And freedom from disturbance [*ataraxia*] is a release from all of this and involves a continuous recollection of the general and most important points [of the system].[2]

In thinking about the "general and most important points" Epicurus recommended continuous contemplation of natural phenomena, seeing them as nothing but the result of interactions between atoms and the void. Thus, in some vague, general way, Epicurus hit upon an intuition, through the sheer audacity of speculative thought, that got something right about the nature of things. His idea that all things are composed of smaller, more fundamental units has turned into an accepted fact about the universe, even if debate still rages about what those units are and how they operate. More remarkably, perhaps, his radical materialism would put him in the thick of contemporary discussions about, for instance, the philosophy of mind. Epicurus was a hardcore naturalist before anyone was even sure what that really was.

But just as soon as one is feeling comfortable with Epicurus as a contemporary thinker, it's important to remember that he did it all for ethics. This, you might say, is the distinctly non-contemporary aspect of Epicurean natural science. It's simply not science in the modern conception of the term. This is the case even though Epicurean atomism has the distinction of guessing right about atoms. He had no interest in experimentation, verification or anything else of the sort. He was a dogmatist of the highest order. The

---

[2]Epicurus, "Letter to Herodotus," in *Hellenistic Philosophy*, pp. 14-15 [Diogenes Laertius 10.81].

doctrine of atoms and voids was to be learned by his pupils like holy writ. Indeed, the three letters – to Herodotus, Pythocles, and Menoeceus – that have survived from all of Epicurus' writings are essentially crib notes for Epicureans looking for the basics of the system. They're the fundamental talking points for being an Epicurean. To Pythocles Epicurus writes:

> Commit all of this to memory, Pythocles; for you will leave myth far behind you and will be able to see [the causes of phenomenon] similar to these. Most important, devote yourself to the contemplation of the basic principles [i.e., atoms] and the unlimited [i.e., void] and things related to them, and again [the contemplation] of the criteria and the feelings and the [goal] for sake of which we reason these things out.[3]

The "goal for the sake of which we reason these things out" is *ataraxia*, the ethical endpoint for Epicurean philosophy. *Ataraxia* is a noun derived from the Greek verb *terasso*. It denotes a state of calmness, a freedom from disturbance. It is sometimes, somewhat clumsily translated as 'unperturbedness'. The Epicurean doctrines of natural science are settled and complete doctrines. Their sole purpose is to create a practical effect, and to change one's life from a state of fear and disturbance to one of *ataraxia*. Epicurus' doctrines are thus primarily tools for living.

Indeed, Epicurus could not have stated this fact more unequivocally than he did to Pythocles, saying, "First of all, do not believe that there is any other goal to be achieved by the knowledge of meteorological phenomenon, whether they are discussed in conjunction with [physics in general] or on their own, than freedom from disturbance and a secure conviction, just as with the rest [of physics]."[4]

There you have it. Epicureanism is a therapeutic philosophy and natural science is nothing more than a tool for that therapy. It is a powerful tool but it has no other purpose, none. The aim of Epicureanism is to live well in a state of *ataraxia*. If there was a better way to reach *ataraxia* than a study of nature, we would discard the study of nature altogether. But there isn't, so we study nature, or at least we study Epicurus' doctrines about nature.

That's precisely the standpoint from which Lucretius wrote *De Rerum Natura*. While differing on points of detail, there is no question that Lucretius is an orthodox Epicurean through and through. His innovation was to put Epicurean philosophy into poetic form. And a beautiful poem it is.

---

[3] Epicurus, "Letter to Pythocles," in *Hellenistic Philosophy*, pp. 22-23 [Diogenes Laertius 10.116].

[4] *Ibid.*, p. 15 [Diogenes Laertius 10.85].

Writing in Latin roughly two hundred years after Epicurus' death, Lucretius was to translate the basic insights and attitudes of his master into a forceful work of dactylic hexameter that was influential to such giants of Latin verse as Horace, Virgil, and Ovid. It's a pleasure to read Bailey's magisterial commentary on the poem simply to learn how well crafted it is, what a subtle use of Latin poetic language is achieved by Lucretius throughout.[5]

But it also helps to remember that the poem is philosophy first and foremost. For reasons that Lucretius is explicit about in Book I of his poem (I, 930-950), he decided that the best way to lead a potential Epicurean through the therapeutic process was to get them involved in an epic poem that mixes classical imagery with hard-nosed philosophical analysis. In fact, the concept isn't particularly difficult to understand. Lucretius had the model of Empedocles (who he openly admires) and Parmenides to look toward. Both philosophers, presumably, saw the poetic form as a kind of heuristic device by which difficult concepts could be delivered in a palatable package. If Lucretius goes further than either of those it is in the extent to which he consciously structures his poem as a continuing, modulated ascent from sensual poetic imagery to a purified language of Epicurean rationalism.

For instance, in an early attempt to convince the reader that nature is acted upon by imperceptible forces, i.e., that atoms exist, Lucretius writes the following lines about the wind.

> ...the wild wind awakened whips the waves of the sea, capsizes huge ships, and send the clouds scudding; sometimes it swoops and sweeps across the plains in tearing tornado, strewing them with great trees, and hammers the heights of mountains with forest splitting blasts. Such is the frenzied furry of the wind, when it shrieks shrill, rages, and menacingly murmurs. Undoubtedly, therefore, there are invisible particles of wind that sweep the sea, sweep the lands, sweep the clouds in the sky, buffeting and battering them with swirling suddenness. The flow of their current and the devastation they deal is no different from that of a river in sudden spate: water is by nature soft, but when swollen by a great deluge racing down from high mountains after heavy rains, it rams together debris of forests and whole trees; even sturdy bridges cannot withstand the sudden shock of advancing flood, so furious is the force with which the river, made to boil by bulk of rain, dashes against the piles; with thundering roar

---

[5] See C. Bailey, *Titi Lucreti Cari De Rerum Natura livri sex*, 3 vols. (Oxford: Clarendon Press, 1947-1950).

it deals destruction, rolling big boulders beneath its waves and sweeping away all that obstructs its course.[6]

This striking passage shows that Lucretius is working in the realm of epic verse – in the territory of Homer, Pindar, and the great tragedians. At the same time, he has also inserted the germs of an argument that will tame his language simultaneously as it tames the emotional impact of these descriptions of natural phenomena. After talking about the shrill, raging wind, he mentions "undoubtedly, there are invisible particles that . . ." The therapy is already under way. Within a few hundred lines the poet is already writing:

> But since I have shown above that nothing can be created out of nothing or, once born, reduced to nothing, the first elements must consist of imperishable substance, into which everything can be resolved at its last hour, so that a constant supply of matter may be available for the renewal of all things. Therefore the primary elements are solid and simple; otherwise they could not have been preserved through the ages and so renewed things from infinite times past.[7]

The transition from poetic sensuality to abstract reasoning and language is rather extreme. But the transition is not absolute. In an evolving dialectic, Lucretius keeps returning to the sensualism, and then drawing it back out into the abstract again in a series of overlapping spirals. That is the paidetic structure of *De Rerum Natura*, how it teaches people to cure themselves and to reach *ataraxia* through Epicurean means.

There is also a deeper reason Lucretius writes in a style that overlaps with the language and imagery of epic poetry, mythology, and the pathetic stories of the great tragedies, however. Lucretius, as Epicurus before him, saw these literary traditions as engaged in similar problems to his own. They were also trying to tame human fear and clear the way for their own form of *ataraxia* in the face of the terrors of the world. Consider the role Hercules plays in Greek mythology. His primary job is to tame the beasts, bring the cosmos into order and make the world habitable for human beings. He is the destroyer of monsters, if you define monsters as the constant looming threat to the sustainability of human life.

Yet for Epicurus and Lucretius, myth and traditional poetry, not to speak of previous philosophies, utterly fail in their mission. They cannot tame the

---

[6]Lucretius, *On the Nature of Things*, trans. Martin Ferguson Smith (Indianapolis: Hackett, 2001), pp. 10–11 [book I, verses 271-90 – hereafter provided in brackets following page references to this edition].
[7]*Ibid.*, p. 17 [I, 542-550].

fears. Often, they create new and different fears even as they attempt to provide weapons against the old ones. Lucretius warns, "The time may come when you yourself, terrorized by the fearsome pronouncements of the fable-mongers, will attempt to defect from us. Consider how numerous are the fantasies they can invent, capable of confounding your calculated plan of life and clouding all your fortunes with fear."[8]

Epicurean philosophy as elucidated by Lucretius doesn't emerge onto the philosophical scene *ex nihilo*. It is itself a response to the intellectual problems and tendencies of thought that had been handed down to it. This dialectic, driven not by some grand Hegelian motif but by the handing down of solutions to various problems that themselves become new problems, is addressed specifically by Hans Blumenberg in his analysis of Epicureanism, in both his more sustained theoretical works *Legitimacy of the Modern Age* and *Work on Myth*, as well as in an elegant essay he wrote in the late 1970's entitled *Shipwreck with Spectator*.

Epicurean philosophy, he argues, can be seen as taking over from and trying to improve on the results of myth insofar as myth had been an attempt to provide intellectual tools in the overcoming of human dependency and the prevalence of fear in human life. Blumenberg writes, in *Work on Myth* and speaking specifically of Lucretius,

> For the philosopher, physics has taken over the distancing function of myth: It neutralizes everything, without exception. But above all it lets us comprehend, for the first time, what had been at issue – with the inadequate means of myth too – all along. Only work on myth – even if it is the work of finally reducing it – makes the work of myth manifest.[9]

Reading *De Rerum Natura*, there is no question that an intellectual project of "distancing" and "neutralization" is at work. The Epicurean will cure the mind troubled by events in the external world by giving it the tools to become, essentially, indifferent to that world. Martha Nussbaum discusses this aspect of Lucretius and Epicurean philosophy as the goal of becoming godlike. She speaks of Lucretius as having the "aim to make the reader equal to the gods."[10] But this means something very specific in the Epicurean framework. The Epicurean gods are strange gods; they are not like the gods of Greek myth or of the various monotheisms. They are idle

---

[8] *Ibid.*, p. 6 [I, 104-109].
[9] Hans Blumenberg, *Work on Myth*, trans. R.M. Wallace (Cambridge, Mass.: MIT Press, 1990), p. 118.
[10] Martha Nussbaum, *The Therapy of Desire: Theory and Practice in Hellenistic Philosophy* (Princeton: Princeton University Press, 1994), p. 194.

gods living in the *intermundi*, the spaces between worlds, lacking any interest in the events of mortals, living a life of permanent lack of disturbance. They are *ataraxia* personified. As Lucretius puts it,

> For it is in the very nature of the gods that they should enjoy immortal life in perfect peace, far removed and separated from our world; free from all distress, free from peril, fully self-sufficient, independent of us, they are not influenced by worthy conduct nor touched by anger.[11]

This is the goal, the *ataraxia* toward which the Epicurean strives. It is constituted by giving up on fundamental features of a life engaged with the normal day-to-day affairs of men and beasts. Nussbaum discusses this in her chapter on Epicureans as 'mortal immortals'.

> The proem to Book II, similarly, promises the diligent reader a life that is in no respect significantly different from the lives of Epicurean gods: a life detached from human care, looking down, upon the world of mortal things without worry or tension. Here the imagery of boundaries takes one more turn: philosophy is said to build round the pupil a wall that sets her off from other humans, until she inhabits 'the lofty serene temples of the wise, well-fortified by doctrine'.[12]

And this, one cannot stress too much, is the sole purpose of the study of nature for Epicureans. A true understanding of nature and its mechanisms will remove concerns for the particulars of this or that event. From the perspective of atoms and voids, from the standpoint of the gods, one arrangement of things is as pleasing as any other. They are all equally meaningless. That is what nature shows us. And when we have learned that lesson we cease to care about things in the way we used to.

For Lucretius, a crucial step in achieving *ataraxia* and becoming like the Epicurean gods is a full recognition of what is really natural, and what isn't. This distinction already exists in Epicurus himself when, in the letter to Menoeceus, he says, "One must reckon that of desires some are natural, some groundless; and of the natural desires some are necessary and some merely natural; and of the necessary, some are necessary for happiness and some for freeing the body from troubles and some for life itself."[13] The study of nature allows one to order these things properly, to step away from a life of concern, and to become like an immortal god.

---

[11] Lucretius, *On the Nature of Things*, p. 4 [I, 44-49].
[12] Nussbaum, *The Therapy of Desire*, p. 216.
[13] Epicurus, "Letter to Menoeceus," *Hellenistic Philosophy*, p. 24 [Diogenes Laertius 10.127].

In this way, and as Lucretius recognizes, it is entirely the opposite approach to previous mythology and philosophy. The thrust of many of the intellectual schools and movements that existed in the generations before Lucretius was to provide tools by which to engage the external world and solve its problems. In the vein of Hamlet, the approach was to take arms against a sea of misfortunes and by opposing end them. Again, we could think of this in Herculean terms. Myth presents Hercules as a figure who takes up and masters the threats of a hostile world. The problem of the world is that it is filled with monsters, monsters who must be destroyed or tamed so as to fit within the parameters of human need. Hercules is the hero of human engagement. That in several versions of the Prometheus myth he is the figure who frees Prometheus from his punishment for giving men fire (i.e., the capacity to fend for themselves) is but further confirmation of that role.

In Book V of *De Rerum Natura*, Lucretius takes up the figure of Hercules explicitly. In speaking of Epicurus he writes,

> If you consider that his achievements are surpassed by Hercules, you will stray still further from the path of sound judgment. What harm could come to us now from those great gaping jaws of the Nemean lion or from the bristly Arcadian boar? . . . And all other such monsters that were destroyed – if they had not been vanquished, but were still alive, what harm could they possibly do? None at all, in my judgment; for the earth swarms even now to repletion with wild beasts: the woods and mighty mountains and deep forests all teem with trembling terror . . . But unless our minds are purified, what strife and what dangers find their way into us against our will! What poignant pangs of passion disturb and distract us, and equally what fears! . . . And will not the man who, using words instead of weapons, subdued all these monsters and banished them from the mind rightly be considered worthy of a place among the gods?[14]

Here, Lucretius presents Epicurus as the new Hercules, the real Hercules. The labors of Hercules would be infinite, suggests Lucretius, because the various arrangements of atoms and void will always produce new monsters. The trick in defeating monsters is in recognizing that they don't really exist in the external world. We see these external threats as monsters because we cannot separate our true opinions from our false ones. We don't see the whole, and because we don't we tremble in fear before things that should be a matter of indifference to us.

---

[14]Lucretius, *On the Nature of Things*, pp. 137-138 [V, 22-50].

True to his basic rationalist approach to natural science, Lucretius treats the biological fact of monsters as something that can be explained to the point of irrelevance. There is no need of a Hercules to deal with any of the strange products of nature for the simple fact that nature itself only provides for and sustains viable species. He writes, "monstrous and prodigious beings were produced by the earth. But they were created in vain, since nature denied them growth and they were unable to attain the coveted bloom of maturity or find food or be united in the acts of Venus."[15]

Similarly, Lucretius' response to the rather more fanciful tales in myth and legend is simply to debunk them. Things like Centaurs, Scyllas, or Chimaeras could never have existed given the fact that they are a logical impossibility. Such creatures are merely fanciful combinations of other existing creatures in the mind. But in reality, "The parts of such creatures do not simultaneously attain their prime or gain physical strength or decline in old age; they are not inflamed with the same sexual desires, they do not agree in their habits; and they do not find the same foods agreeable."[16] Thus, they could never have survived even long enough to procreate.

The intention here, as always in Lucretius, is not to inquire into natural phenomena for their own sake, or even to attempt to verify whether any of these rationalist explanations are empirically substantiated, so much as it is to provide intellectual resources that can dissolve the problem altogether. Nature is shown to be a process that, in the whole, takes care of itself. In the face of that overwhelming sufficiency, the particular affairs of any individual node pale into insignificance.

The monsters, in reality, are not outside. The world is simply all that is the case. The real monsters are internal. They are our judgments, our mistaken apprehensions that put us in a state of disturbance regarding the events of the world. The monsters are the passions. The real Hercules is the figure who can eradicate unnatural passions, and his real weapons are the doctrines of Epicurus.

The radicalism of this position should be apparent. It amounts, essentially, to quietism of an extreme sort, namely, the eradication of a great deal of the attitudes and impulses that would, outside of the Epicurean framework, be most associated with what it is to be human. It makes the everyday world of human activities into something largely if not wholly illusory and the dreamy world of the gods in the *intermundus* the real reality. Politics, business, law, international affairs, are all, as they exist outside of the Epicurean garden, products of the illusions produced from human fears and passions. In reality, they are nothing.

---

[15] *Ibid.*, pp. 159-160 [V, 844-849].
[16] *Ibid.*, p. 161 [V, 893-896].

Now what Blumenberg points out, drawing an insight from Voltaire, is that this radicalism looks a little dubious even from within the Epicurean atomic system. As Voltaire says in *Zadig*, "Everything in this world is dangerous, and everything is necessary."[17] This sentiment is diametrically opposed to that of the Epicurean, for whom the dangers of the world are but an illusion and for whom the human passions are anything but necessary.

As a solution to a specific problem, however, one can understand the appeal of the Epicurean system. If the eradication of fear is your primary goal, and if the insufficiencies of previous thought systems to achieve that task are your motivation, the Epicurean response is powerful. But, if the Epicurean solutions are themselves looked at as a problem, something troubling jumps to the fore. The distinction between the really natural and the falsely natural looks somewhat arbitrary. What prevents Lucretius from considering the passions that drive human beings into their states of disturbance as also natural? They too are outcomes, in the last instance, of atoms and void. How did the Epicurean system end up producing something contrary to the system if there is nothing but the system? Why aren't the human impulses toward engagement with the world as natural as the indifference of the gods living outside of the world? Blumenberg raises the problem thusly in an insightful passage from *Shipwreck with Spectator*.

> Lucretius had stressed humanity's liberation from fear. It was primarily events in nature – and only secondarily events in the human world, as a category of natural events – that could cause fear. Therefore, liberation was to be found, above all, in Epicurus' atomistic physics, which had taught that all possible explanations of natural events should be seen as equally valid and consequently a matter of indifference for men. Because they participate in this, human action and suffering, which are from birth to death processes of this same nature, must leave the man who understands these things unmoved. Shipwreck shows this: it is a natural event, and it is accidental that it involves people along with the ship. That man goes to sea at all and puts himself in such danger must, accordingly, also be a natural event, the results of his drives and passions – if the Roman Lucretius had not intended, by means of this philosophy, to denounce the hypercultivated degeneration of his world. Voltaire, by identifying curiosity as an animal drive, and thus as a natural event, had come closer to the heart of the philosophy than Lucretius had thought he could afford to come. The energy that drives

---

[17] As quoted by Hans Blumenberg in *Shipwreck with Spectator*, trans. S. Rendall (Cambridge, Mass.: MIT Press, 1997), p. 111, n. 48.

us beyond the state of nature and the meager provision of the natural standpoint is itself a part of nature.[18]

What Voltaire objects to in Lucretius, perhaps through his disgust with the Epicureanism latent in Leibniz's atomism and its 'best of all possible worlds', is precisely the extent to which it leaves human beings helpless in the face of an indifferent cosmos. But this objection, taken alone, is not necessarily enough to shake the committed Epicurean. The Epicurean can simply respond that such objections only come from those who haven't fully mastered their indifference, haven't yet reached *ataraxia*. Where Voltaire strikes a more devastating blow against Lucretius is in naturalizing the very impulses that the Epicurean places outside of the system and designates as monstrous. By suggesting that such human motivations as curiosity, inquisitiveness, and acquisitiveness are as much a part of the natural order as anything else, Voltaire undermines the Epicurean distinction between true and false nature that was the lynchpin for achieving *ataraxia*. And by so doing, the materialism of Lucretius loses its direct and causal relation to the quietude of the Epicurean garden. The natural science of the Epicurean system can be re-appropriated as a tool for a transformative and world-engaging set of scientific practices. For Blumenberg, such a shift is at the heart of what makes the modern, modern.

Regarding monsters, one should notice that it is precisely through their redefinition that a difference is drawn between the Epicurean standpoint and the one that Blumenberg defines as properly 'modern'. Lucretius had reacted against the failure of earlier myths and by doing so had redefined Hercules. The real Herculean figure was defined as he who put down his weapons and decided to let the monsters be. In doing so, he became the only one who could really defeat them, simply by recognizing the monsters as our own unnatural passions. If the Epicurean garden is a kind of fortress, as Nussbaum refers to it, it is a fortress not against the brute danger of an inhospitable world, but against what Epicureans take to be the brute practices of complex human social interaction. The Epicurean fortress is a fortress in the heart of the city and its defenses are directed against that city and not against anything in nature more broadly defined. Whereas myth, for instance, had marshaled its conceptual resources to push the monstrous and terrifying aspects of the natural world out to the very boundaries of the world, Epicureanism responds with complete indifference to that set of boundaries at all.

Instead, it creates an oasis within an oasis, a city against the city within the city's walls.

---

[18]Blumenberg, *Shipwreck with Spectator*, p. 51.

Looked at this way, the simultaneous strengths and weaknesses of Epicurean philosophy are that much more pronounced. If there is an aspect of bad faith within Lucretius' poem, it's the extent to which it takes the city walls for granted. Put simply, the Epicurean garden benefits from but refuses to acknowledge the city walls. It pretends that the city and all its turpitude is simply a hindrance to the repose of *ataraxia*. But the city provides precisely the kind of boundary that the Epicurean gods receive from their space of quietude in the *intermundus*. The key difference is that the gods benefit from the boundary of the *intermundus* through no act of their own – it's simply the way the cards fell. The intermundi were a byproduct of the creation of the cosmos out of the interaction of atoms and void. But the Epicureans get their protection, their mini-*intermundus*, from the activities and labors of the city they've turned their backs on. More troubling still, the Epicurean garden gets its conditions of possibility from the very impulses and inclinations that the Epicureans condemn. This inconvenient fact is never really properly addressed either by Epicurus or Lucretius. Indeed, there is a nervous and never fully reconciled Rousseauian attitude in Book V of *De Rerum Natura* where Lucretius speaks of human history and the development of civilization. Essentially, Lucretius treats the state of man before civilization as one of noble savagery. He writes:

> When overtaken by night, they laid their shaggy limbs naked on the branches. They did not roam panic-stricken through the countryside in the shadows of the night, seeking the day and the sunlight with loud lamentations, but waited silent and buried in sleep for the sun's rose-red torch to spread its radiance over the heavens.[19]

This is presented in contrast to lives lived by contemporary humans. Lucretius paints a picture where every seeming advance in civilization is countered by a matching degradation in the human psyche. Lucretius admits that some aspects of material life were improved in the course of human history, but stresses the political and moral corruption that came along with those improvements. The life of Lucretius' contemporaries, he suggests, is one of confusion, fear, dissembling, inequality, brutality, and war. And so we retire to the garden.

But Lucretius also exhibits a moment's hesitation in describing the natural and robust lives of humans before the advent of civilization. Speaking of the early humans, he says that "A much greater cause of concern was the way in which the tribes of wild beasts often made rest perilous and

---

[19]Lucretius, *On the Nature of Things*, p. 163 [V, 970-998].

wretched for them."²⁰ It is an admittance, if somewhat obliquely, that it's difficult to find any repose in a world that hasn't been tamed. A world in which the monsters have not been driven back to beyond the boundaries is one in which there is little rest. He even calls this a 'cause of concern', and, presumably, this concern was also a cause for further action. Sensing this, Lucretius is careful to explain that the action that resulted from this initial concern was almost always counter-productive from the standpoint of *ataraxia*. The trappings of civilization are but the piling on of more and more concerns. But the trappings of civilization are also, effectively, the creation of the conditions of possibility for the Epicurean Garden. As much as civilization has created a whole new set of worries it has also, in an absolute sense, solved the basic problem of existence that had made true *ataraxia* impossible for early humans. It is impossible to live a life of repose in the Garden when you are being torn apart by wild beasts. Indeed, insofar as fear arises naturally as an emotional state, it helps individuals of a species to survive, which in turn further ensures the viability of the species.

It was Voltaire's insight that the chain of causality from primal human fear to the rather more refined human capacity for curiosity exists on a continuum. As such, there is no moment that can be picked out as a leap from natural to unnatural. But making that distinction, isolating that shift from the natural to the non-natural is what Epicureanism is all about. It is the only way for therapy to take hold and for *ataraxia* to set in. And it is what makes Lucretius' historical narrative so utterly strange. By the end of Book V and the preface to Book VI, Lucretius has both condemned and lauded human achievements so many times that it is difficult to know where he stands. Ultimately, though, Lucretius is forced, simply by the development of his own logic, to admit that the developments of human society are both necessary and condemnable. Necessary because the brutality of natural life does not provide enough protection for Epicureanism itself to grow and thrive. Athens, Lucretius seems to admit, is good for at least one thing: it was the breeding ground for Epicurus. He writes,

> It was Athens of glorious name that in former days first imparted the knowledge of corn-producing crops to mortal men and remodeled their lives and established laws; and it was Athens that first bestowed soothing solaces when she gave birth to a man endowed with such great genius, whose lips once gave utterance to true pronouncements on every subject.²¹

This is an explicit recognition by Lucretius that Epicurus was in some

---

²⁰ *Ibid.* [V, 982-984].
²¹ *Ibid.*, p. 178 [VI, 1-6].

ways the result and product of the same civilizing process that goes hand in hand with the unnatural passions of human beings. Epicureans in a state of *ataraxia* are not in a position to 'remodel lives' or 'establish laws'. But they are dependent, within the garden, on the remodeling and establishing that has happened outside. Epicurus' real genius, Lucretius suggests, was the ability to look into the natural apparatus of human beings and perform a kind of conceptual surgery, eliminating those parts of his intellectual make-up that had become tainted with unnatural drives, monstrous inclinations that can only drive man further away from the one benefit of human society: the capacity to withdraw into the garden. His genius, as the Epicureans view it, was in knowing when to stop, when to pull out of the process altogether. The only genuine benefit of a city-state like Athens is that it provided the conditions within which it could be transcended. Epicurus thus marks, simultaneously, an overcoming and a return. That there is an uneasy relationship between the overcoming and the returning is a direct result of the particular strategies that Epicurean philosophy mobilizes against the perceived failures of myth and the ethical philosophies that preceded Epicurus. There is no bite to Epicurean therapeutic philosophy without the distinction between natural and unnatural passions. There is no reason to be moved by the ethical solutions proposed by Epicureans unless the internalization of monsters is seen as a persuasive tactic.

The modern reception of Lucretius and Epicurean philosophy was thus faced with a serious problem: how to reconcile the fascinating materialism and natural science with the *ataraxia* that seemed so foreign to the spirit of curiosity and world engagement that was driving contemporary thought. Voltaire's method is indicative of his ethical commitments. Basically, he says that we need to put the monsters back into the world again. We need to rehabilitate the passions and repair the breach through which Epicurus inserted his *ataraxia*. We need to become Herculeans again, taking arms against a sea of troubles. Lucretius had redefined Hercules as Epicurus and monsters as passions. Voltaire redefines Epicurus as Candide and monsters as those external forces that constrain and determine human beings, i.e., he redefines monsters as fate. Blumenberg expresses these transformations in the following lines from *Shipwreck with Spectator*.

> Against the latter [Lucretius] he [Voltaire] summons up the full pathos of his moral philosophy. He must, however, accept shipwreck as a given, because for Voltaire, too, 'passions' are the energy that puts the human world in motion. Cultivating one's garden in the withdrawal of resignation, as Candide does at the end of his adventures, cannot be represented as the wisdom of the beginning, like Epicurus's philosophical existence turned

away from the world in his 'garden'. Candide, too, must live through his shipwreck near Lisbon, see the righteous Anabaptist sink into the sea while the brutal sailor survives, so that his resignation at the end might not be eaten away by the 'passion' of believing that something in the world might have escaped him. Voltaire does not trust renunciations of the world.[22]

In not trusting renunciations of the world, Voltaire was to express the modern strategy for appropriating Epicurean thought. Broadly speaking, it was to snatch the materialism out of the system while leaving the quietism behind. Indeed, many of the early modern thinkers who became interested in Lucretius and Epicurus and their materialist natural science reversed the order of priorities in the Epicurean system. They essentially ignored the ethical standpoint that is the ultimate goal of natural science and took up the physics and biological investigations as of interest in their own right. Stripped of the ethical endpoint and the basic Epicurean methodology, the materialism could be appreciated from an entirely different set of assumptions and motivations. Materialism unfettered, and driven by the motor of the passions, would then be unleashed against a world of outrageous misfortunes. This strategy was, in turn, to create its own conflicts, dilemmas, and reactions. For this reason alone, it could be argued that a version of Epicureanism always nips at the heels of modern thought.

Lucretius' *De Rerum Natura* culminates in a terrifying, fictionalized account of the plague of Athens in which the city is destroyed as a consequence of the human passions run rampant. That is the Epicurean riposte always available as a counterpoint to Voltaire's attempt to reject and respond to the ethics of *ataraxia*. In mood, it is not dissimilar to the mistrust of and hostility to the passions of the Enlightenment kicked up by the disasters and implosions of the last century. The question is where we think the monsters are now and what we intend to do about it.

---

[22] Blumenberg, *Shipwreck with Spectator*, p. 34.

Nature and its Monsters in the Renaissance. Montaigne and Vanini

TRISTAN DAGRON

ABSTRACT. The Renaissance interest in monsters is a well known fact, particularly in the guise of an aesthetic fascination for deformity and the various improbable productions of Nature. This interest also has to do with the discovery, beyond the borders of Europe, of new animal species. The goal of this paper is to show that this interest is also tied (1) to the questioning of the Peripatetic category of form and species, and its inseparably logical and metaphysical problematization and (2) to the constitution of a new image of Nature, as a virtually infinite productive power. Using two main texts, by Montaigne and by Vanini, I try to show how the monster henceforth appears as a logical problem, rather than a theological scandal, and how it expresses the crisis of a cosmos previously governed by a guiding providence. The Renaissance, in this respect, is less an anticipation of the modern scientific revolution (although it makes it possible), than it is a shake-up, a *mise en crise* of the older metaphysical order, along with its intellectual and philosophical coordinates.

In an essay written already some time ago on "Monstrosity and the monstrous," Georges Canguilhem devotes a few suggestive pages to the 'prehistory' of modern teratology, in order to emphasize how the encounter in the eighteenth century between comparative anatomy and the new, epigenetically oriented embryology gave rise to a new discipline. Taking his inspiration from the beautiful works of Baltrusaïtis, he then shows that "teratology from the Middle Ages to the Renaissance is hardly a catalogue of monstrosities; it is more of a celebration of the monstrous."[1] Canguilhem thus

---

[1] *La connaissance de la vie*, 2nd revised and expanded edition (Paris: Vrin, 1980), p. 176 (the essay, revised for this edition, originally dates from 1952). Canguilhem quotes Baltrusaïtis' *Le Moyen âge fantastique* (Paris: Colin, 1955) and *Réveils et prodiges* (Paris: Colin, 1960). On the question of monsters, one must naturally refer to Jean Céard's very documented work, *La nature et les prodiges. L'insolite au XVIe siècle* (Geneva: Droz, 1977, 2nd edition, 1996). On the origin of rationalist teratology, see Patrick Tort's

distinguishes a rational approach to anatomical anomalies ("monstrosity" proper), which was characteristic of new developments in medicine during the eighteenth century, from the aesthetic of deviance and the monstrous in general. The latter concepts are fueled by the fascination for extraordinary phenomena, as well as imaginary fantastic beings, in an indiscriminate linkage of myth and phantasm. In Canguilhem's story, science does away with this generic category of the monstrous, the persistence of which, today, merely testifies to the residual existence of that "age of fables." Now, his usage of the horizon effect is justified in rhetorical terms, but one would obviously be wrong to believe that this story is sufficient to explain biological speculation during the Middle Ages and the Renaissance.

During the Renaissance, enthusiasm for monsters is a reality. However, it reflects less a fascination or "blind" celebration of all forms of strangeness, than an epistemological crisis which shakes up the notion of the 'normal' itself, based on a doctrine of natural order that had been dominant until then. If monsters are of such interest, and if they come to occupy the forefront of the cultural and artistic scene, it is because there is a new concept of nature which, although it bases itself on ancient and medieval notions of form and essence, nevertheless strongly calls into question their presuppositions. From this point of view, which belongs equally to natural science and to philosophical speculation, the function of monstrosity, far from being nave, as Canguilhem suggests, appears as clearly heuristic: it questions the established norm through singular realizations of nature, and thereby, the conceptual coordinates with which one thought about the world.

1 Montaigne: The monster as a logical problem

This is undoubtedly the meaning of Montaigne's remark, which concludes his essay entitled "Of a monstrous child" ("D'un enfant monstrueux"):

> Those whom we call monsters are not so to God, who sees in the immensity of his work, the infinity of forms he has comprised in it, and one must believe that this astonishing figure is related and linked to some other figure of the same kind, unknown to man. From his omniscience proceeds nothing but that which is good, common and regular, but we do not see its arrangement and relationship. *Quod credo videt non miratur etiam si cur fiat nescit, quod ante non vidit id si evenerit ostentum esse censet.* That which we call contrary to nature is that which goes against custom. Everything is according to nature, no matter what it

---

extremely stimulating *L'ordre et les monstres. Le débat sur l'origine des déviations anatomiques au XVIIIe siècle* (Paris: Le Sycomore, 1980).

may be. Let this universal and natural reasoning drive out of us the error and astonishment brought to us by novelty.²

The monster, and in general, all natural "marvels," present an initially statistical irregularity with respect to what most often or customarily happens. This is a traditional thesis, clearly found for instance in Aristotle, in his *De generatione animalium*: "the monster belongs to the category of phenomena contrary to nature, to nature considered not in its absolute constancy, but in its ordinary course."³ In the above passage, Montaigne is not content with recalling the natural status of monstrosity; rather, he opposes a norm based on humanity's necessarily limited experience, to a divine science, which alone can match the infinite variety of natural forms, and encompass all the genera unknown to us. From an epistemological point of view, this remark is obviously problematic given that the examples he discusses in this way (a child with a "double body," a shepherd deprived of genitals) would seem to highlight defects with respect to a norm of a well-defined species, and thus reject the assimilation of the "monstrous" to an unknown species. However, in its essentially heuristic dimension, Montaigne's remark does convey a newly elaborated relativism with respect to traditional (or 'customary') norms, which is largely responsible for the enthusiasm for monsters in the Renaissance. In a sense, curiosity is perhaps the best antidote to the asinine astonishment that Montaigne denounces.

However, as is clearly seen in the passage from the *Essais*, the problematization of the norm does not come hand in hand with a rejection of the doctrine of forms. To the necessarily finite number of catalogued gen-

---

² "Ce que nous appelons monstres ne le sont pas à l'égard de Dieu, qui voit en l'immensité de son ouvrage l'infinité des formes qu'il y a comprises, et est à croire que cette figure qui nous étonne se rapporte et tient à quelque autre figure de mme genre inconnu à l'homme. De sa toute-sagesse, il ne part rien que bon et commun et réglé, mais nous n'en voyons pas l'assortiment et la relation. Quod credo videt non miratur etiam si cur fiat nescit, quod ante non vidit id si evenerit ostentum esse censet. Nous appelons contre nature ce qui advient contre la coutume. Rien n'est que selon elle, quel qu'il soit. Que cette raison universelle et naturelle chasse de nous l'erreur et l'étonnement que la nouvelleté nous apporte" (*Essais*, II, 30, ed. A. Tournon [Paris: Imprimerie Nationale, 1998], pp. 601-602). The text is an addition to the "Bordeaux copy." The Latin quote is taken from Cicero, *De divinatione*, II, 22: "That which we see often does not surprise us, even if the cause is unknown; but that which we have never seen we believe to be a prodigy."

³ *De generatione animalium*, IV, 4, 770b. Aristotle continues: "because from the point of view of nature which is eternal and subject to necessity, nothing is produced against nature, but this is the opposite in phenomena which are generally one way, but can also be another." The passage is used by Thomas Aquinas to distinguish monsters from real miracles which proceed from divine intervention, completely exceeding the powers of nature: "Monstra licet fiant contra naturam particularem, non tamen fiunt contra naturam universalem" (*De potentia*, q. 6, art. 2, ad 8m).

era, Montaigne opposes the immensity of nature and the infinite number of forms. However, even if this proliferation naturally affects the sense of their function and the normative status of the idea of a natural species, order as such is not denied. Rather, our ability to comprehend order is called into question. In a sense, one can compare Montaigne's criticism to Spinoza's, who, nearly a century later, denounces those whom, "when they see something happen in nature which is not in keeping with the model they conceived for something of the same sort, believe that nature herself is flawed or has sinned, and that it has left its work imperfect."[4] Montaigne, however, preserves the essence of the doctrine of finality and order which Spinoza challenges; and although he targets in the same way the *stulta admiratio* of those who believe that nature has gone insane, Montaigne does not immediately question the principle of their natural doctrine of formalities. His critical dialectic does not break with earlier paradigms, but instead reveals their inherent difficulties, and develops the immanent logic that pushes them to the limit, until it brings to light their aporias and paradoxes, in an infinite commentary.

In fact, it is easy enough to show that Montaigne's text is (literally) very close to some of Augustine's most frequently quoted arguments, which oppose the human norm (according to which we judge the deformity of certain beings), to a divine or universal plane of ultimate perfection and beauty:

> The same explanation that is used to account for [individual] monstrous births among our race can also be applied to certain monstrous races. For God is the creator of all things, and he knows at what place and time a given creature should be created, selecting in his wisdom the various elements from whose likenesses and diversities he contrives the beautiful fabric of the universe. But one who cannot see the whole clearly is offended by the apparent deformity of a single part, since he does not know with what it conforms or how to relate it to the whole (*quoniam cui congruat et quo referatur ignorat*). We know instances of men born with more than five digits on their hands and feet. This, to be sure, is too slight to be considered a serious aberration from the norm, yet far be it from any one to suppose in his folly that the creator made a mistake in the number of human fingers, even though one may not know why God acted as he did. So, even if a greater deformity were to arise, he whose

---

[4] *Ethics*, Book IV, Preface: "Cum itaque aliquid in natura fieri vident quod cum concepto exemplari quod rei ejusmodi habent, minus convenit, ipsam naturam tum defecisse vel peccavisse remque illam imperfectam reliquisse credunt."

works no one has the right to censure knows what he has done.[5]

The monster as contrasted by Augustine with wisdom and divine power, does indeed comprise a singularity with respect to a norm. If it can be integrated into the whole, it is because of a general congruence, that is, a universal harmony in which imperfection has its function, as a part. Augustine clearly distinguishes here between nature considered in its 'normal course', with respect to which monsters are indeed deviations, and nature as it is related to God. With regard to divine will and divine power, no event could be considered to be 'against nature', because it is an immediate effect of divine power, which cannot err: "We say that all prodigies are against nature, but this is false. How can what is produced by God's will go against nature, since it is the will of such a great creator which makes the nature of all created things? A prodigy is not contrary to nature, but contrary to what we know as nature."[6]

Augustine thus relates monsters (like all other wonders) to divine power, which can intervene in its creations in an 'extra-ordinary' way. Whereas in Aristotle, the monster can be said to be unnatural in the sense that it appears contrary to 'nature' as guided by a final cause, in Augustine, the monster is linked more to the miraculous, because it shows above all divine eminence with respect to nature created as such. In this respect, the creation of the monster can be considered as an event endowed with meaning:

> Just as it was not impossible for God to modify the natures that he wanted to create, it is not impossible for him to change the natures he has created, into anything he wishes. Therein lies this abundant forest of miracles, which are called *monstra, ostenta, portenta, prodigia*.... These names justifiably bring out *monstra* from *monstrare*, because they 'show' or 'demonstrate' [*monstrando*] something in signifying it.[7]

The etymology, of Stoic origin, stems here from a conception of nature entirely regulated by a providential order compatible with God's immediate

---

[5] Augustine, *The City of God*, XVI, 8 (trans. E. Matthews Sanford & W. McAllen Green [London-Cambridge: Loeb Classical Library, 1965], p. 45). This reference to Augustine, like the others I shall provide, is an essential locus of medieval and Renaissance reflection on monsters. Jean Céard emphasizes this (in *La nature et les prodiges, op. cit.*).

[6] *The City of God*, XXI, 8 (translation modified). Cf. *De Genesi ad litteram*, VI, XIII, 24: "These prodigies, when they happen do not happen against the laws of nature, unless we simply do not know nature in its normal course, but not for God, for whom nature is what he made."

[7] Augustine, *City of God*, XXI, 8.

intervention. The monster is indeed the indication of a shift between the first cause and the secondary causes.[8]

When he writes "what we call monsters are not so to God," Montaigne is undoubtedly retranscribing Augustine's own terms.[9] But the meaning he gives to the thesis is very different: it is not divine will which is capable of transforming beings at its leisure, nor a providential order which would overstep the natural order itself, but instead divine intelligence which is the only thing possessing the stature of natural order. Montaigne's astonishing formulation is not meant to distinguish between the ordinary unfolding of natural things and a divine will which could transgress this, but between a superior intelligence "who sees in the immensity of his work, the infinity of forms he has comprised in it," and a limited human intelligence, incapable of understanding this infinity of forms. And it is in reference to a "natured" nature, not to the power of its artisan, that Montaigne adds, commenting on Cicero, that "everything is according to nature, no matter what it may be." The Augustinian commonplace idea is clearly reinscribed in a strongly naturalistic context.

Montaigne thus does not relate the "regularity" of monstrosity to divine will and power, but to "omniscience," solely insofar as it distinguishes itself from man's limited intelligence. He does not adopt the point of view of the creative act, but the purely epistemological point of view of instruments of knowledge: the monstrous deviation is no longer the objective indication of divine transcendence, but the mark *quoad nos* of the limits of our capacity of knowledge. If we had more extensive knowledge, we could understand the monster, no longer negatively, as a deviation with respect to the essence, but in all of its positivity, qua possessing its own form. Now, this requirement of positivity leads Montaigne to dispense with another of Augustine's justifications of the monstrous: the argument of harmony. Recall that Augustine relates the existence of the monster to divine providence, which takes into account the total perfection of the divine work. Our error therefore comes from our ignorance with respect to "harmony and relationships"

---

[8]This doctrine of providence as authorizing an immediate intervention of God in the course of the world will quickly enter into conflict with the 'Averroist' Aristotelian tradition which, on the contrary, denies any intervention of the first cause in the sublunary world: the prime mover only has influence via heavenly bodies. This tension between the Christian idea of providence and the peripatetic and philosophical thesis runs throughout the Middle Ages, but is radicalized at the beginning of the sixteenth century with Pomponazzi, for example (cf. the essential discussion in Alfonso Ingegno, *Saggio sulla filosofia di Cardano* [Firenze: La Nuova Italia, 1980], Chapter I: "Da Pomponazzi a Cardano," pp. 1–78). We will see Vanini's position, which is directly based on this debate, later, as well as Montaigne's, which must certainly be familiar to him.

[9]As Jean Céard judiciously notes in his commentary on the passage (*La nature et les prodiges*, pp. 433–434).

of the monstrous part with the "whole" or the universe. In the sense that it contributes to the perfection of the whole, negativity in general (physical pain, privation, even sin) can be saved and reconciled with the goodness of the universal divine scheme: providence. And this applies to monstrosity as well.

At first glance, the same appears to be true of Montaigne as well: knowledge of the "arrangement and relationship" of things should enable us to relate the monstrous to God's "omniscience." However, the invocation of divine wisdom essentially becomes the foundation of the immanent regularity of natural phenomena — which implies an absence of defects or sin in the natural order. For Montaigne, it is no longer a matter of saving the figures of negativity by invoking a providential order in which they 'fit'; instead, he challenges this negativity as illusory. This is why the "arrangement and relationship" of things doesn't refer so much to an eschatological context or a divine economy as such, but rather to a purely physical knowledge of nature. Further, this expression derives its meaning from a specifically *logical* context. If monstrosity is above all a relative effect of our ignorance, this means it must be possible to think of a monster positively as a "perfect" being in the proper sense of the term, i.e., the actuality of a form or essence that "omniscience" can apprehend in positive terms. In other words, it is a being that possesses a definition.

This is the meaning of Montaigne's slightly technical formulation, "one must believe that this astonishing figure is related and linked to some other figure of the same kind, unknown to man." The "figure" or "shape" of the monster is not absolutely singular in itself; it is only specific, but precisely, we are missing the "kind" or "genus" to which it should be related. And if the kind is unknown to us, it is because we are incapable of "arranging" the monstrous shape with the conformations of other, more familiar beings. Montaigne, like Augustine, also ties the question of the monster to that of "monstrous races," and this is precisely a 'topic' procedure for the 'invention' or discovery of species, various examples of which can be found in the narratives of the early naturalists.[10] In order for the singular form of the

---

[10] In a suggestive parallel, Céard (*op. cit.*, pp. 310-312) shows how a naturalist like Thevet describes strange animals of "Antarctic France" by emphasizing their irreducible singularity, which reveals the incomprehensible power of nature: "Here are admirable facts of nature, and as she likes to do things grandly, diversely, and for the most part, incomprehensible, and admirable to men. It would therefore be impertinent to seek their cause and reason, like many try to do on a daily basis: because this is a real secret of nature, whose knowledge is reserved for the creator alone" (*Singularitez de la France antartique* [1558], f. 99a, quoted p. 312). He opposes Thevet to Belon who, in his *Observations de plusieurs singularitez et choses memorables* (1554), maintains that "one must look for the truth of unknown things by that which we know" (f. 3b, quoted p. 311). For Belon, as for Montaigne, "judgment" must be opposed to admiration

monster to be thought of as specific, one must stop being astonished by it, and locate it within the natural order, which means providing a definition of this 'form' which enables one to grasp the "arrangement and relationship" behind it, which can account for it. Montaigne posits the possibility of such a definition *de jure*, in the name of divine "omniscience," yet he notes that it is easier for us to conceive dissimilarity — a source of astonishment or wonder — than similarity — a source of knowledge. However, only our ignorance, and not a defect of nature, prevents us from giving an authentic definition for the monster, that is, discovering both the "arrangement" or similarity between different forms which makes up the common genus, and the "relationship" or specific difference which relates multiplicity to a variation of the common form.[11] In spite of the literal similarity between these passages in Augustine and Montaigne, they are quite different. Although he uses some of Augustine's expressions, Montaigne's relativism in no way asserts or promotes the transcendence of divine will defined as the ultimate 'reason', 'ground' or 'nature' of the creature; rather, he points to the immensity of nature and the infinite variety of its forms. The monster is no longer a theological paradox, but a merely *logical problem* to which philosophy is necessarily confronted, when grappling with the unusual effects of nature.

By defining the monster as a being that we cannot relate to a "figure of the same genus," Montaigne is deliberately locating himself in the general context of a doctrine of classification based on the Aristotelian notion of "form." But he frees himself from this in more ways than one. Aristotle, as we know, thinks of the monstrous in terms of a biology that considers generation as the transmission of the essential constitutive determinations of the species. When he defines the monster as "against nature," what Aristotle understands by "nature" is 'form' insofar as it has an end, 'form' governed by an end, following the analysis of *Physics* II.8 (199a30-199b4).

---

or astonishment. On the same question, prevalent in the eighteenth century, see G. Canguilhem, "Du singulier et de la singularité en épistémologie biologique," in *Études d'histoire et de philosophie des sciences* (Paris: Vrin, 1983, 5th expanded edition), pp. 211–225: the issue is again how to articulate singular species within a 'system', i.e. a reasoned classification of natural beings.

[11] The expression "arrangement and relationship" translates into a physical context the logical requisites of an "authentic definition" (by genus and difference). The "arrangement" here refers to the common element or the genus; the "relationship" which places figures with respect to each other, refers to the series of differences which affect the genus. The term "figure," which could seem surprising, translates here the ambiguity of the Latin species, simultaneously "species" and "appearance," *eidos* and *morphe*. It is the phenomenological correlation of the form included in God's infinite intellect. Precisely, Montaigne's intention is to show that the physiological form of the monster must be thought of as a specific form.

Error is then a "deviation with respect to species" or to the "generic type" (*genous proton*) (*De animalium generatione*, IV.3, 767b6). The monster thus stems from an "accidental necessity" which comes to "prevent" the information of the matter in conformity with the essential and final type, that is, the species that should be produced. Further, the monster indicates the existence of a 'split', 'unevenness' or 'displacement' between the created shape or organic form (*morphe*) and its essential and specific type (*eidos*). In this perspective, entirely governed by this doctrine of species, the definition of monstrosity is obviously very flexible and can embrace altogether banal dissimilarities:

> The same causes explain that certain products resemble the parents, while others do not; some resemble the father, some the mother, be it the ensemble of the parts or each one individually; some resemble the parents more than they do the ancestors, and to the latter more than anyone in general; males look more like their father and females resemble the mother; in certain cases the children resemble no one in the family, but still have a human form; others do not even have human appearance, but already that of a monster. Moreover, he who does not resemble the parents is already, in a certain respect, a monster: because in this case nature has strayed from the generic type in a certain sense. The very first deviation is the birth of a female instead of a male.[12]

All dissimilarity can therefore be considered as a monstrosity. This is the consequence of Aristotle's scheme in which generation is to be understood as the reproduction of a formal type. The flexibility of such a definition naturally opens the field to more or less infinite speculations.

As long as the delimitations of the specific norm are not defined, the biological characterization of the monster ultimately refers to any kind of singularity. Given such arguments, one can obviously assert that, even when nature goes astray, it operates according to an end: the mistake does not cancel out the rationality of the final cause, but produces a determinate variation within the genus. Cardano recalls this in his *De subtilitate* (1550):

> If nature had no end, that which is born would be without form, but this is not always so. Some, like Aristotle, believe that when nature errs, the end lies in the next genus: such as in a female instead of a male, a two-footed animal for a man, or if she cannot create more human-like animals, she makes quadrupeds, and by

---

[12] *De generatione animalium*, IV.3, 767a35–767b9.

this argument, she rarely breeds fish, and never trees .... And when nature intends a genus, she necessarily imagines (*fingere intendit*) some species of this genus. Therefore it seems that when nature cannot reach a certain specific end, she makes out of the genus the closest determinate being to this end, when matter allows it.[13]

Monsters are not without form. To err is not to move around at random, but to orient oneself according to an overly general direction. By virtue of this principle, Cardano notes that when nature makes a mistake, it still manages to approach its end: it may therefore take the next genus as *telos* and, in doing so, creates a species of this genus. This is why human monsters are most often women, bipeds, even quadrupeds, but rarely fish, and never plants. Cardano, obviously inspired by Aristotle, pushes his logic to the extreme, to the point of creating the idea of a deviation relative to a series of metamorphoses: the regulated mistake of nature can lead, in extreme cases, to sophism *par excellence*, to the shift from one genus to another. That this transgression goes from like to like, keeping an order that the mind can follow internally, does not change matters much: the monster indeed displays the fragility of the essential order of the *eidos*, faced with nature's power of metamorphosis. Conversely, the monster also displays the inventiveness or productivity of a nature that "builds" or "imagines" the species of the final genus ("Et cum natura genus intendit, speciem aliquam necessario etiam *fingere* generis illius intendet"). It is certainly a similar thesis that Montaigne defends in the passage quoted: incapable of knowing the "figure" of the same genus forged by nature, our imagination concludes that there is a flaw, where the efficient cause, in its very 'erring', had in fact displayed infinite ingeniousness.

The effect of deviation always remains a specification of the next closest genus. Montaigne's relativism is entirely based on this logical consideration. When he notes, regarding the monster, that "this figure which astonishes us

---

[13]*De subtilitate*, I. XII; *Opera omnia* (Lyon, 1663), III, pp. 568-569: "Si enim prorsus finem nullum haberet, informe esset, quod nasceretur: at non informe est semper. Quibusdam visum est, ut Aristoteli, naturam assequi in proximo genere, cum aberrat, finem suum, utpote fminam loco maris, bipedem loco hominis, aut si non potest, quadrupedem ex humanioribus, eo argumento, quod rarius pisces gignat, arbores autem nunquam . . . . Et cum natura genus intendit, speciem aliquam necessario etiam fingere generis illius intendet. Videtur igitur cum assequi non potest finem aliquem proprium proximorem illi non incertum, sed ex genere fabricare, non reluctante materia." On Cardano, see Ingegno's very important work, *Saggio sulla filosofia di Cardano, op. cit.*, and also N. G. Saraisi, *The Clock and the Mirror. Girolamo Cardano and Renaissance Medicine* (Princeton: Princeton University Press, 1997), as well as the collection *Girolamo Cardano. Le opere, le fonti, la vita*, eds. M. Baldi & G. Canziani (Milano: Franco Angeli, 1999).

is linked to another figure of the same type unknown to man," Montaigne is specifically criticizing the idea that a "figure" (in the sense of *morphe*) is unclassifiable or without its own essence. Every being rightfully has an essence (*de jure*); and the definition of monstrosity as deviation, justified relative to our rough vision of natural realities, cannot grasp the immensity of nature. The monster must be considered as deviant with respect to known species and types; however, considered in and of itself, it represents a completely separate species or essence of which we do not have the knowledge because we cannot know the order of nature itself — the system of differences deployed by the infinity of forms. The spectacle of nature provides us with endless variety, but without knowing the "arrangement and relationship" of things, we remain incapable of relating these forms or figures to a regulated becoming.

It is therefore not, as in Augustine, the point of view of the "whole" and the providential will of God which must justify monstrosity; rather, it is the definition of that which is singular by the infinite series of differences which make it up as *infima species*. The monster's natural status stems from its having to be considered *de jure as index sui*, because it manifests the immensity, or more specifically, the plenitude of nature from which the infinite variety of things emerges. This is the ethical meaning of Montaigne's reintegration of monstrosity in the natural order. Relativism leads to a singular thought which begins by making the monstrous normal by relating it to a rule unknown to us, and therefore describes singularity with the characteristics of a relative monstrosity. This procedure of distancing is nothing like nominalism: far from refusing to classify what is remarkable with respect to the norm of the essence, it draws its strength, on the contrary, from a dialectic of figure and species, which, as we saw, is not foreign to Aristotelian biology itself. And it is precisely this inversion that Montaigne emphasizes in his essay "Of cripples" ("Des boiteux"), when he draws the lesson of the so-called prodigies and miracles which very often are simply due to causes which "escape our sight by their smallness" and concerning which "a very careful, attentive and subtle inquisitor is required ... indifferent and not prejudiced":

> Until this time, all these miracles and strange events were hidden to me — I have never seen monster nor miracle in the world more explicit than myself: One becomes familiar with anything strange over time. But the more I brood and know myself, the more my deformity astonishes me. The less I understand myself.[14]

---

[14]Essais, III, 11, "Des boiteux," ed. cit., p. 373: "Jusques à cette heure tous ces

The motif is too familiar to readers of the *Essais* for us to insist upon this.

2 Vanini and the critique of the defect of nature

Giulio Cesare Vanini, who died at the stake in Toulouse in 1619, is a very different type of author from Montaigne. His writings, and notably his *Amphitheatrum æternæ providentiae*, published in 1615 in Paris, are rooted in the tradition of scholarly peripateticism which discusses Aristotle based on Averroes' commentaries, and are clearly continuous with sixteenth-century Italian naturalism as represented by Pomponazzi and Cardano. In an entirely different context, using different arguments, Vanini nevertheless puts forth a criticism of the thesis of nature's "defect" or "flaw" which is comparable to Montaigne's, by defining the monster as *index sui*. The discussion which interests us here belongs to the series of *exercitationes* in the *Amphitheatrum* devoted to refuting the purportedly "Averroistic" argument according to which the existence of monsters would show that divine providence does not extend to singular beings of the sublunary world.

The thesis according to which *nihil esse in Natura mutilum* ("there is nothing mutilated in nature"), targets the following passage in Cardano's *De subtilitate*, which Vanini quotes in its entirety:

> We are used to calling the mutilated (*mutilos*) those who are blind, deaf or one-eyed, crippled, those who have six fingers and considering them as monsters of nature with bad morals. Astrologers easily explain this by saying that they are subject to a misfortune which is the source of the flood of vices. As for us, we say that if nature has erred in easier things, *a fortiori* she has failed in difficult ones. In the same respect, as all mutilated ones are dishonest, as those who have no physical defects are not all of good morals: because more is needed to shape a soul without sin than a body [without defect]. Therefore, the worst of all are the hunchbacks, because the mistake involves the heart, the main part of the entire body; then come the blind and one-eyed, because nature erred regarding the brain; then the mute and the deaf, because nature erred in a less noble part of the brain; then the crippled who follow and who are defective in a large member, and then those who have six fingers and those who have webbed fingers, where nature erred in less necessary

---

miracles, et événements étranges, se cachent devant moi — Je n'ai vu monstre et miracle au monde plus exprès que moi-même: On s'apprivoise à toute étrangeté par l'usage et le temps, Mais plus je me hante et me connais, plus ma difformité m'étonne. Moins je m'entends en moi."

things.¹⁵

The passage testifies to an ancient and resistant prejudice, mostly based on physiognomy, against beings which have been "truncated" or "mutilated" by nature. Vanini, however, does not stop at the meanness of the humpbacked; he criticizes the scale of perfection which serves, in Cardano, to present moral perfection (the "soul without sin") as a simple natural perfection:

> You call mutilated the blind and crippled. The Ancients called mutilated he who has a defect by nature, the word coming from *mutus (deaf)*, because language is a very noble and highly necessary thing. You who wrote *De subtilitate*, you should have written with more subtlety. More subtly, we say that nothing in nature is mutilated. Because if we consider the oyster as mutilated because the slug crawls, and the slug as mutilated with respect to the mole, the mole with respect to the dog, the dog with respect to man, man will also be mutilated next to the demon and compared to him. And what will become of the demon itself compared to superior intelligences? All of theses things, and I am not even talking about your examples, all the singular things gathered together and put end to end, I say, such that one single being is made out of all of them, if we compare them to God, will not only seem to be mutilated, but like nothing, and even, whether we can say it or not, as less than nothing.

---

¹⁵Cardano, *De subtilitate*, I, XII, ed. cit., III, p. 564: "Mutilos hos solemus vocare, cci, surdi, strabi, claudi, sexdigiti, taliaque monstra naturae, quae moribus pravis praedita sunt. Facillime negotium absolvunt Astronomi, maleficas dominari dicentes, a quibus flagitiorum colluvies ortum habet. Nos dicimus aberrare naturam in facillioribus, ob id verius in difficillimis defecisse: itaque ut omnes mutili improbi sunt, ita non omnes, qui corpore sunt non vitiati integris sunt moribus: nam plus exigitur ad formandum absque culpa animum, quam corpus. Ergo pessimi sunt omnium gibbi, cum error fit circa cor principium totius corporis post cæci, strabique quod circa cerebrum natura delinquerit. Inde muti, surdique nam in minus nobili cerebri parte natura defecit. Inde claudi, hos sequuntur qui in magno membro sunt vitiati, post quos sexdigiti, et qui digitos habent iunctos: nam in minus necessariis aberravit." Text quoted (with some variations) in Vanini's *Amphitheatrum aeternae providentiae*, exerc. XXXIX (Lyon, 1615), p. 266 (cf. G. C. Vanini, *Opere*, ed. G. Papuli et F. P. Raimondi [Galatina: Congedo editore, 1990], p. 257). Cardano's text ends with a last degree which Vanini doesn't mention: warts and scars. "Lastly come the warts and marks which look like scars. But one can rip off warts with oil of vitriol, although they are natural" ("Ultimus locus est verrucis, ac vestigiis, quae cicatrices mulantur. Sed verrucas extirpare licet oleo vitrioli etiam naturales"). The naturalist and materialist interpretation of moral virtue proposed by this passage is obviously more important than the folkloric prejudices it expresses. The idea of a soul, naturally "without sin" (and therefore a sort of natural sainthood) is original enough to be remarked upon.

This is why of all things produced by nature, either none will be said to be mutilated, or all of them will.[16]

The only defect that Vanini admits in nature and which affects all produced beings, is the *defectus in latitudine entis*: no being is absolute, except for nature itself or God, nor has any being, like God or nature, the capacity to be according to the complete and extensive *ratio entis*. All beings receive being according to certain specific determinations. From the point of view of *latitudo entis*, all beings can be said to be mutilated, but if each was related to its own, definite nature, none would legitimately be said to be defective or mutilated. The initial sense of Vanini's thesis is that it exonerates divine providence by the very recognition that nothing other than the absolute is totally all that it can be, in actuality. But the thesis goes much further, because it challenges the very notion of a defect or flaw of nature, and makes each singular entity its own scale of perfection. The same idea is taken up again later, in answer to the "Averroistic" argument according to which, if "monsters are imperfect beings," it follows that "they do not come from God." Vanini retorts: "In its genus, the monstrous animal is at the highest point of perfection (*summe perfectum*). It would not be what it is, if it were not most fully what it is (so to speak), while it is only said to be imperfect in comparison to other beings."[17] The strength of the argument resides in its tautological form.

Far from being imperfect, Vanini adds, monsters are often endowed with unusual skills. One naturally expects here the example of the "genius" or "prophet," but with clear irony, Vanini proposes the most trivial case of "something missing several organs, but which had only two orifices, one by which it sucked in nourishment and the other by which the excrements came out."[18] The idea of the perfection of the monster testifies to the extension

---

[16]*Amphitheatrum*, exerc. XXXIX, ed. cit., pp. 266–267; Opere, ed. cit., p. 257–258: "Mutilos vocas ccos et claudos. Mutilum dixere Veteres, quod esset fraudatum natura sua, deducta voce ab hominibus mutis, quippe homini sermo nobilissima res et maxime necessatia. Tibi vero De subtilitate scribenti subtilius scribendum fuit. Quare nos subtilissime dicimus nihil esse in Natura mutilum. Si enim ostrea mutila videantur, quod limax repat, at limax si talpae, si cani talpa, si canis homini, homo quoque erit mutilus Daemoni collatus et comparatus. Quid ipsi Daemones si ad superiores Mentes referantur ? Omnia vero haec, non dico ista, sed omnia, inquam, et singula conferta ita et conglutinata ut ex iis unum fiat, si cum Deo conferuntur, non solum mutila, sed etiam nihil imo, sive liceat sive non liceat dicere, minus quam nihil; quare eorum omnium quae a Natura procreantur aut nihil erit mutilum aut omnia."

[17]*Ibid.*, exerc. XLI, pp. 281–282; *Opere*, ed. cit., p. 263: "In suo namque genere monstruosum animal est summe perfectum; non enim esset hoc est, nisi in summo suo (ut ita loquar) esset esse, quod, si aliis comparatum dicetur imperfectum."

[18]*Ibid.*, p. 282; *Opere*, p. 263: "Quinimo perfectiones quamplurimas et ipsas quidem admirabiles in monstruosis fuisse legi. Haly refert audivisse de aliquo, quod membris

of the concept of the monster, now covering all of the "prodigies" or "marvels" of nature, and in general all relative exceptions, independently of any evaluative dimension. Again, anything can be considered as "monstrous."

Vanini's example shows to what extent the traditional scale or 'chain of beings' is finally put out of commission. Although the irony of the passage can seem obvious, it shouldn't hide its purpose. What Vanini is placing in the forefront is that nature, by a sort of spontaneous inventiveness, often seems to make up for the defects she has caused. Pushing the reasoning to the extreme, one can go on to say that by her "compensatory" invention, nature can produce monsters "in nobility and in perfection." This is at any rate what is suggested by Cardano's comment, which may be the basis for the thesis of the monster's perfection *sui generis*:

> Men are monstrous in nobility and perfection, like prophets or wise men, or because of the excellent nature of their parents, or by comets, by constellations, or by the concourse of the stars, *or because nature transferred virtue from several members to a single one. Therefore, these are sometimes less powerful in practice.*[19]

The example of the two orifices clearly refers to the last case, wherein the defect of a few members leads to the development of a new faculty.

Vanini's argument concerning "mutilated" beings and the idea of "defects" is even more interesting because it not only contests the norm of the species, but also the norm of the whole. From the standpoint of God and the absolute plenitude of being He constitutes, it is not only determinate beings

---

deficiebatur quamplurimis et non nisi duo habebat foramina, unum per quod sugebat cibum, aliud per quod excrementa emittebat." The comical effect is due to the bringing together of the thesis and the example: the existence of an animal whith two orifices, indeed, is not very remarkable. Vanini is obviously being ironic.

[19] *De subtilitate*, XII, *Opera*, III, p. 569: "Fiunt et montruosi homines nobilitate ac perfectione, seu prophetae dicantur, seu sapientes, vel ob parentum egregiam naturam, aut cometas, et constellationes, seu syderum concursus praecedentes, aut quia natura multorum membrorum vim in unum transtulit. Ob id factum est, ut hi minus quandoque opere valeant." On the influence of the heavens, cf. Pomponazzi's *De incantationibus*, which proposes a doctrine of singularity to explain exceptional "effects" thought to be caused by demons by natural causes: through their individual natures, some people are capable of things beyond the capacity of ordinary men. Some can move their ears at will (*De incantationibus* [Basel, 1567], p. 47, referring to Augustine's *City of God*, XIV, 24), some, like Augustus, can command frogs and make them silent at will (ibid., p. 47; cf. Suetonius, *Life of Augustus*, I, 140) and finally some miracle workers are naturally able to cure certain diseases, and others, to prophesize future events. These powers or properties go beyond ordinary faculties of the species (*eidos*) and are effects of the individual's make-up (*morphe*). Renaissance naturalism thus constantly opposes the normativity of essence with a consideration of "figure."

taken individually which can be considered as "mutilated," but in fact, the whole (as the concatenation of all nature's products) must also appear as imperfect and defective. This does away with the aesthetic or cosmological argument derived from the beauty of the universe, which served to justify monstrosity, notably in Augustine. The latter argument related deviations with respect to the norm of the species to the global harmony of the world, as only God can know "the various elements from whose likenesses and diversities he contrives the beautiful fabric of the universe."[20] Vanini excludes this cosmic norm as he excludes that of the species, in the name of the ontological difference he asserts, between a divine, "naturing" (*naturans*) nature and its multiform effect. In itself, the argument would not go very far if the idea of an ontological difference did not implicitly challenge the notion of an ideal exemplar of the "form of the world" (*forma mundi*) serving as a rule or measure for divine creation. The dignity of the monster can no longer be defended in the name of an originary divine plane which is fulfilled in the concatenation of all natural beings. Instead, the monster must manifest the perfection of its divine cause in and of itself, that is, inasmuch as it displays its 'own' perfection which does not need to be related to any other form of life. When Vanini claims to be defending the idea of a providential order against the objections of the peripateticians, he is actually dispensing with any formal mediation, which was traditionally supposed to guarantee the diffusion of being.[21] Clearly, it is neither the form of the species nor that of the universe which 'gives being' to singular matter.

In response to the "Averroists" who maintain that the monster is an effect of the accidental necessity of matter, and thus is not part of divine providence, Vanini purely and simply brackets the mediation of the essence or *eidos* which is supposed to regulate the production of natural "figures." He does not deny the final cause, but remains silent about it, effectively tossing it out of the theological debate on providence. He concludes as follows: "monsters, whatever be the cause from which they come, fall under divine providence. I show this in the following manner: monsters come from the efficiency of God, because all beings are dependent on the first being, and therefore on divine providence."[22] As in the rest of the *Amphitheatrum*, the ontological perspective is asserted here in order to strip theology itself of its meaning, along with the series of mediations which were to support its

---

[20] Augustine, *The City of God*, XXI, 8.
[21] According to a fundamental formulation of Aquinas' doctrine of substantial forms, which says that 'the form gives being to the matter'.
[22] *Amphitheatrum*, exerc. XL, p. 281; *Opere*, ed. cit., p. 262: "(. . .) dico ultimo, monstra, a quacunque causa proveniant, sub divinam providentiam cadere. Quod ita ostendo: Monstra dependent a Dei efficientia: a primo namque ente dependet omne ens, igitur a Dei providentia."

rationality. Significantly, in the *De admirandis naturæ reginæ deæque mortalium arcanis (Admirable Secrets of Nature Queen and Goddess of Mortals)* published the following year, in 1616, Vanini again evokes the problems of providence, but this time quite unequivocally: "Why is it that nature which is a faculty of God — what am I saying: who is God himself, and should produce everything perfectly, sometimes produces [or 'forms'] prodigious childbirths and monstrous fetuses?"[23]

A being without a purpose, the monster, which in Aristotle was, so to speak, the *ratio cognoscendi* of the articulation of figure and essence, enabling the final cause to be linked to the form as immanent within the composite, here merely displays the arbitrariness of the dialectical edifice with which Aristotelianism was supposed to be adapted to new ends, by presuming to link the order of nature to the creative power of God. If Vanini's discussion seems so significant, it is not because of its deliberately paradoxical and ironic character, but rather because it precisely conveys a constant trait of Renaissance philosophy of nature, in its constant reflection on the tension between the order of 'figures' and the system of the essence, between natural vicissitudes and the realm of meaning which might be able to grasp their seemingly erratic course.

3 The counterfeited beings of a sick world

Montaigne's intention at the conclusion of his short essay on the "monstrous child" is neither to develop a natural question, nor to defend divine providence against its detractors. Rather, he means to contrast human astonishment with a superior intelligence which could perceive the infinity of natural forms and be able to judge or assess them differently from us, by relating the unusual figure or shape of the monster to a determinate genus (yet one which is unknown to us). We have just seen how Montaigne explained our astonishment faced with the monster, not as a theological scandal, but as a logical paradox: the impossibility of relating the individual to a species (that is, a genus and a specific difference). The being which we see as lacking a form is actually an effect of our ignorance; what it is lacking is rather an assignable definition and a name. This is what Cardano emphasizes again, when he comments that even when nature errs, it always reaches a species of a proximate genus. And it is this same paradox that Vanini tries to empty of its theological content when he assures us that the monster is "perfect within its own genus" and must be considered as its own norm. Further, one could even say in this respect that if the Renaissance was so fascinated

---

[23] *De admirandis naturae arcanis* (Paris, 1616), dial. XL, p. 254; *Opere*, ed. cit., p. 414: "Cur Natura, quae Dei facultas, imo Deus ipse cum sit, perfectissime emoliri deberet, prodigiosos tamen partus monstruososque fœtus efformat ?"

with monsters (and all figures of self-reference), it is because they vividly illustrate the limits and traditional aporias of all taxonomic enterprises;[24] the paradox is precisely this: what theater of representation could organize an infinite variety of forms?

Now, Montaigne's response to the formal paradox of monstrosity is in a sense analogous to Vanini's. He lays out a doctrine of essence which is no longer based on the idea of an order guaranteed by divine "will," but on the conviction that the rule of natural production is, on the contrary, immanent to the order of figures and natural vicissitudes. This is what Montaigne's remark suggests, taken literally: from divine omniscience or wisdom, "nothing proceeds but that which is good, common and regular, but we do not see its arrangement and relationship." Although the formulation is clearly Augustinian, the consequence is obviously not, because Montaigne deduces that "everything is according to nature, no matter what it may be," immediately rejecting any kind of 'teratomancy' (prediction by the existence of monsters). He indeed avoids identifying the "nature of things" with divine "will": "this universal and natural reason" — the principle according to which nothing is "against nature" — must "drive out of us the error and astonishment brought to us by novelty." Montaigne's invocation of "omniscience" does not at all mean that all things must be seen in terms of divine will or omnipotence; he is claiming that everything in nature is "good, common and regulated," and nothing happens outside the limits of the ordinary course of things, except in relation to our own ignorance.

Unlike Augustine, who asserts the efficiency and omnipotence of a first cause in order to save the power of the creator against the objections that the philosophers make from the evident imperfections of things, Montaigne defines the perfection of the order of secondary causes as a mere effect of the creator's wisdom or "omniscience," and uses this wisdom as an argument for denying the existence of "defects of nature," as illusory. Divine wisdom clearly has no other function here except to found a perfectly naturalistic epistemology according to which the effects of nature must be explained *iuxta propria principia*, without recourse to any extraordinary supernatural intervention. Far from explaining monsters in terms of God's bare will and his power to show himself through miracles, the conclusion of the essay "Of a monstrous child," on the contrary, targets the "prognostications" Montaigne had mocked in the preceding paragraph and the cliché from

---

[24] Foucault, in the chapter on the "Prose of the world" in *Les Mots et les choses* (Paris: Gallimard, 1966; trans. A Sheridan, *The Order of Things* [New York: Pantheon, 1994]), correctly insisted on the omnipresence of self-referentiality during the Renaissance: the series of logical paradoxes which result from this open and pose the problem of the notion of order with respect to the infinite. Authors of the time do not only accept the twisting of the principle of identity, they call for it.

Augustine according to which "*monstra* [comes] from *monstrare*, because [it] shows [or demonstrates] something in signifying it."[25] Moreover, it is remarkable in this regard that the argument derived from the aesthetic perfection of the whole, which is fundamental in Augustine, is not only absent, but completely invalidated: the postulate of the rule does not govern any harmony of the whole, but only the "arrangement and relationship" of all things in the immensity of a nature which is no longer beautiful for its harmony, but for its variety.

In this respect, Montaigne's aesthetic is representative of a significant mutation which affects Renaissance art forms, its natural philosophy and its theological categories, equally. If there is an 'aesthetic of deviance' in the Renaissance, it is because the problematization of the norm of the essence opens up the field to a completely singular reflection on the "pathological" which then affects all domains of thought. Generally speaking, one can say that in the Renaissance, the various figures of negativity are no longer conceived as external threats, but as the immanent possibilities of beings: contrariness, even contradiction, appear as constitutive. This is perhaps one of the meanings of the success of the Platonic figure of Silenus, or even the famous ambivalence of wisdom and madness, also celebrated by Erasmus. In such a context, one understands that the norm ends up being treated less as a principle of identity than as a principle of variation, and, in turn, that deviance or deviation points less to the dark power of the Other, than to the innocent plasticity of the Same. And it is this point of view which might entitle one to speak of a "celebration of the monstrous," as Canguilhem did. But this fascination does not look backwards to an ancient "age of fables"; rather, it reflects the decline of the mythical universe which Augustine so vigorously reformed.

If monstrosity must be conceived as an immanent possibility of nature and be assigned a positive cause, it is because the natural order largely exceeds the borders of the ancient cosmos. Nature has ceased to be a "world." The rule which governs the arrangement and the relationship of things is no longer that which guarantees the harmony and unity of a totality, but rather the 'rule' of dispersion, variety and vicissitudinous becoming which transforms everything into everything. Of course, this transformation can be interpreted as setting forth the premises of a new science of nature which gradually removes monstrosity from the ancient "fables." But the dialectic from which Montaigne and Vanini's contributions emerge is rather a response to the crisis of these ancient thought-contents, and not an inauguration of the new epistemology of modern times. From this point of view, the "celebration of the monstrous" does call certain notions into question,

---

[25] *City of God*, XXI, 8.

but in a way which largely exceeds the arena of science as such: it primarily targets the notions of "providence" and "world." In a particularly surprising text, Cardano expresses an emblematic worry which, to be sure, displays key tenets of this sixteenth-century "fascination," but above all, allows us to see a crisis, in which the intellectual coordinates inherited from Augustinianism can only be grasped as paradoxical. Here, the monster ceases to be a sign or divine warning, and becomes the symptom of a sick world:

> Because it is a question of prodigies, maybe we will be correct in formulating this doubt: from the moment when they take place, these events depend on their own causes, it would not be possible for the future to depend on the causes of the prodigy, or for us to know it or foresee it by way of this prodigy. For example, if a flock of crows of an altogether unknown type appears and one wants to presage the ruin of a city because of this, the ruin of the city must depend on the cause that led the crows to fly above it. Or yet, to take a clearer example, if a two-headed calf signifies the weakness of a political power, how could this bad luck depend on the cause of the two-headed calf, because it has its own cause? Inasmuch as philosophers recognize that a monster results from a prevention of material and a mistake of nature. We therefore say that nothing happens because of the ineptness of the mass of matter, but because of a chaotic movement due to the vicious effect of opposite causes: because not only does the prevention make the monster, but it prevents the natural progress of things, such that, in animal pregnancies, it expels embryos, during their development, from their usual place. It seems therefore that the cause be a god, this is to say, the soul of the heavens, infinitely more noble and more powerful than a demon, and a servant of the Very High. And just as in the smallest things, these preventions come from small causes, as it happens for the calf, and in average things, they come from average things, like in the case of the city - preventions which are very big when they come from gods. These things do not bother themselves (this would be sacrilegious), but because they function in dispersed order, such that the inferior things which are penetrated by divine power by the Very High by several intermediaries, do not receive it fully and abundantly and are not at all conserved by it as usual. This is also why these monsters happen often following great crimes: because, by this same lessening of divine power, the exhalations and turpitudes abound and the inferior nature, neglected, runs great danger. Sins and

turpitudes, are the disdain of the Very High, the perversion of all justice, fundamental cowardliness, pride to our trust in our own forces, insurrections linked to treachery.[26]

A final and paradoxical attempt at salvaging! Basing divination (and in this case the idea that monsters are "signs") on a doctrine of natural causality, does not lead Cardano to resume the Stoic theme of a linked and unified cosmos, but on the contrary, to blame the causal chain, the vehicle of divine providence whose ministers only act in a dispersed, and often contradictory order. Signs are no longer a manifestation of divine omnipotence, but on the contrary of a relative impotence which is expressed by matter's resistance to the providential order. And this resistance is no longer that of the ultimate receptacle, but characterizes all subjects as such, including the so-called "intermediary" realities.

The starting-point for Cardano's "doubt" is obviously Pomponazzi's thesis that for a thing to be a sign, it must be the effect of determinate causes.[27] In the *De incantationibus*, Pomponazzi, using the Aristotelian theory which relates observable changes in the sublunary world to celestial bodies (*Meteora* I, 2), explains "deficiencies" and monstrosities in terms of astral causal-

---

[26] *De rerum varietate*, XIV, cap. 68; *Opera*, op. cit., III, pp. 272b-273a: "Verum cum ostentis agendum sit, forsan quis merito dubitabit, quoniam cum quae eveniunt, a propriis causis pendeant, non poterit quod futurum est ex ostenti causis pendere, neque ex ipso ostento dignosci aut praevideri. Velut si corvorum multitudo maxime ignoti generis appareat, velis que ex ea excidium urbis praesagire, oportet excidium urbis ex causa illa pendere, quae corvos eo transvolare impulit. Clariore etiam utar exemplo, si biceps vitulus impotentiam dominationis significat, quomodo id infortunium ex vituli bicipitis causa pendere poterit, cum propriam habeat ? Et maxime cum philosophi fateantur hoc monstrum ex materia impedimento atque naturae errore contingere. Dicimus ergo, non ex materia inepta mole id contingere, sed ex motu inordinato haec fieri, qui a causis contrariis pervertitur: neque enim solum impedimentum facit monstrum, sed naturalem tantum processum impedit: ut in ftibus abortus, in motibus animalium, abigat a consueto loco. Videtur ergo causa Deus aliquis, id est animae cli, dmone longe noblior atque potentior, ministrerque altissimi. Et ut impedimenta ex minimis in minimis velut vitulo, ita in mediocribus ex mediocribus in civitate, quae impedimenta sunt Deorum atque maxima: non sibi adversantium (hoc enim nephas) sed diverso ordine operantium, ut haec inferiora numinis vim illam per multos gradus ab altissimo immissam, haud plene et liberaliter excipiant: atque per illam more solito serventur. Quamborem et haec post ingenita peccata sequi solent: nam ab eadem numinis diminutione, afflatus et flagitia exuberant, et destituta inferior natura periclitatur. Sunt peccata atque flagitia, contemptus altissimi, perversio omnis iusti, extrema socordia, superbia cum in nostris viribus confidimus, seditioque quae perfidiae iuncta est." The text is quoted by Vanini, *Amphitheatrum*, exercit. XXXIX, ed. cit., pp. 270–271 (from "Philosophi fatentur monstrum ex materiae impedimento..."). It is translated by Jean Céard, *La nature et les prodiges*, op. cit., pp. 248–249.

[27] Cf. Pomponazzi, *Libri quinque de fato, de libero arbitrio et de praedestinatione*, I, 6, in *Opera*, ed. G. Gratarol (Basel, 1556), pp. 358-360; ed. R. Lemay (Lucani, 1957), pp. 21-23.

ity: "It seems however that celestial bodies are the cause of the defect of the species, blindness and limping for example, because astrologers often predict monstrous years based on the study of the stars, and that these monsters announce the future, because the word monster comes from *monstrare* (according to Saint Augustine, *De civit. Dei*, XXI, 8)."[28] In other words, the defect with respect to the species does not only come from the material or accidental cause, but from a positive cause (such as celestial bodies, according to Pomponazzi), which can therefore be known. Cardano takes up this thesis again, but distorts it, by tying it to another hypothesis of *De incantationibus*, the horoscope of religions, which associates the historical development of human societies and religions with astral revolutions. Hence monsters can be ascribed to a more general cause which affects the sublunary world in its entirety, and the human world in particular. This is the "preventing" of divine nature itself, and not just of matter.[29]

Here, the monster retains its divinatory dimension, but without being linked to any supernatural cause. Above all, the positivity of the monster's celestial cause integrates it into a cosmic order, but if it ceases to appear as an isolated effect, it is because the monster has become a symptom. Biological and moral monstrosity are indeed the effects of the same cause here: the disintegration of the links which make up the world itself. Providence, which guaranteed the cohesion of parts and the diffusion of divine gifts, now becomes the vehicle for deformity and vice. This is perhaps the audaciousness of Cardano's naturalism: to consider the articulation of the individual and the cosmos, no longer with the prospect of reconciliation, but in terms of a general teratology. What are we, except for the 'counterfeit', 'badly made' beings of a sick world?

Vanini responds to Cardano's worry with irony. Monsters, he repeats, are not always "defects"; sometimes they diverge from the species by "excess," as in the case of extra members or when a power of the soul seems over-developed. And he also answers that crimes are more frequent than monsters. However, beyond these objections, it is clearly in the name of another philosophy of nature that he rejects Cardano's thesis. Vanini neu-

---

[28]"Videtur tamen quod etiam corpora clestia sint causa defectu in specie, utpote ccitatis et claudicationis, argumento, quod Mathematici, multotiens ex inspectione siderum prdicant annos monstruosos, et etiam ista monstra prnunciant ventura. Quare a monstrando monstra appellata sunt: veluti 8. cap. 21 lib. de civitate Dei dicit Augustinus" (*op. cit.*, p. 258). On this aspect of Pomponazzi's thought, see in particular F. Graiff, "I prodigi e l'astrologia nei commenti di Pietro Pomponazzi al De Cae lo, alla Meteora e al De generatione," *Medioevo* 2 (1976), pp. 331–361.

[29]Cf. *De incantationibus, op. cit.*, notably p. 286, where Pomponazzi foresees the end of Christianity. Cardano's extract is remarkable because it does not link monsters to human turpitudes, or to any diabolical power, but to higher causes, to divine providence itself and to the disorder of an innocent nature.

tralizes the norm of the ideal species, defines the deviant form as *index sui*, and rejects the "form of the world" in favour of the infinite productivity of nature; he thereby also replaces an aesthetic of harmony with an aesthetic of variety. Similarly, Montaigne, too, opposes "prognostications" with the infinite productivity of a nature that escapes from custom and constantly exceeds our limited knowledge.

Translated from the French by Stacey Dagron

Conjoined Twins and the Limits of our Reason
ANNIE BITBOL-HESPÉRIÈS

ABSTRACT. In treatises on monsters, the sets of human double monsters, in particular conjoined twins, have undoubtedly provoked the most surprise, curiosity and amazement. With their physical peculiarities and varied appearances, conjoined twins have fired our imagination and triggered many debates in which philosophical issues have been important. Double monsters crystallized in an exemplary way the problems we must face with monsters: (i) as regards the reactions towards their extraordinary physical appearance and their place in society, (ii) as regards their ontological status and their place in Nature — which had been for a very long time tightly associated with God, (iii) as regards the issue of their causes, which for a long time were not treated independently from theological concerns. Double monsters have raised some important additional questions: their individuality, i.e. do conjoined twins have one soul or two?, an important question linked with the discussions about the 'life principle' and the seat of the soul, and not only with the decision to baptize either one person or two. In this paper I examine (**1**) the importance of theology and philosophy in the first medical treatises on monsters, (**2**) the changes initiated in such a context by some physicians at the beginning of the seventeenth century, and by Descartes' introduction of a new conception of nature. Lastly, (**3**) I turn to the limitations in the influence of these fundamental changes in the eighteenth century, with a particular focus on theological and teleological arguments in the debates concerning detailed dissections of conjoined twins at the Académie Royale des Sciences.

In writings dealing with monsters, the sets of human 'double monsters', in particular conjoined twins, have undoubtedly provoked the most surprise, curiosity and amazement. With their physical peculiarities and varied appearances, conjoined twins have fired our imaginations and triggered many debates in which philosophical issues have been important.

Double monsters have crystallized in an exemplary fashion the problems we face with monsters overall: (i) the reactions towards their extraordinary physical appearances and their place in society, (ii) their ontological status and their place in Nature, which for a very long time was tightly associated with God, (iii) the issue of their causes, which was not separate from theological concerns for an equally long time. Double monsters have raised additional questions that are equally significant: their individuality, i.e. do conjoined twins have one soul or two, an important question related to the discussions on the "principle of life" and the seat of the soul, and not only with the decision to baptize either one person or two. Another important question regarding human double monsters, when they had lived for a long period of time, concerned their psychology and whether they have different personalities, not to mention the possibility of their being separated by surgery and the details of their autopsy reports, which showed the importance of the fusion of their organs, a dimension which had implications for the mechanics of matter itself. These issues did not arise independently from the accounts of monstrous births and, from the second half of the sixteenth century onwards, from the publication of "canards," pamphlets and broadsides showing illustrations of conjoined twins, or from actual encounters with traveling conjoined twins.

In the first part of this paper, I discuss the conception of conjoined twins in relation to the notions of 'spectacle' and Nature, with a particular focus on the importance of theology and philosophy in the first medical treatises on monsters. In the second part, I examine the fundamental changes brought about in this context by some physicians at the beginning of the seventeenth century, as well as by René Descartes. I emphasize the split between the investigation into monsters and theology, as well as the importance of the new conception of nature introduced by Descartes, especially with regard to matter and to the laws of Nature. In the third part I describe the limitations in the influence of these fundamental changes in the eighteenth century, with a particular focus on the enduring influence of theological and teleological arguments in the detailed debates concerning dissections of conjoined twins at the Académie Royale des Sciences in Paris.

1 With conjoined twins, Nature is a "strange spectacle"

It must first be noted that conjoined twins are not to be mistaken for 'Siamese twins', as has often been said since the birth in 1811 in Thailand (the former kingdom of Siam), of Chang and Eng Bunker. These equally developed twins, conjoined in the area of the sternum, lived to the age of 63, traveled abroad for exhibition and became very famous throughout the world. From the second half of the sixteenth century onwards, texts dealing with monsters generally gave precise illustrations of the various cases of conjoined twins that were to be named and reclassified by the teratologists in the nineteenth century. Since twins may be joined at various points of their anatomies, the illustrations showed the observed types of conjoined twins and their anatomical features. Double monsters, equally developed and with a parallel axis, of which the Siamese twins are a paramount example, may be united at different parts of their bodies, from the head to the hips.

According to the classification proposed by Isidore Geoffroy Saint-Hilaire, if conjoined twins are attached at the head, they are called "cephalopagus"; if they are attached at the hips, they are called "pygopagus." Sometimes, their bodies and their heads may have collapsed and they are called cephalothoratopagus (the suffix "pagus," derived from the Greek "pageis," means "united"; the prefix locates the union). Double monsters may also have a change in their axis, be double in the upper parts of their bodies and simple in the lower part, as in the case of a monster with two heads and necks, a "derodymus" (where "dymus," derived from "didymos" means "double" and "dero," derived from "déré," means "neck"), or of the monster having two heads and two thoraxes on a single pair of legs, a "thoracodymus." The opposite situation may occur, with one head on two trunks and four pairs of limbs, the type of "deradelphus." Double monsters may also be unequally developed, one of the twins being smaller and not so well developed, with a part of its body aborted and thus becoming a "parasitic" twin living on its sibling's body (the "autosite"). These are called "heteradelphia" ("hetero" meaning "alterity" in Greek and "adelphos" meaning "brother").[1]

The variety of double monsters has to be mentioned because all these cases are recorded not only in the illustrations of books dealing with monsters from the sixteenth century onwards, but also in reports both on conjoined twins traveling in Europe to be shown and on autopsies of conjoined twins performed in an increasingly accurate way.

It is a fact that some conjoined twins had lived long lives, which sets them apart from the vast majority of monsters. This physiological peculiarity is emphasized, after the chronicler Pierre Boaistuau, by the French surgeon Ambroise Paré in his treatise *Of Monsters and Prodigies (Des Monstres et prodiges)*, first published in Paris in 1573, expanded several times until the publication of his *Œuvres* in 1585, and translated into Latin and English.[2] It is interesting to note that Paré did not associate monsters' short

---

[1] On these points, see Etienne Wolff, *La science des monstres* (Paris: Gallimard, 1948).
[2] In Latin: Paré, *Opera*, trans. Guillemeau (Paris: Du Puys, 1582); in English: *Works*, trans. Johnson (London: Cotes, 1634), which is mainly based on the 1582 Latin version, and was reprinted in 1649, 1665, and 1678.

lives with their birth defects that rendered them 'non-viable'. He claimed instead that they "do not love themselves and become melancholic when realizing that everyone is filled with scorn."[3] The reference to the pathological influence of the most complex among the humours in the human body, the melancholic one, associated with "fear and sadness,"[4] already appears in Boaistuau's *Histoires Prodigieuses*, first published in Paris in 1560, expanded and reprinted many times and translated into Dutch and English.[5] This explanation aimed to prove that despite their extraordinary physical appearances, monsters were not different in their psychologies.

If conjoined twins were put on display from their early days onwards by their parents who thereby earned a lot of money (as mentioned by Paré, J.G. Schenck and Jean Riolan the Younger; examples range from the two girls joined by their foreheads who were seen "by thousands of people," as stated by Lycosthenes,[6] referring to Sebastian Münster who met them in Mainz in 1501, and by Cardano[7] to Paré's account of a girl with two heads traveling in Bavaria in order to show her strange appearance, and, in the seventeenth century, Lazarus Colloredo or Colloredon and his parasitic twin John-Baptista who traveled in Europe, were seen in Copenhagen and Basel by many people, including the physician Thomas Bartholin,[8] and were a great success in London), if they were drawn on broadsides and served to illustrate many treatises, not only medical ones, it was because of their spectacular physical appearance. In those days these monsters were considered to be a genuine 'spectacle'. For Boaistuau, the "monster" born in Normandy, being double in the upper part and single in the lower part,

---

[3] Ambroise Paré, *Vingt-cinquième livre traitant des monstres et prodiges*, ch. IV, in *Œuvres* (Paris: G. Buon, 1585) (last edition revised by Paré, the first one published in 1573 under the title *Des monstres tant terrestres que marins)*, p. M.XXII. On this treatise, see Jean Céard's critical edition (Geneva: Droz, 1971), and, by the same author, *La nature et les prodiges, l'insolite au XVIe siècle* (Geneva: Droz, 1977, reprint, 1996).

[4] On the pathological effects of the melancholic humor in the sixteenth and seventeenth centuries, see my "Descartes face à la mélancolie de la princesse Elisabeth," in *Une philosophie dans l'histoire, Hommages à Raymond Klibansky*, eds. Bjarne Melkevik & Jean-Marc Narbonne (Québec: Presses de l'Université Laval, 2000), pp. 229-250.

[5] Cf. Boaistuau, *Histoires prodigieuses...* (Paris: Robert le Mangnier, 1566), ch. XXVII, fol. 129 b.

[6] Cf. Conrad Lycosthenes (Theobald Wolffhart), *Prodigiorum ac ostentorum chronicon* (Basel: H. Petri, 1557), pp. 504-505.

[7] Cf. Boaistuau, *Histoires prodigieuses*, ch. VI, fol. 18, and Girolamo Cardano, *De subtilitate*, XII; French translation by R. le Blanc, *Les livres de Hierosme Cardanus Médecin Milannois, intitulés de la Subtilité et subtiles inventions, ensemble les causes occultes et raisons d'icelles* (Paris: Guillaume le Noir, 1556, 1578), pp. 326b-327a.

[8] See Jean Palfyn's comments in his edition and translation of Fortunio Liceti's *De monstrorum caussis ...* (originally published Amsterdam, 1665): *Traité des monstres, de leurs causes, de leur nature...* (Leiden: veuve Schouten, 1708).

was "a strange spectacle in nature."[9] For Paré, the conjoined twins from Verona were "Nature's new spectacle."[10]

Monsters considered as a spectacle were not approached in a uniform fashion; one might say they were 'context-dependent', specifically in terms of society or Nature as possible contexts. Similarly, they were not a topic of inquiry restricted to surgeons, physicians, or even philosophers, and as such were not understood as requiring a specific studies devoted to them alone. It is a fact, confirmed by Caspar Bauhin at the opening of his treatise *On Hermaphrodites and Monsters,* that until the beginning of the seventeenth century, medical writings on monsters were very few.[11] It is thus easier to understand why Ambroise Paré himself borrowed many examples of monsters from non-medical sources, mainly from chroniclers like Lycosthenes and Boaistuau. The explanation lies more in the way monsters were perceived than in the fact that monsters are 'rare'.

In the sixteenth century, monsters, especially conjoined twins, were perceived as the most "strange and marvelous effects" of Nature, very often written with a capital letter. And Nature did not have the same meaning in those days and was not associated with what we call the laws of Nature, because Nature itself was primarily a "show" or "spectacle."[12]

In the show produced by Nature, monsters were closely associated with "prodigies," as was the case in the title Paré chose for the second, expanded edition of his book, *Of Monsters and Prodigies* (the initial title was *Monsters, on Land and Sea — Des monstres, tant terrestres que marins*). In the enlarged edition of Paré's work, human monsters as well as animal monsters, on the earth, in the air and in the sea, were to be found in the same treatises as "celestial monsters,"[13] that is, comets. Comets, parhelia and giant floods were already mentioned with conjoined twins and other monsters and sometimes directly linked with them, before Paré's book, in the editions of the *Prodigiorum ac ostentorum chronicon* of Lycosthenes (1557), and also, to a lesser extent, in the enlarged editions of Boaistuau's *Histoires prodigieuses*. The association of monsters and prodigies, along with their respective links to Nature, was significant but also highly problematic because it in fact excluded possible inquiries into either the medical or the philosophical status of monsters. Let us examine these points.

---

[9] Boaistuau, *Histoires prodigieuses*, op. cit., ch. XIII, fol. 42.

[10] Paré, *Des monstres et prodiges*, op. cit., ch. IV, p. M. XXIII.

[11] Caspar Bauhin, *De hermaphroditorum monstrosorumque partuum natura...* (Oppenheim: H. Galleri, 1614), first pages of the preface.

[12] Boaistuau, *Histoires prodigieuses*, op. cit., ch. XXVII, fol. 129 and fol. 130.

[13] Paré, *Des monstres et prodiges*, ch. XXXVII, in *Œuvres*, op. cit., pp. M.XCII-M.XCVI. This chapter was added to "instruct the young surgeon in the contemplation of celestial phenomena."

The first point to examine is the connection between monsters, in particular double monsters, and the notions of 'spectacle' and of Nature, before turning to the fundamental changes that gradually occurred in both the notion of nature and the perception of monsters, and examining the ultimate limits in the influence these changes had.

Such connections are apparent in Paré's treatise *Of Monsters and Prodigies*, for instance in the long fourth chapter, in which he discusses the illustration of the two female twins joined by their posterior parts, born "in the year of grace 1475" in Verona. Paré mentioned that they had been brought to several cities in Italy by their poor parents, in order to collect money from the people, "who were very eager to see this new spectacle of Nature."[14] Indeed, one of the etymologies of the word 'monster', deriving from the Latin word *monstrum*, means 'show'. This etymology was reasserted in the seventeenth century by Fortunio Liceti in his famous Latin treatise *On the Causes of Monsters*, first published in 1616, then reprinted with many illustrations in 1635 and 1665, and translated into French only in 1708.

According to Liceti the word 'monsters' comes from the fact that "their novelty and their enormity being so important, everyone considering them with as much surprise and admiration, *shows* them to one another."[15] Thus Liceti also confirmed the link between 'monster' and the adjective "admirable." Boaistuau had already used the expression "admirable monsters," with reference to conjoined twins.[16] In the texts dealing with monsters and especially mentioning conjoined twins, the adjective 'admirable' was very often used. It derived from the Latin verb "mirari," expressing a strong feeling of admiration or amazement.

Admiration and amazement were frequently associated with the evocation of conjoined twins in Paré's *Of Monsters and Prodigies*. Just after writing about the conjoined twins from Verona, Paré presented another impressive teratological case, a "heteradelphia," when one of the conjoined twins is not as well developed as the other and is attached to its sibling in the thoraco-epigastric region. This monster, "seen" in 1530 in Paris, was a man, about forty years old, who had the body and members of his brother, except for the head, which came out of his belly. And this man carried his parasitic twin in such a "marvellous" way that people assembled in large groups to "see" him.

---

[14] *Ibid.*, ch. IV, in *Œuvres*, op. cit, p. M.XXIII.
[15] Fortunio Liceti, *De monstrorum caussis*, op. cit., I, ii; *Traité des monstres*, I, ii, p. 6.
[16] Boaistuau, *Histoires prodigieuses*, op. cit., ch. XXVII, fol. 129.

In his *Essais,* Montaigne precisely describes a similar teratological case in his chapter on a "monstrous child" of fourteen months that was displayed by his father, uncle, and aunt, to get some money, because of its "strangeness" (*étrangeté*).[17] Monstrous creatures going from one place to another caused astonishment, amazement, and also fear, as can be seen from the famous example, first quoted by Lycosthenes, of the two-headed girl.[18] According to Paré, echoing Lycosthenes and Boaistuau, these two heads "had the same desire to drink, eat, sleep; had identical speech and had the same emotions." The girl with her two heads was begging from door to door and getting money because, as Paré wrote, of the "novelty of such a strange and new spectacle." However, she was driven out by the Duchess of Bavaria because it was said that she could "spoil the fruit of the pregnant women" by the "apprehension and ideas which might remain" in their imaginations.[19] The "strength of imagination" (*vis imaginativa*) in pregnant women was an important cause invoked in the cases of monsters.

As can be seen from these examples, monsters were, except in Montaigne's *Essais,* described succinctly. Since there was generally very little information about them, illustrations — sometimes full of ambiguity — played a crucial part in the history of monsters. It is also important to observe that in most cases, there was a complete lack of information about the conditions of the births of these monsters.

The fact that monsters and generation were not always closely linked was one of the main features of the conception of birth defects in the sixteenth century.[20] Notably, the focus on the monster's amazing appearance marks a break with the theory of generation derived from Aristotle, which asserted the "reproduction" of "the same" from one generation to another, a kind of substitute for eternity in our world,[21] exemplified in the "resemblance" between children and their parents. In his treatise on the *Generation of Animals,* Aristotle had famously declared that "a monster . . . is unlike its parents."[22]

Human double monsters are indeed characterized by the extreme singularity of their extraordinary physical appearances, which 'astonishes', in

---

[17] Cf. *Essais,* book II, ch. xxx, "D'un enfant monstrueux."

[18] Cf. Lycosthenes, *Prodigiorum ac Ostentarum Chronicon,* op. cit., p. 565.

[19] Paré, *Des monstres et prodiges,* op. cit., ch. IV, pp. M.XXII-M.XXIII.

[20] On this point, see my "Monsters, Nature and Generation in the Early Modern Period," in *The Problem of Generation in Modern Philosophy,* ed. Justin E.H. Smith (Cambridge: Cambridge University Press, 2005).

[21] The ideas come from Aristotle's *Generation of Animals,* trans. A.L. Peck (Cambridge: Cambridge University Press, 1990) and Galen, and can be found, for instance in Paré, *Vingt-quatrième livre traitant de la génération de L'Homme,* in *Œuvres* (1585), op. cit., p. IX.CXXV.

[22] Aristotle, *Generation of Animals,* IV.4, 770b.

the strongest sense of the word, and provokes 'admiration'. It is important to remember that in the medical tradition, in most cases, admiration is the opposite of comprehension. For instance, when Galen marveled at the opening of the uterus during parturition, he wrote that it "surpasses human intelligence," and that "we can indeed marvel at it, but we cannot understand it."[23] At the beginning of the seventeenth century, André Du Laurens (Laurentius) also mentioned that understanding the "admirable" formation of a human fetus in the womb "surpasses the powers of the human mind."[24] At the time, explaining the causes of the peculiarity of monsters such as a two-headed girl and various conjoined twins seemed beyond the abilities or scope of doctors, surgeons, or even philosophers. This was not only due to the great complexity of the question. In fact, the topic was closely related to the question of divine design.

The central role of theology must be emphasized, especially as concerns the question of the origin of monsters. In his *City of God (Civitate Dei)*, Saint Augustine mentioned the case of a man born in the Orient being double in the upper part of his body and simple in the lower part, having "two heads, two chests, four arms, but only one belly and two feet."[25] Augustine added that this monster "had lived enough time so that his fame *(fama)* attracted many spectators." A few lines later, he wrote with "precaution and prudence" that this monster, this source of wonder, was descended from Adam.[26] This example became very famous and was quoted by Boaistuau,[27] Paré,[28] Caspar Bauhin and Liceti.

According to Augustine, who was invoked by both Catholic and Protestant authors in philosophy and also in medicine (such as Caspar Bauhin in the seventeenth century), but not always with an explicit reference to the *City of God*, a monster *(monstrum)*, synonymous with *prodigium*, shows *(monstrat)* God's will.[29] This view must be understood in relation to Au-

---

[23] Galen, *De usu partium* XV.7, in *Galeni Opera Omnia*, ed. C.G. Kühn (Leipzig: C. Cnobloch, 1821-1833; reprint, Hildesheim: Olms, 1965), vol. 4, p. 246ff.: "superat humanum ingenium," "mirari quidem possumus, intelligere autem non possumus."

[24] Du Laurens (Laurentius), *Historia anatomica* (Frankfurt: M. Becker, 1600), VIII, xv, p. 305; *Histoire anatomique*, trans. Sizé (Paris: J. Bertault, 1610), p. 886. This work was translated into French again in 1613 (by Gelée), and reprinted many times throughout the seventeenth century.

[25] Augustine, *The City of God*, XVI, 8 (trans. E. Matthews Sanford & W. McAllen Green [London/Cambridge: Loeb Classical Library, 1965], p. 45).

[26] *Ibid.*

[27] Cf. Boaistuau, *Histoires prodigieuses*, op. cit., ch. XIII (with the title of the chapter explicitly referring to Augustine : "Prodige de deux corps, antés ensemble, comme deux greffes en un tronc d'arbre : Duquel saint Augustin fait mention en sa *Cité de Dieu*"), fol. 42.

[28] Cf. Paré, *Des monstres et prodiges*, op. cit., beginning of ch. IV, p. M.XXII.

[29] Cf. Augustine, *City of God*, XXI, 8.

gustine's denunciation, in *De Trinitate*, of the philosophers who tried to seek for causes other than God's will in order to explain monsters (and eclipses): "sometimes they found true causes, but [merely] immediate ones, because they were not at all able to see the supreme cause, i.e. God's will."[30]

Since monsters were understood in relation to God and as a divine "remonstrance," the explanation of their generation, i.e. of their conception and of their development in the womb or gestation, not only brings together medicine and theology but in fact clearly subordinates medicine to theology. It is all the more significant since, in the sixteenth century, the "generation" of human beings (what we call conception and embryonic life) still belonged to the "secrets of Nature" (*Naturæ arcana*). At the beginning of the seventeenth century, echoing Galen, Du Laurens wrote in his *Historia Anatomica* that trying to know how the parts form in the womb was "such a difficult question and so full of obscurity that only God or Nature can comprehend it." He added: "What could be more divine than the first form of man? What could be more admirable? What could be more secret and hidden?"[31] At the time, the problem of generation produced the same assertions and questions as that of the movement of the heart,[32] to which they refer as the "principle of life."[33]

In this context, however, some hypotheses emerged. The conception of twins posed difficult problems such as whether they came from a single coupling or two different couplings, and the division of the superabundant seminal material in the womb. This was called "superfetation" and was invoked in the case of "distinct and separate" twins, conjoined twins being produced by "too great a quantity of seed."[34] In the Renaissance, the life of the fetus in the womb was a deep mystery. It was also strongly linked with "souls" as approached through the ideas of Aristotle and Galen, or with a soul divided into a "vegetative" soul, found in plants as well, a "sensitive" soul, found in animals, and a rational soul or understanding found in human beings alone. The Zürich surgeon Jacob Rüff explained this in *On the Conception and Generation of Man* (*De Conceptu et generatione hominis*),[35] and so did Paré in his treatise on the *Generation of Man*, first

---

[30] Augustine, *De Trinitate*, III, 2.

[31] Du Laurens, *Historia anatomica*, op. cit., VIII, xv, p. 305; *Histoire anatomique*, op. cit., p. 886.

[32] Cf. Du Laurens, op. cit., VIII, xv, p. 305 and IX, vii, p. 352; translation, pp. 886, 1068.

[33] Cf. A. Bitbol-Hespériès, *Le principe de vie chez Descartes (et ses prédécesseurs)* (Paris: Vrin, 1990).

[34] Paré, *Génération*, in *Œuvres*, op. cit., ch. XXXIX, p. IX.CLXXI. This is confirmed in the title of the fourth chapter of *Monsters and Prodigies* : "Examples of monsters caused by too great a quantity of seed."

[35] J. Rüff (Rueff), *De conceptu et generatione hominis*. German editions were printed

published in 1573 and preceding the treatise on monsters, then included in his *Œuvres*.³⁶

For Rüff, the study of monsters was part of an illustrated treatise on conception and generation, in which he first provided many illustrations of fetuses in the womb before moving onto various illustrations of monsters. In book V, chapter 3, he showed many human double monsters, such as a two-headed man, two-headed children, and conjoined twins joined at different parts of their bodies. But, among these precise illustrations, some were also quite ambiguous, such as the one, on the same page as the picture of a two-headed child with two arms (where the text mentions "four arms"), of an elephant-headed boy born "somewhere."³⁷

Rüff mentioned the "physical" or "natural" causes of monsters, such as the "lack" of seed (for a child with only one arm) or the "excess" of seed (for a child with two heads or three legs), but ultimately related all these causes to God's will. When introducing the famous 'monster' born in 1552 in England, not far from Oxford, i.e. conjoined twins fused ventrally in the pelvis region, with four arms and three legs, one ending with ten toes — a genuine case of ischiopagus — Rüff asserted that the "providence of God almighty" allowed the birth of monsters to "punish and admonish human beings."³⁸ Rüff referred incidentally to the second etymology of the word *monstrum*, that of *monestrum*, derived from the Latin verb *moneo* whose infinitive *monere* means "to warn."³⁹

But more fundamentally, the surgeon from Zürich confirms his previous assertions regarding the importance of God's will in generation: God either allows parents to have either descendants, or he allows monsters to be born in order to "castigate" the vices of the "wicked."⁴⁰ Rüff's treatise shows the tremendous influence of theology in sixteenth-century medicine and the enduring link between the existence of monsters and God's will.

---

in 1554 and 1569, and Latin editions in 1554, 1580 and 1587 (our reference edition). Dutch editions were printed in Amsterdam in 1591, 1616, and an English edition was published in London in 1637. Here, *De conceptu...* (1587), I, iv, "De tribus facultatibus corpus dispensantibus et ipso spiritu," f.4, b-f.6, b.

³⁶Cf. Paré, *Génération*, ch. XI, "De l'âme," in *Œuvres*, op. cit., p. IX.CXXXVI.

³⁷Rüff, *De conceptu...*, op. cit., f. 44a. The elephant-headed boy was influenced by Ganesha.

³⁸*Ibid.*, V, iii, f. 37 b, 42 b.

³⁹ On this point, see Cicero, *De divinatione libri*, I, 93 — a text often quoted in writings on monsters —, where the word *monstrum*, "prodigious fact" is synonymous with a "warning sign given by gods." For more recent links between *monstrum*, *monstrare* and *monere*, see Emile Benvéniste, "The Latin Vocabulary of Signs and Omens," in *Indo-European Language and Society*, trans. E. Palmer, Miami Linguistics Series No. 12 (Coral Gables: University of Miami Press, 1973).

⁴⁰Rüff, *De conceptu...*, op. cit., book V, beginning of ch. III, f. 37 b.

Rüff also maintained, significantly, that human beings can conceive with animals. This was explained primarily by the "attractive virtue" of the "matrix" (the uterus) being "the same" among "human beings and animals." This assertion, followed by examples, written in one of the very first treatises of gynecology and obstetrics, were all the more influential since the great importance given to Pliny the Elder is pointed out. Pliny's vast compilation, including the most fantastic monsters, was much more important in those days than Lucretius' denial of the existence of centaurs, for instance.[41] When rejecting the possibility of crossing between two "different species," Lucretius was echoing Aristotle's analysis in *On the Generation of Animals*. In the sixteenth century, and in some books in the seventeenth century, it was as though both Aristotle's and Lucretius' statements had been completely forgotten. In Paré's *Of Monsters and Prodigies*, many monsters are half-human and half-animal. At the beginning of a chapter dealing with the "mixture of seed," Paré asserts that they are "produced by sodomists and atheists joining together."[42] One of the best-known in those days was the child "engendered" in 1493 by a woman and a dog. This child with human upper parts and animal lower parts, "was very complete, without Nature's having omitted anything."[43] Paré agreed that these "monstrous and marvellous creatures proceed from the judgment of God, who let fathers and mothers produce such abominations from the disorder in their copulation like beasts."[44]

After Paré, this example was to be found in the seventeenth century in the treatises of the physicians J.G. Schenck, Liceti, Aldrovandi and Ambrosini. It is no wonder then that in the sixteenth century, regarding twins, we find illustrations such as children conjoined with a dog in their backs, in Lycosthenes. This extraordinary conjoined monster having been produced, in the year 854, "in the times of Emperor Lothair" from two couplings, one of a man, one of a dog, and the narrowness of the womb produced the conjunction in the backs of the small boy and of the puppy... This case was destined for success, as its illustration was still found in the seventeenth century, in Liceti's *On the Causes of Monsters* and in Aldrovandi and Ambrosini's *History of Monsters*.

On the contrary, before the editions of Liceti and Aldrovandi's books, Caspar Bauhin, in his treatise on *Hermaphrodites and Monsters* deemed the birth of a compound monster having the parts of two or three animals "impossible" — with reference to Aristotle.[45] Bauhin insisted that it is

---

[41] Cf. *De Rerum Natura*, book V, verses 872-900.
[42] Paré, *Des monstres et prodiges*, op. cit., beginning of ch. XIX, p. M. XLVII.
[43] *Ibid.*, p. M.XLVIII.
[44] *Ibid.*, beginning of ch. III, p. M.XXI.
[45] Cf. Caspar Bauhin, *De hermaphroditorum...*, op. cit., ch. VI, pp. 62-63.

impossible for an animal to be born after a length of time different from its proper gestation.

Returning to Paré, it is a fact that the extraordinary morphological variety of bodies shown in this book appeared for the most part as a demonstration of the true might of Nature. And it is important to take into consideration the very strong link existing at that time between Nature and teleology, which reveals the importance of the Aristotelian legacy in medicine.

According to Aristotle, Nature "always does the best she can in the circumstances," and does "nothing superfluous nor in vain."[46] Monstrosities, "though not necessary in regard of a final cause and an end," are "necessary accidentally."[47] In the medical tradition, Galen strengthened the teleological point of view, especially in his treatise *De usu partium,* in which each organ is praised both for itself and for its usefulness for the whole. In Renaissance medicine, this tradition was still very much alive, as shown by Vesalius' famous treatise first published in 1543, *De humani corporis fabrica.* The word *fabrica* precisely conveyed a link between Nature and the perfectly crafted human body she produces. In the sixteenth century, Paré's *Anatomy,* which was placed at the beginning of his surgical treatises in his works, was influenced by this tradition and by Vesalius. In the beginning of the seventeenth century, Du Laurens' *Historia Anatomica* and Fabricius' two treatises in embryology[48] were the heirs of this tradition.

Paré was interested in perfect bodies and fascinated by the way Nature produced monsters. So fascinated that he kept in his house the corpses of two pairs of conjoined twins: first, the 'monster' born in Paris in 1546 after a six-month pregnancy, having two heads, two arms, four legs but only one heart, and that had been anatomized by Paré. Secondly, conjoined twins born in Tours in 1569 with only one head, that had been given to Paré, "dried and anatomized" by a surgeon.[49] In the first edition of his text, Paré wrote that he kept the Parisian monster "as a monstrous thing."[50] It is significant to note that he used the same expression "comme une chose monstrueuse" for the vertebra of a whale brought to him from the

---

[46] Cf. Aristotle, *On the Parts of Animals,* IV.10, 687 a 10-16; *Gen. Anim.* II.6, 744 a 37.

[47] Aristotle, *Gen. Anim.* IV.3, 767 b 13.

[48] Cf. Fabricius ab Aquapendente, *De formato fœtu* (Venice, 1604), and *De formatione ovi et pulli* (Padua, 1621) (posthumous publication). On this point, see my "Descartes, Harvey et la médecine de la Renaissance," in *Descartes et la Renaissance,* ed. Emmanuel Faye (Paris: H. Champion, 1999), pp. 323-347, especially pp. 341-342.

[49] Paré, *Des monstres et prodiges,* op. cit., ch. IV, p. M. XXV.

[50] *Ibid.,* ch. IV — in the first edition (Paris, 1573), but no longer in the 1585 edition —, p. M.XXV.

southwest part of France that he also kept in his house.⁵¹ This parallel illustrates that defining a philosophical status for monsters and especially for conjoined twins was in that period quite irrelevant. Instead of a true philosophical categorization which would imply using objective criteria, Paré contents himself with a subjective mark of astonishment towards extraordinary 'monsters and prodigies'. This is all the more obvious since we realize that Paré's aim in writing his treatise was not to comment with precision on the differences between perfect human bodies and very deformed bodies. In his view, the illustrations of monsters sufficed. Paré's aim was to "acknowledge the greatness of Nature," described as "the chambermaid to this Great God."⁵² Though personified, Nature remained mysterious, especially regarding the question of monsters. For Paré, when producing monsters, Nature was "playing" ("Nature se joue") and had to give rise not only to wonder but also to amazement and awe.⁵³ Paré agreed with the excellent formula of Pierre Boaistuau, author of the *Histoires extraordinaires,* one of Paré's source books, that with monsters, Nature presented us with "a strange spectacle."⁵⁴

It is very significant that this expression is found in a chapter dealing with conjoined twins, Boaistuau having referred to the famous human double monster mentioned by Augustine in his *City of God.*⁵⁵

For Paré, as shown by the title of his treatise, and despite the different definitions of "monsters" and "prodigies" he gives early on, monsters and prodigies are closely linked because they are related to the tremendous powers of Nature. Monsters, such as "a child born with one arm or another with two heads" exceed the usual course of Nature ("outre le cours de Nature"), while "prodigies" ("a woman giving birth to a serpent or a dog") are "contrary to Nature."⁵⁶ For Paré, more important than the search for causes for monsters and prodigies is his will to include and to show in his book all the monsters living on the earth, in the sea and in the air, which means that his inquiry concerns nature in its entirety. Monsters with their "rare" appearance are variations and metamorphoses revealing the infinite power

---

[51] Cf. Paré, *Des monstres et prodiges,* op. cit., ch. XXXIV (Appendix, ch. I in 1st ed.), end of the "Description de la baleine," p. M. LXXXII.

[52] This expression appeared in the "Dédicace" to the Duke of Uzès, for the first edition of 1573. Paré's aim has remained the same from the first edition to the last one revised by the author (1585). See for instance, ch. XXXVI, p. M.XCI, "pour admirer la grandeur de ses Œuvres."

[53] Cf. Paré, op. cit., e.g. ch. XXXIV (Appendix, ch. I), first paragraph: "Nature se joue en ses Œuvres," p. M.LXVI, and ch. XXXVI, p. M.XCI.

[54] Boaistuau speaks of an "étrange spectacle" (with regard to conjoined twins) in his *Histoires Prodigieuses,* op. cit., ch. XXVII, fol. 130.

[55] Cf. Augustine, *City of God,* XVI, 8.

[56] Paré, *Des monstres et prodiges,* op. cit., p. M.XX.

of Nature and of God. Some of these monsters are also perceived as 'signs' sent by God to those who lead a sinful life. These expressions of God's might exceed the limits of human reason, which Paré acknowledged when asserting that "there are things divine and hidden and admirable in monsters" ("Il y a des choses divines, cachées et admirables aux monstres").[57]

2 Important changes in the relation between monsters, God and Nature

From the very end of the sixteenth century and during the seventeenth century — leaving aside Aldrovandi's posthumous treatise on monsters published by Ambrosini *(Monstrorum Historia,* 1642) — some doctors and surgeons began to write about monsters and conjoined twins in a more specific way. Thus, without being explicit, they gradually rejected two of the three adjectives that Paré had associated with monsters: "divine" and "hidden." Then, in his vast enquiry into *The World* and *Man (Le Monde, L'Homme)*,[58] the philosopher-scientist René Descartes made a considerable breakthrough in redefining nature and putting forward the importance of the laws of Nature. He confirmed these aims in his first published book, *The Discourse on Method* and *Essays* (Leiden, 1637), in explaining the 'method' for rightly conducting human reason in science, and eradicate admiration.

Marin Weinrich promoted the split between medicine and theology in his *De ortu monstrorum commentarius,* published in 1595. Weinrich explained that the theory of monsters needed to become "physiological," since it belonged to the study of nature by means of human reason. He insisted on the specificity of his task, since being a "physician," meant (by reference to the Greek etymology of the word) dealing solely with nature (*physis*) and "physical" explanations. He contrasted "physicians" with "theologians," and explained that their principles as well as their aims were different, because theologians "based their knowledge on the word of God and raised it to the heights," while physicians "relied on the grounds of reason alone" and dealt with the immediate causes of things.[59] In one of his chapters, Weinrich argued against both Augustine and the Stoics, who claimed the necessity of less perfect bodies and of monsters in the world, and asserted that they did not destroy the "beauty" of the world. According to Weinrich, monsters are "ugly" but studying monsters is important because it

---

[57] *Ibid.*, ch. XIX, p. M.LI.

[58] René Descartes, *Le Monde & L'Homme*, critical edition and introduction by A. Bitbol-Hespériès with J.-P. Verdet for the astronomical part of *Le Monde* (Paris: Seuil, 1996).

[59] Cf. Marin Weinrich, *De ortu monstrorum commentarius* (Breslau: sumptibus M. Osthesii, 1595), I, f. 6a.

improves our knowledge of nature,[60] since, in his view, monsters are to be traced back to "natural" causes and "physiological" explanations.[61]

This shift is also apparent in Du Laurens' *Historia anatomica*. After having stated that the theologians relate monsters to God's vengeance, and astrologers to the stars, he explained that he himself had put aside theological causes as well as metaphysical causes, to relate monsters only to "natural" causes ("physica" in the Latin text).[62] Du Laurens explicitly explained the birth of two-headed children by the presence of excessive quantities of seed.

Highlighting the importance of 'natural' causes did not seem to be Caspar Bauhin's main objective when, in 1614, he published in Frankfurt his treatise on hermaphrodites and monsters, *De hermaphroditorum monstrosorumque partuum natura et Theologia, Jurisconsultorum, Medicorum, Philosophorum et Rabbinorum sententia libri II* (first edited in Oppenheim in 1600). In his book, Bauhin, a famous teacher of anatomy in Basel, wanted to free hermaphrodites from any suspicion of the curse of God. He made an inventory of all writings about monsters and hermaphrodites and emphasized the small place then occupied by the medical writings therein, in comparison to those of theologians, philosophers, and jurists. However, in offering a table summing up the causes of monsters, either "superior," i.e. coming from God, or "inferior," for instance linked with the "matter" (of the parents), the "place" (the size of the womb), the "efficient" causes, arising from the weakness of the "formative faculty," Bauhin gave much more prominence to the inferior causes.[63]

Referring to Rüff, Bauhin explained that the generation of monsters was linked with the judgment of God. Theology remained an important topic in his vast historical inquiry, even though he discussed many medical arguments. According to Bauhin, infants born with too many limbs, for instance too many feet, and many heads, are to be classified as monsters. He explained that in monsters the matter "is conserved," while the "natural form" is changed, as shown by the examples of monsters having "four eyes, four arms and four legs."[64] His treatise was important insofar as Bauhin questioned the status of monsters as *contra naturam*. The question echoed Aristotle's assertion in *On the Generation of Animals*, that "monsters are beings contrary to nature, not contrary to all of nature but to nature such

---

[60] *Ibid.*, II, fol. 86 a and b.

[61] *Ibid.*, I, fol. 46b.

[62] Cf. Du Laurens, *Historia anatomica*, VIII, xiv, "De monstris et hermaphroditis," op. cit., p. 302; *Histoire anatomique*, op. cit., pp. 877-878.

[63] Cf. Bauhin, *De hermaphroditorum monstrosorumque...*, op. cit., beginning of the book for this table linked to chapter V.

[64] Bauhin, *De hermaphroditorum...*, op. cit., VI, p. 63.

as it most often shows itself to us."[65] Bauhin explained that monsters are *secundum naturam* precisely because of this conservation of matter and this change in the form.

The question whether monsters are *contra naturam* was also explicitly raised by Jean Riolan the Younger in his *De monstro nato a Lutetiae anno Domini 1605, Disputatio Philosophica*. The publication of this 'philosophical disputation' in Paris, in 1605, followed the public dissection of a pair of two female twins born in Paris in the same year. It was illustrated by a folded engraving with two drawings showing both the internal and external conformations, first the twins in front with their insides displayed and with letters corresponding to the joined organs and to some vessels, and secondly the twins before dissection, seen from the side. These twins with two heads, four arms and four legs, were joined from the middle of their chests to their navels, having only one heart, one diaphragm, and one liver. According to Riolan, monsters such as the Parisian conjoined girls did not seem to be *contra naturam* insofar as they were produced by nature, which intended to make a perfect product but had been unable to do so as a result of some cause, such as a defect in matter.

The influence of the Aristotelian, teleological conception of Nature can easily be identified here; Riolan explicitly quotes Aristotle's *Physics*.[66] As for the question whether these "remarkable deformities" observed in the conjoined twins deserved the denomination 'monster', Riolan answered positively. According to him, the generation of monsters is linked with "errors" (*errata*) committed by nature.[67] In the third chapter, Riolan explained that these conjoined twins belong to the category of monsters "in individuo," not of monsters "in specie." Monsters "in individuo" belong to the same "species" as their parents, but have an important deformation, while monsters "secundum speciem" (according to the species) are different from their mothers. Here Riolan referred to famous examples, e.g. the one described by Plutarch, recalling that Ariston of Ephesus, who hated women, mated with a she-ass who gave birth to a beautiful young lady appropriately named Onoscele, which means 'having the legs of an ass'.[68]

---

[65] Aristotle, *Gen. Anim.* IV.4, 770b.

[66] Cf. Riolan the Younger (Riolan fils), *De monstro nato a Lutetiae...* (Paris: O. Varennaeus, 1605), ch. II, f. 2b and 3b. I shall hereafter refer to Riolan fils (1580-1657) simply as 'Riolan', since his father, also named Jean Riolan, plays no role in this story.

[67] Riolan, *De monstro...*, op. cit., fol. 4a.

[68] *Ibid.*, fol. 7b-fol. 8a, and again quoted in fol. 21 (ch. VII). The example already occurs in a medical text (Rüff's), and is also quoted by Liceti, who displays it in a spectacular engraving (*Traité des monstres*, op. cit., p. 232).

Riolan also mentioned that physicians call something "divine" (*divinum*) when they are ignorant of its causes,[69] recalling the famous "divinum quid" in the medical tradition and more precisely in Hippocrates' *Works*. The "divinum quid" refers to the limits of human reason because it is related to a totally unknown cause in a very serious illness.

In his *Disputatio philosophica,* Riolan also asked whether these conjoined twins have a single soul or two. The question was not raised within a theological framework, focusing on the decision to baptize either one person or two, but rather within the philosophical tradition of inquiring into the "vitæ principium" (principle of life), and its localization in the human body, either in the head or in the heart — as these conjoined twins had two heads but only one heart. In his *Monsters and Prodigies* (chap. IV), Ambroise Paré had already mentioned that the monster he dissected in Paris in 1546, having two heads, two arms, four legs, but one heart was to be considered, according Aristotle, as a single monster.[70] On the contrary, and against Aristotle who associated the heart with the principle of life, Riolan asserted that the Parisian twins have two distinct souls because they have two distinct heads. The principle of life being also the seat of the affections and passions, Riolan explained that the twins with two heads had different personalities. Thus he mentioned the Oxford monster born in 1552, who lived two weeks, already quoted by Rüff. This monster had two heads, one being awake while the other one was sleeping, one showing happiness while the other one looked sad. But Riolan mostly referred to the "memorable story" of a monster born in Northumberland, with two heads and four hands but having the lower parts in common, who lived more than a few days. The king of Scotland wanted this monster to be brought up and well educated, especially in music, where "wonderful" progress had been made, and in languages. The two bodies differed in their inclinations. "They had distinct wills and sometimes quarreled," when one liked something that displeased the other. But "most remarkable" was the fact that when they were hurt in their thighs or their kidneys, both felt pain, while when they were hurt in their superior parts, only one of them could feel it. When this monster was 28, "one body having died some days before the other, the surviving one progressively declined as the other half was rotting away."[71]

Riolan also examined, in reference to the Romans who threw monstrous creatures into the Tiber, whether monsters should be destroyed at birth. He rejected such an attitude but suggested that monsters have to be kept apart

---

[69] Riolan, *De monstro...*, op. cit., fol. 11.
[70] Cf. Paré, *Des monstres et prodiges,...*, , op. cit., ch. IV, p. M. XXV.
[71] Riolan, *De monstro...*, op. cit., ch. VI, fol. 18a –fol. 19.

from society.[72] The reference to the Romans throwing "the small monstrous creatures in the Tiber" already occurs in Boaistuau and contrasts with the Christian context. In Boaistuau's book, the presence of Catholicism is prominent from the beginning (the "prodigies of Satan") to the end (the last word is "sins"). Boaistuau emphasized that since "we are trained in a better school, we consider monsters more humanely and knowing they are God's creatures, we allow them to become members of his Church thanks to the regeneration and sacrament of the holy baptism." His example was the conjoined twins joined by their foreheads, born in 1495 in the Rhine valley, who had been "seen by thousands of people," including Münster in 1501 in Mainz, and who lived for ten years. One of the conjoined twins having died, she was separated from the other, but the surviving one died soon after because of the wound received from the separation.[73] This is apparently the first recorded case of surgical separation of conjoined twins. Despite Boaistuau's assertion, what is striking in the case of monsters and of conjoined twins, is that they were generally referred to by their birthplaces, not by their Christian names. Some exceptions can be mentioned, such as in chapter IV of Paré's treatise, the conjoined twins born in Paris on July 20th, 1570, baptized Louis and Louise at St Nicolas des Champs, or the case (added to Liceti's edition of 1665, mentioned by Blasius, after Bartholin), of Lazarus Colloredo or Colloredon and his unequally developed brother, John-Baptista, growing out of his body.

In his book, Riolan also rejected the association of monsters with prodigies and their being bad omens. This contrasts with the beginning of Paré's *Of Monsters and Prodigies,* where the French surgeon stated that "monsters are very often signs of some forthcoming misfortune."[74] At the end of his book, Riolan claims that "there is nothing to be afraid of" with the birth of these conjoined twins. He also adds that the exhibition of the monstrous twins allowed their parents to earn a good deal of money, since they showed the twins only to those who could afford the price for the show; according to Riolan, the conjoined twins saved their parents from poverty.[75]

The link between monsters and nature was also addressed in the *Monstrorum historia memorabilis,* published in Frankfurt in 1609 by Johann Georg Schenck, who described himself as a "physician doctor" ("physicus medicus"). In his book, fine engravings displayed the "miracula" of nature, monsters that occurred as an "error" in relation to the "genius of nature,"

---

[72] *Ibid.*, ch. VII, fol. 19b-fol. 22b.
[73] Cf. Boaistuau, *Histoires prodigieuses,* op. cit., ch. VI, fol. 17b-18b, and Paré, *Des monstres et prodiges,* op. cit., ch. IV.
[74] Paré, *Des monstres et prodiges*, op. cit., p. M.XX.
[75] Riolan, *De monstro...*, fol. 27b-28a.

and that deviated from the "law" or the "norm" of nature.[76] Pursuing the work initiated by his father Johann in his *Observationum medicarum, rararum, novarum, admirabilium et monstrosorum,* Johann Georg Schenck also began to classify the illustrations of monsters in relation to the pathologies in the different parts of the human body, beginning with the head. By presenting monsters as examples of various pathologies in the bodies of human beings and animals, whose causes were to be explained by "natural" reasons alone, Schenck sought to introduce a new teratological discourse into medicine. This new discourse contained no references to the traditional "supernatural" or "supranatural" causes, i.e. divine signs, especially "God's wrath" or "the curse of God," as were invoked at length by Lycosthenes and Boaistuau[77] and strongly echoed, as we have seen, in the treatises on monsters by the surgeons Rüff and Paré.

The tradition of subordinating medicine to theology was also directly questioned by Fortunio Liceti in his famous treatise *De monstrorum causis, natura et differentiis,* first published in 1616 in Padua without any illustrations, then printed in 1634 with several engravings, and reprinted again in 1665 in Amsterdam and translated into French in 1708. The illustrations were often presented in a spectacular manner, befitting the taste for monsters and the long-lasting association between monsters and 'spectacle'. Liceti rejected the conception of monsters produced by God's will. He asserted this clearly, although without openly refuting Augustine. The study of monsters was, Liceti argued, within the proper scope of physicians. He also focused on the extension of the word 'monster' as distinct from 'prodigy', a question that mattered for "those wanting to speak about monsters in a proper way," as an inquiry into nature ("physice vero ac proprie dicuntur").[78] According to Liceti, a monster is an animal, rather close to a man, "whose disposition and arrangement, considering its members, is extraordinary; who is different from those from whom it has been begotten," and whose birth can only occur "rarely." Monsters raise "surprise" and "admiration."[79]

Liceti rejected the connection established by Cicero and the common opinion between monsters and "signs of misfortune."[80] He insisted upon the "true" etymological link between 'monster' and the verb *monstrare,*

---

[76] Cf. J.G. Schenck, *Monstrorum Historia memorabilis...,* (Frankfurt: M. Becker, 1609), p. 14.

[77] Cf. Boaistuau, *Histoires prodigieuses,* op. cit., ch. 5, fol. 14 b, where Boaistuau writes that in most cases, "monstrous creatures proceed from the will, justice, punishment and curse of God."

[78] Liceti, *De monstrorum caussis,* book I, ch. i, p. 4; *Traité des monstres,* I, i, p. 2.

[79] Liceti, *Traité des monstres,* op. cit., p. 4.

[80] *Ibid.,* I, ii, pp. 4-5.

which Ambrosini, the editor of Aldrovandi's notes on monsters, confirmed when asserting that a monster is named this way because it triggers surprise and is pointed to.[81] After Riolan, Liceti asserted that monstrous children are put on display by their parents who can thereby earn money.

While explaining that monsters are "effects" and "works" of Nature, Liceti emphasized with meticulous subtlety their Aristotelian causes.[82] But Liceti's explanations of the causes of monsters were still underpinned by anthropomorphic statements concerning "Nature," "mother of all things and thereby of monsters."[83] In Liceti's opinion, nature, when producing monsters, can "sin and wander in a marvelous way." If the religious notion of sin was present in this sentence, the following parts of the text insisted more on the notion of 'wandering' or 'erring', Nature producing what she was intended to make — the "admirable fabric of the living body" — but in a different way, either by reducing or increasing the number or the mass of the parts, or by transposing some members apart from their "natural situation." According to Liceti, "Monsters are nothing more than defects or wanderings of Nature."[84] He also wrote that what is distinctive about monsters is that their "matter [is] organized in a different way," and that the "error of nature when producing monsters may be seen in the disposition of the organs."[85]

The anthropomorphic conception of nature was very common in medical treatises of the time, and particularly, as we have just seen, with the question of monsters; it was precisely what Descartes wanted to eradicate in the first work he wrote in French, which he decided not to publish when he learned of Galileo's condemnation. In *Le Monde,* which includes *L'Homme* (the so-called treatise on Man being an important part of *Le Monde* in Descartes' project),[86] Descartes asserts that by "nature" he does not "mean some goddess or any other sort of imaginary power."[87] Rather for Descartes, nature signified "matter itself."[88] These claims, at the beginning of the important chapter explaining "the laws of Nature," were not only significant for physics, but also for medicine. The conception of nature being a "goddess" or "dame Nature," as Paré wrote in his treatise on generation,[89] or alterna-

---

[81] Cf. Aldrovandi/Ambrosini, *Monstrorum Historia* (Bologna: N. Telaldin, 1642), p. 325.
[82] Cf. Liceti, *Traité des monstres,* op. cit., I, chs. vi-x and II, chs. iii-xxix.
[83] *Ibid.*, I, vii, p. 29.
[84] *Ibid.*, I, viii, pp. 33, 34, and beginning of ch. ix, p. 34.
[85] *Ibid.*, I, viii, p. 33.
[86] On this point, see my Introduction to Descartes, *Le Monde, L'Homme,* op. cit.
[87] Descartes, *Le Monde,* beginning of chapter 7, AT XI, 36 / *The World,* CSM I, 92. In the cases where the text cited does not appear in CSM or CSMK, I refer only to AT.
[88] *Ibid.*
[89] Cf. Paré, *Génération,* in *Œuvres,* op. cit., ch. I, p. IX.CXXV.

tively as "the chambermaid to our Great God" in the treatise on monsters, and of nature being a "mother" as Liceti put it, was unambiguously rejected by Descartes.

This entailed Descartes' rejection of the conception of Nature as "playing" when producing monsters, an influential conception in the medical treatises on monsters, as we have seen. As he explains in the *Discourse on Method* and the *Dioptrics*, our link with nature is no longer to be considered as that of mere "onlookers." Nature is no longer to be regarded as a 'spectacle'; rather, we have to "make ourselves, as it were, the lords and masters of nature."[90]

Descartes also insisted that scientific thought, in physics and astronomy as well as in medicine, must lead to the eradication of the admiration of natural phenomena. This is clearly written at the beginning of the First Discourse of *Les Météores*.[91] In this text, admiration is linked to the ignorance of the causes of the phenomena, which is rather close to the uses of the adjective "admirable" we have seen in Paré, in Du Laurens and in Riolan.

On the contrary, Descartes wanted to "explain all the phenomena of nature, that is to say the whole of physics"[92] and to "explain all the main functions in man."[93] When describing the human body and explaining its organic functions, Descartes insisted on the "disposition of the organs," on the importance of the circulatory pattern, for the blood as well as for the "animal spirits" — i.e. the most subtle particles of blood — and made use of mechanical models instead of praising Nature and viewing the body as containing occult "faculties." These mechanical models were linked with the mechanistic definition of the "principle of life," in contradistinction to the Aristotelian tradition, which is still vivid in Harvey's *On The Movement of the Heart and Blood in Living Creatures* (*De motu cordis et sanguinis in animalibus*),[94] and the hierarchy of souls. They are found in Descartes' writings from *L'Homme* (see, for instance the famous example of

---

[90] Descartes, *Discours de la méthode*, part VI, AT VI, 62 / CSM I, 142-143.
[91] AT VI, 231.
[92] Letter to Mersenne, November 13th, 1629, AT I, 70 / CSMK, p. 7.
[93] Letter to Mersenne, November or December 1632, AT I, 263 / CSMK, p. 40. On the "onlookers" ("spectateurs," "regardants"), see my "*L'Homme* de Descartes et le *De Homine* de Hobbes," in *Descartes, Hobbes et la métaphysique* (Paris: Vrin, 2005), op. 155-186, especially pp. 163-173.
[94] On these points, see my *Le principe de vie chez Descartes*, op. cit.; "Cartesian Physiology," in *Descartes' Natural Philosophy*, eds. Stephen Gaukroger et al. (London / New York: Routledge, 2000), pp. 349-382; "Descartes Reader of Harvey: The Discovery of the Circulation of the Blood in Context," in *The Renewal of Materialism*, ed. Charles T. Wolfe (*Graduate Faculty Philosophy Journal* 22:1, New School for Social Research, 2000), pp. 15-40.

the hydraulically-powered statue)[95] onwards in order to explain physiological functions, often associated with Descartes' use of the expression "there is no wonder" ("ce n'est pas merveille"), for instance, in *L'Homme*, in the *Description du Corps Humain* (*The Description of the Human Body*, an up-to-date version of *L'Homme*, published posthumously with it in 1664) and in his correspondence.[96]

Descartes' medical explanations were grounded in the laws of physics, which included physiology. They represent a new way of considering medical questions, which is also significant with regard to the generation of monsters. In his *Primae cogitationes circa generationem animalium*,[97] Descartes reflected on the causes of the generation of monsters and, in an important passage, evoked the laws of Nature that he had discussed in *Le Monde*. He explicitly subsumed monsters under to "the eternal laws of Nature."[98] The novelty of this statement is remarkable when contrasted with the traditional importance of theological explanations and anthropomorphic assumptions about Nature. Certainly, Descartes was not the first to use the expression "laws of Nature" in medicine. But if such an expression can be found in medical treatises, for instance in Du Laurens' *Historia anatomica*, its meaning is very different from the one Descartes intends. When Du Laurens spoke of the "laws of Nature," he had in mind regular movements, the causes of which remained completely unknown to human beings.[99] In contrast, for Descartes, the laws of mechanics that rule the human body are identical to the laws of Nature, and are derived from the immutability of God. This is stated in *The World*, alluded to at the beginning of the fifth part of the *Discourse on Method*, and explained at great length in the second part of the *Principles*. And in his *Primae cogitationes,* Descartes attempted to explain the generation of man, including cases of hermaphrodism, with reference to mechanistic principles alone.[100] Descartes' texts on embryology, as well as his anatomical descriptions of the heart and of the eye, for instance, eliminated both teleological and theological assumptions.[101]

---

[95] Cf. AT XI, 120. A statue inspired by Salomon de Caus, *Les raisons des forces mouvantes* (Frankfurt, 1615).

[96] Cf. AT XI, 153, 268; AT III, 262.

[97] On all the fragments of the *Excerpta anatomica*, on *La Description du Corps humain*, and on their links with *L'Homme* and the fifth part of the *Discourse*, see my annotations in Descartes, *Œuvres complètes* (in French) (Paris: Gallimard-Pléiade, forthcoming).

[98] AT XI, 524. Not in CSM.

[99] Du Laurens, *Historia anatomica,* op. cit., VIII, x, p. 297; *Histoire anatomique,* op. cit., p. 859.

[100] Cf. AT XI, 524. Not in CSM.

[101] Cf. my notes on the heart and sight in the *Treatise of Man*, in Descartes, *Le Monde, L'Homme, op. cit.*, and my "La médecine et l'union dans la *Méditation sixième*,"

The new approach to medicine Descartes prescribed was linked with the rejection of the search for final causes, so common in medical treatises from Galen onwards, especially when considering the teleological overtones of the invocation of nature. Descartes contrasts physics and physiology where "such conjectures are futile" with ethics "where we may often legitimately employ conjectures" and where "it may admittedly be pious on occasion to try to guess what purpose God may have had in mind in his direction of the universe."[102]

It must also be noted that the Cartesian method for the sciences which have to include the knowledge of what is "rare" in nature, and therefore of monsters, is different from a compilation, as explained by Descartes in an extract from the incomplete dialogue *The Search for Truth By Means of the Natural Light.*[103] This does not only sound new when contrasted to Paré's vast compilation of monsters and prodigies. It also sounds original when compared to Bacon's program for the reform of human knowledge in the *Novum Organum*, his methodological treatise published in 1620 to replace Aristotle's method in the investigation and the "interpretation of nature." Here, a rigorous compilation plays a major part in the study of monsters, the causes of natural things remaining "secret."[104] In Bacon's works, this echoes the beginning of the second book of the *Advancement of Learning* (London, 1605), dealing with the three sorts of "History of nature," "nature" being still associated with the word "history,"[105] nature still "erring" and "wandering" when producing monsters, while Descartes puts forward the word "philosophy" and the laws of Nature, and rejects the anthropomorphic conception of nature.

---

in *Union et distinction de l'âme et du corps, Lectures de la VIe Méditation*, ed. Delphine Kolesnik-Antoine (Paris: Kimé, 1998), pp. 18-36, especially pp. 27-35.

[102] AT VII, 375; cf. my "La médecine et l'union dans la *Méditation sixième*," op. cit., pp. 32-35.

[103] *La Recherche de la vérité par la lumière naturelle*, published posthumously (AT X, 503 / CSM II, 404).

[104] The Baconian program on monsters is emphasized in K. Park & L. J. Daston's paper, "Unnatural Conceptions: The study of monsters in 16th and 17th-century France and England," *Past and Present* 92 (1981). It begins with a quotation from the *Novum Organum (The New Organon, or true directions concerning the interpretation of nature)* asking the natural philosopher that: "a compilation, or particular natural history, must be made of all monsters and prodigious births in nature. This should be done with rigourous selection, so as to be worthy of credit." On Baconian reforms, see also Daston & Park's *Wonders and the Order of Nature* (New York: Zone Books, 1998), chapter 6, in which they study the process of the naturalization of wonders, emphasizing how ideas on wonders (not only on monsters) relate to the institutional context, and the Enlightenment overall.

[105] *The Two Books of Francis Bacon, of the Profience and Advancement of Learning, Divine and Human*, beginning of the Second Book.

William Harvey did not question the anthropomorphic conception of Nature in his Latin treatise *On the Generation of the Animals (Exercitationes de generatione animalium)* in 1651.[106] In this important work, Harvey, a great observer and still an Aristotelian,[107] respectfully praised Nature, "perfect Nature."[108] Teleology was not absent from his book.[109] Harvey also referred to "the Divine Architect," and the "divine mystery in the generation of animals."[110] He expresses disagreement with Fabricius of Aquapendente, his famous former teacher at the University of Padua and the author of two embryological treatises, regarding embryos with four legs and wings, two heads, "monsters in short": they are not produced by a double-yolked egg, but by twin eggs.[111] According to Harvey, who insists on the numerous dissections of human embryos of almost every size, and the even more numerous dissections of various animals, important malformations come from a truncation of embryonic development.[112]

3   The limited impact of these changes in the eighteenth century: reports on dissections of conjoined twins at the Académie Royale des Sciences

Descartes' *Primæ Cogitationes* on generation were published in 1701, and his remark on the connection between the generation of monsters and the laws of Nature found an echo in 1703 at the Académie des Sciences. That year, in the *Histoire* of the Académie, that is, in a synthesis written by the Académie's Secretary on its most important papers, printed before the *Mémoires* themselves, Fontenelle (who was then the Secretary) stated that monsters are not to be regarded as the games of Nature (*jeux de la nature*), as the common man does; philosophers know that nature does not play (*que*

---

[106] On this point, see my paper "Monsters, Nature and Generation," op. cit.

[107] On Harvey's influences, see Jacques Roger, *Les sciences de la vie dans la pensée française au dix-huitième siècle, La génération des animaux de Descartes à l'Encyclopédie* (1963; expanded edition, Paris: Albin Michel, 1993), pp. 112-121, and Walter Pagel, *William Harvey's Biological Ideas, Selected Aspects and Historical Background* (Basel/New York: S. Karger, 1967).

[108] W. Harvey, *Exercitationes de generatione animalium* (London: O. Pulleyn, 1651), Exercises 10, 26, 40, 44, 48, and 61. Note that in this edition there is an error of numbering, from *Exercitatio* 4.

[109] *Ibid.*, Exercises 40, 57, pp. 111, 198-199.

[110] *Ibid.*, p. 125.

[111] *Ibid.*, Ex. 23, pp. 73-74, with a quotation from Fabricius' treatise *De formato ovi et pulli*; cf. Aristotle, *Hist. An.*, VI.3, 562a25-562b, and Harvey, Ex. 12, p. 41.

[112] Harvey, Ex. 56, 57, 69.

la Nature ne se joue point).¹¹³

It would be inaccurate to believe that this statement expresses the views of the vast majority of the members of the Académie Royale des Sciences. If we examine the context of this statement and survey the reports to the Académie on monsters, mostly conjoined twins, not only that year, but also in subsequent years, a more finely shaded situation appears.

Fontenelle was referring to the case of a monstrous fetus of a lamb, born dead, without head, chest, vertebrae and tail, while the other one was alive and well "formed in all its parts." The case was reported by Antoine, a surgeon, and the main question he raised about the monstrous fetus lacking a heart concerned the circulation of the blood from the mother to the fetus and *vice versa*. Since this monstrous fetus was "deprived of all the most necessary parts, such as the heart, the lungs and the liver, how could he have been formed and be fed"? The questions that follow this one are noteworthy because they reveal a more complex context than Fontenelle's first assertion tying the existence of monsters to "general rules." These questions bear witness to an entanglement between the anthropomorphic conception of Nature (still very vivid among doctors and surgeons), teleological assumptions, admiration of the *fabrica* of an animal, and references to the Cartesian mechanics of the body. This is all the more significant since it is linked with the importance of the Aristotelian influence in medicine, which contrasts strongly with the relinquishment of the Aristotelian references in physics. These questions were: "How could Nature remove the half of a Whole so well bound and so indivisible as an Animal? How did she remove the most dependent half from the one that governs and that contains the principal springs of the Machine"?¹¹⁴ Fontenelle stated that because of this monstrous case, Antoine had preferred to "abandon the system than to admit an exception to the ordinary laws of circulation."¹¹⁵

That year, a short report on a monster by a physician from Blois was also read in the Academy, on twins joined at the head so their faces looked in different directions. All the other parts of the conjoined twins' bodies were distinct and well formed. Their common skull led one to believe that they had just one brain, and this was discussed with the curate who had baptized them as "two distinct individuals."¹¹⁶

The place of the "extraordinary" as contrasting with the "ordinary structure" of the parts; the role of God in creating monsters; the possibility of chance (*hasard*) as a distinct factor: all of these matters were discussed in

---

¹¹³ This expression refers to Paré's "Nature se joue." See *Histoire et Mémoires de l'Académie Royale des Sciences*, année 1703 (published in Paris in 1705), p. 28.
¹¹⁴ *Histoire de l'Académie Royale des Sciences*, année 1703, op. cit., p. 30.
¹¹⁵ *Ibid.*, p. 31.
¹¹⁶ *Ibid.*, p. 29.

the year 1706, when Du Verney (Duverney) presented to the public inaugural session of the Académie, on November 13, the detailed observations he had made when he had carefully dissected the conjoined twin babies joined end to end, ventrally united by the posterior parts, having four arms and four legs, born on September 19th, and who died a short time after. The conjoined twins were born alive thanks to a midwife "skilful in her art,"[117] but died on September 26th, at four in the morning for the one who looked stronger, and three hours afterwards for the other one. According to Duverney, the death had three causes: first, the bad manner in which the conjoined twins were swaddled, which cramped the part of the belly they had in common; secondly, the fact that they never suckled and that the cow's milk they were given curdled in their stomach and intestines, as seen during the dissection; thirdly, "they were too often uncovered in order to satisfy the curiosity of several people" and each time they were turned in various ways.

What is striking in the reasons given for their early death is the lack of reference to important malformations incompatible with post-natal life. What is also important is that the causes are all *human* causes, a significant detail which must be related to the detailed anatomical description of this "extraordinary fetus," compared to the "ordinary" ones, and with the precise drawings of this impressive teratological case that illustrate the paper, and more deeply with the paragraphs following the precise account of the dissection.

Duverney deemed any explanation of the way the twins were joined that relied either on "chance," "a blind formative virtue" or "a fortuitous alteration of the natural workings"[118] impossible. In his long *Mémoire*, Duverney referred to a similar monster in Paré's *Works*, the one born in Paris on July 20th 1570, a true "ischiopagus."[119]

Despite all the differences between Paré's treatise *Of Monsters and Prodigies* and Duverney's *Mémoire*, — the precise comparison between an "ordinary" fetus and the "monstrous" or "extraordinary" one being of paramount importance in the *Mémoire*, as well as the remarkable quality of the engravings —, for Duverney, as well as for Paré, monsters raised admiration. Moreover, for Duverney and Paré, the descriptions of monsters were not incompatible with teleological and theological assumptions. But in his paper, Duverney never presented monsters as the curse of God. On the contrary, the end of his paper was exemplary in the way it traced the entire partic-

---

[117] Cf. "Observations sur deux enfants joints ensemble" par M. Du Verney l'aîné, in *Mémoires de l'Académie Royale des Sciences* (hereafter MARS), année 1706 (Paris: Jean Boutot, 1707), pp. 418-419.

[118] *Ibid.*, p. 431.

[119] *Ibid*, p. 421. Paré's monster is described in ch. IV of his treatise.

ular conformation of these conjoined twins, either external or internal, to an "intelligence": "everything (in this monster) is of a design guided by an intelligence free in its purpose, omnipotent in execution and always wise and organized in its means." It must be noticed that the adjectives "free," "omnipotent" and "wise" traditionally refer to God's main characteristics and point towards the divine attributes. According to Duverney, this "intelligence . . . wanted to produce two human bodies joined together . . . One cannot help assuming this will, since its execution is so clearly visible."[120] As for the reasons for such a creation, Duverney left this to the "theologians." But he was convinced that

> the inspection of this monster displays the richness of the Creator's mechanism, at least as much as the most regular productions . . . , being outside the common rules, it displays more fully both the freedom and the fecundity of the Author of this Mechanism so various in these kinds of productions.[121]

The conclusion of Duverney's anatomical paper turned into a lyrical hymn to the "Creator." Such an attitude was not new: since Galen, the links between anatomy and teleology had been very strong, and in the sixteenth and seventeenth centuries, these links had included theology. But what does not fit the medical tradition[122] in Duverney's paper, is the link established between the extraordinary structure of the body of a monster and the praises to the Creator. Equally novel is the reference to the mechanics of the body. Let us examine these points.

Traditionally in medicine, such praises concern an "ordinary" body — what we would call a "normal" body, but this adjective was not used in the texts I am referring to — and always refers to Nature, God, or the Creator.

Du Laurens' *Histoire anatomique* and Riolan's *Anthropographie* begin in the same way, with praise for the human body, its dignity and "admirable" structure.[123] In these thick anatomical treatises, as well as in Caspar Bauhin's *Theatrum anatomicum*, Nature was praised for having built the human body, the most remarkable and most admirable work in the whole created world. With these assertions, the famous anatomists followed ideas grounded in Galen's *De usu partium,* and brilliantly renewed

---

[120] *Ibid.*
[121] *Ibid.*, pp. 431-432.
[122] On this point, see my "Connaissance de L'Homme, connaissance de Dieu," *Études Philosophiques* (octobre-décembre 1996), pp. 507-533, especially pp. 516-526, and "La médecine et l'union dans la *Méditation Sixième*," op. cit., especially pp. 30-31.
[123] Du Laurens, *Histoire anatomique,* op. cit., I, chs. i, ii, and the first pages of Riolan's *Anthropographie* (in his *Œuvres anatomiques en français,* trans. P. Constant [Paris: Denys Moreau, 1629]).

in Vesalius' famous treatise *De Humani corporis fabrica.* The word "fabrica," preferred in the title to the word "structura," which appeared in the treatise, referred to a conception of the body as a remarkable piece of work made by an "Opifex" or by "Nature," which was frequently associated with Providence.[124] Du Laurens and Riolan praised the human body, that was not made "by chance"; in Du Laurens' eyes, this amounted to a refutation of Epicurus.[125] At the end of his anatomical treatise, in the "Graces to God" ("Action de grâces à Dieu"), Du Laurens mentioned the divine attributes in relation to a perfect human body: God's "admirable omnipotence, unbelievable wisdom and infinite goodness."[126]

In his praise of the conjoined twins, Duverney undoubtedly had in mind this anatomical tradition, refuting "chance" and reinforcing the link between anatomical demonstrations and teleological assumptions, very vivid in medical treatises. But instead of mentioning the "goodness" of the Creator, — an odd reference when describing a monster —, Duverney insisted on the Creator's "freedom." No doubt that, despite his admiration for the "extraordinary" anatomical structure of these conjoined twins, he had to admit the fact that, for instance, they would not have been able to walk, or more precisely that, as Duverney stated, they could only have walked "with great difficulty."[127] This euphemism hardly tempered Duverney's admiration for the mechanism of the junction of these twins, as well as, more generally, for the variety of the works of God, more important in his eyes than the question of order in Nature.

It is thus less difficult to understand why Fontenelle did not mention Duverney's detailed *Mémoire* in the *Histoire* of the Académie des Sciences for the year 1706. It is easy to realize why a priest, the abbé Bignon, could have congratulated Duverney for such an analysis, as it appeared in Father Le Brun's letter published in the *Journal des Savants* for the year 1707. Prolonging Duverney's statements, the abbé Bignon explained that "if monsters have led some inattentive or unlearned people to make difficulties for Providence, they must now serve as an admirable proof in favor of that same Providence." He even did not hesitate to introduce God's wisdom in relation to monsters, claiming that "as Providence varies bodies as it pleases, it knows how to give them arrangements so marvelous and regular

---

[124] On this theme, see my "Descartes, Harvey et la Renaissance," in *Descartes et la Renaissance,* op. cit., pp. 341-342, and "Cartesian Physiology," in *Descartes' Natural Philosophy,* op. cit., especially pp. 366-367.

[125] Cf. Riolan, *Anthropographie,* op. cit., p. 17, also stated in Du Laurens' *Histoire anatomique,* op. cit. pp. 13-14, with a refutation of Epicurus.

[126] Du Laurens, *Histoire anatomique,* op. cit., end, n.p., in fact, pp. 1415-1416.

[127] Duverney, "Observations sur deux enfants monstrueux," in *Mémoires...,* 1706, op. cit., p. 430.

in their apparent irregularity, that they can make us admire the wisdom and omnipotence of the Author of nature as much as the objects that seem to us the most regular."[128] Once again, facing monsters, the bounds of human reason were clearly set.

The *Mémoires* of the Académie des Sciences concerning monsters, and not only conjoined twins, in the eighteenth century, illustrate the entanglement between, on the one hand, very precise anatomical descriptions of the peculiarities observed in these "extraordinary" bodies — using comparisons with "ordinary" bodies and taking into account the mechanics of ordinary and monstrous bodies — and, on the other hand, philosophical thoughts, teleological assumptions about Nature and/or theological convictions.

The important part still played by teleological assumptions about Nature, often still personified, and by theology in the anatomical part of the works at the Académie des Sciences contrasts with the content of the *Mémoires* on physical subjects. It is especially striking when considering the reports about eclipses and comets, subjects that had traditionally been included among prodigies, and therefore closely associated with monsters. This is probably why, in 1712, Fontenelle, faced with the great number of monstrous births studied in the Académie, judged that the history of monsters was "endless and not very enlightening."[129]

Theological assumptions can again be found in the 1716 *Mémoire* to the Académie by the physician Marcot, of the Société royale de Montpellier, on a monstrous child born without a brain and without a cerebellum.[130] But for Marcot, God, or more precisely the Creator, was not to be held responsible for having originally produced a monstrous egg, without a brain or a cerebellum. Marcot holds that the egg "is the work of the Creator, through whom they were all placed in the ovary of the first woman, and from whose hands come nothing imperfect or unfinished."[131] He stated this as though it were obvious, without discussing Duverney's opposite assertions openly. For Marcot, the reason for the lack of brain and cerebellum lay "in the lack of nourishment," i.e. in the absence of blood, — "the nourishing liquor of all the parts" —, together with the compression of the arteries, which prevented the brain from being nourished in the womb and thereby from

---

[128] *Journal des Savants,* Supplément pour janvier 1707, Seconde lettre du R.P.*** à M.*** touchant les jumeaux monstrueux, p. 10.
[129] *Histoire de l'Académie...*, année 1712, p. 39.
[130] Cf. Marcot, *Mémoire sur un enfant monstrueux, MARS* 1716 (Paris: Imprimerie Royale, 1718), pp. 329-347. [As all of the *Mémoires* were printed at the Imprimerie Royale I will henceforth merely indicate 'Paris' followed by publication date when citing them.]
[131] *Ibid.*, p. 340.

growing.¹³² Although the title of Marcot's paper did not mention conjoined twins, he nevertheless tackled the question of their origin. In his view, conjoined twins arise when two eggs join together. If these joined eggs grow equally in the womb, the children are conjoined and equally developed, and are double either totally or partially. If the joined eggs grow unequally and penetrate into each other and "incorporate," so to speak, then a child would have two heads, four arms on a single body.¹³³ In his paper, Marcot did not mention Duverney by name, but he quoted Malebranche, because his main thesis was to refute the alleged prodigious effects of the imagination of pregnant women in producing monsters. Marcot referred to Malebranche's famous book *La Recherche de la vérité* (*The Search after Truth, in which is treated the nature of the human mind and the use that must be made of it to avoid error in the sciences*, 1ˢᵗ edition 1674 — a title suggested by Descartes' manuscripts known thanks to Clerselier). In the second book of the *Search*, Malebranche championed "the force of the imagination of the mothers" or "the disturbances of the maternal imagination" in the generation of monstrous children.¹³⁴ Marcot refuted the alleged communication between the imagination of the mother and her fetus and the role of maternal imagination made responsible for birthmarks or monstrosities.¹³⁵ It is noteworthy that Marcot's analysis rejecting the alleged influence of maternal imagination on the carried child came in the Académie three years after the reported birth of a child with a beef kidney in the place of its head because it was said that its mother had not been able to satisfy her craving for kidneys,¹³⁶ and shortly after Malebranche's death.¹³⁷

The year 1724 was not only an important one in the debates on monsters, particularly conjoined twins, at the Académie des Sciences, because Lémery confirmed Marcot's analysis and directly challenged Duverney's assertions; it was also essential in order to understand the importance of the strong link still existing between anatomy and teleology, as seen in Marcot's paper. Such a link became obvious in the *Histoire* section with a subject that was not monsters, but rather the organs of respiration, and its assertions concerning the complementarity of "two anatomies" proved very illuminating. They shed a new light on the debates concerning the origin

---

[132] *Ibid.* , pp. 340-341.
[133] *Ibid.*, p. 333.
[134] Cf. Malebranche, *De la recherche de la vérité*, II, i, ch. 7, §§ 1, 2 and especially 3, in *Œuvres*, I, ed. Geneviève Rodis-Lewis (Paris: Gallimard-Pléiade, 1979), pp. 174-183.
[135] Cf. Marcot, *Mémoire sur un enfant monstrueux*, op. cit., p. 335.
[136] Cf. *Histoire de l'Académie...*, *Diverses observations anatomiques*, année 1713, pp. 20-21.
[137] Malebranche had been elected to the Académie in 1699. He died on October 13ᵗʰ 1715.

of monsters that precisely took place in the Académie from 1724 on, when Lémery wrote a *Mémoire* against Duverney, putting forth his observations on a fetus with two heads and two necks, culminating in 1733 with the intervention of Winslow, after Duverney's death.

When, in 1724, the Académie distinguished between "two anatomies, one *material*, displaying the structure and the movements of the parts, the other one *spiritual*, displaying the uses of this structure and the design of these movements," and claimed that they were truly complementary, the idea was not an original one.[138]

To be sure, this way of qualifying these two anatomies was new, but Riolan, for instance, had already advanced the distinction they referred to. In his *Anthropographia*, the famous French physician stated that before being "médicinale" and explaining the characteristics of the healthy human being, anatomy has to be initially "physicienne." This anatomy "physicienne" (dealing with Nature, *physis* in Greek) "teaches the structure of each animal, to show that Nature did not act without any purpose."[139] This finalist concern often mingled with theology, especially among French Catholic physicians. Riolan emphasizes that "Christian theologians (Lactantius, Ambrose, Basil, John Chrysostom) did not feel ashamed of drawing their most important arguments in favor of the divine providence from the fabric of the human body."[140]

More profoundly, all this referred to the structure of the human body having been called by "some of the Ancients," the "Book of God." And Du Laurens, who made such an assertion after having written lyrical pages on the human body, maintained that anatomy served to "know God."[141] Du Laurens, Riolan as well as Caspar Bauhin were also full of admiration towards Nature, which undoubtedly acted according to a teleological principle.

These considerations indicate that the Cartesian articulation of a link between monsters and the laws of Nature, as well as the rejection of the search for final causes (not to mention admiration) was too far-reaching, especially in regard to medical issues. Descartes' physics, which included physiology, was grounded on metaphysics, but was not mixed up with it.

---

[138] "Sur les organes de la respiration," *Histoire de l'ARS*, 1724, Paris, 1726, p. 24 (emphasis mine).
[139] Riolan, *Anthropographie*, op. cit., ch. VII, p. 86, and the Latin original, *Anthropographia* (Paris: Plantin, 1618), p. 48.
[140] Riolan, *Anthropographie*, op. cit., p. 34.
[141] Du Laurens, *Histoire anatomique*, op. cit., pp. 21, 27-28. On this point, see my "Connaissance de L'Homme, connaissance de Dieu," op. cit., and "La médecine et l'union dans la Méditation sixième," op. cit., pp. 18-36.

In the *Histoire* at the beginning of the volume for the year 1724, Fontenelle provided a good summary of the two different conceptions of the origin of monsters with "some parts in excess," such as a monster having two heads, and declared himself in favor of the first and therefore against Duverney's views. The first conception of the origin of monsters having parts in excess, appealed to accidental causes: the "accidental crushing of two eggs," in which "each of them having lost some parts that have remained in the other one, it happened by chance that other parts have remained in both at the same time."[142] Fontenelle wrote that "this system, though likely enough, was even so not that of M. Du Verney" and he referred to the *Mémoire* of 1706. The second position was therefore Duverney's, who "believed" that conjoined twins were originally, "naturally monstrous" eggs ("des œufs naturellement monstrueux"), which, in his view, demonstrated "the fecundity and the variety of the infinite art of the Creator and at the same time his freedom."[143]

Fontenelle acquiesced that monsters need to have "an organization as regular and at least as complex as in other animals" but noted that it did not seem "easy for the remains and ruins of two mixed-up eggs, which therefore are nearly destroyed by one another, to gather luckily enough and right enough to form this new, absolutely necessary organization. It was just as likely, or even, if you like, much more likely that smashing two good clocks violently together would produce a third one, with regular movements."[144] However, Fontenelle added that Lémery's statements about the crushed eggs had been well confirmed with "a fact he had in his hands": the fetus he observed.

In his *Mémoire*, Lémery wrote that this fetus was born on March 15th 1721, that it died shortly after painful labor, mainly because of the efforts made in order to take the two heads out of the womb. He mentioned that the two heads of the fetus were well formed.[145] The chest of the fetus was larger, which, according to Lémery, indicated several anatomical peculiarities to be discovered with the dissection. But this dissection did not occur immediately after the death. No doubt that the reason Lémery gave in order to explain this delay hurts our sensibilities, but he did not comment upon it. The midwife's attitude towards this monster was undoubtedly close to Paré's conception of the "monstrous thing," as seen above. According to Lémery, the "Mistress midwife, Mrs Aubert, to whom the monster had been given, would not allow it to be opened up . . . her aim was to keep

---

[142] *Histoire de l'Académie Royale des Sciences*, année 1724 (Paris, 1726), p. 20.
[143] *Ibid.*
[144] *Ibid.*, p. 20.
[145] Cf. Lémery, "Sur un fœtus monstrueux," *MARS* 1724, op. cit., p. 44.

it complete and therefore she had put it in a big earthenware vessel full of brandy, which preserved it for over two years." She would have preserved it for much longer if she had not in the end got tired of topping up the brandy as it evaporated. "So the midwife contented herself with having it (the monster) painted," and since Lémery had often asked her to dissect it, she let him know that he could do as he wished.

Before reporting his observations on the dissection of the monster with two heads, Lémery asserted that "the careful examination" of the very strange facts seen in this case seemed to him to give "a very clear and mechanical explanation of their strangeness."[146]

The most striking fact was that this "monstrous child" was "double with his head and some other parts," though having the same number of arms and legs as an "ordinary child."[147] Among the anatomical peculiarities of this monster described by Lémery, and remarkably illustrated by Simonneau, I shall only mention that the spine was double, and not only in the upper part, and that there was also another spine, the "third spine," a "false" one, because it had no marrow and no canal. In the middle of the double trunk, there was only one heart. After the anatomical description, Lémery mentioned other similar cases recorded in medical treatises and he referred to Paré. But he mainly quoted Duverney's *Mémoire* of 1706, and referred to the 'third volume of Régis' philosophy', a direct allusion to Pierre-Sylvain Régis' *Système de Philosophie,* published in 1690, after the great controversy between Malebranche, an Oratorian, and Antoine Arnauld, a Jansenist, both of whom were great readers of Descartes' works. In this important philosophical debate what was at stake was not only the human hope of attaining the truth, but the very idea one should have of God and his Providence: two problems with a direct impact on the question of monsters. Malebranche was looking for the order visible in divine wisdom, while Arnauld wanted to demonstrate God's infinite freedom and the radical impotence of human beings. In his *Système de Philosophie,* Régis took Arnauld's side against Malebranche, and explained that it was impossible to consider that "God's understanding and will are two faculties distinct from each other."[148] For Régis, "God truly produces Monsters" and "is obliged to create some in order to satisfy the simplicity of the laws of Nature." Further, "the laws of Nature are in no way different from God's will"[149]; this assertion was Cartesian. Régis' book raised an important controversy among philosophers and scientists as can be seen in the *Journal des Savants*

---

[146] *Ibid.*, p. 45.
[147] *Ibid.*, p. 46.
[148] Pierre-Sylvain Régis, *Système de Philosophie, contenant la logique, la métaphysique, la physique et la morale,* 3 vols. (Paris: Anisson, Posuel et Rigaud, 1690), I, p. 89.
[149] *Ibid.*, III, pp. 29-30.

for the year 1694.

The controversy was not totally extinct thirty years later, in 1724, at least with regard to the origin of monsters, as seen with Lémery's *Mémoire*. Lémery rejected both Régis' and Duverney's assertions when explaining that the originally monstrous eggs and the monstrous germs were a shocking and obvious attack on "the order, simplicity and uniformity of nature in the principles of the generation of the animals."[150]

For Lémery, the "system of monstrous germs is useless," since monstrous fetuses can be explained by a "constant pressure," either moderate or stronger in the womb, as the womb is "a kind of hollow muscle, capable of an infinity of movements and of irregular contractions in every direction." This pressure can join different parts of the two fetuses in the womb, and thereby produce "monstrous patterns" ("arrangements monstrueux").[151] Thus, the third spine in the skeleton of the monstrous fetus was a "vestige" of some broken parts belonging to the two fetuses, and especially of their broken ribs. It was a "monument of the rupture or of the defect in the development of the two ranks of ribs." This was made by "Nature."[152] According to Lémery, the "extraordinary structure" of the unique heart in this monstrous fetus was also produced by the fact that two identical parts had constantly pressed on each other, had merged and produced a third part.[153]

In May 1733, the origin of conjoined twins was debated again at the Académie, with the first *Mémoire* written by Winslow. In his *Remarks on Monsters, with reference to the case of a twelve-year old girl whose body was attached to the lower half of another body; and to the case of a fawn with two heads, dissected by order of the King,* Winslow also included a new classification of monsters. At the beginning of his *Mémoire*, he mentioned that some years earlier, he had been called to the *Hôpital Général* to visit a very ill twelve-year old girl that was said to have two bodies, and to decide whether extreme unction was to be administered to one or two girls. After having described the smaller of the two bodies growing out of the body of the other well developed twin — what we now call a "parasitic" twin —, Winslow stated that since it had neither head, nor arms, nor the appearance of a heart, it could not be considered as a particular "animated subject."[154] This analysis was confirmed by the fact that the well-developed

---

[150] Lémery, *Sur un fœtus monstrueux*, MARS, op. cit., p. 51.
[151] *Ibid.*, pp. 52-53.
[152] *Ibid.*, pp. 55-58.
[153] *Ibid.*, pp. 59-61.
[154] Winslow, *Remarques sur les monstres, à l'occasion d'une fille de douze ans, au corps de laquelle était attachée la moitié inférieure d'un autre corps, et à l'occasion d'un faon à deux têtes, disséqué par ordre du Roy* (= 1st Mémoire), in *MARS* 1733 (Paris, 1735), pp. 366-368.

twin could feel when the limbs of the smaller twin were scratched. Winslow emphasized his interest in the "communication of the sense of touch between two bodies conjoined against nature."[155] In his second *Mémoire*, published a year later, this interest either in same or in different feelings in conjoined twins was shown when Winslow quoted the examples of the Oxford monster and of the Northumberland monster from Riolan's Latin treatise on the conjoined twins born in Paris in 1605.[156]

After the death of the twelve year-old girl, Winslow's description of her dissection was detailed, at least when considering the difficulties that arose due to the very hot weather. In his remarks, Winslow sided with Duverney, after having reread all the *Mémoires* of the Académie on monsters, emphasized those written by Duverney in 1706 and Lémery in 1724, and added some recent cases. Among these cases was a two-headed fawn he received in May 1729,[157] the drawings of which were to be found in a new *Mémoire*, the second part of the *Remarques sur les monstres*, written the following year. The title "second part" referred to Winslow's classification of monsters — described in the first *Mémoire* with three classes, but summed up at the beginning of the second part with only two —, the first class being that of "simple monsters," having an "extraordinary conformation or by defect," and the second one being that of "double, triple," — either totally or by portions —, or "compound" monsters (*monstres composés*).[158] In his *Réflexions* which followed precise anatomical descriptions of double monsters, Winslow confirmed his rejection of the "system of accidents" while pointing out how this thesis of the crushing of two originally complete and separated subjects was incapable of explaining double monsters.[159] Winslow's explanations were remarkably well grounded on precise anatomical arguments detailing all the difficulties he encountered in his observations of the two-headed fawn and the twelve year-old girl, as well as in his careful readings of Duverney's and Lémery's *Mémoires*. His arguments focused on rejecting the "system of accidents" much more than on approving the thesis of monstrous germs. What was also remarkable in Winslow's anatomical demonstration was his reluctance to bring in any theological or teleological arguments. It is all the more noticeable since his first *Mémoire* began with the theological question he was asked, about the extreme unction to be administered in one or two girls.

---

[155] *Ibid.*, pp. 368-369.
[156] Cf. Winslow, *Remarques sur les monstres, seconde partie*, in *MARS* 1734 (Paris, 1736), pp. 488-489. On these examples, see the second part of this paper.
[157] Cf. Winslow, *Remarques sur les monstres* (1st Mémoire), op. cit., pp. 369-373.
[158] *Ibid.*, p. 453.
[159] *Ibid*, pp. 463- 486.

Lémery only answered in 1738, first without mentioning Winslow's name, but referring to Duverney, and polemically rejecting Duverney's "praise of the design and structure of the parts of his monster." In his *Mémoire*, when considering the anatomical peculiarities of Duverney's monster, Lémery wondered how "an omnipotent Intelligence," how "the Author of Nature" could have produced them. He claimed that the "monstrous structure" of the monster was "ridiculous," and asked whether the "contradictions" observed in the parts destined for generation, such as displaced testicles and empty scrotums, could "be imputed to the Author of Nature?" Lémery could see nothing in this monster except "disruption, disorder, trouble, and confusion — failed productions." He was convinced that the two children joined in the same monster came from the Creator, and were separated. This happened because "the fortuitous and immediate action of some accidental causes . . . corrupted and disfigured two works of nature and made a monster."[160]

In his second *Mémoire* on monsters, published the same year in the same volume,[161] Lémery's aims were to refute the system of originally monstrous eggs and to provide arguments in favor of the action of accidental causes on monstrous parts. Lémery announced the publication of four *Mémoires*, and this time, Winslow's name was quoted after Duverney's.[162] In his paper, Lémery raised the question of the bounds of human knowledge: "Can we read clearly enough into the productions of Nature to be able to see perfectly how each of their causes has managed to produce everything we perceive?"[163] He quoted examples of efficient remedies the causes of which remained unknown and he maintained the scientist's right to attribute an effect to causes whose way of being efficient was ignored.

Lémery also claimed that the question of monsters was not an anatomical one that could only be decided by anatomists, but that it was a mere "question of Physics which requires merely common sense and reason."[164] He had to acknowledge that it was easier to explain the causes of monsters in general anatomical terms than at the level of "the most particular details of the monstrous structures."[165] In his long refutation of "originally monstrous eggs," Lémery was undoubtedly aware of being less anatomically competent than Winslow.

---

[160] Lémery, *Sur les monstres, Premier Mémoire*, in *MARS* 1738 (Paris, 1740), pp. 269-272.
[161] Cf. Lémery, *Second Mémoire sur les Monstres*, in *MARS* 1738, op. cit., pp. 305-330.
[162] *Ibid.*, p. 306.
[163] *Ibid.*, p. 308.
[164] *Ibid.* pp. 316-317.
[165] *Ibid.* p. 320.

According to Lémery, what monsters show is "disorder, confusion, disturbance, depravity and abolition of some different functions, certain ridiculous relations among parts that were not made to go together . . . in a few words an infinite number of peculiarities all the more extravagant" in that they are clearly against "life or health, or the uses of the parts." Even if it is "a design," "one may regard it as very bad, since its products are so erratic, so faulty . . .." Thus, "these causes are blind." What is therefore "established" is the action of "accidental causes."[166] When pointing out all the faulty structures in the anatomical description of monsters, Lémery turned the arguments about God's omnipotence against Duverney. But for Lémery, as well as for Duverney, theological and teleological arguments were superior to anatomical ones in this unabated controversy.

In 1738 and 1740, Lémery wrote more than 150 pages in the *Mémoires*. In the first part of his third *Mémoire* read in 1740, he repeated his arguments against Winslow and put forward some anatomical "proofs" in favor of the accidental causes and against the "monstrous eggs . . . , chimerical and imaginary beings." "Observations of compared anatomy" have to be used to fill "the depths of ignorance" concerning the question of the origin of monsters.[167] In the second part of his third *Mémoire*, read in the same year, Lémery tried to put forward the intervention of Nature "capable of carrying out her designs despite unfavorable circumstances." The new Secretary to the Académie, Dortous De Mairan, also invoked this argument in the *Histoire*. He even wrote that the "system of accidental pressure," shown in the new detailed investigation of the conjoined twins already examined in 1724, "seemed truly written by the hands of Nature."[168]

In his fourth *Mémoire*, read the same year, Lémery wanted to explain the origins of monsters in relation to what is now called the fixity of species. He stated that "the Author of Nature had given to each species of animals on earth a particular conformation that brings its distinct features, hence the individuals of a same species must be alike as perfectly . . . as they differ with these particular conformation from all the individuals of other species." He invoked the "laws prescribed by Nature," hence the "fixed and permanent . . . specific conformation" through generations from the beginning of the world.[169] Monsters, with their "bizarre, variegated and often horrifying, ugly, always amazing, and extremely different shapes from the fetuses having not degenerated," can be seen as various "examples

---

[166] *Ibid.* pp. 323-324.
[167] Lémery, *Troisième Mémoire sur les monstres à deux têtes*, in *MARS* 1740 (Paris, 1742), pp. 116, 121.
[168] Lémery, *Seconde partie du Troisième Mémoire*, in *MARS* 1740, op. cit., pp. 233-234, and D. de Mairan, "Sur les monstres," in *Anatomie*, section '*Histoire*', p. 43.
[169] Lémery, *Quatrième Mémoire*, in *MARS* 1740, op. cit., pp. 433-434.

of organic diseases," – with "serious causes" — affecting a fetus in the womb.[170]

According to Lémery, since doctors name diseases in relation to "the figure (the form), the size, the number, the place and the connections between the parts," monsters can be named and classified in the same way. He illustrated this new definition and classification of monsters with examples that had already been mentioned in the Académie's papers. In the second part of his fourth *Mémoire,* Lémery praised Nature, her "variety" and "fecundity," and introduced the notion of "organic disease" in his more complete definition of monsters. He first mentioned that a monster has always been an animal with an extraordinary structure, different from those from whom they have been begotten, a structure that surprises and amazes. Then, he explained that monsters issued from a male and a female of the same species are characterized by a "disarrangement in their organs, a genuine organic disease which, while attacking more or less the structure of the parts and their uses, more or less attack health and even life." Monsters offer "only disorder, confusion, diseases that lead them very often to perish in their mother's womb or within a short time after their births." This definition clearly connected the question of monsters to pathology, which also meant, in Lémery's mind, that the "anatomical way" was not the sole method of investigating monsters. But this investigation was not separate from theological controversies or teleological themes, as can be seen from the end of the paper, when Lémery concludes that monsters "cannot be attributed to the Author of Nature, without insulting him proportionally to all that is hideous and irrational in these monsters, . . . without attributing often ridiculous designs to him, that he cannot fulfill or that he fulfils rather poorly."[171]

Lémery's conclusions were that monsters did result from accidental causes, and that "reason could never allow attributing (them) to the Creator."[172] On the contrary, in the same year, at the Académie, Winslow returned to the pre-eminent meaning of an "anatomical detail" to close the matter.[173] He however admitted that in some cases he was ready to accept the "system of accidents," but wanted "explanations that truly correspond to a perfect anatomical knowledge of the structure of the parts."[174] When the "traces or vestiges either of a loss or of a joining, or of the two together" could

---

[170] *Ibid.*, pp. 437-438.

[171] Lémery, *Seconde partie du Quatrième Mémoire...*, in *MARS* 1740, op. cit., pp. 530-533.

[172] *Ibid.*, p. 538.

[173] Winslow, *Observations anatomiques... avec des réflexions sur cette conformation extraordinaire,* in *MARS* 1740, op. cit., p. 596.

[174] *Ibid.*, p. 597.

not be found in the dissection or in the study of the skeleton of a monster, then the only possible attitude was "the wise Pyrrhonism" recommended by Fontenelle in 1699.[175] Hoping in the advance of anatomical knowledge, Winslow sided with those who, far from thinking that their idea of "extraordinary originals shocks the uniformity of Nature and hurts the wisdom and other divine attributes of the Creator, rather believe that they are thereby paying full homage to his omnipotent and sovereign freedom."[176]

Lémery answered briefly emphasizing the importance of the metaphysical context in the debate on monsters in the French Académie. In his view, the divine attributes could not be dissociated from one another.[177] This argument was repeated by the Secretary to the Académie, as can be seen from the end of his account echoing the metaphysical disagreement between Winslow and Lémery. Dortous de Mairan asserted that "The divine attributes never part," after having written that in monsters, "the freedom of the Creator" could be recognized, "if one wanted to," "but not his wisdom."[178]

Despite this assertion, the theme of the "wisdom" of the Creator in relation to monsters was once more debated at the Académie in the year 1742, when Winslow analyzed two 'dissertations' on monsters, originally written in Latin, concerning conjoined twins. The first one, published anonymously in Lyon in 1702, had been written by a physician from Lyon, Goëffon (Goiffon), and dealt with a monster with two heads, two necks, two arms, one belly, two legs and two feet. The second, published more recently in Hanover in 1739, had been written by Albrecht von Haller, a teacher of anatomy in Göttingen and concerned two girls joined by their chests and epigastria, born on the 2nd of May, in the region of Bern.

After having reiterated that he wanted neither "to exclude in every occasion the extraordinaries by accident, nor to admit in every occasion the extraordinaries by origin," Winslow carefully examined the "motives" that had grounded Goëffon's anatomical explanations in favor of the system of accidents. These motives were theological. Since it was very difficult to explain the junction of the intestines in the conjoined twins, it appeared to the physician from Lyon "much more inconceivable that God could have wanted to leave some confusion in his works and some defects in the formation and organization of the animals. That would be an insult to his Wisdom to consider defects, monsters, and imperfect productions as the effects of a particular design of his Providence."[179]

---

[175] *Ibid.*, pp. 598, 606.
[176] *Ibid.*, pp. 603, 606.
[177] Cf. Lémery, *Remarques sur un nouveau monstre, dont M. Winslow a donné depuis peu la description à l'Académie*, in *MARS* 1740, op. cit., p. 606.
[178] D. de Mairan, *Sur les monstres*, in *Anatomie, Histoire*, op. cit., p. 50.
[179] Winslow, *Remarques sur deux dissertations touchant les monstres, l'une de 1702 par*

Before commenting on this text, Winslow explained the second *Dissertation*. He first gave precise anatomical details about the two conjoined twins with four lungs and one heart, carefully described by Haller who performed the dissection. Winslow noted that Haller, in the second edition of his *Dissertation,* had gathered information on conjoined twins. Among the main authors quoted by Haller, Winslow mentioned only one name: Saint Augustine, who described a monster with two heads.[180] Then, looking for the causes of monsters, Haller summed them up in two classes, divided into 6 headings for the accident opinion, and into 7 headings to show that a "singular conformation did exist in the first lineaments and therefore could not have been the product of an ordinary structure corrupted by external violence or other cases."[181] This point directly referred to Haller's *Dissertation*, and especially to his remarkable analysis — both anatomical and embryological — of the single heart in these conjoined twins. Since the heart was considered as a "principium vitae" according to Harvey, who first saw the *punctum saliens* as the "first organ in a human being" according to Maitrejean (Maître-Jan) and to Malpighi, this single heart had been different from the very beginning, "from the first lineaments," and therefore had not been the result of some pressure or of some accident.[182]

In the two sections carefully analyzed by Haller with many precise references and briefly summarized by Winslow, there were both theological and moral arguments. For the first class it was reported that it "seemed unworthy of the divine Wisdom to directly form creatures that can live only very unfortunately. According to these authors [i.e. the authors quoted by Haller in this class — A.B.-H.], the Creator granted the fortuitous case and the second causes the power to produce diseases and death, and by himself did not produce with his hands anything that was not perfect." For the second class, Winslow reported Haller's conclusion: "the Creator did not bind himself in such a way that he could not allow the formation of fetuses without the parts that are the most useful for life, and that one must not conclude injustice in the Creator from defectiveness in such a case."[183] According to Haller, who took into account scarce reliable observations displaying the internal structure of monsters, one could find different things obviously showing "a true design and causes directed towards this same design." For Haller, the singular arrangement of all these bizarre parts seemed

---

M. Goëffon, médecin de Lyon, l'autre en 1739 par M. Haller, professeur à Gottingue (...), in *MARS* 1742 (Paris, 1745), pp. 92, 96.

[180] *Ibid.*, pp. 97-101.

[181] *Ibid.*, pp. 101-105.

[182] Cf. Haller, *Descriptio fœtus bicipitis ad pectora connati ubi in causas monstrorum ex principiis anatomicis inquiritur* (Hanover, 1739), pp. 26-27.

[183] *Ibid.*, pp. 102-103.

to be made with "science and art, with the idea of a perfection of the whole"; thereby "the constancy of such an economy could not be attributed to any fortuitous case, but to the providence of the Creator."[184]

According to Haller, "it was not too harsh a thing to attribute the direct creation of monsters to God," since they displayed "arrangements" that "proved the Wisdom of the Intelligence that formed them, and since it is not a proof of harshness on the part of the Creator that there be some individuals formed in such a way as not to be able to live, or only to be able to live miserably." Once again, the question of the origin of monsters was addressed through a careful linkage of theology and precise anatomical arguments. Once more also, the praise to God concerning monsters was associated with the limits of our minds, as well as with teleological concerns, as seen in the end of Haller's *Dissertation*: it was "not up to us to know why God has given these extraordinary conformations to some rather than to others." Haller also thought that there was "nothing denying the fine agreement and the general aims of the Universe in recognizing that the Author by forming several archetypes or different models, impresses upon men a greater and a nobler idea of his Power and his Wisdom, which are bound neither by the laws of Nature nor subject to any necessity in the formation of creatures."[185]

Even if Winslow would have preferred to avoid crossing "the boundaries of academic sciences into difficulties the discussion of which belongs to higher sciences," he nevertheless quoted Régis, Duverney, the Abbé Bignon,[186] and also Saint Augustine. The quotations of the latter were given in Latin, as they were in Haller's *Dissertation,* and they were taken from *The City of God* and the text *Against Julian the Pelagian*. The sentences extracted from *The City of God* came from Book XVI, 8, on monstrous beings. Their aim was to exonerate God from erring when producing monsters, such as the one born in the Orient with two heads, two chests, four hands, one belly and two feet. The second text echoed "God true and good," the fact that monstrous things are often called "errors of Nature" by those who are unable to disentangle the ways the divine might acts and the weakness of our minds. These quotations precede Winslow's own conclusion consisting first in some questions:

> which of the two sentiments honors the Supreme Being more: to claim that He has a particular reason in his wisdom to act as He does, or to say, as others do, that He has been stopped in the course of his general laws by the secondary or occasional causes

---

[184] *Ibid.*, pp. 104-105.
[185] *Ibid.*, p. 105.
[186] For the references, see *supra*.

which prevent the execution of his initial designs? . . . Does [this] system not seem to acknowledge some sort of impotence in the All-Powerful?

Then Winslow asserted both the impossibility for human beings to fathom the divine attributes, and God's wisdom, unaffected by the "extraordinary effects of his omnipotence."[187]

In 1743, at the beginning of the *Anatomie* section, Dortous de Mairan gave a summary of the debate between Lémery, who had just died, and Winslow, who had just published another *Mémoire*, the "last one about the question of monsters." In his *Mémoire,* Winslow confirmed the preeminence of his theological point of view with regard to the origin of monsters. He agreed that "the true Physics rises to become a kind of theology" and he closed with a quotation from Saint Augustine about "God good and just." This time Winslow did not only agree with his brilliant colleague Haller when quoting Saint Augustine, but he also emphasized the importance of Augustine's text in theological terms, explaining that the Council of Trent had confirmed the text, which related all misfortunes in the world, including physical ones, to Original Sin.[188]

Dortous de Mairan did not say a word about this theological reference. In his exposition of the two available theses, he emphasized that in the crushing of germs, "an amazing amount of chance" was required to produce a monster,[189] and appealed to examples from probability theory. He explained that faced with "such enormous difficulties" only "reasons grounded in analogy and suitability" were asserted:

> One cannot conceive that the Author of Nature, so wise, so regular and so constant in his productions had directly wanted to produce monsters when creating monstrous germs... We seek the Creator's will within our lights whereas it manifests itself in execution, and instead of attributing the formation of these wonderful creatures, despite the odious name of monsters that we have imposed upon them, to an infinite Wisdom that hides its motives from us, we prefer to see them as the product of chance or of a blind formative virtue. And if anyone should insist that the Creator produced monsters merely to satisfy the simplicity of the laws of Nature..., we shall reply that the laws of Nature are in no way different from the Creator's wills.[190]

---

[187] *Ibid.*, pp. 119-120.
[188] Cf. Winslow, *Remarques sur les monstres, cinquième et dernière partie,* in *MARS* 1743 (Paris, 1746), p. 358.
[189] Cf. Dortous de Mairan, *Sur les monstres,* op. cit., p. 61.
[190] *Ibid.*, pp. 64-65.

This clearly echoed Régis' philosophical position on monsters. According to Mairan if the lives of monsters were short, it was because we did not take care of them — which was a way of asserting that God was not responsible for this, a reason already given by Duverney. In addition, he rejected the idea of monsters being the products of a "game of Nature," recalling Fontenelle's position in 1703, in his synthetic report to the Académie des Sciences.

Despite Fontenelle's assertion and Dortous de Mairan's echo forty years later, and in contrast to the great interest shown in the mechanics of the human body; despite Voltaire's article "Nécessaire" in the *Dictionnaire philosophique* (added to the 2nd edition published in 1755), in which he confirmed that "the general laws of Nature brought some accidents which created monsters," the reports of very precise dissections of conjoined twins in the Académie des Sciences still bear some influence of the Aristotelian conception of Nature, closely tied to teleology and also theology, as was the case in the anatomical treatises of the sixteenth and seventeenth centuries, dealing with ordinary bodies. What is also very striking in these debates, is the enduring link between much more precise observations of the external and above all the internal parts of the different monsters studied, and the admiration expressed by the anatomists for these extraordinary bodies as well as for the artful junctions in conjoined twins, even when these junctions were not compatible with life. This attitude led the physicians, anatomists and surgeons to admire not only the variety of Nature but above all, as we have seen, to praise God's freedom and wisdom. The enduring link that had been established for centuries between God and the origin of monsters has changed inasmuch as in the eighteenth century, in the *Mémoires* to the Académie des Sciences, it was no longer the curse of God that was invoked, but God's wisdom even more than his freedom. Even though the theological framework was still prevalent, the atmosphere had radically changed. God had become a being of supreme reason rather than a being of judgment and punishment. What also seemed remarkable in the *Mémoires* on monsters, as contrasted with the *Mémoires* in physics, was also the fact that facing monsters — as well as when invoking the divine wisdom — the weakness of our minds had to be acknowledged. What was also noticeable in the anatomical *Mémoires* on monsters, and especially on conjoined twins, was the discussion of the divine attributes and the explicit reference to Saint Augustine.

These debates about monsters in which God, Nature and the limits of our reason played a crucial part had to be mentioned because they had been discussed not only in France, as it is well known, by Buffon, Maupertuis and Diderot, for instance, and also in the *Journal des Savants* as well as in some articles in the *Encyclopédie*, but also in the European learned societies and by some excellent anatomists such as Haller.

The debate on monsters did not end, as it is commonly believed, with the fifth and last part of Winslow's 1743 *Mémoire*. At the end of December 1775, Bordenave — a surgeon who had translated the third edition of Haller's *Primae lineae physiologiae* into French — read one *Mémoire* about a monstrous child born at term, having two faces on a single head and two bodies joined in the upper part, one being well and the other one badly conformed.[191]

The tone of this *Mémoire* was different because neither God nor the divine attributes were questioned; only Nature itself was in question. In his introduction, Bordenave asserted that, "Though the production of Monsters has often seemed to display bizarre effects the causes of which are unknown, however, the careful observation of facts has sometimes led us to follow Nature in her processes and to surprise her, so to speak, in her productions." Bordenave then claimed that admiration was "useless for the progress of science,"[192] an idea clearly expressed more than a century before by Descartes. After a precise description of the external parts of the monstrous stillborn fetus, Bordenave asserted that "such a conformation cannot be attributed to imagination, nor can it be the product of an egg monstrous by origin. It seemed much more natural to believe that it resulted from the pressure and some various accidents felt by the two germs at the time of gestation." The two germs, "distinct at the very beginning, came closer together, contracted a union against nature, and from this union a bizarre production resulted." Bordenave concluded that "monstrous productions are most often the effect of Nature disturbed at the beginning of the gestation," such that "One does not believe that Nature is capable of producing *écarts* [*sc.* going 'off track'], and one will be persuaded that it remains uniform even in the midst of such apparent disorders."[193]

This conclusion was important when related to the immediate context. The dismissal of the notion of "écarts" contrasted with the title of the recently published illustrated book, *Les écarts de la nature ou recueil des principales monstruosités que la nature produit dans le règne animal*.[194] In this work, with colored plates carefully drawn and painted by the authors

---

[191] Cf. Bordenave, *Description d'un enfant monstrueux né à terme, ayant deux visages sur une seule tête, et deux corps réunis supérieurement, l'un bien et l'autre mal conformés*, in *MARS* 1776 (Paris, 1779), pp. 697-699.

[192] *Ibid.*, p. 697.

[193] *Ibid.*, p. 699.

[194] Nicolas-François Regnault and Geneviève Regnault, *Les écarts de la nature ou recueil des principales monstruosités que la nature produit dans le règne animal* (Paris: chez l'auteur, 1775).

who were artists, monsters (human or animal) were presented as if they were in a show performed by Nature, not only to satisfy the curiosity of readers and fill them with admiration for its productions, but above all, to please them. This book had no scientific purpose. Its text consisted only of captions to the large illustrations of monsters. Among the human monsters, the illustrations featured some conjoined twins that had been shown in public, such as the ones 'seen' in Paris in 1775 and the others seen the same year in Spain. This book was undoubtedly intended to familiarize the learned public with monsters. The painters had been fascinated by their dead models, and had wanted to convert the ancient terror associated with monsters into pleasure by showing in most cases baby monsters with lively facial expressions and with chubby bodies, displayed in a quiet landscape where there was no longer room for prodigies. The traditional feeling of ugliness associated with monsters has been converted — not into beauty, but more fundamentally, into a fascinated sympathy for these monsters, many of which came from private cabinets, such as Pinson's, a surgeon in Paris.

Bordenave's conclusion was also important because he articulated a notion of "apparent disorders" that opened the way to Etienne Geoffroy Saint-Hilaire and his son Isidore, and also to the physician Etienne Serres,[195] the founders of teratology. In his *Philosophie anatomique*, published in 1822, Etienne Geoffroy Saint-Hilaire demonstrated that the "organization" in monsters "does not produce an extravagance."[196] He paid tribute to Harvey and especially to Duverney, who had argued, in his 1706 *Mémoire*, that monsters were organized with "as much art and wisdom and for a design as well defined as" those we call "perfect animals."[197] Saint-Hilaire père stated that being astonished when seeing monsters was not at all a kind of knowledge (an idea he repeated in 1826),[198] and added that Nature could no longer be seen as "playing" when producing monsters, such that we could no longer agree with the lines quoted by Leibniz in the *New Essays*, about "Nature unwise and undoubtedly leading a debauched life" ("Nature peu sage et sans doute en débauche") when associated to monsters.[199] Saint-Hilaire recommended that if one wanted to draw conclusions on the case of

---

[195] Cf. Etienne Serres, *Recherches d'anatomie transcendante pathologique* (Paris: J.-B. Baillière, 1832).
[196] Etienne Geoffroy Saint-Hilaire, *Philosophie anatomique. Des monstruosités humaines...* (Paris: Méquignon-Mervis, 1822), pp. 29, 31, 104.
[197] *Considérations générales sur les monstres* (Paris, octobre 1826), p. 29.
[198] Cf. *Philosophie anatomique*, op. cit., p. 104. See also *Considérations générales sur les monstres*, op. cit., p. 6.
[199] *Considérations générales sur les monstres*, *op. cit.*, p. 6 (the quotation is from Leibniz, *Nouveaux Essais sur l'entendement humain*, III.vi.27).

a monster, one should combine very careful and precise anatomical description of the case with a study of similar cases,[200] as had already been clearly illustrated by Haller in the eighteenth century. But in his will to distinguish admiration from knowledge, and understand the mechanics of monstrous bodies, Saint-Hilaire père showed a kind of bold confidence inherited from Descartes. When examining the conjoined twins born in Prunay-sous-Albis, in the district of Rambouillet, on October 7th 1838 and who died a month later — a case of ischiopagus — he wondered whether this monster had not been given to us by God to "unveil the mysteries of the essence of all things."[201]

4 Conclusion

Even if we can share a feeling of legitimate frustration when reading the *Histoires* and *Mémoires* of the Académie and acknowledging that they fail to make real progress in the debate on the origin of monsters, as well as on the status of conjoined twins, the importance here was to show how these anatomical discussions on dissections of monsters were enduringly tied to teleology and theology, not least since these texts were also much discussed in the nineteenth century by the founders of teratology.

The term 'teratology', already found for instance in Aldrovandi's and Ambrosini's *History of Monsters,* was used to identify the "science of monsters," in 1832, by Isidore Geoffroy Saint-Hilaire in his *Histoire générale et particulière des anomalies de l'organisation chez L'Homme et les animaux (...), ou Traité de tératologie*. Saint-Hilaire fils restricts the term "monstrosity" to the "most serious anomalies." These "very complex" and "very serious" anomalies produce "beings remarkable enough to catch everyone's eye." The appearance of these beings "astonishes," and their life after birth is generally impossible."[202] After these definitions, the author provides a classification of "double monsters." When restricting the use of the word "monster" he was reviving attempts already made by physicians at the beginning of the seventeenth century. When making use of the verb "astonish," he was repeating a word with a strong meaning, frequently found in sixteenth and seventeenth century treatises on monsters.

---

[200] *Ibid.*, p. 16.
[201] *Etudes sur la monstruosité bicorps de Prunay...*, lues à l'Académie des Sciences, les 22 octobre et 5 novembre 1838 (Paris: F. Maleste, n.d.), p. 5.
[202] Isidore Geoffroy Saint-Hilaire, *Histoire générale et particulière ... ou Traité de tératologie* (Paris: J.-B. Baillière, 1832), I, Prolégomènes, pp. 33, 41.

Hence these remarks, as well as the virtual exhibition on monsters out of which they emerged, should lead one to nuance the histories of monsters we are most familiar with, whether Saint-Hilaire's[203] or Foucault's.[204]

Acknowledgements

This paper is based on the online exhibition on monsters that has been on the website www.bium.univ-paris5.fr of the main medical library in Paris (the BIUM, Bibliothèque Interuniversitaire de Médecine) since January 29th, 2004, entitled *Les monstres de la Renaissance à l'âge classique, métamorphoses des images, anamorphoses des discours. De l'admiration, souvent mêlée de peur pour ces signes divins et prodiges de la nature aux bases d'une lecture plus "scientifique": l'émergence d'un discours "médical" sur les monstres*. Texts, bibliography and selection of the illustrations (from rare books in the BIUM) by Annie Bitbol-Hespériès. Concept, web design and image editing by Jacques Gana, webmaster and librarian, BIUM.

All translations are my own, unless a published English translation of the text is cited.

I would like to thank Charles Wolfe, for many linguistic emendations. The remaining mistakes are mine.

---

[203] *Ibid.*, pp. 4-27.

[204] Cf. M. Foucault, *Les anormaux*, Cours au Collège de France, 1974-1975, leçon du 22 janvier 1975 (Paris: Gallimard-Seuil, coll. "Hautes Études," 1999), pp. 51-74.

Degeneration and Hybridism in the Early Modern Species Debate: Towards the Philosophical Roots of the Creation-Evolution Controversy

Justin E. H. Smith

ABSTRACT. Early modern nominalism partially maps on to what is today often referred to as "species anti-realism" in the philosophy of biology, according to which, because what we think of as species are but snapshots in time of various, ever-evolving lines of descent, there can be no justification for treating them as real natural kinds. Anti-realism is strongly motivated by evolutionary theory, which takes animal species out of the class of relatively stable, fixed entities and historicizes them. In the seventeenth century the possibility of change in a species over time was generally associated with change for the worse, and thus was closely connected in the minds of some with the threat of moral decline. The perception of the fluidity of species, in contrast, may in large measure be associated with those authors most intent on promoting new empirical methods of natural-scientific investigation that would be entirely independent of ancient authority, whether that of pagan philosophy or of revealed scripture. This essay pursues the connection between the early modern mechanist account of generation and the problem of the ontological status of species. When reproduction was conceived by premodern science as the imparting of a fixed and eternal form that endows the offspring with some, to use Locke's language, real essence, there was no problem in accounting for the ontological status of species or in asserting with certainty the membership of an individual within a species. But now, in the absence of such a real essence, species membership can at most be conceived as a taxonomical, but not an ontological matter. The mechanization of embryogenesis, which is to say first and foremost the removal from this process of a role for a formal principle, effectively put all species on the endangered list, and threatened to give us only a world of individuals. Thus the question of the mechanisms of sexual generation was at the heart of the recrudescence of nominalism in the early modern period.

In the seventeenth century, the possibility of change in a species over time – and most relevantly the human species — was generally associated with change for the worse, and thus was closely connected in the minds of some with the threat of moral decline. In 1658, for example, the now largely forgotten British pietist John Bulwer complains of a new intellectual fashion among free-thinkers: "[I]n discourse," he writes,

> I have heard to fall, somewhat in earnest, from the mouth of a Philosopher ... that man was a meer Artificial creature, and was at first but a kind of Ape or Baboon, who through his industry ... by degrees in time had improved his Figure & his Reason up to the perfection of man.[1]

The philosopher remains regrettably unidentified, and there is every indication that his account of human origins was meant more to shock than to explain. Yet Bulwer takes the suggestion of man's descent from apes seriously enough to rail against it at length. And he is not alone. By the middle of the seventeenth century, the controversy about the origins of biological species, about the authority of the biblical account of origins, and about the human being's place in the animal kingdom, was already in full swing.

Bulwer's treatise was published eight years after the death of René Descartes, the figure who, perhaps more than any other, spearheaded the modern reconceptualization of animals, which transformed them from substantial, hylomorphic compounds of soul and matter, into machines of nature, well organized but in the end ontologically no different from the things of the inorganic world, and subject to all the same physical laws. Elsewhere, I have argued that we may discern a connection between the mechanization of animal generation and animal physiology on the one hand, and the new and distinctly modern problem of the origins and ontology of biological kinds on the other. In other words, Bulwer's anxiety was in large measure precipitated by the appearance some decades earlier of the *bête-machine* doctrine and the corollary mechanist account of embryogenesis. For when reproduction was conceived by premodern science as the imparting of a fixed and eternal form that endows the offspring with some, to use Locke's language, real essence, there was no problem in accounting for the ontological status of species or in asserting with certainty the membership of an

---

[1] John Bulwer, *Anthropometamorphosis: A view of the people of the whole world, or, A short survey of their policies, dispositions, naturall deportments, complexions, ancient and moderne customes, manners, habits, and fashions: a worke every where adorned with philosophicall, morall and historicall observations on the occasions of their mutations & changes throughout all ages : for the readers greater delight, figures are annexed to most of the relations* (London: Thomas Gibbs, 1658), p. 455.

individual within a species. But now, in the absence of such a real essence, species membership can at most be conceived as a taxonomical, but not an ontological matter.

This paper stems from research into the rather immense topic of the relationship between embryology and the species debate in the early modern period. I cannot hope to cover all of the important facets of this topic here. Instead, I shall limit myself to a consideration of one rather curious problem that emerged in connection with the species debate in the wake of the mechanization of embryogenesis: if biological reproduction is no longer conceived, as Aristotle had had it, as the approximation of eternity by an individual representative of an eternal species through a teleologically driven self-duplication "in kind if not in number," what is there in nature that ensures that reproduction may only occur between members of one species? If members of different species are close enough with respect to the size range of their fetuses and the length of gestation, what is there to guarantee that cross-species reproduction will not happen, and indeed, what justification is there in saying, when it does happen, that it is unnatural? Finally, if hybridism is admitted as a natural phenomenon, what is there to ensure that species, which had always been taken to be fixed and eternal, will not, over time, transform or degenerate?

In the first section, I shall briefly sketch out the connection between the mechanist theory of biological reproduction and the problem of the ontology of species as it was understood in the late seventeenth century, focusing particularly on the reflections upon this problem of John Locke. In the second section I will survey the views of early modern thinkers concerning the kinship of humans and apes, in the aim of showing that this new discourse was closely bound up with an equally new concern about the fluidity of species boundaries, and in particular about the threatened integrity of the human species. In the third section, I will consider some of the ways this concern informed the discussion of the possibility of biological hybridism between humans and apes. I will conclude with some observations on the continuity between the early modern controversy surrounding human-ape kinship and the debate that continues to rage today, in politics if not in real science, over the question of human origins.

1 Embryogenesis and species reproduction in the seventeenth century

The mechanization of embryogenesis, which is to say first and foremost the removal from this process of a role for a formal principle, effectively put all species on the endangered list, and threatened to give us only a world of individuals. This is precisely what Nicolas Malebranche had feared when he noted in 1676 that Cartesian embryology is adequate to account for reproduction in general but wholly unable "to explain why a mare does not give birth to a calf, or a chicken lay an egg containing a partridge or some bird of a new species."[2] But what Malebranche feared, Locke celebrated. For early mechanist theories of embryogenesis, in seeking to banish active immaterial agents from scientific explanation, unwittingly brought about a crisis in the ontology of biological kinds that could not be adequately dealt with until the emergence of the theory of natural selection. Late-seventeenth-century heirs to the mechanist tradition, such as Locke, were the first to fully grasp the consequences of the new theory of sexual generation for the ontology of species.

Interestingly, in Darwin's *Descent of Man* of 1871 we find a compelling statement of the connection I am claiming between the metaphysics of embryology and the nature of species. Darwin writes of his basic argument in this work — namely, that man is descended from what he calls 'lower forms' — that this thesis is no more shocking than the view already widely accepted in the seventeenth century that man is generated anew at each conception, out of ordinary matter following the ordinary laws of the physical world. "I am aware," he writes,

> that the conclusions arrived at in this work will be denounced by some as highly irreligious; but he who denounces them is bound to shew why it is more irreligious to explain the origin of man by descent from some lower form, through the laws of variation and natural selection, than to explain the birth of the individual through the laws of ordinary reproduction. The birth both of the species and of the individual are equally parts of that grand sequence of events, which our minds refuse to accept as the result of blind chance.[3]

For many in the seventeenth century, the acceptance of the view that embryogenesis proceeds from 'the laws of ordinary reproduction' is indeed, as Darwin suggests, at least as offensive to traditional natural theology as the view that humanity has descended from lower forms. With respect to both questions, the position one took up in the period generally flowed from one's view of the relationship of God to creation: the more avowedly pious the author, the more will he bemoan the view that inorganic nature can, on its own, organize into discrete, living units.

Thus for Walter Charleton the emergence of complex organic forms bespeaks God's role as both designer and builder, and the corollary of this view

---

[2]Nicolas Malebranche, *De la recherche de la vérité*, OC I, p. 243.
[3]Charles Darwin, *The Descent of Man*, in *Darwin: A Norton Critical Edition*, ed. Philip Appleman (New York: W.W. Norton, 1979), p. 202f.

is that the reduction of reproduction to a sequence of mechanical causes, from primordial, homogeneous fluids to complex structures, is tantamount to a denial of God's wisdom. As Charleton writes in his *Natural History of Nutrition, Life, and Voluntary Motion* of 1659:

> Who can observe, that so magnificent a pile is rais'd only *e luto*, out of a little slime; that from a few drops of the Colliquamentum or Genital humor, of a substance Homogenous or simple, are formed more than two hundred bones, more Cartilages, very many ligaments, membranes almost innumerable... Who can, I say, observe this, without being forced to acknowledge the infinite Power of the Divine Architect, who makes the very Materials of his building? [Who can look on this] and not discern an infinite Wisdom in the design and construction of them?[4]

Of course, not everyone who believes in the firm reality of species in the seventeenth century believes in formative principles or seeds in nature that would make embryogenesis something more than 'blind chance'; and not everyone who denies that formative principles or seeds are at work in embryogenesis would deny that there are species (indeed, Descartes does not seem much concerned about the problem of species). But the connection is clear: if there is no immaterial guiding blueprint or formative principle ensuring that the colliquamentum take the shape it is destined to take, then little sense remains to the claim that breeding true is the proper or fitting outcome of conception, or to the claim that breeding *true* is in any sense true in virtue of the membership of individual organisms in a real kind.

As with the opposition to 'blind' or unguided embryogenesis, the figures most committed to the fixity of species are also those most committed to traditional theology. Thus the pious natural theologian John Ray insists unequivocally that "the number of true species in nature is fixed and limited and, as we may reasonably believe, constant and unchangeable from the first creation to the present day."[5] The perception of the fluidity of species, in contrast, may in large measure be associated with the *novatores*, those authors most intent on promoting new empirical methods of natural-scientific investigation that would be entirely independent of ancient authority, whether that of pagan philosophy or of revealed scripture. Thus in the *Novum Organum*, Francis Bacon notes that there are natural beings "which appear to be composed of two species, or to be the rudiments

---

[4] Charleton, *Natural History*, Preface, no page numbers.
[5] John Ray, *Historia plantarum* (1688), cited in John C. Green, *The Death of Adam: Evolution and its Impact on Western Thought* (Ames: Iowa State University Press, 1959), p. 129.

between one and the other." He offers as examples of these "Moss, which is something between putrescence and a plant," and "Flying Fishes, between fishes and birds," and, finally, "Bats, between birds and quadrupeds." He goes on to suggest that sometimes these transitional individuals may emerge by way of degeneration: "plants," he writes, "sometimes degenerate to the point of changing into other plants."[6]

Following in Bacon's path, Locke speaks in the *Essay Concerning Human Understanding* of creatures that "have shapes like ours, but are hairy, and want Language, and Reason.... If it be asked," Locke reasons,

> "whether these be all Men, or no, all of humane Species; 'tis plain, the Question refers only to the nominal Essence: For those of them to whom the definition of the Word Man, or the complex Idea signified by that Name, agrees are Men, and the other not. But if the Enquiry be made concerning the supposed real Essence; and whether the internal Constitution and Forme of these several Creatures be specifically different, it is wholly impossible for us to answer."[7]

Elsewhere in the same work, Locke again attempts to draw empirical evidence in favor of his nominalism from what he takes to be the common natural phenomenon of cross-species reproduction. "I once saw a Creature," he maintains,

> that was the Issue of a Cat and a Rat, and had the plain Marks of both about it; wherein Nature appear'd to have followed the Pattern of neither sort alone, but to have jumbled them both together. To which, he that shall add the monstrous Productions, that are so frequently to be met with in Nature, will find it hard, even in the race of Animals to determine by the Pedigree of what Species every Animal's issue is; and be at a loss about the real Essence, which he thinks certainly conveyed by Generation, and has alone a right to the specifick name.[8]

Here Locke offers us a paradigmatic statement of his nominalism, and he takes the apparent fluidity of species boundaries as evidence for the truth of this theory. Early modern nominalisms, including Locke's, partially map on to what is often referred to today as "species anti-realism" in the philosophy

---

[6] Bacon, *Novum Organum*, II, 30.
[7] Locke, *Essay Concerning Human Understanding*, III.vi.22, pp. 450-451.
[8] *Ibid.*, pp. 451-452.

of biology,⁹ according to which, insofar as what we think of as species are but snapshots in time of various, ever-evolving lines of descent, there can be no justification for treating them as real natural kinds. Anti-realism about species is strongly motivated by evolutionary theory (though, to be sure, many evolutionists remain realists), which takes them out of the class of relatively stable, fixed entities, like the elements on the periodic table, and historicizes them, placing them more on a par with, say, nation-states or car models. In general, species anti-realism today is an issue rather distinct from the much more general issue of the ontological status of natural kinds. An evolutionist can believe that species are historical collective entities, or individuals designated by *de facto* proper names, while staying altogether out of the debate as to whether, e.g., water is essentially H_2O. If species anti-realists in the philosophy of biology steer clear of the water problem it is not the case that those involved in the more general discussion of the problem of natural kinds steer clear of biological species. These are regularly adduced, alongside naturally occurring elements, as though these two different examples presented all and only the same problems.¹⁰ Of course, as Elliott Sober points out, atom smashers can now transform one element into another, but this is not in itself proof that elements are not, after all, natural kinds. And yet the immense difference between the relative ephemerality of, say, a species of finch on the one hand, and the relative fixity of, say, gold on the other, does at least problematize their interchangeability as stock examples for the discussion of natural kinds.¹¹

What has often been overlooked in the study of the history of nominalism from antiquity through the eighteenth century, is that prior to the universal acceptance (among serious inquirers, anyway) of an evolutionary account of the origins of biological species, animal kinds were taken as instances of natural kinds *par excellence*. In this context, it is entities from the inorganic world that appear ontologically unstable or questionable, and animal species that are seen as the most fixed and certain. The landscape was thus very nearly the opposite of what it is today: today, we can comfortably deny

---

[9] See, for example, Robert A. Wilson, "Realism, Essence, and Kind: Resuscitating Species Essentialism?"; Richard Boyd, "Homeostasis, Species, and Higher Taxa," both in Robert A. Wilson, ed., *Species: New Interdisciplinary Essays* (Cambridge, Mass: MIT Press, 1999). Both authors argue, in different ways, that some kind of modified realism can be made to fit with an evolutionary account of species. For a classical statement of the view that evolutionary theory renders essentialism about species untenable, see David Hull, "The Effect of Essentialism on Taxonomy — 2000 Years of Stasis," *British Journal for the Philosophy of Science*, vols. 15 (1965), pp. 314-326 and 16 (1965), pp. 1-18.

[10] See, e.g., S. A. Kripke, "Identity and Necessity," in M. K. Munitz, ed., *Identity and Individuation* (New York: New York University Press, 1971).

[11] See Sober, *Philosophy of Biology* (Boulder: Westview Press, 1993), ch. 6.

the fixity of animal species while nonetheless not going so far as to say that there are no real natural kinds out there; in the tradition of thinking about nature that goes back at least as far as Genesis and extends into the eighteenth century, if discrete and stable animal kinds are bid *adieu*, we lose those entities that have generally been perceived as the most basic ingredients of the world. Speculatively, it may be suggested that cross-species reproduction is so offensive to our sense of what is right and decent, and monsters have such a power to disrupt social order, precisely because such phenomena would threaten to obliterate those boundaries between species that have evidently given all human cultures a sense of stability and regularity in the world around them. In this light, Locke's nominalism, and his arguments for it, appear far more radical than those of us living comfortably in the post-Darwinian world are able to easily recognize.

For obvious reasons, purported ape-men constitute even more of an affront to traditional piety than cat-rats. Cross-species breeding would disrupt the order of nature, but only the unnatural coupling of a human and a beast could amount to an ontological and a moral transgression at once. Yet new data from sundry sources was pushing European science to an understanding of humans and apes as closer than had earlier been thought, and as quite possibly close enough to interbreed. Increasingly in the late seventeenth century, the study of primates in general was seen as relevant to the study of man, notwithstanding the confrontation with traditional, religiously grounded anthropology this was bound to provoke. Before approaching the question of ape-human hybrids in particular, perhaps it will be useful to survey a bit of the history of the early modern assimilation of anthropology to primatology, and of the confrontation this brought about with traditional theology.

2 The birth of modern primatology

Ancient and medieval interest in apes had been mythological and speculative, and the legacy of Herodotus' fantastic fables about half-men remained so strong in the seventeenth century that even Edward Tyson, in writing his 1699 work, *Orang-Outang, sive, Homo sylvestris*, felt compelled to divide it into 'anatomical' and 'philological' sections.[12] The philological part of his work pursues such questions as who the dog-headed men of Africa are

---

[12] The very earliest works that we may believe to offer genuine reports of observations of apes stem from the turn of the seventeenth century. These include Filippo Pigafetta, et al., *Regnum Congo hoc est, Warhaffte und eigentliche Beschreibung dess Königreichs Congo in Africa und deren angrentzenden Länder* (Frankfurt: Verlag Hans Dietrich und Hans Israel von Bry, 1597); followed by Samuel Purchas, *Hakluytus posthumus, or Purchas his Pilgrimes. Containing a History of the Worlde, in Sea Voyages & Lande Travells*, 20 vols. (London, 1625; reprint, New York: AMS Press, 1965).

(the 'Cynocephali' mentioned as early as Herodotus — baboons, as it turns out), and whether the 'Pygmies' who battled the cranes in Homer ever really existed. In this respect, seventeenth-century primatology straddles two different eras' very different conceptions of our closest relatives: the semifabulous conception, which paid very little attention to the question of our fundamental similarity to the higher primates, and emphasized only how strangely different they were; and the new conception, which would seek to ground the lines of taxonomical affinity in sound comparative anatomical research. Many authors continue in the old, fabulist vein. Olfert Dapper, for example, does not make any advances over Herodotus in his description of the baboon; for both, they are "[l]es Cynocephales, gens qui avoient une tete et des pattes de chien et abayoient comme ces animaux."[13]

While the cynocephali would turn out to be baboons, it was the ancient satyr that would be redescribed as an 'orang-outang' in the seventeenth century — with the alternative "homo sylvestris" literally translating the original Malay term. In the mid-seventeenth century Walter Charleton and Nicolas Tulpius both continue to explicitly identify the creature as 'orang-outang, sive satyrus indicus'. In his taxonomical compendium, the *Onomasticon zoikon*, Charleton identifies all simians as belonging to the "Classis digitatorum semiferorum." Among these he lists in last place the "Satyrus Indicus," also known as "homo sylvestris" or "Orang-Outang," citing the authority of Tulpius, who attests to its "admirable intellect [*ingenium admirandum*]."

In antiquity, Pliny had written of the satyr that it is "an animal, a quadruped, in the tropical mountains of India, a most pernicious one; with a human figure, but with the feet of a goat; and with a body hairy all over. Having none of the human customs; rejoicing in the shadows of the wood; and fleeing from intercourse with men." In the seventeenth century, Tulpius praises Pliny's account, while giving a rather different one of his own: "[I]f you explore [the descriptions of the ancients] ... you will see them not far wrong. There will be found still this lascivious animal in the tropical mountains of India; it rejoices in rough corners; avoids human comforts, and one hears, not undeservedly, salacious, hairy, fourfooted, bearing a human face; and furnished with nostrils turning inward."[14] Roughly equidistant in time between Pliny and Tulpius, Nizami al-Arudi describes the satyr in quite different terms, but like Pliny and Tulpius both attributes to it the capacity, and desire to generate hybrid offspring with humans:

---

[13] Olfert Dapper, *Description de l'Afrique* (Amsterdam: Wolfgang, Waesberge *et al.*, 1686), p. 3.

[14] Nicolas Tulpius, *Observationes Medicae* (Amsterdam: Ludovicum Elzevirium, 1641), p. 274.

> [The highest animal] is the satyr, a creature inhabiting the plains of Turkistan, of erect carriage and vertical stature, with wide flat nails. It cherishes a great affection for men; wherever it sees men, it halts on their path and examines them attentively; and when it finds a solitary man, it carries him off, and it is even said that it will conceive from him. This, after mankind, is the highest of animals, inasmuch as in several respects it resembles man.[15]

Similar stories continue to be related by Olfert Dapper in 1686,[16] and by Louis le Comte in 1697,[17] describing their journeys to Africa and Asia respectively. Gassendi as well relates tales of creatures straddling the boundary between humanity and beastliness. In *La vie de Peiresc*, a desultory tribute to the prominent French civic leader Nicole Peiresc, relates a story of a creature

> of a middle nature, between Men and Apes. Which because many could not believe, Peireskius told what he had heard chiefly from Africa. For Natalis the Physician before mentioned, had acquainted him, that there are in Guiney, Apes, with long, gray, combed Beards, almost venerable, who stalk at an Aldermans pace, and take themselves to be very wise: those that are the greatest of all, and which they terme Barris, have most judgement; they will learn any thing at once shewing; being cloathed they presently go upon their hind legs; play cunningly upon the Flute, Cittern, and such other Instruments (for it is counted nothing for them to sweep the house, turn the spit, beat in the Morrer, and do other works like Household Servants).[18]

---

[15] Edward G. Browne, ed. & trans., *Chahar Maqala of Nizami-i-Arudi* (Gibb Memorial Series, vol XI-2), pp. 6-9 (reprint, Cambridge: Cambridge University Press, 1925).

[16] Dapper, *Description de l'Afrique*, op. cit.

[17] Louis le Comte, *Nouveaux mémoires sur l'état present de la Chine*, 2 vols. (Amsterdam: de Lorme, 1697); translated as *Memoirs and observations topographical, physical, mathematical, mechanical, natural, civil, and ecclesiastical made in a late journey through the empire of China* (London: Benjamin Tooke, 3^d revised edition 1699). Le Comte reports that in Borneo "the People of the Country assure us, as a thing notoriously known to be true: That they find in the woods a sort of Beast, called the Savage Man; whose Shape, Stature, Countenance, Arms, Legs, and other Members of the Body, are so like ours, that excepting the Voice only, one should have much ado not to reckon them equally Men with certain Barbarians in Africa, who do not much differ from Beasts" (cited in Edward Tyson, *Orang-outang, sive Homo sylvestris; Or the Anatomy of a Pygmie compared with That of a Monkey, an Ape, and a Man* [London, 1699], p. 23).

[18] Pierre Gassendi, *The Mirrour of true Nobility & Gentility. Being the Life of The Renowned Nicolaus Claudius Fabricius Lord of Peiresk, Senator of the Parliament of Aix*, trans. W. Rand (London: Humphrey Moreley, 1657), p. 91.

Dapper, for his part, tells of "une Espece de Satyre que les Negroes appellent Quoias-Morrous, & les Portugais, Salvage." He offers a proto-adaptationist account of how these creatures, descended originally from humans, grew physically ape-like as a result of the degenerative effects of living the life of an ape:

> They have a large head, a large and weighty body, nerve-ridden arms, they have no tail, and they walk now fully upright, now on four feet. The animals eat fruit and wild honey, and at any moment will begin fighting with one another. They are descended from men, according to the Negroes, but they became such half-beasts as a result of staying always in the forest.[19]

Increasingly, in the seventeenth century, apes and men were thought to have common origins, and this both by those who bemoaned the possibility of physical and moral degeneration from human into beast, as well as by those who evidently saw humans as having risen from a beastly state to our current human one. The latter view, of course, is harder to fit into an interpretation of origins in scriptural terms. The view that apes are degenerated humans is but a variation of the myth of the fall, while the claim that humans are excellent apes seemed to have no religious precedent at all. Many authors consequently chose to pay lip service to scripture while ultimately treating it as irrelevant to the study of affinities between humans and apes.

John Wallis's natural-philosophical consideration of the question of human carnivorism provides a fine example of the sort of un-pious consideration of the relation of humans to apes against which Bulwer had railed some decades earlier. Wallis begins his 1699 letter to Edward Tyson, on whether humans are naturally carnivorous, by noting that it is the "Opinion of many Divines that before the Flood, Men did not use to feed on Flesh, because of what we have in Gen[esis 9:3], where God says to Noah, (after the Flood,) Every moving thing that liveth, shall be meat for you, even as the green Herb have I given you all things: Compared with Gen[esis 1:29] where God says to Adam, I have given you every Herb bearing Seed, and every Tree in the which is the fruit of a Tree yielding Seed, and every Tree in the which is the fruit of a Tree yielding seed, to you it shall be for Meat." So much for scriptural considerations. Wallis turns from here to consider the structure of the teeth and the length of the colon, arguing that the latter is longer in herbivorous creatures such as sheep than in carnivores such as foxes, wolves,

---

[19] Dapper, *Description de l'Afrique*. "Ils ont la tête grosse, le Corps gros et pesant, les bras nerveux, ils n'ont point de queue, et Marchent tantot tout droit, et tantot à quatre pieds. Les Animaux se nourrissent de fruits et de Miel Sauvage, & se battent à tout moment les uns contre les autres. Ils sont issu des Hommes, à ce disent les Negroes, mais ils sont devenus ainsi demi-bêtes en se tenant toujours dans les Forets."

and dogs. Where do humans stand in this comparison? Interestingly, they are placed with the other primates: "Now it is well known, that in Man, and, I presume, in the Ape, Monkey, Baboon, &c. such Colon is very remarkable." The distinguishing feature of the human colon is the relative smallness of it, in proportion to the whole body, in contrast with the relative size of the fetal colon: "'Tis true, that ... in Man [it] is very small, and seems to be of little or no use: But in a Foetus, it is in proportion much larger than in persons adult."

Wallis conjectures that this contraction is brought about by dietary factors: "And it's possible, that our Customary change of Dyet, as we grow up, from what originally would be more natural, may occasion its shrinking into this contracted posture." In other words, our colons are more naturally like those of sheep; meat-eating transforms them into something more closely resembling the colons of wolves. This transformation, Wallis speculates, "Seems to be a great Indication, that Nature, which may be reasonably presum'd to adapt the Intestines to the different sorts of aliments that are to pass through them, doth accordingly inform us, to what Animals Flesh is the proper aliment, and to what it is not."[20]

Wallis's correspondent Edward Tyson would certainly appreciate the invocation of anatomical similarities to the other primates as a way of answering the question concerning the proper diet of human beings. Tyson is the first modern scientist to perform an anatomical study of a great ape, in 1698, and it is with this study that, as Ashley Montagu puts it, "for the first time in human history, [it was] suggested by a scientist to a scientific audience that a creature of the ape-kind was structurally more closely related to man than was any other known animal." In Montagu's view, Tyson's realization that human beings are anatomically, if not by way of ancestry, related to other animals — are, as it were, variations on the same theme, "was one of the greatest and most far-reaching advances to be made in the thought of Western civilization."[21] Tyson's work is certainly different from prior writing on the topic of apes in that it is firmly devoted to the extraction of a core of empirically based facts from the mountain of myths and rumors that had accumulated since the ancient period about satyrs, half-men, etc. Tyson's "chief design," as he himself describes it, "is the Improvement of the Natural History of Animals; so I have made it my Business more, to find out the Truth, than to enlarge Mythology; to inform the Judgement, than to please the Phancy."[22]

---

[20] John Wallis, "A Letter to Edward Tyson," *Philosophical Transactions* 22 (1700), p. 772.

[21] M. F. Ashley Montagu, *Edward Tyson, M. D., F. R. S., 1650-1708* (Philadelphia: American Philosophical Society, 1943), p. 227.

[22] Tyson, *Orang-outang*, p. ix.

In his lengthy 1943 study of Tyson's life and work, Montagu maintains that while Tyson was a firm believer in gradation, he did not, and could not, have had any inkling of evolution. Gradation, for Montagu, is an unchanging state, and not a process. Tyson's insight, Montagu contends, is only that the closest link to man is the great ape, and not that these two are linked by ancestry. The distinction is not so clear, however. Tyson does not explicitly deny that similarities may be accounted for in terms of common lineage. Indeed, he seems positively to affirm adaptation in the case of porpoises, of which he also did an anatomical study some 18 years before his much better known study of the chimpanzee:

> The structure of the viscera and inward parts have so great an Analogy and resemblance to those of Quadrupeds, that we find them here almost the same. The greatest difference from them seems to be in the external shape, and wanting feet. But here too we observed that when the skin and flesh were taken off, the fore-fins did very well represent an Arm... the Tayle too does very well supply the defect of feet both in swimming as also leaping in the water, as if both hinder feet were colligated into one.[23]

The relationship between porpoises and quadrupeds is one matter, but for Tyson it is a fundamental truth that "inter hominem et non-hominem medium non datur [there is no intermediary between man and non-man]" All the same, he can't help but acknowledge the remarkable resemblance between human and ape bodies. After dissecting a chimpanzee (which he variously calls a 'pygmie' and an 'orang-outang'),[24] Tyson concludes: "notwithstanding our Pygmie does so much resemble a Man in many of its Parts, more than any of the Ape-kind, or any other Animal in the World that I know of: Yet by no means do I look upon it as the Product of a mixt Generation; 'tis a Brute-Animal *sui generis*, and a particular Species of Ape."[25]

When writing about apes — as opposed to porpoises — Tyson is very concerned to turn back the trend in his contemporaries' thinking toward blurring the line between man and ape. But the fact that he feels compelled

---

[23] Edward Tyson, *Phocaena, or the Anatomy of a Porpess, dissected at Greshame Colledge; with a Praeliminary Discourse concerning Anatomy, and a Natural History of Animals* (London: Benjamin Tooke, 1680), p. 16f.

[24] Tyson's identification of the chimpanzee as an 'Orang-Outang', was not the result of any confusion on his part, since he took this to be a generic name which included both African and Asian 'Orang-Outangs' as two distinct species. The name today properly designates only the Asian species.

[25] Tyson, *Orang-outang*, p. 5.

to enter into this battle at all might be taken to show, against Montagu, that to think about apes and men as having shared ancestry was, if offensive to Tyson's sense of human dignity, nevertheless possible. Indeed, for Tyson there is so much evidence for human-ape kinship that in the end the only way he could secure this fundamental difference, while acknowledging physiological similarities, is by locating human uniqueness in something altogether unconnected to physiology:

> The Organs in Animal Bodies are only a regular Compages of Pipes and Vessels, for the Fluids to pass through, and are passive. What actuates them, are the Humours and Fluids: and Animal Life consists in their due and regular motion in this Organical Body. But those Nobler Faculties in the Mind of Man, must certainly have a higher Principle; and Matter organized could never produce them; for why else, where the Organ is the same, should not the Actions be the same too? and if all depended on the Organ, not only our Pygmie, but other Brutes likewise, would be too near akin to us.... In truth Man is part a Brute, part an Angel; and is that Link in the Creation, that joyns them both together.[26]

As we have seen, some decades earlier Bulwer had argued differently: saying that we could be certain of the absence of a soul in apes, in view of their anatomical difference from us. "Indeed, the bodies of other Creatures," Bulwer writes, "are not capable of mans soul, because they are not of that Fabrick, temper, and constitution, if they were capable; yet, for want of fit Organs the soule could not exercise her actions."[27] In 1672, similarly, Thomas Willis identifies the complexity of human action and deliberation with the elaborately folded surface of the human brain:

> Those Gyrations or Turnings about in [the brains of] four footed beasts are fewer, and in some, as in a Cat, they are found to certain figure and order: wherefore this Brute thinks on, or remembers scarce any thing but what the instincts and needs of Nature suggest. In the lesser four-footed beasts, also in Fowls and Fishes, the superficies of the brain being plain and even, wants all cranklings and turnings about: wherefore these sort of Animals comprehend or learn by imitation fewer things, and those almost only of one kind; for that in such, distinct cells, and parted one from another, are wanting in which the divers

---

[26] *Ibid.*, p. 54f.
[27] Bulwer, *Anthropometamorphosis*, p. 445.

Species and Ideas of things are kept apart.[28]

For Willis, as for Bulwer, there are sufficient physiological markers of a profound difference between humans and animals to assure us of our unique place in nature without having to leave the bounds of empirical science and engage in metaphysical disputations about the possession of a soul. Tyson offers an account of a current regrettable trend towards thinking of humans and apes as kin that at first may appear to be an echo of Bulwer's statement in the previous section to the effect that any change in the physical traits of humans is change for the worse, which is to say degeneration into animality. For Tyson, upon completing his anatomical study, it does not appear so easy to establish the radical difference between humans and apes by appeal to their respective parts and structures.

Tyson observes that "the Ancients were fond of making Brutes to be Men: on the contrary now, most unphilosophically, the Humour is, to make Men but meer Brutes and Matter." But, unlike Bulwer, Tyson does not hope to base the claim to tremendous difference in anatomical difference, since this latter sort of difference is, in his view, trivial.[29] In comparing Tyson's statements about the crucial difference between apes and humans with those of his close predecessors, we find reason to affirm Montagu's assessment of Tyson's work as revolutionary. Tyson holds on to a fundamental difference between humans and apes, but acknowledges that the scientific evidence will not permit him to ground this difference in anatomy or physiology. Bulwer and Wallis, in contrast, continue to hope to establish the fundamental difference between the moral or intellectual status of humans

---

[28]Willis, *De anima brutorum* (1672) in *Opera omnia* (Lyon: J.-A. Huguetan, 1676), p. 76. For an interesting discussion of Willis's easy passage between anatomy and psychology, see William F. Bynum, "The Anatomical Method, Natural Theology, and the Functions of the Brain," *Isis* 64:4 (December 1973), pp. 444-468. The view that the apparent simplicity and grace of animal behavior, in contrast with the relative clumsiness of humans, is attributable to their lack of higher cognitive faculties, appears widespread in the early modern period. Thus, Descartes observes early in his career that "The high degree of perfection displayed in some of their actions makes us suspect that animals do not have free will" (CSM, I 5), and makes similar claims again in the *Discourse on Method* (CSM I, 139) and the *Principles of Philosophy* (CSM I, 205).

[29]It is worth noting that the effort to ground profound moral differences between humans and apes in arguably inconsequential features of each continues today. These features are no longer anatomical; instead, today certain linguistic abilities are taken as a shibboleth of moral status. As Richard Sorabji wryly observes, "It sounded grand enough when Aristotle and the Stoics declared that man had reason and animals did not. But as the debate progressed, it began to appear that animals might lack only certain kinds of reasoning, and a stand was taken on their not having speech. When this defence too began to be questioned, a retreat was made to the position that they lacked syntax. 'They lack syntax, so we can eat them', was meant to be the conclusion" (*Animal Minds and Human Morals: The Origins of the Western Debate* [Ithaca: Cornell University Press, 1993]), p. 216.

and apes by appeal to the evidence of physical traits. The vastly greater part of Tyson's study, the anatomical part, speaks to the tremendous similarity of man and ape; the metaphysical part that insists upon an essential difference could easily seem to be a message drowned out by the wealth of physiological information within which it is embedded.

As we have seen, by the late seventeenth century, many natural philosophers, as well as travel writers, are taking sides on the question of the possibility of transitional beings lying between humans and apes, as well as between other animal species. Bulwer, Ray, and Tyson say 'no'; Dapper and Locke say 'yes'.[30] Tyson, again, protests more against the possibility of transitions between apes and humans than between quadrupeds and porpoises, and the crux of his argument is a Cartesian distinction between the immaterial soul and the mortal body, which for its part is now conceived as only slightly different from that of a chimpanzee. In sum, while writing about apes in the seventeenth century continued to be mixed with a good deal of exaggeration and embellishment of the sort characteristic of many ancient and medieval writers, the body of accurate knowledge about apes increased steadily over the course of the century, and was most greatly advanced by Tyson; and this new accurate knowledge of primate anatomy and behavior strongly militated in favor of a view of species boundaries as fluid and not fixed.

3 The spectre of hybridism

Traditionally, hybridism was thought to be possible in sufficiently similar creatures. Thus, a claim to the possibility of hybrid offspring in early biology may give us insight into a perception of similarity, and into taxonomic links that may otherwise have remained unelaborated. Thus in the 12th century, in his *De animalibus*, Albertus Magnus identifies the 'hybrid' as any quadruped that is dual-genused, and maintains this is possible "for animals which have the same gestation period, an appropriately sized uterus, and are not very far apart as to shape."[31]

In the Renaissance, the subject of animal-human hybrids had generally served as little more than a pretext for the denunciation of sin. Nonetheless, in the course of this denunciation we are often given inadvertent insight into the era's conception of the nature of species and their boundaries. Paracelsus's comments in the 15th century on bestiality, and what can issue

---

[30] For a defense of the importance of Dapper's work in response to similar criticism, see Adam Jones, "Decompiling Dapper: A Preliminary Search for Evidence," *History in Africa* 17 (1990), pp. 171-209.

[31] Albert the Great, *On Animals: A Medieval summa zoologica*, ed. & trans. Kenneth F. Kitchell and Irven Michael Resnick, 2 vols. (Baltimore: Johns Hopkins University Press, 1999), vol. 2, Book 22, 1511.

from this, are particularly revealing. He believes that humans can be born of animals, and vice versa. He thinks that the first sort of birth must be a result of 'unnatural', and 'heretical' union, "when a man mixes with an animal and this animal takes in and retains the sperm of the man with lust and greed, like a woman, the sperm becomes rotten and through the constant warmth of the body another human will arise, and not an animal."[32] The other possibility, however, when an animal is born of a human, may be the result of a rather more innocent process:

> It is also possible and not contrary to nature, that a woman and a man can give birth to an animal. In such a case the woman should not be judged in the same way as the man. She should not be taken for a heretic, as if she had acted contrary to nature; rather, this should be attributed to her imagination. For her imagination is often to blame in such a case. The imagination of a pregnant woman is so strong, that in the conception she can transform in various ways the seed and the embryo [*die Frucht*] in her body, for her inner stars have such a strong and powerful influence on the embryo as to bring about an effect and an influence.[33]

For Paracelsus, then, animals can be born of humans without bestiality, but humans can only be born of animals as a result of unnatural sexual contact. The reason for the difference is that human females have a greater power of imagination, so that they are able to transform the fetus into an animal as a result of the communication of images, while female animals are unable to bring about such effects in a fetus they are carrying.

---

[32] "Es ist auch in der Natur moeglich, dass Menschen von Tieren geboren werden können. Dies hat auch seine natürliche Ursache. Ohne Ketzerei kann dies aber nicht geschehen. Wenn sich ein Mensch mit einem Tier vermischt und dieses Tier als ein Weibsbild das Sperma des Mannes mit Lust und Begehrlichkeit in seiner Gebärmutter empfängt und einschliesst, dann mus das Sperma in Fäulnis gehen und durch die ständige Wärme des Körpers wird wieder ein Mensch und kein Tier daraus..." (Paracelsus [Theophrastus Bombastus von Hohenheim], *Sämtliche Werke*, nach der 10 bändigen Huserchen Gesamtausgabe, 1589-1591 [Leipzig: Zentralantiquariat der Deutschen Demokratischen Republik, 1975], 4 vols., here, vol. 3, p. 223f.).

[33] "Es ist auch möglich und nicht wider die Natur, dass ein Weib und Mensch ein Tier gebären kann. Das Weib ist darin nicht so wie der Mann. Es ist auch möglich und nicht wider die Natur, dass ein Weib und Mensch ein Tier gebären kann. Das Weib ist darin nicht so wie der Mann zu beurteilen. Man soll sie darum nicht für eine Ketzerin halten, als ob sie wider die Natur gehandelt hätte, sondern dies soll ihrer Einbildung zugeschrieben werden. Denn ihre Einbildung ist oft daran schuld. Die Einbildung einer schwangeren Frau ist so stark, dass sie bei der Schöpfung den Samen und die Frucht in ihrem Körper in verschiedener Weise verwandeln kann, denn ihre inneren Gestirne wirken so stark und kräftig auf die Frucht, dass sie eine Wirkung und Influenz liefern" (*ibid.*).

Without wishing to be crude, it is undeniably significant that Paracelsus's examples of bestiality are all of a decidedly barnyard variety, while by the seventeenth century imaginations had drifted not just from the farm, but from the continent, in coming up with ways in which humans might transgressively blur the boundary between us and the beasts. Why this shift from horses and goats to chimpanzees and gorillas? It may be suggested, speculatively, that the particular concern we see in the seventeenth century about the possibility of ape-human hybrids is a symptom of a growing awareness of the possibility of kinship between the two species. The important historical developments that served to bring this awareness about were (i) increased contact with the parts of the world in which great apes live, and their consequent demythologization on the one hand, and on the other their distinction from monkeys; (ii) towards the very end of the century, the vastly expanded anatomical knowledge of apes that resulted from Tyson's work.

One particularly important part of the perception of apes in the early modern period concerned their reportedly voracious sexual appetite. As Dapper observes (based, unsurprisingly, on hearsay), "On dit qu'ils forcent les femmes & les filles, & qu'ils ont le courage d'attaquer des Hommes armez."[34] According to Tulpius, the desire for human women "burns so ardently that not seldom do they ravish them when captured. In fact they are so greatly inclined to venery (even among themselves, as was common with the licentious Satyrs of the ancients) that they are at all times wanton and lustful: so that the Indian women therefore avoid the woods and forests, worse than dog and serpent, where these shameless animals roam."[35] Gassendi too reports that "the males exceedingly desire the company of Women."[36] Castanenda, for his part, reports in the *Annals of Portugal* of a woman who has had two children by an ape,[37] and Clauderus relates the story of a veritable Baroque King Kong, "which grew so amorous of one of the Maids of Honour, who was a celebrated Beauty, that no Chains, nor Confinement, nor Beating, could keep him within Bounds; so that the Lady was forced to petition to have him banished the Court (*sic*)."[38]

Tyson, wishing ever to replace myth with fact based in observation, suggests he may even have found an anatomical basis for the ape's concupiscence:

---

[34] Dapper, *Description de l'Afrique*, p. 18f.
[35] Nicolas Tulpius, *Observationes Medicæ*, p. 274.
[36] Pierre Gassendi, *The Mirrour of true Nobility & Gentility*, p. 91.
[37] As reported by Fortunio Liceti in his *De monstrorum causis, natura, et differentiis, libri duo* (Patavii: apud Paulum Frambottum, 1634), lib. 2. cap. 68, p. 217.
[38] This is Tyson's paraphrase of an account offered by Gabriel Clauder in the *Miscell. Curiosa Germanae*, Decur. 2. Ann. 5. Obs. 187; Tyson, *Orang-outang*, p. 42.

[W]hether the Testes being thus closely pursed up to the Body, might contribute to that great salaciousness this Species of Animals are noted for, I will not determine: Tho' 'tis said, that these Animals, that have their Testicles contained within the Body, are more inclined to it, than others. That the whole Ape-kind is extreamly given to Venery, appears by infinite Stories related of them. And not only so, but different from other Brutes, they covet not only their own Species, but to an Excess are inclined and sollicitous to those of a different, and are most amorous of fair Women.

But just what did people imagine the apes wished to do with these fair women? It would seem the underlying concern was with the prospect of hybrid offspring. As we've already seen, Tyson thought it urgent to argue against the suggestion that his Orang-Outang might be 'the Product of a mixt Generation'. For Locke, in contrast, important empirical evidence for the non-reality of species, or at least purported empirical evidence, is what he takes to be the common phenomenon of cross-species reproduction or hybridism. For him, one potential hybrid is that between humans and apes; "if History lie not, he writes, "Women have conceived by Drills; and what real Species, by that measure, such a Production will be in Nature, will be a new Question."[39]

Clearly, much of what was said about apes in the seventeenth century was based in completely unsubstantiated rumor; male apes have no particular interest in human women, and plain observation of them in the presence of women would have been enough to demonstrate this. But again, the very appearance of the rumor is telling: no one worried about what might happen to a woman in the proximity of a bull, say, or a stallion. The perception of a threat may be a perfect illustration of what has been called "the narcissism of minor differences," where it is feared similarity itself that prompts one group of people, or creatures, to exaggerate their difference from another group and insist on radical separation, whether geographical or taxonomical.

In traditional embryology, which posited a formative principle, there was a comprehensive way of dealing with monstrosities and with the exceptional case of mules (Aristotle, unlike Locke, never saw a cat-rat), that did not do too much harm to this ontology: monstrosities were simply the failure of the form to reach full actualization. But once reproduction is reconceived as a mechanical process, breeding true comes to look like a merely regular, but by no means certain, outcome of mating, an outcome that could have nothing

---

[39] Locke, *Essay*, III.vi.22, p. 451.

to do with the membership of the parents in a really existing natural kind; and consequently, change in a population over time, as a result of cross-species mating, or of change in environmental factors, becomes thinkable. For Locke and others of like mind, hybrid or monstrous offspring cannot in any way be accounted for as nature's occasional misfiring, since there is no longer any justification for claiming that nature is firing towards any particular target or other.

4 Conclusion

It would be no exaggeration to say that Tyson's work, and more generally the discovery of human kinship with apes — of which the fear of hybrids may be seen as a sort of cultural shockwave — is the only great breakthrough of the scientific revolution with which society has not been able to come fully to terms. There have been other elements of the premodern world view that have been forever displaced by new evidence, to no one's great sorrow. Some decades before Tyson, famously, the church found the suggestion that the sun has spots to be heretical in the extreme, since, as we all know, the celestial bodies are made of æther, as opposed to the four earthly elements, and thus must be uniform throughout. But within a few decades of Galileo's condemnation, sunspots had been unproblematically incorporated into the religious world view, to the extent that no one today could even imagine worrying about their theological implications.

At some point, anyone seriously engaged, on either side, in the evolution-creation controversy must ask why supernatural and instantaneous creation of species, with men occupying a special place among creatures in virtue of their possession of their creation in the image of God, is so widely seen as preferable to a universe that has the remarkable capacity — perhaps given it by God, perhaps not — to organize itself over time into complex units possessing self-consciousness, emotional depth, and concern for others. It seems reasonable to suggest that in order to unearth the philosophical roots of the creation-evolution controversy, and in order to understand why — in spite of the massive consilience of evidence that has accumulated in favor of evolution — it is still with us, we must understand the controversy as but one part of the much broader problem of whether the design of the world can justifiably be said to point to a designer. This is a problem that is coeval with modernity.

It seemed easy enough to concede that the sun, a unique entity in the world, may come with or without spots, and that either way there is really no greater or less evidence for the existence of a designer. But if, by contrast, the leopard kind has spots, or the human kind reason or the ape kind the gift of imitation, it has seemed much harder to dispense with the view that these traits issue from species essences, and that these essences in turn issue from some sort of wisdom. Philosophically, the divergent histories since the seventeenth century of sunspots and leopard spots, as it were, suggests something very fundamental about the different ways in which individuals are conceived, on the one hand, and kinds on the other. Individuals have always been unstable and evasive. They come into existence for a while, represent a kind as best they are able, and fade. Kinds are fixed and eternal. When an individual representative of a kind disrupts its fixity, in, for example, generating a hybrid monster, the very order of the world is imperiled, and not a mere matter of fact about the world, as, arguably, in the case of sunspots.

This order has been decaying steadily since the demise of Aristotelian teleological embryology in the early seventeenth century, through Locke's nominalism, and then, decisively, with the theory of natural selection. The pristine and orderly scenario of the Garden of Eden, in which Adam zeroed in on the fixed essences of instantaneously and supernaturally created animal kinds and named them accordingly, has been lost, but we should not be surprised that after several centuries this scenario commands the nostalgic passion of a significant number of people.

Ultimately, their reasons for taking up this cause are probably more anthropological than philosophical, let alone scientific. From the work of Durkheim and Mauss in the early twentieth century, it is now a commonplace in anthropology that animal kinds have provided the basic schema for organizing the external world for most pre-scientific human cultures.[40] It is not unreasonable to see the folk zoology of Genesis, as well as its more detailed elaboration in the cleanliness rules of Leviticus,[41] as a literate continuation of this 'primitive' classificatory practice, and the same may be said for Aristotle's zoology, Linnean taxonomy, and so on. But the view of kinds as sharing lines of descent, as fluid and historical, makes a mess of this primitive habit of mind. And 'primitive' here is meant in the sense of 'most likely ineliminable', which is to say that, whatever the scientific evidence tells us, the descendents of Bulwer will no doubt continue to fulminate for some time to come.

---

[40] Émile Durkheim and Marcel Mauss, *Primitive Classification*, ed. & trans. Rodney Needham (London: Cohen and West, 1969 [1903]).
[41] The most convincing argument to this effect is Mary Douglas's "The Abominations of Leviticus," in *Purity and Danger: An Analysis of Concepts of Pollution and Taboo* (London: Routledge, 1966).

Acknowledgements

Many thanks to Charles T. Wolfe for the invitation to write this paper, and especially to Catherine Wilson for her comments.

Leibniz on the Unicorn and Various Other Curiosities

ROGER ARIEW

ABSTRACT. I discuss some of Leibniz's pronouncements about fringe phenomena — various monsters; talking dogs; genies and prophets; unicorns, glossopetrae, and other games of nature — in order to understand better Leibniz's views on science and the role these curiosities play in his plans for scientific academies and societies. However, given that Leibniz's sincerity has been called into question in twentieth-century secondary literature, I begin with a few historiographical remarks so as to situate these pronouncements within the Leibnizian corpus. What emerges is an image of Leibniz as a sober, cautious interpreter, a skeptic one might say, but one who is prepared to concede the possibility of many strange phenomena. Leibniz expects these fringe phenomena to take their place among the natural curiosities catalogued as part of a hoped for empirical database intended as means toward the perfection of the sciences.

There is a flourishing literature on the culture of natural curiosity in the early modern period.[1] My interest is not about that culture as such, but rather about Leibniz himself, his pronouncements with respect to various natural curiosities, what these can reveal to us about his views on science, and the role they play in his plans for scientific academies and societies. However, before discussing Leibniz's statements concerning such fringe phenomena, given that his sincerity about even the gravest subjects has been called into question in Leibnizian twentieth-century secondary literature, I begin with a few historiographical remarks in order to situate these pronouncements within the Leibnizian corpus.

---

[1] See, for example, T. Leinkauf, *Mundus Combinatus Studien zur Struktur der barocken Universalwissenschaft am Beispiel Athanasius Kirchers SJ (1602-1680)* (Berlin: Akademie Verlag, 1993), P. Findlen, *Possessing Nature* (Berkeley: University of California Press, 1994), W. Eamon, *Science and the Secrets of Nature: Books of Secrets in Medieval and Early Modern Culture* (Princeton: Princeton University Press, 1994), P. Smith, *The Business of Alchemy: Science and Culture in the Holy Roman Empire* (Princeton: Princeton University Press, 1995), and A. Blair, *The Theater of Nature: Jean Bodin and Renaissance Science* (Princeton: Princeton University Press, 1997).

1 Historiographical preliminaries

In his "Eloge de Monsieur Leibnitz," Bernard de Fontenelle complained that Leibniz's interests were very wide-ranging, so broad, in fact, that he could not write about Leibniz's works chronologically because "Leibniz wrote about different matters in the same years, and this almost perpetual jumble, which did not produce any confusion in his ideas, these abrupt and frequent transitions from one subject to another completely different subject, which did not trouble him, would trouble and confuse this history." Clearly, Leibniz's interests were broad even by eighteenth century standards: "In the same way that the ancients could manage simultaneously up to eight harnessed horses, Leibnitz could manage simultaneously all the sciences" — and by all "the sciences" Fontenelle meant all the traditional sciences of mathematics, metaphysics, natural philosophy, and theology. So, Fontenelle proposed to split Leibniz up: "we will make several savants from only one Leibniz."[2] Modern commentators, such as Bertrand Russell and Louis Couturat, have been more parsimonious. They have conceived of Leibniz not so much as a universal genius working all the sciences at once, but as a systematic philosopher, a logician applying his intuitions to metaphysics, who was forced, because of his diplomatic position or his desire for persuasiveness, to write more popular essays about theology and science for the general public. They have argued that there were two Leibnizes, an esoteric, systematic, logician-metaphysician, who deserves to be studied carefully, and an exoteric, shallow, theologian-natural philosopher, who barely needs to be read.[3] Nowadays we have rejected this dual Leibniz as not meshing very well with our image of the whole Leibniz: the relations between Leibniz's logic and metaphysics were not as close as Russell and Couturat thought;[4] changes in Leibniz's physics corresponded well with changes in his metaphysics;[5] and, in any case, it hardly seems possible to understand Leibniz's metaphysics without reference to his theology.[6]

There is no real danger of returning to the turn-of-the-century image of Leibniz, but there is still the possibility of thinking that there is a dual Leibniz. We can find the esoteric/exoteric distinction invoked, with more

---

[2]Fontenelle, "Eloge," in G. W. Leibniz, *Opera Omnia*, ed. L. Dutens (Geneva: Fratres De Tournes, 1768), 1: xx.

[3]See B. Russell, *A critical Exposition of the Philosophy of Leibniz* (Cambridge: Cambridge University Press, 1900) and L. Couturat, *La Logique de Leibniz* (Paris, 1901; reprint ed., Hildesheim: Olms, 1969).

[4]See G. H. R. Parkinson, *Logic and Reality in Leibniz's Metaphysics* (Oxford: Clarendon Press, 1965).

[5]See D. Garber, "Leibniz: Physics and Philosophy," in *Cambridge Companion to Leibniz*, ed. N. Jolley (Cambridge: Cambridge University Press, 1994), 270-352.

[6]See R. C. Sleigh, *Leibniz and Arnauld, A Commentary on Their Correspondence* (New Haven: Yale University Press, 1990).

plausibility, in some recent essays. Leibniz himself may be the cause of this situation, for he sometimes talked of there being deep reasons hidden below the surface in his works, of not accepting his proclamations about other philosophers at face value, of saying different things to different people depending upon the appropriateness of the forum.

A recent article, discussing Leibniz's seeming contradictions about corporeal substance in his later metaphysics, quotes him as saying to Bartholomew Des Bosses:

> I do not think that those things we have discussed concerning philosophical matters are suited for communication in any public way.... I have written these things for you, namely for the wise, not for any one at all. And thus they are hardly appropriate for the *Mémoires de Trevoux*, which is intended more for a popular audience; I hope that you, in virtue of your goodwill towards me, would not allow them to appear in such an unsuitable place.[7]

The article then attempts to diminish the apparent contradictions by discounting various Leibnizian pronouncements; those of the *Theodicy* are said to be from a popular book: "But we must remember that this is the *Theodicy*: a book that Leibniz was prepared to release to the general public and for which he craved the widest possible support."[8] A similar judgment is applied to the *Principles of Nature and Grace*, as compared to the *Monadology*, that is, the former is a "less abstract" summary of Leibniz's philosophy, not intended for the "wise."[9] And Leibniz's assertions to René-Joseph de Tournemine are said to be "a masterly exercise in diplomacy," given that Tournemine is a leading Jesuit and that Leibniz, being respectful of the Jesuits' authority, did not wish to appear overly innovative. Leibniz is said to have been "disingenuous" in his response.[10]

Another recent article quotes a Paris-period Leibniz as saying:

> A metaphysics should be written with accurate definitions and demonstrations, but nothing should be demonstrated in it apart from that which does not clash too much with received opinions. For in that way this metaphysics can be accepted; and once it has been approved then, *if people examine it more deeply later, they themselves will draw the necessary consequences...* In this

---

[7] Leibniz, G II, 328.

[8] D. Rutherford, "Metaphysics: The late period," in *Cambridge Companion to Leibniz*, p. 158.

[9] *Ibid.*, p. 163.

[10] *Ibid.*, pp. 156-157.

metaphysics, it will be useful for there to be added here or there the authoritative utterances of great men, who have reasoned in a similar way.[11]

The "especially important lesson" to be derived from the above is that "as students of Leibniz, we must not be satisfied with the definitions and demonstrations that he offers, nor should we accept at face value his proclamations about other philosophers. Rather, we must be willing to dig beneath these definitions and comments in an attempt to discover the more fundamental assumptions beneath."[12]

Whatever one decides about such theses,[13] it is clear that one has to tread carefully as one is reading Leibniz. We may have to accept a dual Leibniz; it is just possible that he is not always forthcoming with his best considered view or his most precisely formulated theory and that he changes his presentation depending upon his audience. But the distinction between an esoteric and an exoteric Leibniz cannot cut between philosophy narrowly considered, on the one hand, and science or theology, on the other, as Russell and Couturat would have wanted it. We might have to pay attention to Leibniz's chosen mode of dissemination, but that would hold true for all of Leibniz's endeavors. What is important for the purposes of this essay is that, further, whatever one thinks of the natural curiosities Leibniz discusses and whatever one thinks of his accounts, there is no reason to think *by these criteria* that Leibniz was not just as serious when working on the natural sciences as when working on any of the other sciences (broadly construed).

There is, in fact, no demarcation in Leibniz's thought between philosophy and science and among the various sciences. Whenever Leibniz uses the word "science" (in Latin or French, of course), it means "knowledge," as opposed to the explanation of natural phenomena (or a human endeavor dealing with natural phenomena). For Leibniz *scientia* is a technical term signifying knowledge in the strict sense, normally entailing certainty or truth, to be contrasted with *cognitio*, or knowledge in the weak sense, something close to understanding, acquaintance, or even cognition.[14] In the seven-

---

[11] G. W. Leibniz, *Sämtliche Schriften und Briefe* (Darmstadt / Leipzig: Reichl, 1923-), vol. 6-3, p. 573. Also cited in a discussion of Leibniz's sincerity by R. M. Adams, *Leibniz: Determinist, Theist, Idealist* (Oxford: Oxford University Press, 1994),p. 52.

[12] Mercer, in C. Mercer and R. C. Sleigh, Jr., "Metaphysics: The early period to the Discourse," in *Cambridge Companion to Leibniz*, p. 71.

[13] There is a fair amount of evidence for the proposition that Leibniz might have tailored his various pronouncements to fit his audience. There are even a couple of stories that Leibniz repeated which indicate that he would not have been embarrassed to have been seen as doing so. See the early episode about his writing a letter of entrance to an alchemical society and the later episode about his pretending to be a devout Catholic in R. Ariew, "Leibniz: Life and Works," in *Cambridge Companion to Leibniz*, pp. 21, 31.

[14] See Leibniz, "Meditation on Knowledge, Truth, and Ideas," *Philosophical Essays*,

teenth century, one could use "science" in a relatively modern sense to refer roughly to the human activities to which we presently refer, namely, physics, biology, and perhaps mathematics, but along with physics, biology, and the mathematical sciences, the "sciences" would also include much of philosophy, together with metaphysics and theology.[15]

Leibniz can also refer to the sciences in this more or less modern sense. What we call sciences, Leibniz would think as belonging to two of the three parts of philosophy. This is made clear by one of Leibniz's classification schemes for libraries. He divides books into various fields: theology, medicine, jurisprudence, philology, history, etc. What we would call philosophy corresponds with what he calls intellectual philosophy, divided into theoretical, that is, logic, metaphysics and philosophy of mind, and practical, that is, ethics and political philosophy). What we would call mathematics and the mathematical sciences, he calls the philosophy of imaginable things, or mathematics, divided into arithmetic, algebra, geometry, but also including, in good seventeenth century fashion, musical theory, physical astronomy, geography, optics, mechanics, etc. And what we call science, he calls the philosophy of sensible things, or physics, including physics, chemistry, and other physical or biological investigations — specifically including also the mineral and vegetative realms.[16]

---

ed. and trans. R. Ariew and D. Garber (Indianapolis: Hackett, 1989), pp. 23-34 or "Discourse on Metaphysics," sec. 24, *Philosophical Essays*, pp. 56-57. *Scientia* or *science* is also applicable to God, as divine knowledge (*la science divine*), with a distinction to be drawn between God's knowledge of possibles, that is, his simple understanding (*scientia simplicis intelligentiae*), and his knowledge of actuals, that is, his knowledge by intuition (*scientia visionis* or *la science de la vision*) — see Leibniz, "Letter to Arnauld, May 1686," *Philosophical Essays*, p. 74, and "The Source of Contingent Truth," *Philosophical Essays*, pp. 98-101.

[15] For example, two of the volumes of S. Du Pleix's multi-volume collegiate textbook, written around 1603-1610, concern the "sciences": *La Physique, ou science des choses naturelles* and *La métaphysique, ou science surnaturelle*. Here "science" encompasses much that we wouldn't consider as science; given that another of Dupleix's volumes is entitled *La logique, ou art de discourir et raisonner*, in this tradition, the main contrast for "science" is "art" or "practice"; see Dupleix, *La logique* (Paris: Fayard-"Corpus," 1984), I, chaps. 8-11.

[16] "Philosophia Intellectualis: Theoretica, Logica, Metaphysica, Pneumatica; Practica, Ethica & Politica. Philosophia rerum imaginationis, seu mathematica: Mathesis pura, ubi Arithmetica, Algebra, Geometria, Musica; Astronomia cum Geographia generali, Optica, Gnomonica; Mechanica, bellica, nautica, Architectonica; Opificiaria, omnigena a vi imaginationis pendentia. Philosophia rerum sensibilium seu Physica: Physica massarum, & similarium, quo pertinet etiam Chymia, de aqua, igne, salibus, &c.; Regni mineralis; vegetabilis, quorsum Agricultura; animalis, quorsum Anatomica quoque; Oeconomica, & opificiaria artificialis physicis nitentia." *Idea Leibniziana Bibliothecae ordinandae contractior, Opera Omnia*, vol. 5, pp. 213-214.

2   Various monsters

Leibniz wrote about various natural curiosities to the most scholarly audiences, to the *Journal des savans*, to the *Acta Eruditorum* of Leipzig and to the *Mémoires de l'académie Royale des sciences de Paris*. These are the very same journals in which Leibniz published his mathematical works, his dynamics, and his philosophy; the Académie Royale is the institution to which Leibniz dedicated his *Theoria motus abstracti* and of which he became a member in 1700. During his mature period at Hanover, the 40 years from about 1676 to his death in 1716, Leibniz published more than 100 articles in learned journals.[17] He published over 25 of them in the *Journal des Savans*, including some of his crucial papers on physics and mathematics[18] but also letters concerning "une expérience considérable d'une eau fumante,"[19] "La manière de perfectionner la medecine,"[20] and "La relation et la figure d'un chevreuil coiffée d'une manière fort extraordinaire." He published over 50 papers in the *Acta Eruditorum*, again including some of the essays intended as rivals to Newton's *Principia*,[21] but also "Meditatio de separatione salis et aquae dulcis" and a summary of the *Protogaea*.[22] He likewise issued another 25 articles or so, many of them polemics, in various other journals;[23] for the *Mémoires de l'académie Royale des sciences de Paris*, Leibniz wrote "Explication de l'Arithmetique binaire qui se sert des seuls caractères 0 et 1, avec des remarques sur son utilité, et sur ce qu'elle donne le sens des anciennes figures Chinoises de Fohy," "Mémoire sur les pierres qui renferment des plantes ou des poissons desséchés," and "Exposé sur un chien qui parle." There is no reason to treat Leibniz's work in natural history other than as seriously as he seems to have intended it — as seriously as one might treat anything else he tried to accomplish. Certainly, Leibniz's correspondents

---

[17] Ravier — in E. Ravier, *Bibliographie des Œuvres de Leibniz* ([1937] reprint ed., Hildesheim, 1966) — lists 115 articles, together with 60 monographs, 68 chapters in edited works, and 56 reviews.

[18] Such as "Si l'essence du corps consiste dans l'étendue," "Nouvelles remarques touchant l'analise des transcendantes," and "Système nouveau de la nature" and its subsequent "Eclaircissements."

[19] "Nous avons vu icy une expérience considérable d'une eau fumante. Elle fume a froid et ne cesse point de fumer qu'elle ne soit tout a fait exhalée. Cependant, on la peut conserver tant qu'on veut dans une bouteille bien bouchée. Quand on la verse sur quelque chose, il en sort d'une fumée si épaisse qu'on jugeroit a la voir de loin qu'il y a en cet endroit quelque chose qui brûle."

[20] Leibniz asked for a history of medicine at Paris and the Isle de France and other provinces, proposing to write annual histories of illnesses in France.

[21] Such as "Brevis demonstratio," "Tentamen de motuum caelestium causis," "Specimen Dynamicum," and "De ipsa natura."

[22] *Acta Eruditorum* (January 1693, erroneously dated 1692), pp. 40-42.

[23] Such as the *Nouvelles de la République des lettres*, *Histoire des ouvrages des savans*, and *Mémoires de Trevoux*.

dealt with this material as if it were important. Perhaps a good illustration of such an exchange would be the one described in the "Extract from a letter of Leibniz to the author of the *Journal des Savans*, written from Hanover on 18 June 1677, containing the account and picture of a goat whose hair is arranged in an extremely unusual manner."

The exchange is a simple report by the editor of the *Journal des Savans*, l'Abbé La Roque, containing a few paragraphs and a picture. The first paragraph is a flattering gesture to duke Johann Friedrich, Leibniz's employer, together with a request that he share more of his curiosities.[24] There follows an account of Leibniz's letter. Apparently, the duke, seeing a monstrous hare depicted in the *Journal des Savans*, gave Leibniz the picture of a goat whose hair
was arranged in a strange manner. According to Leibniz,

> Sr. Winckel got the goat from Dessau in the land of Anhalt and raised it at Meest, a land that belonged to him. At first there was nothing out of the ordinary with it; but afterwards it needed to be tied down because it kicked passersby, then this headdress that appeared around his head grew.

Leibniz speculates about the cause of the "headdress":

> I do not know whether the grief it had by being deprived of freedom contributed to it; for you know what the stories teach us, that a great unhappiness or worry was able to change the color of a prisoner's hair in one night and make an old man out of a young one. The doctors made some even more extraordinary observations, which have greater bearing on the headdress or growth with which we are concerned, about a substance which is not very hard, but which can nevertheless be called *rudimentum cornuum*, because it is this substance from which the horns are formed.

---

[24] "L'Honneur que nous fait S. A. S. M. le Duc d'Hanovre de donner à la lecture de nos Journaux quelqu'un de ces momens précieux qu'il emploie avec tant de succès au bonheur de ses Etats, et à la gloire des belles-lettres, est un effet de cette curiosité que lui donne une vaste étanduë d'esprit, qui au milieu des plus grandes affaires qui l'occupent, lui laisse encore plus du tems pour les belles choses. Mais la bonté avec laquelle ce Prince si intelligent et si éclairé daigne enrichir nôtre travail, par la part qu'il veut qu'on nous fasse des choses les plus rares qui se trouvent dans ses Etats, est une suite de l'estime qu'il fait de celui de tous les sçavans, qui peut-être pourroit un jour l'obliger à nous faire communiquer les choses merveilleuses de Physique et de Mécanique qu'il fait voir tous les jours avec admiration aux gens de sa Cour, qui ont l'honneur de l'approcher de plus près," "Extrait d'une lettre de M. L. à l'Auteur du Journal des Savans, écrite de Hanover le 18 Juin 1677, contenant la relation et la figure d'un chevreuil coiffée d'une manière fort extraordinaire" (*Opera Omnia*, vol. 2b, p. 175).

The picture of a monstrous goat transmitted by Leibniz to the **Journal des Savans** on behalf of his employer, Johann Friedrich as published in L. Dutens, *Opera Omnia*

The picture of the goat (as published in *Journal des Savans*

> Be that as it may, his majesty intended to send this goat to the king, as he had done in similar circumstances; but the goat died a few months later. A picture was made of it from life, of which a faithful and exact smaller copy is enclosed.

The editor of the *Journal* accepted Leibniz's generally sober account, published the picture, and even embellished upon Leibniz's remarks:

> We can add to Mr. Leibniz's reflections that the physical cause of this growth could be attributed to the aqueous humor of this animal not being able to be dissipated when it was tied down, as it is ordinarily through the heat these kinds of animals acquire through their leaps, their bounds, and their running around; this great humidity which was mixed with the juice and volatile salt that form the horns, then drove down this matter by its weight and rendered it soft, with a colder temperament.[25]

---

[25] *Ibid.*

None of this seems unusual by seventeenth century standards. In fact, what should come across in the contrast between Leibniz and the editor of the *Journal des Savans* is Leibniz's hesitancy and caution.

A similar attitude was shown by Leibniz in his account of a talking dog. In an initial letter to Pierre de Varignon, who reported the phenomenon to him, Leibniz spoke skeptically about the matter, though he allowed its possibility, especially given that the account came from "a Prince who has seen the dog speak at a fair, where a multitude of other people can testify to the truth of the matter."[26] Two years later, Leibniz wrote that he "has now seen and heard the talking dog; it pronounced well the words *thé, caffé, chocolat*, and *assemblée*, among others."[27] In the report to the Académie, Leibniz described the dog as a common, middle-sized dog owned by a peasant. According to Leibniz, a young girl who heard the dog make noises resembling German words decided to teach it to speak. After much time and effort, it learned to pronounce approximately thirty words, including *thé, caffé*, etc., French words which had passed into German unchanged. The dog, described as having had a disposition which is rarely found in other dogs, was three years old when it was trained. Leibniz also adds the crucial observation that the dog speaks only "as an echo," that is, after its master pronounced the word; "it seems that the dog speaks only by force, in spite of itself, though without ill-treatment."[28]

Leibniz's stand concerning the possibility of a talking dog is mirrored in what he says about prophets and genies. In a letter to Pierre Coste, he defends himself against an intimation that the existence of prophets would be contrary to his hypothesis of pre-established harmony.[29] Leibniz asserts that the existence of prophets "would strongly agree with it. I have always said that the present is pregnant with the future, and that there is a perfect interconnection between things, no matter how distant they are from one another, so that someone who is sufficiently acute could read the one from the other." He elaborates:

> I would not even oppose someone who maintains that there are spheres in the universe in which prophecies are more common than in ours, just as there might be a world in which dogs have noses sufficiently acute to smell their game at 1,000 leagues; perhaps there may also be spheres in which genies have greater leave than they have here below to interfere with the actions of

---

[26] *Mathematische Schriften*, ed. C. I. Gerhardt (Berlin, 1849-55), vol. 4, p. 194.
[27] *Ibid.*, p. 199.
[28] "Exposé d'une lettre de Mr. Leibniz à l'Abbé de St. Pierre, sur un chien qui parle," *Hist. de l'Académie Royale des Sciences de Paris* (1715); *Opera Omnia*, vol. 2b, p. 180.
[29] G III, pp. 393-394.

rational animals. But when it is a question of reasoning about what actually happens here, our presumptive judgment must be based on what is usual in our sphere, where these kinds of prophetic views are extremely rare. We cannot swear that there are no such prophets, but, it seems to me, it is a good bet that those in question are not.

Leibniz then reproaches Coste for having gotten his facts about prophets from newspapers, instead of getting them directly from a reliable source; he adds, paraphrasing the facts that Coste recited,

If you yourself have observed, with all due attention, a gentleman with a yearly income of two thousand pounds sterling who prophesies well in Greek, Latin, and French, although he only knows English well, there would be nothing to criticize. Thus I beg you to send me some more information about this very curious and important matter.[30]

3 The unicorn

Having hopefully established Leibniz as a sober, cautious interpreter, a skeptic or a debunker, one might say, though clearly not a close-minded person, but one who is prepared to concede the possibility of many strange phenomena, we are in the position to analyze his belief in unicorns. There is a strange picture appended to *Protogaea,* chapter 35, "Concerning the horn of the unicorn and the monstrous animal dug up at Quedlinburg."

The *Protogaea, or on the primitive aspect of the earth and on the traces of a most ancient history enclosed in the very monuments of nature,* is Leibniz's volume of natural history or geology. It happens to be the first volume of Leibniz's history of the house of Hanover, which the Princes of Brunswick had delegated him to write. Leibniz intended to preface his history with a dissertation on the state of Germany as it was prior to all histories, taking as evidence the natural monuments, shells petrified in earth, stones with the imprint of fish or plants, and even fish and plants not from the country itself, but bearing the marks of the flood. As he says at the beginning of the book, "Even a slight notion about great things is worthwhile. Thus, in order to trace our state back to its first beginnings, we should say something about the first configuration of the earth and about the nature of the soil and what it contains."[31]

---

[30] *Ibid.*, pp. 403-404; "Letter to Coste, on Human Freedom," *Philosophical Essays*, pp. 195-196. Coste's undated reply relates that the prophets lost all credibility because of their rash prediction of the resurrection of one of their members (G III, p. 405).

[31] G. W. Leibniz, *Protogaea, oder Abhandlung von der ersten Gestalt der Erde und den*

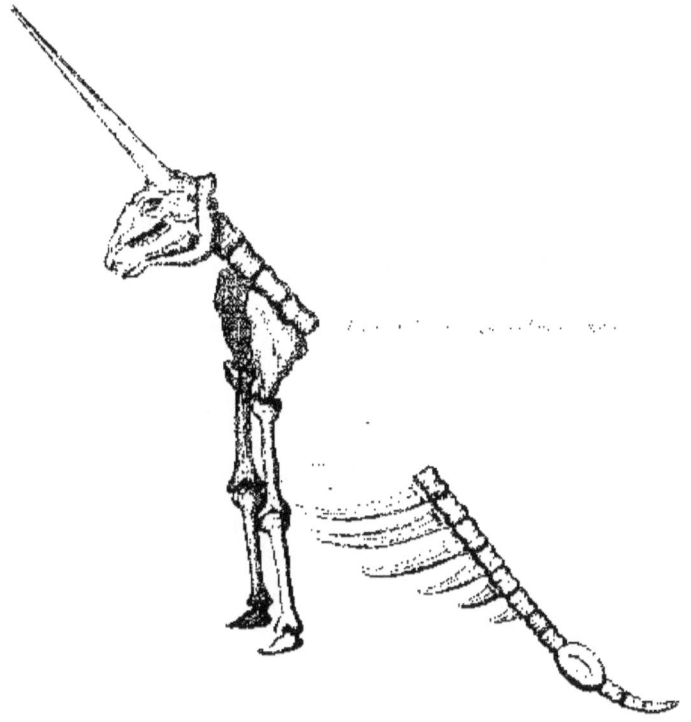

Figure 1. The Quedlinburg monster or unicorn

Spuren der Historie in den Denkmaalen der Natur, ed. Christian Ludwig Sheid (Leipzig: Vierling, 1749), 1. Leibniz intended to continue his history by treating the oldest known people, then the different peoples that succeeded one another in that country, treating their languages, and the mixtures of these languages, to the extent that they can be judged by etymologies. The origins of Brunswick would begin with Charlemagne and continue with the Emperors descended from him and with the five Emperors of the House of Brunswick. This segment of time would encompass the ancient history of Saxony through the House of Witikind, of Upper Germany through the House of the Guelfs, and of Lombardy through the Houses of the Dukes and Marquis of Tuscany and Liguria, tracing the descent of the Princes of Brunswick. After these origins would come the genealogy of the House of the Guelfs, with a short history up to the seventeenth century. This genealogy would be accompanied by those of the other great Houses, including the House of the Ghibellines, ancient and modern Austria, and Bavaria. To accomplish his design and to amass sufficient materials, Leibniz scoured the whole of Germany, visited ancient Abbeys, searched town archives, and examined tombs and other antiquities. He never completed the *History of the House of Brunswick*, which was probably an important reason for why he was out of favor with his employer toward the end of his life. But we should not think that Leibniz balked at the project, preferring instead to write a volume

The text of chapter 35 on unicorns is brief. Leibniz begins with a skeptical remark:

> Since it has been demonstrated by Bartholin that unicorns (once one of the most curious and rarest ornaments of natural history cabinets but now surrendered to the people's admiration) come from fish from the Northern ocean, we are allowed to think that the unicorn fossil found in our countryside has the same origin.[32]

But Leibniz does not think that all the remains of unicorns can be accounted for in the same way, as remains of aquatic animals, that is, as narwhal teeth:

> However, we should not hide the fact that a quadruped unicorn of the size of a horse can be found in Abyssinia, if we have to believe the Portuguese Hieronimus Lupo and Balthasar Tellesio;[33]

---

of geology. In fact, Leibniz took on the project with his customary optimism, that is, he took on much more than he could reasonably accomplish. One cannot look upon the masses of corollary materials he did publish and think that he was not completely given to the project, including the first volume. Among other works, Leibniz brought out the *Codex Juris Gentium Diplomaticus*, a volume containing the acts of nations, declarations of war, peace treaties and marriage contracts of various sovereigns, in 1692; and in 1700, he published a supplement to the volume; from 1707-11, he published a three-volume collection of original pieces related to the history of Brunswick, *Scriptorum Brunsvicensia illustrantium*. (Leibniz also published *Lettre sur la connexion des maisons de Brunsvic et d'Este*, 1695; *Specimen Historiae Arcanea sive Anectodatae de Vita Alexandrii VI*, 1696; *Dissertatio de Origine Germaniorum*, 1697; *Accesiones Historicae*, vol. 1, 1698, vol. 2, 1700; *Alberici Monachi Trium Fontium Chronicon*, 1698.) Leibniz left behind enough materials that G. H. Pertz, a Hanover librarian and editor of Leibniz's works was able to put it all together and finally publish the history in four fat volumes during the nineteenth century. The only complete unpublished manuscript was the preface, the *Protogaea*; but it was not totally unknown. Leibniz disseminated bits and pieces of it in letters, various articles in learned journals, and inserted a few paragraphs of it in his *Theodicy*. He appeared most proud of his account of fossils, having written a letter about fossils, the aforementioned report to the Académie des Sciences de Paris about fossils, and various sections of *Protogaea*, particularly chapter 18, "Where do the imprints of various fish in clay come from?" which I discuss below. ("Epistola ad autorem dissertationes de figuris animalium quae in lapidibus observantur, & lithozoorum nomine venire possunt," *Opera Omnia*, 2b: 176-77, and *Mémoire sur les pierres qui renferment des plantes & des poissons desséchés*, *Opera Omnia*, 2b: 178-79.

[32] The note by Bertrand de Saint-Germain refers to "Gaspar Bartholin, the noted Danish physician and naturalist from the first half of the 17th century." Leibniz might have been referring to "De unicornu eiusque affinibus et succedaneis," from *Opuscula quatuor singularia* (Hafniae [Copenhagen]: Georgius Hantzschius, 1628) of Caspar Bartholin (1585-1629), but he also could have been referring to its revision in *De unicornu observationes novae accesserunt de aureo cornu* (Poitiers: Typis Cribellianis, 1645) by Thomas Bartholin (1616-1680).

[33] According to J.-M. Barrande, Tellesio was a Portuguese Jesuit who wrote *Historia general de Ethiopia Alta* (1660), translated and summarized by Thévenot (*Protogaea: de l'aspect primitif de la terre*, ed. J.-M. Barrande, trans. B. de Saint-Germain [Toulouse: Presses universitaires du Mirail, 1993], p. 242).

and similarly, the skeleton extracted from limestone in 1663 on Mount Zeunikenberg, next to Quedlinburg, looked more like a terrestrial animal than anything else.

Moreover, the 1663 skeleton was discovered by Otto von Guericke, an observer with impeccable credentials, as Leibniz reminds us:

> This fact was certified by Otto von Guericke, Burgomaster of Magdeburg, who has ennobled our era by his discoveries. He was the first inventor of a pump capable of aspirating the air from a container, making remarkable demonstrations of it in 1653 to the Diet of Ratisbon, in the presence of the Emperor himself. This invention was then marvelously perfected by the rare genius of the Englishman, Robert Boyle, that illustrious man, brother of the Irish Count of Cork, who has enriched us with a new treasury of experiences.

Leibniz continues,

> Thus Guericke, in the book he published on the void, relates incidentally that a skeleton of a unicorn animal was found with a lowered back, as is common with animals, but with its head raised and its forehead armed with a horn of almost five ells, of the size of a man's thigh, but tapering by degrees. This skeleton was broken and extracted by pieces, because of the ignorance and carelessness of the diggers. But the horn, united with the head and some ribs, as well as the backbone and some bones, were brought to the abbess of the place.[34]

If I may be permitted a presentist comment: The figure to which we have been referring was originally printed in 1704 by Michael Bernhard [Valentini], who drew it from notes and sketches by von Guericke and descriptions of it by Johann Mayer;[35] it was then reproduced by

Leibniz and printed with the original edition of the *Protogaea* by C. L. Sheidt in 1749 and included in Louis Dutens' *Leibnitii Opera Omnia*, volume II, in 1768. The editor and translator of the nineteenth century French edition of the *Protogaea,* Bertrand de Saint-Germain, refused to reproduce the drawing and other such figures without comment, but elsewhere proclaimed

---

[34] Chap. 35, in *Opera Omnia*, vol. 2b, p. 230: De cornu Monocerosis et ingenii animali Quedlinburgi effosso. Von Guericke's book is *Experimenta nova, ut vocant Magdeburgica, de pauco spatio.* . . (Amsterdam, 1672). See *Protogaea: de l'aspect primitif de la terre,* pp. 242-243.

[35] B. Accordi, "The Museum Calceolarium (XVIth century) of Verona Illustrated in 1622 by Ceriti and Chiocco," *Geologica Romana* 14 (1977), p. 42.

with respect to Steno's drawing of glossopetrae and a monstrous shark that "il s'eloigne trop de la nature pour qu'il soit utile de la reproduire ici."[36] However, accompanying the unicorn is another figure, which, it is alleged, is sufficiently natural that contemporary geologists can identify it as a fossil elephant molar.[37] The inference is then drawn that Leibniz's unicorn was an imaginative reconstruction of the bones of an elephant with only one tusk.[38]

Chapter 35 of the *Protogaea* is preceded by some chapters relevant to Leibniz's account of the unicorn. Chapter 31 is entitled "Glossopetrae are shark teeth." Leibniz sometimes gets the credit for demystifying glossopetrae in the secondary literature, but, as he himself indicates, he was simply repeating the views of previous Italian naturalists.[39] In chapter 31, he compares favorably glossopetrae with shark teeth and reaffirms the conclusions of the Italian painter-naturalist Agostino Scylla and of his countryman Nicolaus Steno.

In chapter 32, "The Use of Glossopetrae in Medicine is well-known," Leibniz continues the removal of glossopetrae from the realm of magic; he relates the various claims made for their curative properties: an antidote against poisons, a medicine for stomach aches, sore throats, blisters that arise from sour humors, and internal acids. He claims that "one cannot refuse a certain medicinal value to them, but that this value is very exaggerated by credulity. . . . In my opinion, glossopetrae are most useful as toothpaste, either because the powder obtained from them is sufficiently hard and rough, or because this dental matter seems to be what is least harmful for teeth." Chapter 33 details a classification of shells,[40] and chapter 34 discusses various fossils from the Baumann and Scharzfeld caves.[41]

The chapters following the one on the unicorn are also quite revealing. Chapter 36 concerns a "description of Scharzfeld cave and of the bones found in it" and chapter 37 is a "description of Baumann cave and of what

---

[36] *Protogée*, ed. & trans. B. de Saint-Germain (Paris: L. Langlois, 1859), p. 80n.

[37] Accordi, "The Museum Calceolarium": "the same drawing next to which is a fossil elephant's molar."

[38] "C'est de reste à la suite de la découverte par Otto von Guericke à Quedlemburg, dans le Harz, en 1663, des fragments d'un squelette (les ossements d'un éléphant, mais avec une seule défense), que Leibniz fut convaincu de la réalité des licornes" (A. Schnapper, *Le géant, la licorne et la tulipe. Collections et collectionneurs dans la France du XVIIe siècle* [Paris: Flammarion, 1988], vol. 1, p. 94).

[39] Cf. Accordi, "The Museum Calceolarium," p. 33, who credits Fabio Colonna as the first to recognize glossopetrae as shark's teeth.

[40] Chap. 33: "De Belemnitus, Osteocolla, Corallio, Strombitis, Conchytis, Trochitis, Entrochitis, Ebore fossili."

[41] Chap. 34: "De offibus, maxillis, et dentibus minoribus et majoribus, quae in antro Baumanniano et alibi etiam apud nos inveniuntur."

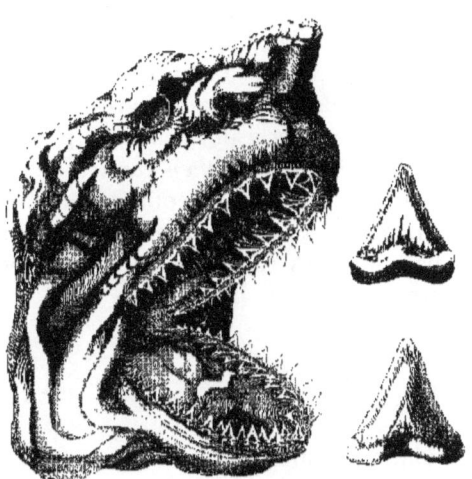

Steno's drawing, reproduced by Leibniz, which Bertrand de Saint-Germain refused to reproduce as "too unnatural"

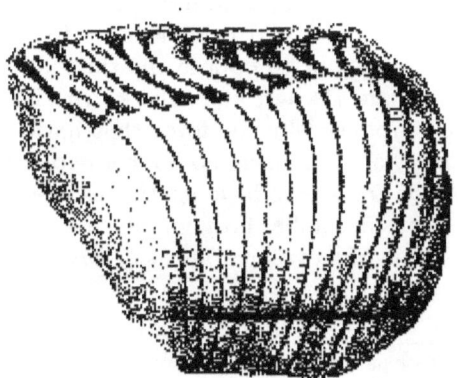

The reproduction of a fossil identifiable as an elephant molar

it contains." From the personal account these chapters contain, it appears that Leibniz actually visited these caves: "My subject invites me to speak most particularly of the two caves of my country which I have visited in person. . . Scharzfeld . . . is called by the people who live in the area the cave of the dwarfs, because a person of ordinary height cannot enter it except by crawling." (Thus, one has to imagine Leibniz on his stomach entering Scharzfeld cave.) He states "one also finds there a great number of teeth of various color, often white, and frequently implanted on pieces of jawbones; some of them are of such magnitude *that they cannot be referred to any actually known animal.*" He continues, "on one of the columns [stalagmites] it is believed one sees the image of a monk; on another the image of Moses with horns." But Leibniz concludes that "as for the games[42] of nature which one calls to the attention of the visitor, they need the help of the imagination."[43]

4 Fossils

Thus, the chapters surrounding chapter 35 are sober reflections, from the demystification of glossopetrae and their medicinal use to the debunking of various games of nature. If so, then why should Leibniz be, as it were, "taken in" by Von Guericke's "unicorn"? The answer lies in Leibniz's account of fossils. For Leibniz, fossils are the remains of animals. They are the real products of a natural furnace, the earth, created on analogy with goldsmiths who produce a golden insect by pouring gold into a mold made by covering an insect with some suitable metal and driving away its ashes.[44] Leibniz's thesis was a conscious attempt to oppose the then-fashionable views of Athanasius Kircher, Joachim Becher, and others, who held that fossils are mere games of nature produced by the force that nature has of making stones (the *vis lapidifica)* and requiring no further explanation. "Those who hold a different opinion from ours have let themselves be seduced by the frivolous accounts, set out in somber fashion, in the writings of Kircher, Becher, and others, who speak of *marvelous games of nature* and of *nature's formative force.*"[45]

---

[42]Throughout, what I translate as "games of nature" is *lusus naturae,* more properly "sports of nature"; this is perfectly good English, as in "the little dog laughed to see such a sport" — sport as genetic mutation – but slightly archaic. The example is due to Richard Arthur.

[43] *Protogaea*, chap. 29: "ludicra imaginationis"; "fictas pleraque aut semivisa . . . imaginatio in rerum signaturis ludit"; "sed haec imaginationis judicia sunt, non occulorum."

[44] *Ibid.*, chap. 18.

[45] *Ibid.*, chap. 29; see also chap. 20.

Leibniz summarizes his thoughts on fossils in his *Mémoire* to the Académie on *Stones Containing Dried Plants and Fish*. There he argues that some kind of earth has covered up various lakes and buried plants and fish. That earth then hardened into clay, and time, or some other cause, then destroyed the delicate matter of the plants or fish, in the same way flies and ants wither away in amber. The matter of the plants or fish, having been consumed, left behind in the clay an imprint which was then filled by some other matter and baked by the subterranean fire or by some other chemical process. Having given his naturalistic account of fossils as the petrification of the remains of animals, Leibniz then takes on his opponents:

> Several authors have called these kinds of representations of fish or of plants in stones, *Games of Nature;* but that is a purely poetic idea. . . . If nature played, it would play with greater liberty; it would not subject itself to express so exactly the smallest traits of the original, and, what is still more remarkable, to conserve their dimensions so strictly. When this exactness is not found, the things can be games, that is, arrangements that are in some sense fortuitous.[46]

We can see why Leibniz discusses the games of nature found in his caves and underscores that they require help from the imagination to be seen as the head of Moses, etc., what is not the case for fossils and other remains.[47] It is also clear that Leibniz is not dogmatic about the nature of the process resulting in petrification. Although he denies the accounts of contemporary scholastics, such as Kircher and Becher, he specifically allows the account of older scholastics, suggesting that he could accept fossils as remains of creatures *transformed* by some petrifying force (*vis lapidifactiva*):

---

[46] *Opera Omnia*, vol. 2b, p. 179. The opposition to the poetical thesis of Kircher and Becher was a new development in Leibniz's thought. C. Cohen cites an undated and unedited Leibnizian manuscript (probably from before 1678, the year of Leibniz's first meeting with Steno); there Leibniz writes: "I find it difficult to believe that the bones one sometimes finds in the fields, or that one discovers by digging in the earth, are the remains of real giants; similarly, that the maltese stones commonly called serpent teeth are parts of fish, and that shells often found rather far from the sea are the certain marks of the sea having covered these places, and upon withdrawing, left behind these shells, which then became petrified.

If that were true, perhaps the earth would have to be much older than is reported by the holy scriptures. But I don't want to stop there, and we need to give natural reasons here. Thus, I believe that these forms of bones of animals and shells are often only games of nature which have been formed apart without having come from animals. For it is invariable that stones grow and take on a thousand strange forms, as testify the stones that the reverend father Kircher has amassed in his Subterraneous World" (C. Cohen, *Le destin du mammouth* [Paris: Seuil, 1994], p. 79).

[47] Cf. chap. 29 of *Protogaea*.

> If someone refuses to admit that nature formed these stones by cooking them, and prefers to assume that after some silt has covered the fish, the silt was changed into stone, either by the effect of its own constitution, or by a kind of petrifying virtue, or by some other cause, . . . although that is hard to understand, I would not deny this. I do not claim to establish anything in this respect, other than that *these impressions come from real fish.*[48]

This looks like Leibniz at his most conciliatory.[49] But it would be a superficial judgment. We can better understand Leibniz's account by contrasting it with a standard conservative account of fossils from a contemporary textbook, the *Philosophy, Following the Principles of Saint Thomas*, of the Dominican, Antoine Goudin. According to Goudin, fossils (or minerals) are bodies formed in the bowels of the earth; they can be reduced to three classes: stones, metals, and fossils (properly speaking):

> Their common matter comes from earth and water; but these elements are first purified and reduced into variously tempered exhalations, then distilled and combined among themselves, and finally concretized into these bodies. Their efficient cause is, on the one hand, the heat that produces certain exhalations from within the depths of the earth, and on the other, from the action which the sun and stars from above exercise on terrestrial products by modifying them secretly; finally it is also a certain force earth itself possesses variously, following the different places in which the mixed body is formed. This force, similar to the maternal bosom from which animals arise, assuredly plays a great role in the formation of these bodies; this is why, according to Aristotle and Saint Thomas, earth and water furnish to everything arising from the bowels of the earth their matter and bosom, as would a mother, while heaven and the stars fulfill the office of the father, who imparts the form.[50]

We can see from the above that, without specifically stating it, Leibniz accepts only the material and efficient cause from the scholastic theory of

---

[48] *Protogaea*, chap. 20. See also R. Ariew, "A New Science of Geology in the Seventeenth Century?" in *Revolution and Continuity: Essays in the History and Philosophy of Early Modern Science*, ed. P. Barker and R. Ariew (Washington, DC: Catholic University of America Press, 1991), pp. 81-92.

[49] Cf. Leibniz, Letter to Remond, G III, p. 607.

[50] A. Goudin, *Philosophie suivant les principes de Saint Thomas,* trans. T. Bourard (Paris, 1864 [original ed. Paris: Poussielgue-Rusand, 1668]), p. 301: *Des corps mixtes inanimés, dit fossiles.*

fossils, implicitly rejecting the formal cause. This is, of course, consistent with his restoration of forms only to metaphysics, giving purely mechanistic explanations at the level of physics: "to separate the use one should make of them from the abuse that has been made of them."[51] And it is the real lesson of the unicorn. Leibniz wants to remove such phenomena from the realm of astrology as usually interpreted in his time, that is, phenomena considered as contraventions of the ordinary course of nature, monsters that are not to be fully explained, but marveled at for what they portend in a fortuitous world regulated by the stars, which incline, but do not necessitate.[52] He wants to treat all such phenomena as regularities. His unicorn is, after all, no different than any other animal whose remains can be examined; he realizes that he is committed to there having been animals which no longer exist;[53] and the remains of his unicorn have been described by an unimpeachable observer. The unicorn can therefore take its place among the

---

[51] "New System of Nature," *Philosophical Essays*, p. 139; see also "Against Barbaric Physics," and others.

[52] For more on monsters as contraventions of the ordinary course of nature, see P. Dear, "Jesuit Mathematical Science and the Reconstitution of Experience in the Early Seventeenth Century," *Studies in History and Philosophy of Science* 18 (1987), pp. 133-175. Following Dear, the basic point is this: the essential properties of an acorn explain why it grows into an oak tree, given that it actually does; if it does not, accidental impediments must have prevented it: an acorn failing to grow into a oak tree would shed no light on the nature of acorns. Deviations from the ordinary course of nature, if sufficiently spectacular, would be dubbed "monsters," and far from being regarded as providing privileged insight, they would be taken to be portents or omens, literally supernatural occurrences due to God's intervention; whether portents or not, they were by definition contrary to nature, and hence not illuminating of the natural order. See also L. Daston & K. Park, "Unnatural Conceptions: The Study of Monsters in 16th and 17th century France and England," *Past and Present* 92 (1981), pp. 20-34.

[53] According to C. Cohen, it is impossible for Leibniz to conceive of extinct species; for him, the world was created perfect (*Le destin du mammouth*, pp. 83-84). Cohen repeats the thesis on p. 248: "But since God has created the world perfect and immutable, the disappearance of species remains unthinkable for him." To support the thesis, she quotes again from Leibniz's unedited manuscript: "we find stone shells of several unknown species which we would seek in vain in the sea, a mark that these are games of nature, unless one holds that they are lost species, something not likely" (*Le destin du mammouth*, 315-16). But this is mistaken. First, Cohen's thesis is too strong. Leibniz is giving probabilistic arguments. There is no question about what is conceivable or what is possible. Second, Leibniz has changed his mind about every other aspect of the matter under discussion: accepting the bones as petrified remains of aquatic origin and rejecting the thesis that they are games of nature. There is no reason to believe that Leibniz would continue to hold it is not likely that they are lost species. Third, and most important, when giving a metaphysical account, Leibniz does not deny the physical phenomenon. Nothing follows about the physical extinction of species, even if Leibniz believed that there are no extinctions *in a strict metaphysical sense*. The same holds for the physical phenomena of birth and death, given Leibniz's metaphysical account of birth and death (see *Philosophical Essays*, p. 141).

natural curiosities that Leibniz catalogues as part of a hoped for empirical database.

5 Scientific Societies and Museums

This is where Leibniz the collector and creator of scientific societies enters into the account. In the same way that in his "Manner of Perfecting Medicine" Leibniz proposed to write annual histories of illnesses in France in order to provide the data for perfecting medicine, Leibniz proposed scientific societies and museums as repositories of information for perfecting science. In his plan for Russia's first public museum, Leibniz had written to Peter the Great in 1708: "Concerning the Museum and the cabinets and *Kunstkammern* pertaining to it, it is absolutely essential that they should be such as to serve not only as objects of general curiosity, but also as means to the perfection of the arts and sciences."[54] The various plans for scientific societies he drew up for the Elector of Hanover in 1680, for the Elector of Brandenburg in 1700, for Peter the Great in 1708, and for the three Austrian Emperors, as well as an earlier plan of 1671, allotted an important place to cabinets of medals, antiquities, instruments, and anatomy, zoological and botanical gardens, and an *iconothèque*, all of which would illustrate "the great works of art and nature."[55] In his proposal for a Royal Academy of Sciences in Berlin, Leibniz writes:

> It would be rather important to give Tableaux of the Sciences and of the liberal as well as mechanical Arts, and to erect a Theater of Nature and Art. . . And the Theater of Nature and Art, which would contain the very things of nature, or models of them, would have an even greater effect. It would enrich the imagination by presenting it with a quantity of distinct ideas.
>
> Moreover, it would be better to study the bodies of humans, animals and plants, and other natural things in the three realms, which serve as remedies, nourishment, or instruments for people, analyzing them through anatomy as well as chemistry; these require well furnished laboratories, and above all microscopes,

---

[54] Gerje, *Otnoschenje Leibnitza k Rossii i Petru Velikomu* (1871), p. 76, as quoted in O. Neverov, "His Majesty's Cabinet and Peter I's Kunstkammer," *The Origins of Museums, The Cabinet of Curiosities in 16th and 17th Century Europe*, eds. O. Impey & A. MacGregor (Oxford: Clarendon Press, 1985), p. 56. The full text is available in *Nouvelles lettres et opuscules inédits*, ed. A. Foucher de Careil (Paris, 1857), vol. 7, pp. 473-474.

[55] *Nouvelles lettres et opuscules inédits*, vol. 7, p. 79, as quoted in W. Schupbach, "Some Cabinets of Curiosities in European Academic Institutions," in *The Origins of Museums*, p. 166. See also Leibniz, "An Odd Thought Concerning a New Sort of Exhibition (1675)," in *Selections*, ed. P. Wiener (New York: Scribner, 1951), pp. 585-594.

which allow us to discover in the sensible world another insensible world, in which the causes of sensible things are very often hidden. . . . By these means we will soon have an inestimable treasure concerning the workings of inner nature. The king's or the country's mines, gardens, parks, and cabinets of rarities will furnish the matter for research into the three realms, mineral, vegetal, and animal, if the inspectors, officers, and custodians of the various relevant professions are required to assist in this.[56]

The philosopher who told Peter the Great that you cannot have enough books obviously meant it in the broader sense that you cannot have enough data.[57]

With his unicorn, Leibniz himself takes his place within a culture of natural curiosity, stretching from Jean Bodin and Scipion Dupleix to Marin Mersenne and the various scientific academies.[58] But Leibniz does not hawk curiosities for their own sake; his spirit is more like that of his fellow dreamer of scientific academies, Mersenne, who asks whether we are able to walk on water without miracle and without magic, debunking the claims of those who brag of secrets from China or Persia — for "they are normally so deprived of science and reason that one does not like to hear them or see them a second time" — but who answers in the affirmative, that is, as long

---

[56] "Discours de M. Leibniz, sur le projet d'érection d'une Académie Royale à Berlin, sur les moyens de fonder et de faire fleurir cette Société" (*Histoire de l'académie de Berlin*, t. VII, 1752), *Opera Omnia*, vol. 5, pp. 176-177.

[57] "Il est indispensable de fonder des bibliothèques, un théâtre de la nature et de l'art, y compris des cabinets des arts et des raretés, des jardins de plantes et ménageries, des observations et des laboratoires. . . . Une bibliothèque ne peut pas être ni trop grande ni trop rare, car souvent, dans les moindres livres, on peut trouver quelque bonne chose que les meilleurs mêmes ne renferment pas" (*Nouvelles lettres et opuscules inédits*, vol. 7, pp. 470-471; cf. *ibid.*, pp. 138-154).

[58] Obviously, the curious come in many stripes (and from divergent contexts): some are collectors, others not, some explain their phenomena using powers and virtues, others invoke various mechanisms. The point is that the interest in curiosities was extremely widespread at the time. However, an exception to the culture was Descartes, who clearly disliked the whole business. See K. Pomian, "La culture de la curiosité," *Collectionneurs, Amateurs et Curieux. Paris, Venise: XVIe-XVIIIe siècles* (Paris: Gallimard, 1987), pp. 61-80. In pp. 78-80 he points out that in *Regulae*, but especially in *La Recherche de la Verité*, Descartes is anti-curiosity; cf. title: "par la lumière naturelle qui toute pure et sans emprunter le secours de la religion ni de la philosophie, determine les opinions que doit avoir un honeste homme, touchant les choses qui peuvent occuper sa pensée et penetre jusque dans les secrets des plus curieuses sciences" (AT X, 499): "tout ce qu'on vous peut enseigner de meilleur sur ce sujet, c'est que le désir de savoir, qui est commun à tous les hommes, est une maladie qui ne peut se guérir car la curiosité s'accroit avec la doctrine." Cf. also *Discours*, pt. vi.

as one is wearing big rubber boots filled with air.[59]

This Leibniz cannot be described as dual. While this Leibniz may be variable – he changes his mind about various theories, for example, rejecting Kircher and his games of nature, having previously been seduced by him, and he writes differentially to various correspondents depending upon their social status and/or political persuasion — there is no evidence of a radical duality that cuts across genres. Fontenelle was right; it was he who was constructing the several savants from only one Leibniz. Similarly, it was Russell and the others who constructed dual Leibnizes from one complex seventeenth century thinker.

Acknowledgements

This essay originally appeared in *Early Science and Medicine* 3:4 (1998), pp. 267-288, and is reprinted with the permission of Brill Academic Publishers (Leiden).

---

[59] M. Mersenne, *Question Inouyes* (Paris: Fayard-"Corpus," 1985 [original ed. 1637]), pp. 13-14.

The Creativity of God and the Order of Nature: Anatomizing Monsters in the Early Eighteenth Century

ANITA GUERRINI

ABSTRACT. This essay challenges the generalization that monsters were "naturalized" in the eighteenth century because attention shifted from supernatural to natural causes. Anatomical accounts of monsters in the first half of the eighteenth century in fact paid little or no attention to causes. Within the teleological schemes of the anatomists, monsters, like animals, displayed nature's ingenuity. Examination of monstrous humans could help to define normal humanity while also demonstrating the extremes of nature's possibilities, and the language of wonder, if not attribution to the supernatural, continued to be employed. Nature may have been subject to laws but the laws were yet beyond human understanding. A close study of two accounts of monsters from 1700 and 1748 demonstrates the peculiarly anatomical point of view in contrast to attention to causes. They also point up the distinction between the display of monsters and their description in print, and the intersection of learned and popular culture in the study of anomalous human forms.

> Why should the poor Minotaur be suffering in hell?
> It was not the Minotaur's fault that it had been born a monster.
> It was God's fault.
>
> Iris Murdoch, *The Flight from the Enchanter* (1956)

Much has been written in recent years about the interpretation of monsters (defined here as human anomalies) in early modern Europe. Attention has focused particularly on the de-sacralization of monsters in the seventeenth century. In this process of naturalization, their meaning changed from portents of earthly events to natural, if unusual, phenomena. By the eighteenth century, it is generally agreed, human anomaly had lost any supernatural significance because it was now attributed to natural causes, and attention shifted to proving the authenticity of claims to novelty. Natural philosophers employed human and animal monsters mainly as evidence to buttress one or another theory of generation. The Winslow-Lémery debate of the 1720s and 30s is usually cited as the paradigmatic discussion of monsters in this era.[1]

In this essay I wish to challenge this generalization by looking at anatomical accounts of monsters in the late seventeenth and early eighteenth centuries. These accounts, which filled the pages of journals such as the *Philosophical Transactions* and the *Histoire et Mémoires* of the Paris Académie des Sciences, lacked reference to causes. I suggest, based on a survey of articles in the *Philosophical Transactions* and the *Histoire et Mémoires*, that this lack of attention to causes on the part of anatomists was not only deliberate but highly meaningful. Within their teleological schemes, monsters, like animals, displayed nature's ingenuity. "When the uniformity of nature seems to deny itself, nothing ought more to excite the attention of philosophers," began an account in the *Histoire*.[2] Examination of monstrous humans could help to define normal humanity while also demonstrating the extremes of nature's possibilities, and the language of wonder, if not attribution to the supernatural, continued to be employed. The dissection as well as the display of monsters in cabinets and in print took place in the full gaze of the public, but there were important differences between actual display and its description in print. In the second half of the paper I will focus on two accounts of monsters, from early and mid-century. The first is the Irish physician Thomas Molyneux's "Essay concerning Giants," published in 1700, while the second is the 1748 essay on conjoined twins of James Parsons, a well-known London physician and fellow of the Royal Society. While these essays differ in their emphases, they demonstrate a peculiarly anatomical point of view in contrast to attention to causes. I will conclude with a few observations on the relationship between public and private natural philosophy and popular culture in this era.

---

[1] Patrick Tort, *L'ordre et les monstres* (1980, 2nd ed. Paris: Editions Syllepse, 1998); Lorraine Daston and Katharine Park, *Wonders and the Order of Nature* (New York: Zone Books, 1998); Michael Hagner, "Enlightened Monsters," in *The Sciences in Enlightened Europe*, ed. William Clark, Jan Golinski, and Simon Schaffer (Chicago: University of Chicago Press, 1999), pp. 175-217; Palmira Fontes da Costa, "The making of extraordinary facts: authentication of singularities of nature in the Royal Society of London in the first half of the eighteenth century," *Studies in History and Philosophy of Science* 33 (2002), pp. 265-288; idem, "The understanding of monsters at the Royal Society in the first half of the eighteenth century," *Endeavour* 24:1 (2000), pp. 34-39.

[2] "Sur une matrice double," *Histoire de l'Académie Royale des sciences avec des Mémoires de mathématique et de physique* (1705), pp. 47-49, at p. 47: "Quand l'uniformité de la Nature semble se démentir, rien se doit exciter l'attention des Philosophes."

1

In *Wonders and the Order of Nature*, Lorraine Daston and Katharine Park briefly refer to the descriptive side of monster studies in the eighteenth century. They note the numerous scholarly accounts of monsters in the period between 1670 and 1740, the great majority of which did not discuss either the origins of monsters or their larger significance, but simply described, in great detail, their anatomy. Daston and Park point out that "these anatomical observations did not converge in any single theoretical explanation for monsters. In the early eighteenth century, anatomists could not even agree on the definition of a monster, much less on a classification."[3]

While acknowledging this lack of theorizing among anatomists, Daston and Park nonetheless subsume anatomical accounts under the more general category of the generation debates. But, enraptured by the complexity of form, anatomists ignored questions of cause and secondarily of viability, since many of the monsters they dissected were incapable of survival, however ingeniously crafted. Within a teleological framework, monsters were not anomalies but examples of the creativity and fecundity of nature, which, far from being increasingly confined to laws, was viewed, in the words of Thomas Molyneux, as "uncontrollable" in her productions. Maria Teresa Monti has argued, "by deviating from the usual construction plans, the monster celebrated the richness and freedom of divine providence rather than its regularity."[4] Rather than accidents or mistakes, monsters were part of God's plan, the extent of which surpassed human understanding.

Monsters were natural and rational in cause, but more complex, and therefore more instructive, than the normal. To many anatomists, the study of morphology itself was sufficient. In his "Preface sur l'utilité des mathematiques et de la physique," written at the time of the "renouvellement " of the Paris Académie des Sciences in 1699, Fontenelle argued that monsters, like animals, played important roles in the exploration of human anatomy:

> The anatomy of animals ought to be a matter of indifference, since we only need to know the human body. But such a part which in the human body is so delicate or complex, so that it is invisible, is visible and evident in the body of a certain animal. Thus monsters too should not be neglected. The mechanism

---

[3] Daston and Park, *Wonders and the Order of Nature*, p. 204.

[4] Thomas Molyneux, "An Essay concerning Giants. Occasioned by some further Remarks on the large Humane Os Frontis, or Forehead-bone, mentioned in the Philosophical Transactions of February, 1684/5. Number 168," *Philosophical Transactions*, 22 (1700-01), pp. 487-508, at p. 499; Maria Teresa Monti, "Epigenesis of the Monstrous Form and Preformistic 'Genetics' (Lémery-Winslow-Haller)," *Early Science and Medicine* 5 (2000), pp. 3-32, at p. 12.

hidden in a particular species or in a common structure is evident in another species, or in an extraordinary [ie monstrous] structure, and one could almost say that Nature is forced to multiply and vary her works, not being able to keep, sometimes, from giving away her secrets.[5]

Later in the same essay, Fontenelle asserted that anatomy, in revealing the "mechanism of animals," also offered to the observer the best means of appreciating the "infinite intelligence" of the Creator. He added, "True physics raises itself to become a kind of theology."[6]

During the Renaissance, natural philosophers such as Ambroise Paré viewed monsters both as portents of earthly events and as examples of the fecundity of nature. By the end of the seventeenth century, the portentous aspect of monsters had fallen away.[7] Monsters continued to be preternatural, but not unnatural or supernatural; they were, somehow, within the ordinary course of nature. If, by 1700, it was assumed that nature was or would eventually be comprehensible, then monsters were a part of that comprehensibility.[8] Fontenelle commented in the *Histoire* for 1703, "One ordinarily looks upon monsters as jokes of nature, but philosophers believe that nature does not play, but always follows inviolably the same rules... it is often therefore the most extraordinary that give the most opportunity to discover the general rules by which they are all understood."[9] As the "hid-

---

[5] Bernard le Bovier de Fontenelle, "Préface sur l'utilité des mathématiques et de la physique, et sur des travaux de l'Académie des sciences," in *Éloges des académiciens. Avec l'histoire de l'Académie Royale des sciences en M.DC.XCIX ..*, vol. 1 (The Hague: Isaac vander Kloot, 1740), pp. xii-xiii: "L'anatomie des Animaux nous devroit etre assés indifferente, il n'y a que le Corps humain qu'il nous importe de connoitre. Mais telle partie dont la structure est le Corps human si délicate ou si confuse, qu'elle en est invisible, est sensible & manifeste dans le corps d'un certain Animal. De-là vient que les Monstres memes ne sont pas à negliger. La Mechanique cachée dans une certaine espece ou dans une structure commune se developpe dans une autre espece, ou dans une structure extraordinaire, & l'on diroit presque que la Nature à force de multiplier & de varier ses ouvrages, ne peut s'empecher de trahir quelquefois son secret."

[6] Fontenelle, "Préface," p. xxi: "La véritable Physique s'éleve jusqu'à devenir un espece de Théologie." Cf Hagner, "Enlightened Monsters," p. 177.

[7] Jean Céard, "The Crisis of the Science of Monsters," in *Humanism in Crisis. The Decline of the French Renaissance*, ed. Philippe Desan (Ann Arbor: University of Michigan Press, 1991); see also his *La Nature et les prodiges* (Geneva: Droz, 1977).

[8] On the distinction between preternatural and supernatural, see Lorraine Daston, "Marvelous Facts and Miraculous Evidence in Early Modern Europe," in *Questions of Evidence: Proof, Practice and Persuasion across the Disciplines*, ed. James Chandler, Arnold I. Davidson, and Harry Harootunian (Chicago: University of Chicago Press, 1994), pp. 243-274.

[9] "Sur un Agneau foetus monstrueux," *Histoire* (1703), pp. 28-32, at p. 28: "On regarde ordinairement les Monstres comme des jeux de Nature, mais les Philosophes sont très-persuadés que la Nature ne se joue point, qu'elle suit inviolablement les mêmes

den mechanisms" of nature were revealed, monsters would be understood. But in this period, that understanding had not yet occurred; monsters were cut off from supernatural or other causes, but were not yet integrated into another order. They remained extraordinary, anomalous.

The act of describing monsters in print contributed to this gradual comprehension. On display in cabinets or side-shows, monsters could accrue layers of portentous meaning. The hydrocephalic child on display in the cabinet of Frederik Ruysch (and illustrated in his *Thesaurus anatomicus* of 1702) looks toward heaven with an otherworldly expression and cradles his placenta in his arms. The illustration is at once an anatomical description and a moral lesson.[10] Ruysch was well known for his moralizing anatomical tableaux, but even less pointedly didactic displays shared the emotion-producing qualities of a spectacle. As anatomical displays shaded into natural history museums, the older meanings of anatomical objects, including monsters, jostled for attention with newer ideas of classification and critical discourse. Display did not necessarily demystify monsters.[11]

In contrast, the narrative of display was easily controlled in print. In 1699, the Oxford physician and natural philosopher John Freind described his dissection of a hydrocephalic child in strictly impersonal terms. He measured the head and described its interior in minute detail, and he offered only those personal facts about the child while alive — age, health, disposition — which were relevant to the anatomical description. He did not speculate about the cause of the anomaly.[12]

Freind was notoriously skeptical about supernatural causation in particular, and he debunked a supposed case of possession a few years later.[13] But in avoiding discussion of causes, he followed the norm in anatomical description. Nor was this a particularly English characteristic, since accounts in the *Histoire et Mémoires* and those in the *Philosophical Transactions*

Règles.... Ce sont même souvent les plus extraordinares, qui donnent le plus d'ouverture pour découvrir les règles générales où ils sont tous compris." On "jokes of nature," see Paula Findlen, "Jokes of Nature and Jokes of Knowledge: The Playfulness of Scientific Discourse in Early Modern Europe," *Renaissance Quarterly* 43 (1990); *idem*, "Between Carnival and Lent: The Scientific Revolution at the Margins of Culture," *Configurations* 6 (1998).

[10] See discussion and illustration in Hagner, "Enlightened Monsters," pp. 181-182.

[11] Hagner, "Enlightened Monsters," p. 186, argues that display was a way to control the deviance of monsters; Barbara Stafford, "Voyeur or Observer? Enlightenment Thoughts on the Dilemmas of Display," *Configurations* 1 (1993). See also Anita Guerrini, "Duverney's Skeletons," *Isis* 94 (2003).

[12] John Freind, "Concerning a Hydrocephalus," *Phil. Trans.* 21 (1699), pp. 318-323; Fontes da Costa, "The making of extraordinary facts," who argues that written description helped establish the authenticity of monsters.

[13] John Freind, "Epistola D. Johannis Freind ad Editorem missa, De spasmi rarioris historia," *Phil. Trans.* 22 (1700-01), pp. 799-804.

from outside Britain displayed the same characteristics. In the *Philosophical Transactions* for 1670, for example, Jacomo (Giacomo) Grandi, who identified himself as the public anatomist of Venice, wrote about "two odd births" he had come across — conjoined twins and an infant, "terrible to behold," born with his internal organs outside the body. Grandi described his dissections but offered no further commentary. In the same year, Dr. William Durfton of Plymouth recounted the birth and subsequent dissection of another set of conjoined twins in rather more detail but with a similar lack of speculation about causes. A 1705 account of a double womb in the *Histoire* listed a number of possible causes but came to no conclusion.[14] Causes were outside the purview of the anatomist.

Steven Shapin and Simon Schaffer (as well as others) have argued that the plain and "functional" style of scientific narratives in the mid-seventeenth century, including the *Philosophical Transactions*, served simply to establish "matters of fact," in contrast to the speculation about causes deemed to be characteristic of scholastic philosophy.[15] Bacon's notion of a natural history that catalogued all the characteristics of an object or a phenomenon is applicable here. Each report in this genre was of a particular "local" event, not of a generalized theory of how the world behaves.[16] Each description of a monstrous birth or other anomalous form was singular in two senses: the author described a single event which was, apparently, a singularity when considered in more general terms. But this supposedly value-neutral description was laden with unspoken theories, for the assumption of anomaly or singularity rested on a notion of what was normal, while at the same time the monstrous helped to define the normal. This brings to mind Foucault's discussion of discourse as the "already-said" that is superimposed upon the "not said" which he defines as "a hollow that undermines from within all that is said." In this context, the assumption of a norm as defined by the

---

[14] Jacomo Grandi, "An Extract of an Italian Letter Written from Venice by Signor Jacomo Grandi, to an Acquaintance of his in London, concerning some Anatomical Observations, and two odd Births: English'd by the Publisher, as follows," *Phil. Trans.* 5 (1670), pp. 1188-1189; William Durfton, "A Narrative of a Monstrous Birth in Plymouth, Octob. 22. 1670; Together with the Anatomical Observations, Taken thereupon by William Durfton Doctor in Physick, and Communicated to Dr. Tim. Clerk," *Phil. Trans.* 5 (1670), 2096-2098; "Sur une matrice double," *Histoire* (1705), pp. 47-49.

[15] Steven Shapin & Simon Schaffer, *Leviathan and the Air Pump. Hobbes, Boyle, and the Experimental Life* (Princeton: Princeton University Press, 1985), pp. 66-67; Brian Vickers, "The Royal Society and English Prose Style: A Reassessment," in Brian Vickers & Nancy Streuver, *Rhetoric and the Pursuit of Truth: Language Change in the Seventeenth and Eighteenth Centuries* (Los Angeles: Clark Library, UCLA, 1985), pp. 3-76; Anita Guerrini, "The Eloquence of the Body: Anatomy and Rhetoric in the Early Eighteenth Century," in press.

[16] Peter Dear, "*Totius in verba*: Rhetoric and Authority in the Early Royal Society," *Isis* 76 (1985).

not-normal, therefore, destabilizes the meaning of normality.[17]

Even when an article was illustrated, the illustration continued the unadorned style of the text. In contrast to Ruysch's illustrations of his cabinet — and indeed the cabinet or dissection room itself — the illustrations in the *Philosophical Transactions* and, to a lesser extent, the *Histoire*, were stripped of context and emotional associations. Often the image was of a part rather than a whole, identifiable only to the cognoscenti; and even an image of a whole was often on a page with illustrations for other articles. The image of one of two "monstrous pigs, with the resemblance of humane faces" related by John Floyer to Edward Tyson in 1699 was in the corner of a page with illustrations of various mechanical devices. The French anatomist Duverney's description of his dissection of conjoined twins in the 1706 *Mémoires*, whose illustrations were by far the most detailed and explicit in this genre, showed the twins whole (and apparently alive) before dissection and then the dissected parts detached from the whole. This "normalizing" of the monstrous rested on the assumption of the objective nature of the singular.[18]

What did anatomists find in the late seventeenth and early eighteenth centuries? Monsters seem to have fallen into a few general categories. Unusual human births formed one large group, including conjoined twins and hydrocephalic and anencephalic infants. Another group consisted of unusual human body formations or organs, in the sense of number or size, often discovered only in the course of autopsy: thus several cases of double wombs, a man with three bladders, the "preternatural" appearance of the kidneys of a certain Mr. Smith of Highgate and the lacking kidney of a French child. In these cases, the anomaly did not seem to disturb the functioning of the body. A third category consisted of humans whose unusual traits did not manifest themselves fully until adulthood: giants of course were obvious examples, but so too were hermaphrodites, whose peculiar attributes often were not noted until puberty. A final category consisted of monstrous animals, such as the human-faced pig or the sheep consisting only of stomach and legs. Although many of the latter were reported on at meetings of the Royal Society and the Paris Academy between 1670 and 1730, relatively few made it into the pages of the *Philosophical Transactions* or the *Histoire et Mémoires* in comparison to accounts of human monsters.

The Huguenot anatomist Paul Buissière described an anencephalic infant

---

[17] Michel Foucault, *The Archaeology of Knowledge* (1969, translation, London: Routledge, 1972), ch. 1.

[18] This is a somewhat different argument than that given in Lorraine Daston and Peter Galison, "The Image of Objectivity," *Representations* 40 (1992), whose emphasis on anatomical atlases ignores other forms of anatomical illustration. On Duverney's essay and illustrations, see Monti, "Epigenesis of the Monstrous Form," pp. 11-14.

in the *Philosophical Transactions* in 1699, and his account is quite typical of the genre.[19] Buissière immigrated to London around 1688 and was well-known as a surgeon and a teacher of anatomy. He was elected a fellow of the Royal Society in 1699 and frequently contributed items to the *Philosophical Transactions* based on his anatomical experiences, as well as to the *Mémoires* of the Paris Academy and to *Acta eruditorum*.[20] According to Buissière's account, a French woman living near Shoreditch in east London gave birth to a child in October 1698. His narrative emphasizes the normality of the situation: the woman was healthy, the pregnancy normal, the process of birth usual. The child itself was of normal size, "well-shap'd in his Body . . . without the least mark of Corruption" except for the odd position of the eyes on the top of the forehead and the "unequal" shape of the skull.

While Buissière did not trust the midwife's account that the child was born alive, he did believe the parents' claim that the child moved while in the womb. He did not witness the birth, but was called in to dissect the head after death. He described the head and skull in minute detail, noting that not only were both the upper portion of the skull and the brain itself missing, but there was no sign that either had ever existed; the edges of the existing bones, for example, looked smooth, not "corroded or gnawn." He found a medulla and the nerves leading to it, but no other part of the brain, and the nerves of the eye were in their usual places but not attached to anything. The eyes looked normal, as did the face and the rest of the body. Buissière refused to speculate either on the cause of the anencephaly or on the evidence that the child was alive at least up to the time of birth: "I leave it to others to explain how this Child could live, and move so long, without a Brain." Although the article was not illustrated, Buissière had kept the child's skull, and "any Body may have a view of it, to satisfy their Curiosity, when they please."[21]

Buissière therefore did not question the origin of the deformity, but simply described its existence. As Fontes da Costa has pointed out, the circumstantial detail of the account enhanced its credibility. The anatomist's language indeed emphasized the ordinariness of the child, particularly externally, its

---

[19] [Paul] Buissière, "An Anatomical Account of a Child's Head, Born without a Brain in October last, 1698. By Mons. Bussiere," *Phil. Trans.* 21 (1699), pp. 141-144.
[20] George Peachey, *A Memoir of William and John Hunter* (Plymouth: Brendon, 1924), pp. 9-10; *Oxford Dictionary of National Biography*, s.v. "Buissière or Bussière, Paul." He published six papers in the *Philosophical Transactions* between 1694 and 1712.
[21] Buissière, "Anatomical account." A similar case was described by William Smellie in the 1740s in his *Treatise on Midwifery*. Although the mother attributed the defect to the influence of maternal imagination, Smellie dismissed this idea. See Dennis Todd, *Imagining Monsters* (Chicago: University of Chicago Press, 1995), pp. 49 and 283n.27.

soundness and the order of his well-crafted other organs, so that the lack of the brain comes across as an oversight — a serious one, to be sure — and the overall impression is of the skill of nature in crafting the rest of the body. This emphasis on the ordinary outward appearance as opposed to the extraordinary (the word most commonly used) anomaly revealed by dissection constituted a particular literary genre in these accounts. Thus another child whose viscera were in his thorax gave signs of unease during life but ate and excreted as a normal child. The only clue that something was amiss was the "odd sort of working in its Breast . . . a Crawling round the Ribs and Breast . . . as if a Knot of small Eels, or large Earth-worms had been penned up within the Cavity." The dissection of the child's corpse revealed the anatomical anomaly which led to the child's "extraordinary" death, but the description itself is again very detailed yet expressed in neutral, even emotionless, language.[22]

The physician and anatomist James Douglas, in describing an overly large ventricle of the heart of a young man, affected a more breathless style, yet even he used a limited, if expressive, vocabulary. The ventricle was of "stupendous magnitude," the heart while in life beat "violently" with a "prodigious" motion, "And, which is almost incredible, at sometimes the trembling and throbbing made such a Noise in his Breast, as plainly could be heard at some Distance from his Bedside."[23] But his description of the heart used the same words as did others, such as "uncommon," "preternatural," and of course "extraordinary." The French account of a woman with a double womb described her as "an extraordinary contrivance of nature," the key word here being "nature": while extraordinary, it was not unnatural. In his 1706 account of conjoined twins, Duverney spoke of "a plan designed by an intelligence free in its goals."[24]

These words denote wonder, but neither supernatural causation nor horror; the creativity of nature led to admiration, not to disgust. In fact, monsters seemed so commonplace that they could seem dull; the *Histoire*

---

[22] Fontes da Costa, "The making of extraordinary facts"; Charles Holt, "Part of a Letter from Sir Charles Holt to the Publisher, concerning a Child who had its Intestines, Mesentery, &c. in the Cavity of the Thorax, and a further account of the person mentioned to have swallowed Stones, on No. 253 of these Transactions," *Phil. Trans.* 22 (1700-01), pp. 992-996, at p. 992.

[23] James Douglas, "Ventriculus cordis sinister stupendae magnitudinis, lately communicated to the Royal-Society by James Douglass, M.D. and R.S.S.," *Phil. Trans.* 29 (1714-1716), pp. 326-329, at p. 326.

[24] "An Account Concerning a Woman having a Double Matrix; as the Publisher hath Englished it out of French, lately printed at Paris, where the Body was opened," *Phil. Trans.* 4 (1669), 969-970. Joseph-Guichard Duverney, "Observations sur deux enfans joints ensemble," *Mémoires* (1706), 418-432, at 431: "un dessein conduit par une intelligence libre dans sa fin."

of the Paris Academy reported in 1712 that "We will only report on the most singular [anomaly in the case under discussion] because the story of monsters is infinite and little instructive." By the end of the seventeenth century, monsters no longer seemed either supernatural or horrific — as they had a century earlier — but it is not at all clear, as some historians have claimed, that explaining the causes of monsters was responsible for this change of focus. Lorraine Daston has argued that "causal knowledge drove out wonder," but the anatomical accounts here under review pointedly ignore causes and embrace wonder.[25] Here we can debate methodological differences between natural history, the kind of detailed description we find in anatomical accounts, and natural philosophy, the ascription of cause; is one more "scientific" than the other, or is that a meaningless question? Or does it indicate that the current historiographic emphasis on causal explanation does not tell the whole story? Like Daston, Arnold Davidson asserts that "the displacement of horror [was] a result of causal explanation," but gives as his example the Floyer-Tyson account of the human-faced pig. While it is true that Floyer and Tyson gave a natural cause for the pig's deformity (a result of external pressure on the womb), this was to refute not a supernatural cause but another, although to them less probable natural cause, that of inter-species sex.[26] Other historians have argued that detailed descriptions such as Buissière's were a way "to distance scientific observers from the idly curious," to separate the wondrous — the province of the vulgar — from the natural and analytic.[27] But this distinction is overdrawn for the early eighteenth century, when the wondrous and the analytic existed simultaneously.

2

In 1684, Thomas Molyneux (1661–1733), an Irish Protestant medical student, encountered a "most prodigiously large" forehead bone in the cabinet of the medical school of the University of Leiden. He wrote a short account of the dimensions of the bone which he sent to Francis Aston, secretary of the

---

[25] "Diverses observations anatomiques," *Histoire* (1712), 37; Daston, quoted in Arnold I. Davidson, "The Horror of Monsters," in *The Boundaries of Humanity: Humans, Animals, Machines*, ed. James J. Sheehan and Morton Sosna (Berkeley: University of California Press, 1991), 36-67, at 51.

[26] Davidson, "The Horror of Monsters," pp. 51-53; see also Julia Kristeva, *Pouvoirs de l'horreur* (Paris: Seuil, 1980).

[27] Stephen Pender, "In the Bodyshop: Human Exhibition in Early Modern England," in *"Defects": Engendering the Modern Body*, ed. Helen Deutsch & Felicity Nussbaum (Ann Arbor: University of Michigan Press, 2000), p. 112; Daston, "Marvelous Facts and Miraculous Evidence," pp. 270-274; Fontes da Costa, "The making of extraordinary facts"; cf. Hagner, "Enlightened Monsters," pp. 185-186.

Royal Society, who published the letter in the *Philosophical Transactions*.[28] By 1700, when his extended essay on this topic appeared, Molyneux was a successful physician and well known as a natural philosopher. His brother William had founded the Dublin Philosophical Society in 1683 and Thomas Molyneux was also an active member as well as a frequent correspondent of the Royal Society of London.[29]

The bone struck Molyneux's imagination, and he wrote his essay after years of thought about the significance of "gigantick bones." He even sent a friend to Leiden to measure the bone again, in case his earlier measurements were faulty. Since, as he truly believed, nature produced nothing that was not "admirable," how did one explain such a production? The huge bone demanded attention for several reasons: it was an extraordinary product of nature; if it was indeed both real and human (as Molyneux set out to prove), it implied that there had been a huge man who possessed this huge forehead; if such a man existed, he must somehow be fit into our view of nature; and the existence of such a man or men might confirm biblical statements about giants. Molyneux carefully distanced himself from more credulous reporters. Most previous accounts of giant bones he deemed "improbable," noting that most "pretended Giants Remains" were in fact the bones of large quadrupeds such as elephants or other "cheats." The forehead bone, in contrast, could only be human, and Molyneux presented anatomical evidence and detailed measurements to make his case.[30]

By means of analogy and also of synecdoche, he concluded that the giant to whom this head belonged must have been eleven or twelve feet high: "a goodly stature, and such as may well deserve to be called Gigantick." Molyneux then considered other circumstances which might have led to the

---

[28]Thomas Molyneux, "Part of 2 Letters from Mr. Thomas Molyneux concerning a Prodigious Os Frontis in the Medicine School at Leyden. Dec. 29th 1684 and Febr. 13th 1684/5," *Phil. Trans.* 15 (1685), pp. 880-881. According to Jan Bondeson, Molyneux was correct in assuming the bone was human; he surmises that it may have been from a hydrocephalus (*A Cabinet of Medical Curiosities* [1997; rept. New York: Norton, 1999], pp. 83-84. Molyneux seems to have been fascinated by big things; besides measuring the giant Edmond Malone (see below), he wrote about the Irish Elk and the Giant's Causeway (arguing that the latter was natural, not man-made).

[29]On Molyneux see K. Theodore Hoppen, *The Common Scientist in the Seventeenth Century. A Study of the Dublin Philosophical Society 1683-1708* (London: Routledge & Kegan Paul, 1970); *Oxford Dictionary of National Biography*, s.v. "Molyneux, Sir Thomas." Molyneux was made a baronet in 1730.

[30]Thomas Molyneux, "An Essay concerning Giants. Occasioned by Some Further remarks on the Large Humane Os Frontis, or Forehead-Bone, mentioned in the Philosophical Transactions of February, 1684-/5 number 168," *Phil.Trans.* 22 (1700-1701), pp. 487, 489-490; Antoine Schnapper argues that most ancient authors did not count giants as monsters, since they only differed from ordinary humans in dimensions, in his *Le géant, la licorne, la tulipe. Collections et collectionneurs dans la France du XVIIe siècle, I — Histoire et histoire naturelle* (Paris: Flammarion, 1988), p. 97.

production of such a large head, but dismissed them; this head was so large it could only have been a part of a proportionately large body. The question of proportion and symmetry fit Molyneux's idea of how nature must work, and therefore,

> Nor do I apprehend so great a stature as this in a Humane Body, tho it be indeed extraordinary, any way absurd or repugnant to the course of nature, but rather, if duly weighed, very conformable to a certain Anomalous method, if I may so call it, that she apparently affects in the producing most of her Works . . . does she not always tye herself up to the observance of such strict Laws, but that she sometimes falls very much short of her usual standard, and at other times goes as far t'other extreme, by vastly surpassing the common bounds of her Workmanship.[31]

Although there was a norm for any given species, nature, fundamentally "uncontrollable," was free to surpass it or otherwise modify it. Trees, for example, could vary greatly in size within a species, and Molyneux also cited the difference in size between Manx ponies and the largest horses as an example of wide variation within an animal species. Among humans, dwarfs were well-documented, as were humans of prodigious age. With such variations accepted as natural, "I think it at least appears that Humane Gigantick Bodies are in no way inconsistent, but rather easily reconcilable with the course of Nature." Molyneux then cited evidence of the existence of giants – if none as large as his *os frontis* required — including Edmond Malone, the famous "Dublin giant" of the late seventeenth century, whom Molyneux had measured in 1682. The closest he approached to discussing causes was his speculation that differing climates and soils may have an influence on size; in this regard, he particularly noted the account of André Thevet, a sixteenth-century French explorer, who in 1559 claimed to have seen the bones of an eleven-foot giant in North America. Molyneux surmised that the Leiden bone might have been taken from the New World; "but this I only conjecture." After a brief survey of biblical giants, he concluded on a note of skepticism that still larger giants may once have existed.[32]

Molyneux's account amounts to a natural history of giants, characterized by descriptive detail and lack of theorizing. Once one accepted that the bone was both real and human, he needed to explain not its causes but how it fit into the chain of being. Like contemporary natural historians, he was concerned with classification: were nature's categories flexible enough to accommodate human giants? In giving examples from other species, both

---

[31] Molyneux, "Essay Concerning Giants," pp. 495, 498-99.
[32] *Ibid.*, pp. 502, 506.

animal and plant, Molyneux assumed that nature was constant and symmetrical while at the same time unrestrained in her creativity. His description of the bone emphasized its "conformity to the Symetry or common rules of Nature," particularly in proportion to a normal skull: the forehead bone was perfectly proportioned, but simply larger than normal, and by analogy, the human to whom it belonged must also have been proportionately larger. However improbable an eleven-foot tall human might have been, to Molyneux this was the inevitable conclusion of his chain of reasoning. Yet this implied that nature encompassed anomaly rather than that monsters were normal.[33]

Molyneux's essay fit squarely into the ongoing discussion of classification. If classification was to be based on a single or essential characteristic, what was that characteristic? Shape, color, age, or even size did not define the essence of humanness for those who agreed with Aristotle that essential characteristics existed and must determine the order of nature. But those who argued that only a natural classification — based on consideration of all the qualities of a given organism — truly represented nature increasingly challenged the notion of essences.[34] Molyneux implied that the essence of humanness did not lay in size, but in other characteristics. But what were these? Anatomists seemed to locate human identity in external appearance; Buissière was surprised that the anencephalic infant had survived (for however short a time), but he did not doubt that it was human and indeed emphasized how much the infant resembled a normal human infant. Yet, without a brain, the infant lacked what most would have agreed was an essential aspect of human identity. Similarly, other monstrous births did not usually long survive, but anatomists nonetheless found them to be morphologically human, again assuming that morphology defined the meaning of the human even in the absence of the ability to sustain life. Patrick Tort has commented, "The fact that, for the most part, monsters were stillborn or lived only a short time did not constitute, according either to medicine or theology, a sufficient proof of their essential non-viability."[35] As Molyneux stated, the creativity of nature allowed for wide variation within a loosely defined morphological framework.

---

[33] *Ibid.*, p. 493.

[34] Phillip R. Sloan, "John Locke, John Ray, and the Problem of the Natural System," *Journal of the History of Biology* 5 (1972).

[35] Tort, *L'ordre et les monstres*, p. 22: "Le fait que, pour leur plus grande part, les monstres soient mort-nés ou ne vivent que très peu de temps ne saurait constituer, ni sur le plan de la médecine, ni sur celui de théologie, une preuve suffisante de leur non-viabilitié essentielle." For an interesting discussion of the construction of human identity in the seventeenth century, see Eve Keller, "Embryonic Individuals: The Rhetoric of Seventeenth-Century Embryology and the Construction of Early-Modern Identity," *Eighteenth-Century Studies* 33:3 (2000).

Almost fifty years later, the English physician James Parsons (1705-1770) read a paper to the Royal Society on a case of conjoined twins, later published in the *Philosophical Transactions*. Parsons was one of the many protégés of the anatomist James Douglas, and specialized, like Douglas, in obstetrics. He published a number of articles on a wide variety of topics, ranging from anatomy to antiquities, in the *Philosophical Transactions*.[36] Hermaphrodites were a particular interest, and he published a book on this topic in 1741, the same year he was elected a fellow of the Royal Society. In his *Mechanical and Critical Inquiry into the Nature of Hermaphrodites* he debunked the entire notion of hermaphrodites, arguing that those labeled as such were either male or female, "having only some Deformity or Disease in the Parts of Generation."[37]

Parsons read his lengthy and detailed account of conjoined twins to the Royal Society about two months after their birth in September 1748. Although Parsons included a section of "observations" in which he speculated on the cause of the conjunction, he did not use the case to prove a particular theory of generation. The tone is sharper and more matter-of-fact, and the language is subdued — the word "extraordinary" is missing — but in many ways his essay resembles those at the beginning of the century. Parsons spent much time describing "the Care of preparing these Children for keeping in Spirits," including the injection of the vascular system with some substance, probably colored wax or mercury, to make it more prominent. His dissection and inspection was even more painstaking than that of his predecessors, and he added instructional asides on proper techniques and critiques of those who had not been as careful. If an argument was to be made from morphology, then the morphology must be very thoroughly understood.[38]

Although the twins were apparently stillborn, or only survived for a short time after birth (Parsons was not present at the delivery), like other writers,

---

[36] *Oxford Dictionary of National Biography*, s.v. "Parsons, James." Parsons served as Douglas's amanuensis for a time; see C. Helen Brock, *Dr James Douglas's Papers and Drawings in the Hunterian Collection, Glasgow University Library A Handlist* (Glasgow: Wellcome Unit for the History of Medicine, University of Glasgow, 1994). He published 36 articles in the *Philosophical Transactions* between 1739 and 1768.

[37] James Parsons, "A Letter from James Parsons, M.D.F.R.S. to the Royal Society, giving a short Account of his Book intituled, A Mechanical Critical Inquiry into the Nature of Hermaphrodites. London, 1741 in 8vo.," *Phil. Trans.* 41 (1739-1741), pp. 650-652. James Parsons, *A Mechanical and Critical Inquiry into the Nature of Hermaphrodites* (London: J. Walthoe, 1741). He published an account of another hermaphrodite in the *Philosophical Transactions* in 1752.

[38] James Parsons, "A Letter from James Parsons M.D.F.R.S. to the President, containing an Account of a preternatural Conjunction of two Female Children," *Phil. Trans.* 45 (1748), pp. 526-27.

Parsons emphasized the "regular and natural" condition of much of the body. Like Duverney, he explained the complexity and ingenuity of the conjoined systems and how they might have worked in a living infant; how did nature compensate for missing or extra parts? Like Molyneux's giant, Parsons's twins fit within a flexible category of "natural."[39]

Unlike anatomists earlier in the century, however, Parsons explicitly addressed the question of causes. For over two decades, controversy had raged on the continent, particularly in France, over the origins of monsters. The debate between Louis Lémery and Jacques-Benigne Winslow was known throughout Europe, and it would be surprising if Parsons had not commented on origins in his essay, although he did not mention this debate. Both Lémery and Winslow accepted the theory of preformation to explain generation, and Parsons thought this was so obvious as barely to merit mention: "both these Parts of the Creation [i.e. animal and vegetable] are daily propagated from Organizations already formed and treasured up in natural Receptacles provided for them, till they come to be removed into proper Places of Nourishment." In other words, the embryo or seed was preformed, and required only nutrition in the womb or in the ground to grow. Parsons stated this as both a physical and a metaphysical principle: it was the best theory because it was the simplest and most subject to proof, but it was also the best theory because it agreed with the "the Ordination of Providence . . . that all should be good." The theory of epigenesis allowed too many opportunities for mistakes to occur, which was contrary to the divine character.[40]

Parsons then explained the circumstance of conjoining in much the same way that Tyson and Floyer had explained the human-faced pig: it was simply the mechanical effect of pressure. In the cases of conjoined twins, the two embryos in the womb simply came too close together and grew into each other. "We have many Facts to corroborate this Opinion, and to shew that the Fibres of Animals and Vegetables have a wonderful Capacity of extending and insinuating themselves into one another." Parsons compared the phenomenon to grafting trees and other such phenomena. He seemed to think that most cases of monstrous births could be attributed to such a cause; as we have seen above, he did not believe that hermaphrodites were truly monstrous in the sense he defined.[41]

---

[39] *Ibid.*, p. 531.

[40] The Lémery-Winslow debate has received much historiographical attention; the most recent account is Monti, "Epigenesis of the Monstrous Form." Parsons, "Preternatural Conjunction of two Female Children," p. 533.

[41] Parsons, "Preternatural Conjunction of two Female Children," p. 536.

3

What can we conclude from these accounts? They demonstrate the particular and peculiar interface, or overlap, between natural history and natural philosophy in the late seventeenth and early eighteenth centuries, as well as the intersection of learned debate and popular display. Daston and Park's assumption of a split between popular and learned culture in this era, a dichotomy between wonder and analysis, does not quite hold water, for wonder and analysis went hand in hand. The obsession of learned men with monsters of every sort has been dismissed as a trivial and lingering relic of the past. Although popular display of curiosities diverged from learned culture by the end of the eighteenth century, the collection and display of anatomical curiosities continued to be a respectable enterprise for the learned well into the nineteenth century. The anatomical examination of human (and animal) anomalies at the Royal Society and the Paris Academy earlier in the eighteenth century represents what some historians have called a transition from wonder to curiosity. Through attention to anomaly, natural philosophers explored how to define the normal, the human, the real. The eighteenth century was the great era of classification, of putting nature's productions into a logical order that would tell us something about the purposes and order of nature, and the anatomists sought to find the purpose of the singular in the overarching order of nature.[42]

---

[42] On display, see Richard Altick, *The Shows of London* (Cambridge, Mass: Harvard University Press, 1978); on the idea of a transition from wonder to curiosity, see Barbara Benedict, *Curiosity: A Cultural History of Early Modern Inquiry* (Chicago: University of Chicago Press, 2001); for a different view, see Palmira Fontes da Costa, "The Culture of Curiosity at the Royal Society in the First Half of the Eighteenth Century," *Notes and Records of the Royal Society* 56 (2002). I discuss this point further in Anita Guerrini, "The Hermaphrodite of Charing Cross," in progress.

The Status of Anomalies in the Philosophy of Diderot

ANNIE IBRAHIM

ABSTRACT. Diderot's reflections on monsters — not so much the perception of monstrosity or the relativity of our judgments on monstrous and 'normal' form, but rather the occurrence of 'sports' or 'freaks of nature' as a part of biological functioning overall — are in good part a reflection of his 'Lucretianism', that is, his vision of a universe in constant transformation, in which non-viable forms are regularly produced but just as quickly, removed. Two paradoxes emerge as a result of this vision: first, that Diderot sees monsters everywhere but also strips the notion of its normative content; second, that we are tempted to understand it as a 'proto-transformism', or alternately, as a proto-teratology. I suggest that this approach is misguided, because Diderot's materialism never departs from a fascination with *fictions*: his 'proto-scientific' ideas are inextricable from the 'dream' format in which they are presented.

The marked interest in the living world that is a noticeable trait of eighteenth-century French thought, can also be seen as a confrontation with the problem of biological monstrosities, one which reveals both 'curiosity' and a sense of uneasiness: thinkers, scholars, philosophers and physicians share the ancient conviction that Nature is ordered. Long before Diderot addresses the question, monsters are 'contradictory facts' that must be brought back to order, since these interruptions or subversions of mechanism undermine the perfection of the universe and our capacity to rationalize it. It is worth noting that, during the Enlightenment, the problem of monsters led to the gradual failure of (then) predominant theories, particularly mechanistic materialism; it revealed the inability of those theories to resolve such contradictions. Diderot sheds light on the significance of this failure by showing that the fact that blind people and six fingered-hands do exist demonstrates an *other* order of Nature, and demands an *other* metaphysics. In the *Principes philosophiques sur la matière et le mouvement* (1770), challenging the philosophers who mistakenly believe that matter is indifferent to motion and rest, Diderot has Nature itself draw the line between appearance and reality. It is up to us to locate this line of demarcation, provided that we follow Nature, instead of imposing pre-established systems on it: "While they argue for the indifference of a body to motion and rest, they forget that the block of marble tends towards disintegration."[1] If we follow the path from Diderot's early *Pensées philosophiques* (1746) to his late, unfinished *Éléments de physiologie* (which he worked on from the mid-1760s until approximately 1780), what concept of the monster will we see being formed?

The unclassifiable nature of Diderot's position on this issue, especially in his later works, has had a 'seductive' effect on a number of historians of philosophy: paradoxically, while using the traditional vocabulary of 'monster', 'oddity' (*bizarrerie*), 'defect', 'disorder' or 'deviation' (*écart*, really a 'gap'), his works effectively try to strip the notion of monster of any normative content. The profound influence of Lucretius' 'transformism', especially on the *Rêve de D'Alembert* (1769), enables monsters to be understood as merely *de facto* irregularities, as products of *chance*: this is a purely empirical assessment, free of any normative intention. Yet the transition from the term 'monster' to 'anomaly'[2] (along with the advent of embryology and comparative anatomy) was one of the epistemological conditions of the birth of positive teratology. In his *Histoire générale et particulière des anomalies*,[3] Isidore Geoffroy Saint-Hilaire, one of the founders of the discipline, strongly emphasizes this condition, along with the importance of terminology in any approach to monsters.[4]

From that point on, in a number of studies, we can see scholars succumb to this seductive effect, and rely excessively on that time-worn artifact,[5]

---

[1] References to Diderot's texts are given either to the DPV or the Versini editions (the latter indicated as V), except for the *Éléments de physiologie*, which is cited in J. Mayer's edition (Paris: Didier, 1964). Here, *Principes philosophiques sur la matière et le mouvement*, V 681.

[2] See G. Canguilhem, *Le normal et le pathologique* (Paris: PUF, 3rd edition, 1975 – translated as *The Normal and the Pathological*, by C. Fawcett & R.S. Cohen [New York: Zone Books, 1989]), especially pp. 81-90, on the play of the two etymologies *a-nomos* and *an-omalos*; an etymological confusion that helped to narrow the gap between anomaly and abnormal, the latter giving the former the adjectival form that it was missing, and vice versa. To eliminate the confusion between the Greek *nomos* and the Latin *norma* thus means rigorously defining the anomaly as a descriptive *fact*, and radically distinguishing it from the abnormal, which is always an axiological, value-laden term.

[3] *Histoire générale et particulière des anomalies de l'organisation chez l'homme et les animaux ... ou traité de tératologie*, 3 vols. (Paris: J.-B. Baillière, 1832-1837).

[4] See Beate Ochsner's essay in this volume.

[5] G. Canguilhem, *Études d'histoire et de philosophie des sciences* (Paris: Vrin, 1968), Introduction.

the concept of 'precursor'[6]; after all, Diderot's texts seem to give more than sufficient grounds for interpreting him as a 'precursor' of the science of monsters. But a careful reading of the texts speaks against the relevance of this notion[7]; for those who would naïvely insist on having Diderot put on trial retroactively by 'established' science, the 'straw man' of teratology seems more than adequate.[8] The essential reason for which the *Rêve* or the *Entretien*[9] could never serve as a propaedeutic for the works of Isidore Geoffroy Saint-Hilaire has to do with Diderot's critique of the traditional usage of 'monster' as a concept. If I anachronistically attribute the concept of 'anomaly' to Diderot, it is because he has the terms 'monster', 'disorder', 'illness', or 'oddity' converge in the thesis that the products of matter are wholly random, at the absolute mercy of chance and accident. Labeling Diderot a 'precursor' is obviously inappropriate here: how could an early nineteenth-century teratology or a theory of evolution allow for mere anomalies pure chance, when their project entails the twin assumptions of the objectivity of the study of living beings, and the existence of a teleology in organisms?[10]

Hence Diderot's position is a singular one: on the one hand, he denounces

---

[6] This image of Diderot as a precursor of nineteenth-century evolutionism can be found in F. Paître, *Diderot biologiste* (1904, reprint, Geneva: Slatkine, 1971); S. Doublet, *La médecine dans les œuvres de Diderot*, thèse de doctorat en médecine (Bordeaux: Imprimerie de l'Université, 1934); L. Germe, *Le philosophe Diderot, le médecin Bordeu et la médecine* (Arras: Maréchal, 1884); J. Mayer, *Diderot, homme de science* (Rennes: Imprimerie bretonne, 1959); the articles by N. Laidlaw ("Diderot's teratology," *Diderot Studies* 4 [1963]) and M. Wartofsky ("Diderot and the Development of Materialist Monism," *Diderot Studies* 2 [1952]). Also, in general studies such as P. Ostoya's *Les théories de l'évolution* (Paris: Payot, 1951) and E. Callot's *La philosophie de la vie au XVIIIe siècle* (Paris: Marcel Rivière, 1965).

[7] Authors who recognize this include J. Roger, *The Life Sciences in Eighteenth-Century French Thought*, trans. K. Benson (Stanford: Stanford University Press, 1997; originally published 1963), and F. Jacob, *The Logic of Life. A History of Heredity*, trans. B. Spillmann (New York: Pantheon Books, 1974). Also, L.G. Crocker, "Diderot and Eighteenth-Century French Transformism," in *Forerunners of Darwin, 1745-1859*, eds. B. Glass, O. Temkin & W.L. Straus (Baltimore: Johns Hopkins University Press, 1959); *id.*, *Diderot's Chaotic Order* (Princeton: Princeton University Press, 1974), and E. Hill, "The role of *le monstre* in Diderot's thought," *Studies on Voltaire and the Eighteenth Century* 97 (1972).

[8] Indeed, one can wonder if the term or concept of 'precursor' is ever really useful (or usable), especially in the life sciences. See A. Fagot's "Le transformisme de Maupertuis," in *Actes Maupertuis*, ed. O. Bloch (Paris: Vrin, 1975), and M. Barthélémy-Madaule, *Lamarck ou le mythe du précurseur* (Paris: Seuil, 1979).

[9] [The *Rêve de D'Alembert* is divided into three parts: first, the "Entretien" between Diderot and D'Alembert; second, the "Rêve" proper; third, the "Suite de l'Entretien."— Ed.]

[10] Thus Isidore Geoffroy Saint-Hilaire could just as well have targeted Diderot as Lémery, when he criticized the latter in these terms: "He could only treat abnormal beings as the blind and disordered products of chance" (*op. cit.*, vol. 3, p. 491).

the inability of mechanistic materialism to account for contradictions in the order of things, and recasts the notion of 'monster' as the yet unformulated 'anomaly' while, on the other hand, he does nothing to lay the grounds for the science of teratology. How do we then define the content of Diderot's investigation of the concept of disorder, both within his work and more broadly, in the relations between his work and other eighteenth-century theories of living beings? I suggest that Diderot provides a *radically materialist* definition of anomalies. Indeed, in the *Rêve* and in the *Entretien*, oddities are reduced to merely random or chance differences. But are these Diderot's 'thoughts' on the matter, in the sense of his reflective positions? Or is he rather formulating — indeed, yielding to — a series of *metaphorical* anticipations, as he himself suggests?[11] On this reading, Diderot, instead of trying to provide a systematic treatment of anomalies, instead works at constructing an elaborate apparatus (particularly the *Rêve*, both as a 'dream' and in its complex dialogic structure) to show that his materialism ends — and culminates — in *fiction*.

Be that as it may, the impossibility of any direct lineage between Isidore Geoffroy Saint-Hilaire and Diderot emerges through a 'matter of words'. I will first consider the divide, terminological and conceptual, between the two thinkers, then briefly review Diderot's stance toward monsters, in order to show how it is based on his conception of the relation between the Whole and its variations. Finally, I will examine the way his position ultimately takes the form of a conjecture, that of the inventions or creations of chance.

Apart from any philosophical criteria, the tone of the *Lettre sur les aveugles* (1749) and the existence of the *Neveu de Rameau* (first drafted in 1761, and revised possibly until Diderot's death in 1784) would be sufficient proof that Diderot's interest in monsters went well beyond the mere role of an academic hypothesis meant to resolve the theoretical difficulties of the period. On the contrary, these texts convey his concern with the uniqueness and the irreducibility of the individual, which he violently defended. under the rubric of the *original*, the 'singular' personality, against Helvétius in his *Réfutation* of the latter's ideas (V 821). From the genius to the 'doctor of oneself' through the blind man, beings are formed that are in no way determined by the laws of the universe; rather, it is the 'singular' or 'original' beings that provide a 'rule' for the world. In this respect, the objection against Helvétius is also an objection against Isidore Geoffroy Saint-Hilaire, for whom eccentricity or originality has no place in the world of living beings. For him, like for many positivist physicians, the pathological depends on the physiological, which serves as a *norm*. As he states in the Preface to

---

[11] On this see my "Matière des métaphores, métaphores de la matière," *Recherches sur Diderot et l'Encyclopédie* 26 (1999).

his treatise: "I will show how the laws and the relations between anomalies are themselves mere corollaries of the more general laws of organization" (p. xi). Each teratological law has a counterpart law in the order of normal things, and monstrous aberrations never cross certain boundaries. The rule to which all living things are reduced is the "affinity of oneself for oneself"; monsters are 'permanent embryos' that Nature puts at our disposition to help us recreate the formation of organized beings. Thus there is no exception to Nature's laws.

If it were a matter of choosing between the two etymologies of the word 'monster', it is clear that Diderot, like Isidore Geoffroy Saint-Hilaire, would be more attracted to the less common: *le monstre est ce qui montre*, the monster is that which 'shows' (in the sense of 'de-monstrates'). In the *Lettre sur les aveugles*, this is expressed by the blind man whose existence 'shows' us something about origins. But in the *Lettre*, the origin is not a simple organ that ends up developing harmoniously; it is chaos, and maimed worlds. The blind man's demonstration has several negative impacts on what would otherwise be the linear development of teratology: first, he shows that it is a false metaphysics that posits order in Nature. Moreover, this order exists no more today than it did at the time of the 'maimed worlds': passing symmetry, momentary order. Geoffroy's "natural method" which reduces natural living forms to the unity of an organizational schema, is thus just an illusion. Furthermore, that which comes first is not the simplest, the rule or the norm, to which exceptions could be reduced, but disorder. An attempt to understand the living world should then take differences or deviations as a point of reference, at the risk of sacrificing the dream of a theoretical unity, and abandoning the hope of an ideal homology between the rational and the real. This is the difficulty Diderot faces when confronted by the 'mutes by convention'[12]: which of them can be described as following the natural order (which itself would have then to be defined *a priori*!)? He expresses a similarly skeptical attitude in the sixth 'Pensée' of the *Interprétation,* when noting the disproportion between "the infinite multitude of the phenomena of Nature" and "the limits of our understanding and the weakness of our [sense] organs." We can thus perceive only "some broken, separate pieces" of the Whole.[13] Similarly, the doctor uses sickness as a point of reference, which is actually why pathological cases are so important in Diderot's eyes: "Everything being equal otherwise, he who best understands the human body will be in the best position to keep it safe from illness; and the

---

[12]The "muet de convention," as opposed to the person who is mute by birth, is part of Diderot's thought experiment in the *Lettre sur les sourds et muets* (1751): if someone were to express themselves only through gestures, might we be able to learn something about the origin of language, by inference?

[13]Diderot, *Pensées sur l'inteprétation de la nature*, § 6, V 562.

best anatomist will certainly be the best physician" (*Encyclopédie*, article "ANATOMIE"[14]). Favoring what Georges Canguilhem called the 'dogma' of the dependence of the pathological on the physiological, Geoffroy writes:

> All anomalies have been considered by all authors mainly from the practical point of view; by myself, from the theoretical. They proposed healing as their goal; me, a deepened understanding and through that, the confirmation and extension of the general laws of organization.[15]

Whereas Geoffroy systematizes anomalies by treating them as corollaries of the unity of composition, Diderot posits the precedence of differences over the rule, the primacy of the pathological over the physiological, and thus arrives instead at an atomistic theory of the living world and its movements. This atomism could give one the illusory impression of a disorganized scattering of individuals that is irreducible to any imaginable unity, flowing from an original, non-purposive chaos lacking any movement towards harmony. But Diderot himself rules out this interpretation in the famous 'Pensée' 11 of the *Interprétation de la nature*: "The absolute independence of a fact is incompatible with the idea of the Whole" (V 564). It is thus appropriate to try to understand how the idea of the Whole relates to that of the primacy of differences and deviations, by examining texts where the question of the anomaly is addressed most pointedly. Here we can only consider them summarily.

The world of Diderot's 1746 *Pensées philosophiques* is one of natural harmony, where mechanisms of compensation are always at work 'balancing out' any disorders, as in the case of Racine's meanness, which is 'balanced out' or compensated for by his genius. At the same time, physicians and anatomists in the Académie des Sciences begin the debate that will span almost the whole century, on the nature of monsters, in which Lémery in particular distinguished himself against Duverney, then Winslow.[16] We know how this debate over the nature of monsters belonged to the famous 'querelle des germes', in which partisans of pre-existence confront partisans of epigenesis. Thus, faced with the birth of monstrous fetuses, it was necessary to summon metaphysics to the dissecting tables. All this is at work in Diderot's text, which 'inherits' the philosophical debate in which theories of generation were used as proof or denial of this essential compensating mechanism. In the background is the philosophy of Malebranche, whose

---

[14] Hereafter all such references in small capitals are to articles in the *Encyclopédie*.

[15] I. Geoffroy Saint-Hilaire, *op. cit.*, vol. 3, p. 444.

[16] See my "Métaphysique et anatomie au XVIIIe siècle (la théorie des monstres accidentels dans les *Mémoires* de Louis Lémery à l'Académie des sciences)," *Recherches sur le XVIIe siècle* 8 (1986).

defense of the thesis of maternal imagination,[17] with the famous image of the *enfant roué*,[18] was the standard reference until at least 1740.

Malebranche was deeply opposed to Arnauld and to Jansenism[19] on the question of the distance between God's will and the movement of natural laws. Malebranche leaves nature the possibility of a "game," a "necessary consequence of the laws of communication between movements." Hence he resorted to maternal imagination to account for the monstrous formation of these 'accidents', for which God is innocent. In 1690, Régis reasserts Cartesian orthodoxy against Malebranche and the renaissance of Augustinian thought, by denying that one could distinguish between God's understanding and God's will, since "the laws of nature are indistinguishable from God's will, and if one said that by following the laws of nature, God creates things that he would not want to create, we would again reply that this would be tantamount to asserting that God's will is contrary to itself, a repellent assertion."[20] Even if monsters are the result of accidents, that is, chance disorders made possible by the play of natural movements, it is impossible not to integrate these accidents into God's will. From then on, since the intentions of this (Cartesian) God go far beyond our understanding, does it even make sense to speak of monsters? From the very beginning of the 'querelle des germes', Fontenelle boldly and precisely formulates the notion of accident:

> Monsters are commonly seen as games of nature, but philosophers are quite persuaded that nature does not gamble, that it always, invariably follows the same rules, and that all its cogs

---

[17] See M.-H. Huet, *Monstrous Imagination* (Cambridge, Mass.: Harvard University Press, 1993).

[18] "Seven or eight years ago, one could see at the Hospital of the Incurables a young man who was born insane, and whose body was broken in the same places as the body of a criminal who has been tortured with the wheel.... The cause of this unfortunate accident..., is that the mother of this young man, having heard that a criminal was to be put to death, went to watch the spectacle. Every blow received by the criminal forcefully struck the mother's imagination, and by ricochet (*par une espèce de contrecoup*), the tender and delicate brain of the child she was bearing" (Malebranche, *De la recherche de la vérité*, II, i, ch. 7, § 3, in *Œuvres*, ed. G. Rodis-Lewis, vol. 1 [Paris: Gallimard-Pléiade, 1979], p. 178). The idea is that the child's body bore the same marks as those of the criminal who was subjected to the torture of the wheel. Voltaire quotes Malebranche to this effect in his *Dictionnaire philosophique* ('London' [Avignon]: Cramer frères, 1769), article "Originel (explication du péché originel), and even La Mettrie refers favorably to Malebranche on this point, in *L'Homme-Machine* (in A. Thomson, ed. & trans., La Mettrie, *Machine Man and other Writings* [Cambridge: Cambridge University Press, 1996]).

[19] See H. Gouhier, *La philosophie de Malebranche* (1926; 2nd edition, Paris: Vrin, 1948).

[20] Régis, *Système de philosophie* (Paris: Denys Thierry, 1690), vol. III, pp. 29-30.

are, so to speak, equally serious. Some of them may be extraordinary, but not irregular.[21]

Among the various possibilities of allowing for some 'play' between the extraordinary and the irregular, Diderot, at the time of the *Pensées*, opted for the solution of equilibrium by compensation. All the way to his article "MÉDECINE," Diderot, like Boerhaave, maintains a notion of illness in which therapeutics is understood as supplementing that which is lacking, and subtracting from superfluous elements.

The atheist in the 21st 'Pensée' and the blind man in the *Lettre* are living transgressions of the watchmaker's order (that is, the ordered world understood on the model of a rationally designed watch or a clock). For the atheist, "the world is the result of the chance motion of the atoms" (V 25); the blind man speaks of "the irregular agitations" of the ocean of the universe (V 167). Monsters are deviations from the Epicurean vertical line, which is itself the result of a throw of the dice, that is, of chance motion. Diderot brings together here, in a materialist and mechanistic framework, all the conditions required for the 'abnormal' to be redefined or even reconfigured as 'anomaly' (*an-omalos*, without regularity, away from the set path, which happens to also be the etymology given in the *Encyclopédie* for the word *delirium*: *aberrare de lira*). The possibility of moving away from the set path without this amounting to something 'abnormal', and thus without there being a need for mechanisms of compensation, is explicitly stated by Saunderson, the blind man, on his deathbed, in accordance with a certain number of conditions, all of which are dependent on the notion of time: the current ('ordered') state of the universe was preceded by an original chaotic ('disordered') state. Order came after the fact.

It is not easy to equate this 'after the fact' dimension of the gradual filtering or purification (Diderot uses the odd term *dépuration*) of living forms through the elimination of 'vicious' combinations, with a temporality that would be compatible with the notion of evolution, or even of history. In fact, the relevant tradition here is that of Empedocles and Lucretius,[22] to whose authority Diderot appeals in his article "EPICURISME": "The world is the result of chance and not the realization of a design." In the infinity of worlds, organic matter arises from the inorganic by degree, but the conditions for this development are "circumstances" like those that allow

---

[21] *Histoire de l'Académie des Sciences*, in *Mémoires de l'Académie Royale des Sciences* (Paris: Imprimerie Royale, 1703), p. 28 [hereafter simply cited as *Mémoires*]. See G. Canguilhem, "Fontenelle, philosophe et historien des sciences," *Annales de l'Université de Paris*, 27th year (July-August 1957), pp. 384-390.

[22] Empedocles had already defended this principle, according to Aristotle (*Physics* II, 8, 198b). Lucretius, *De rerum natura*, V, 837-850, 855 and II, 870-901.

for purification: "as we see, a combination of many circumstances is required to enable a species to spread by reproduction" (Lucretius, *De rerum natura*, V, 850). Following in the footsteps of Epicurus and Empedocles, Diderot launches an attack on all explanations that appeal to final causes ('finalism'). The criterion for a successful form is simply the lucky 'fact' that it endures, the length of time it survives, as, for Lucretius' image of the primitive nature that produced a great number of monsters condemned to perish, since "they were unable to reach their much desired prime of life, or find food, or have relations by the act of Venus" (*ibid.*, 847-848). A summary application of the laws of probability, which Diderot calls *l'analyse des sorts*, leads to the claim that since the laws of matter are infinite, there is a certain chance that monsters will appear, side by side with successful combinations. But monsters are rare.

Probability thus construed loses all relevance in Diderot's mature writings, between 1754 and 1770 when, having posited the dynamism of matter, he replaces the earlier, harmonious system of mechanical compensation with the hypothesis of organic regulation. The Whole is no longer a universe or a world, but a dynamism or a sensitivity that moves toward the production of living forms. These combinations are only 'variations' or 'differences' from each other and in relation to the whole. D'Alembert says in the *Rêve* that "Man is but a common result,[23] the monster, a rare result; both are equally natural and equally necessary in the universal and overall order" (DPV XVII, 138). This Spinozist conception of totality does away with the possibility of anything being *contra naturam*, and sets forth a theory of difference as a mere variation of the Whole.[24] Besides the system of the *Ethics*, the other crucial influence on Diderot here is Bacon, his experimental 'mentor'.[25] Diderot's homage to Bacon in the article "ENCYCLOPÉDIE" also shows up in his conception of natural and necessary variation. In fact, for Bacon, the elaboration and application of the method, together with the key role of experience and experiment, render explanations in terms of final causes completely barren, like those remoras who have 'slowed down the march of the sciences'. In Bacon's second subdivision of natural history, the history of monsters describes modifications of natural phenomena, in exactly the same way as the history of generations (rivers, volcanoes, earth, meteors), and explainable just like them, *per causas,* as so many natural determinisms, "for history and experience are one and the same thing; so

---

[23][Actually, "un effet commun." — Trans.]

[24]On the usage of Spinoza in the elaboration of a biologically oriented ontology in the eighteenth century, see my "Sur le spinozisme dans les philosophies du vivant," in O. Bloch, ed., *Spinoza au XVIIIe siècle* (Paris: Klincksieck, 1990).

[25]See J. Varloot's introduction to Volume II of Diderot's *Œuvres choisies* (Paris: Editions sociales, 1972), p. 14.

are philosophy and the sciences."[26] Contrary to the old project of natural history, which created a heterogeneous juxtaposition of the ordinary and the extraordinary, it is appropriate to verify the regularity of the phenomena from a "model of the universe, as it is in fact, and not such as a man's own reason would have it to be."[27] This is also the anatomical thesis of the vitalist physician Théophile de Bordeu,[28] who explains the organization of living beings starting from sensation, according to a purposiveness without purpose, which produces health "justly"; the only medical philosophy here is a Hippocratic naturalism, which allows one to make out "a quite considerable and indeterminate number of combinations that introduce many different variations of ways of being healthy."[29] Thus one can only follow nature, all the more so since whenever it runs up against itself, producing contradictory forms, the ultimate outcome is always a reconciliation.

The *Éléments de physiologie* clarify Saunderson's notions of "temporary symmetry" or "momentary order" as described in the *Lettre*, albeit in a rather curious way. "But the overall order changes incessantly. The vices and virtues of the preceding order lead to the present order, whose vices and virtues will lead to the order that follows, without one's being able to say that the whole is improving or deteriorating" (*Éléments*, p. 209). Henceforth we can surmise that within the overall thesis of an unpredictable naturalism,[30] which serves as a unifying principle of Diderot's thought, he defines the status of anomalies in accordance with a 'vitalist materialism'. Abandoning the image of the dice-throw, he attributes the origin of living forms to the "mute uneasiness" of the molecule,[31] which rules out any rational reply to the question of what nature is 'looking for', and even whether it is looking for something at all, not to mention avoiding a possible 'failure'.

Thus, when inquiring into Diderot's position on anomalies, one cannot help noticing that he hesitates between the hypothesis of a mute purposiveness oriented toward utility, and the hypothesis of games of pure chance. His hesitation is most apparent with (and perhaps motivated by) the ques-

---

[26] Bacon, *On the Dignity and Advancement of Learning* (1605), II, § 1.

[27] Bacon, *Novum Organum* (1620), I, 124.

[28] Paragraph 108 of the *Recherches anatomiques sur les glandes* (Paris: Quillau père, 1751) is the original source for the image of the bee-swarm that Diderot uses in the *Rêve*. (Bordeu also appears as a character in this text.)

[29] Article "Santé."

[30] ["Naturalisme aléatoire," an expression reminiscent of Althusser's "matérialisme aléatoire"; a naturalism which emphasizes chance, randomness and unpredictability rather than order, laws and predictability.—Ed.]

[31] Diderot sometimes speaks of a "mute sensitivity" in 'atoms' or 'molecules', which also expresses itself in the unpredictable behavior he describes as their "automatic uneasiness" (*Pensées sur l'interprétation de la nature*, § 51); cf. also the article "Chaos" (by Diderot) and his *Principes philosophiques sur la matière et le mouvement*.

tion of the formation of organized bodies and the process of individuation: has everything already been played out? Have all the anomalies already been produced? Could there be new ones? (Indeed, can there be anything new at all?) Because of the 'modern' aura of these questions, Diderot has had yet another 'seductive' effect, this time more recently, on some of the key theoretical assessments or rather reassessments in biological thought.[32] This sort of influence could very well produce yet another mythology of 'Diderot as precursor', one quite distinct from that created by the founders of teratology!

Diderot's probabilistic view that chance plays a constitutive role in the creation of organized beings seems to imply — again, anachronistically — an intersection between his standpoint and that of modern genetics. Namely, he seems to be the first to recognize the contradictory-seeming tenet of biology (as Jacques Monod puts it), that it is necessary to posit *both* objectivity *and* teleonomy.[33] Further, Diderot seems to appear again when we consider the prehistory of the discovery of 'microscopic deviations' in the genetic code, and the usage of the term 'lottery' to describe how a program is encoded. His figure also seems to appear when Léon Brillouin describes the brilliant maverick surgeon, inquiring into the meaning of his fascinating operations, in which the random assemblage of an animal's organs, which had been previously separated and kept alive, can end up producing either a viable being or a monstrous being that is destined to die.[34] How should one then define a notion of *value* that would be appropriate for judging the difference between these two possible results? Why, indeed, should we fall back on the notion of value at all? Why not be content with probabilistic thinking? Diderot's response to these troubled aporias is somewhere in between bravado and bravura, as he imagines Mlle de Lespinasse's "playing" at making a cyclops or a hermaphrodite, by manipulating the sensitive "threads" of the molecule — a manipulation of Nature which is meant to refer to Nature's own deviations and combinations (the processes by which Maupertuis, in his *Système de la nature*,[35] had explained the formation of an infinite variety of animals).

---

[32] See J. Monod, *Chance and Necessity. An Essay on the Natural Philosophy of Biology*, trans. A. Wainhouse (New York: Knopf, 1971), and F. Jacob (*op. cit.*) on the notions of chance and lottery in theories of heredity. On the role of the 'Diderot model' in more general scientific/conceptual matters, see I. Prigogine & I. Stengers, *Order out of Chaos* (New York: Bantam Books, 1984), and M. Serres, *Genesis*, trans. G. James & J. Nielson (Ann Arbor: University of Michigan Press, 1995).

[33] Monod, *op. cit.*, chapter 1.

[34] L. Brillouin, V*ie, matière et observations* (Paris: Albin Michel, 1959), p. 105.

[35] Maupertuis, *Système de la nature ou Essai sur les corps organisés*, § 45, in *Œuvres* (Lyon: J.-M. Bruyset, 1768; reprint, ed. G. Tonelli, New York-Hildesheim: Georg Olms, 1987).

In the procession of monsters we see marching through Diderot's 1769 *Rêve de D'Alembert*, when he addresses the case of the carpenter Jean-Baptiste Macé and his inverted organs (*situs inversus*), Diderot appeals entirely to the role of chance: "Now let someone speak of final causes!"[36] The strangeness or "irregularity" of such deformations, as Bordeu terms it, can "leap" to a distant descendant. Chance is actually twofold: there is the *situs inversus* itself, and its inheritance according to the formation of the network of threads. These spiderweb threads (in Diderot's metaphoric terms), juxtaposed with Albrecht von Haller's notion of the fiber (which is meant to refer to the molecule's organic sensitivity),[37] result in the character Bordeu's theory of the bundle of sensitive threads which, combining with each other in an infinite number of unforeseeable ways, produce the six-fingered hand and the cyclops (the former by an excess of threads, the latter, by mutilation). Anomalies are thus not irregularities or residues of the past that recall the original chaos and the gradual process of 'elimination' or 'filtering out' (*depuration*) of monsters and failed combinations. As Mlle de Lespinasse says of hermaphrodites: we must expect the unknown (V 641). This is because the image of a leap applies not only to heredity, but also to the observed and inexplicable passage from the thread to the organ; the two terms that Diderot uses to 'fill in' this explanatory gap are nowhere near an explanation, namely, "nutrition" and "structure" (*conformation*). That is, the shift from an individual 'thread' to a whole organ has to do with both the "nutrition" and the "structure" of the thread (*ibid.*). So, in the *Rêve*, the thread of Mlle de Lespinasse's eyes when she was just a molecule, becomes the beautiful eyes that Bordeu presently sees; likewise, the extremity of an anemone's stalk will be an anemone; and, in the *Éléments*, even though there is nothing in common between the molecule of a willow's bark and the willow itself, it is still this molecule that gives rise to a willow.[38] It seems that in rejecting preformationism, the theory of the thread runs into the same problem that confronted ancient atomism: the formation of visible bodies over time, out of eternal and invisible atoms, occurs by a kind of leap. It is precisely because of this inexplicable leap that any anomaly is imaginable in the future. The new, the unknown, is to be expected; it can be imagined. But can all of this be 'thought'?

---

[36] *Rêve de D'Alembert*, V 644.

[37] See Haller, *De partibus corpori humani sensilibus et irritabilibus* (1753), translated as *A Dissertation on the Sensible and Irritable Parts of Animals* (London, 1755; reprint, Baltimore: Johns Hopkins Press, 1936; also in S.A. Roe, ed., *The Natural Philosophy of Albrecht von Haller* [New York: Arno Press, 1981]); *id.*, *Primae lineae physiologiae* (1747, 3^d revised ed. 1765), trans. & ed. W. Cullen, *First Lines of Physiology* (Edinburgh, 1779 / New York: Johnson Reprint Corp, 1966).

[38] *Éléments de physiologie*, p. 193.

In fact, that would require nothing less than conceiving an infinite, heterogeneous matter, eternally agitated by the unforeseeable movement of molecules combining with each other to form organized bodies. A false metaphysics, accustomed to trusting appearances more than reality, detects monsters among these combinations. If these monsters are nothing but variations, it is because the anomaly is, in the end, one of the definitions of the heterogeneity of matter. Whence Diderot's skepticism about anomaly as a *theory*, and his conviction that it should remain a matter of *conjectures*. This is how he concludes his consideration of monsters in the *Éléments*: "Why couldn't man, indeed, all animals, simply be a more enduring form of monster?" (p. 208). The rhetorical question here is meant to echo Diderot's skeptical tone in the *Pensées sur l'interprétation de la nature*, when he declared that organized bodies are nature's most incomprehensible mystery, and the dogmatism of ancient metaphysics is completely inappropriate ('Pensée' 10, V 564). The true metaphysics thus lies in being 'skeptically' confident in 'blind' experimental philosophy, which proceeds blindfolded, by groping steps, taking anything that falls into its hands and, finally, finding some valuable things ('Pensée' 23, V 568). This is how Diderot describes the method that he uses in his philosophical texts, a blind man's method that neither resembles the dogmatism of the past, nor foresees Geoffroy's "natural method." Especially in the *Rêve* and in his correspondence with Sophie Volland, Diderot alludes frequently to a philosophy of gaps, leaps, disorder, and haphazard ideas — the only methodology capable of understanding the monster as a chance variation, since it takes the same theoretical path. Diderot thus opens the way for *metaphors* to show what, for him, takes the place of a theory of anomalies. I shall mention two such metaphors. The first is famous, and occurs throughout Diderot's work, so I shall say only a few words about it here; it is the metaphor of *play*, and therefore also of *games*, especially games of chance. The second is the metaphor of *grafting* or transplanting.

Games allow a kind of theoretical access to the knowledge of nature's processes, since nature itself plays and plays with the philosopher. Or consider the case of the genius, whose 'playful' spirit indicates that s/he is like Nature itself, or again, the physician, who also learns to 'play' with nature when s/he relies on 'instinct' to make a diagnosis. In the background of all of this is Diderot's distinction between a type of game that he disparages and even condemns as strictly formal (mathematical games and probabilities) and a concrete, living, creative game (the game of the bundle of sensitive threads, the mute uneasiness of the molecule, and the harpsichord). It is more a game of prescience than a calculation of probability in a lottery: "In nature as in all games, there are elements of prescience which are felt and not at all calculated."³⁹

But the metaphor of games is not enough to account for the processions of monsters, or the possibility that they are (or can bring about) the production of something *new*. This is where Diderot uses the image of the graft, bringing us back on the one hand to Mlle de Lespinasse manipulating her threads, and on the other hand, to the problem of curing illnesses. In fact, grafting is an idea that belongs equally to gardening and to surgery, as is described in the article "NATUREL," in a discussion of the difference between the natural and the artificial. Referring back to the article "ART," two examples are used to point out that the natural is not opposed to the artificial: lifting water with pumps is natural *and* artificial, as is crossing plums and cherries on a grafted tree. In Chapter 24 of the *Éléments*, on generation, the Great Gardener, having replaced the Great Clockmaker, is asked, regarding the successive exfoliations of the matrix, if two fruits can be born at the site of a first peduncle? (p. 193). Nature itself shows us that the possibility for new variations depends on the art of the graft that is spontaneously produced by hybrids. In 1740, Trembley presented reveals his discovery of the regeneration of polyps in botanical terms: if they are cut, they reconstitute themselves; if cuttings are taken, they reproduce themselves. Even Lémery, who favored the mechanistic analogy of the clock, also drifted toward the botanical analogy in the *Mémoires* he presented to the Académie des Sciences. While using Duverney and Winslow's argument (the perfection of the clock), he wonders what kind of a clockmaker would, by premeditated design, "go to such pains to make bad clocks instead of producing perfect ones."⁴⁰ The well-regulated mechanism of the clock prevents us from ever hoping to see extraordinary or irregular clocks: the only possibility is that they be broken. The apparent irregularity of a clock whose parts have been inverted by a fanciful clockmaker (from right to left) disappears as soon as one can confirm its correct functioning as compared to the non-inverted clock.⁴¹ However able he may be, the artisan could never astonish us with an invention, whether or not he inverted the clock-parts. However, the plant, even without the gardener's help, suddenly produces something new. The same goes for the "singular trait" appearing

---

³⁹Diderot, letter of 1769 (believed to be to Mme de Maux), in *Corr.*, vol. 9, p. 245. On this theme, see *Le Jeu au XVIIIe siècle*, Colloque d'Aix (Aix: Edisud, 1976); E. de Fontenay, *Diderot, Reason and Resonance*, trans. J. Mehlman (New York: Braziller, 1982); E. Hill, "Materialism and monsters in *Le Rêve de D'Alembert*," *Diderot Studies* 10 (1968), and my "Les adversaires de la métaphore du jeu de dés," in A.-M. Chouillet, ed., *Les ennemis de Diderot* (Paris: Klincksieck, 1993).

⁴⁰Second part of the "Quatrième Mémoire sur les monstres," *Mémoires de l'Académie des Sciences* 1740 (Paris, 1742), pp. 517-538.

⁴¹*Ibid.*, p. 521.

in the Bois de Boulogne, where two oaks grow together as one, because of the proximity of their branches.[42] Producing something new is the monster's injunction to nature; invention is the category eminently occupied by the monster in natural history, thus disturbing the method of inventory and classification. But "two apples, two pears, two cherries or any other fruits that one finds united together on a tree and that form a kind of monster"[43] are not really an exception in comparison with ordinary formations.

The gardener is not really a technician; horticulture is not a form of artifice, but of art. At the level of animals and of man, the physician who could claim to be a gardener of organs rather than a surgeon, would be a lucky physician! Further, someone for whom surgery was like gardening would be even luckier, since this would repeat, imitate and prolong nature's possibilities by analogy with the vegetal realm, since each spontaneous graft is simply nature imitating itself. This is the guarantee of order and completeness for Lémery: animal monsters and vegetal monsters are "continual examples" of one and the same mechanics. Thus, by way of gardening, any singularity, any extraordinary structure is eliminated from the accidentalist etiology by the mere "contact" and "union" of two originally separate seeds. Like the graft, the 'in-between' cases in the catalogue of animals can make a case for the idea that the monster is, in the end, natural and banal. Somewhere in between the clock and the plant, but closer to the graft, the hybrid is the living proof of the strength of the system of accidents against that of 'originally' monstrous eggs. Such is the meaning of the "fortuitous" coupling of a cat and a dog in the Second Mémoire; the blatant process of the accidental generation of hybrids uses the analogy as an identification of the two individuals that are involved: "If an anatomist with eyes as perceptive as his mind went to the trouble of looking into the extraordinary structure of these monsters, in order to see how the monstrous parts were produced, [s/he would conclude] that the cause of their particular characteristics is only a kind of accident."[44] When considered as an accidental hybrid, the monster and its extraordinary structure display no more than "particular characteristics."

The idea that nature merely repeats its own processes, including its errors (which are themselves analogous to its ordinary productions), also had an impact on Maupertuis: dreaming of being a kind of Dareste before his time,[45] artificially producing new monsters, he, too, understands this dream

---

[42] "Premier Mémoire sur les monstres," *Mémoires* (1738), p. 266.
[43] *Ibid.*, p. 272 (see also p. 260, and "Second Mémoire," pp. 310-311).
[44] "Second Mémoire sur les monstres," *Mémoires* (1738), pp: 305-330.
[45] See Camille Dareste, *Recherches sur la production artificielle des monstruosités, ou, Essais de tératogénie expérimentale* (Paris: Reinwald, 1877). Dareste (1822-1899) was a correspondent of Darwin and an early partisan of his theory in France.

as the extension of the gardener's art — but a gardener who accentuates the fortuitous variations that appear in nature by 'accident' or 'chance': "The basis for their existence lies in nature, but they are only brought about by chance or by art. New species of dogs offer an example of this."[46] Variations are thus not exceptional relative to this gardening which "further extends" nature: "Extremely tall and extremely small men are a type of monster; but if we strove to multiply them, they would comprise [entire] peoples."[47] Nature's prodigality, breaking the chain of continuity (also of the elementary memory of particles), gives rise to other possibilities that will be perpetuated as long as the "order and agreement" of the organs is respected. Maupertuis posited this idea, and from it derived both contradictions and discoveries which led him far beyond a strictly spatial combinatorics. However, he too continued to be seduced by this absorption of monsters into the analogical game of variations, that is, into a self-imitating nature (but one which obeys the rule of "order and agreement").

Diderot, in contrast, introduces savagery into the vegetal image, shaking up the composition of the picture. Thus he gives his gardener-demiurge the possibility to produce — by 'playing with threads' and taking cuttings — beings that are much more fantastic, like the ape-men or the goat-men (*chèvre-pieds*) described in the "Suite de l'Entretien." The idea of 'engineering' such fantastic beings was Bordeu and Mlle de Lespinasse's answer to a question of 'poetics', or how to create beings along the lines of Nature's own process of cutting and grafting. In the article "JARDIN," Jaucourt advises suppressing the strong inclination of the tree to work for its own benefit, and to prune it in order to obtain fruit instead of leaves. Considering the domestic role of the goat-men as beasts of burden, one might think that nature invites these gardeners, the anatomists, to produce variations that would be useful, not in terms of the 'animal economy', but of the economy of societies as a whole! Art, when it is imitation of nature and not bad artifice, enables the uneasiness of the molecule to regenerate itself and give rise to new variations — a fiction which serves as a 'theory' of mutant anomalies. Kant actually held this view, when, in the third *Critique*, he described the formation, in a tree suffering from lesions, of completely new parts in accordance with processes of self-preservation, as an anomalous creation (*anomalisches Geschöpf*).

Without the activities of art, the inventive resources of the molecule would be exhausted. Hence the importance of the graft as a model and gardening techniques as a fiction of the variation of species. In the *Vénus*

---

[46] Maupertuis, *Vénus Physique*, in *Œuvres, op. cit.*, vol. II, Table analytique, article "Variétes."

[47] Maupertuis, *Lettre sur le progrès des sciences*, § XIII, in *Œuvres*, p. 421.

physique, Maupertuis writes: "One thing that is sure, is that all the variations that might be characteristic of new species of animals and plants tend to die out: they are gaps of Nature in which it perseveres only by art or regimen. Its works always tend to get the upper hand" (*op. cit.*, p.110).

The natural art of grafting allows us to understand what might otherwise seem contradictory in Diderot's medical conceptions as expressed in the character of the physician Bordeu: it is in fact a matter of ambivalence regarding the difference between bad artifice and legitimate art. There is an apparent contradiction: on the one hand, Hippocratic naturalism and what Claude Bernard was to call "expectative medicine" (i.e. a non-interventionist, holistic position of expectation rather than modification); on the other, an interventionist medicine, focusing especially on two issues: the *apologia* for surgeons, and the affair of the vaccine against smallpox: we know that Diderot supported the vaccine and that he urged Sophie Volland's mother to campaign for its use on her estate. In the famous quarrel Diderot had with D'Alembert, when the latter expressed reservations in his two *Mémoires* of 1761 because of his calculations concerning the risk of death due to the vaccination, Diderot sided with Tronchin and Bordeu. In the article "INSERTION DE LA PETITE VÉROLE," Diderot stressed the importance of the enterprise, emphasizing its victory over prejudice and art's triumph over nature, "causing death to take a step back": "Nature decimates us, art allows us to age gracefully." In the article "HOMME," he asserts Buffon's position on the issue of prolonging life.[48] In the article "MORT," Ménuret de Chambaud speaks of prognosis and cures with respect to the distinction between imperfect and absolute death; curing death would display the omnipotence of a medicine that can reinvent the course of life. On the question of capital punishment as a way to regulate disorder, Diderot, in the letter to Landois, indicates that the idea of natural necessity does not exclude the human capacity to modify it: "although man, whether good or evildoer, is not free, man is nevertheless a modifiable being: because of this, the evildoer must be publicly destroyed" (DPV IX, 257). The ambivalence between an interventionist medicine and an "expectative" medicine is very explicit in Diderot's letter to Morand, in which he defends the necessary collaboration between medicine and surgery: against the artifice of remedies and bleedings, Diderot speaks in favor of the art of surgery. Human capacities for modification are as infinite as the games of the molecule.

---

[48] Condorcet also contested the idea of a natural life-span; Deparcieux challenged the idea of an order of death in his *Essai sur les probabilités de la vie humaine* (1746; reprint, Paris: Éditions d'histoire sociale, 1973). On this question, see R. Favre, *La mort au siècle des Lumières* (Lyon: Presses universitaires de Lyon, 1978).

Faced with the issue of anomalies, Diderot does not respond so much with a *theory* of monsters, as he turns towards the materialist *fiction* of the uneasiness of the molecule, an unpredictable uneasiness from which unexpected variation and novelty arise, through grafts and spontaneous hybridizations. In the article "GREFFE," he alludes to the triumph of art over nature: we force nature to take on other arrangements; we can even transform a species. But can we create other species? If so, that would mean following nature's own processes, leaving everything up to chance, and encountering "circumstances that are as rare as they are extraordinary." This fiction of games and grafts can accompany a completely Promethean vision of medicine, which is how the *Éléments de physiologie* concludes — with the undefined possibility of further advances in the art of healing through surgery. Thus, if we can say that Diderot *dreams* his theory of monsters, he dreams of it in the way that he imagines the production of satyr-like men with goat's hooves, and also in the way that he projects a medical utopia, one which paradoxically could remake nature by obeying the orders that it gives.

translated from the French by Lynn Niizawa.

Acknowledgements

An earlier version of this essay appeared in *Dix-huitième siècle* 15 (1983). Similar material can also be found in my "Diderot ou le paradoxe du développement aléatoire," in O. Bloch *et al.*, eds., *Entre forme et histoire* (Paris: Klincksieck, 1988); "The Life Principle in Diderot," in C.T. Wolfe, ed., *The Renewal of Materialism* (*Graduate Faculty Philosophy Journal* 22:1, 2000), as well as my discussions in Ibrahim, ed., *Diderot et la question de la forme* (Paris: PUF, 1999) and *Qu'est-ce qu'un monstre ?* (Paris: PUF, 2005).

The Materialist Denial Of Monsters
CHARLES T. WOLFE

ABSTRACT. Locke and Leibniz deny that there are any such beings as 'monsters' (anomalies, natural curiosities, wonders, and marvels), for two very different reasons. For Locke, monsters are not 'natural kinds': the word 'monster' does not individuate any specific class of beings 'out there' in the natural world. Monsters depend on our subjective viewpoint. For Leibniz, there are no monsters because we are all parts of the Great Chain of Being. Everything that happens, happens for a reason, including a monstrous birth. But what about materialism? Well, beginning with the anatomical interest into 'monstrous births' in the French Académie des Sciences in the first three decades of the eighteenth century, there is a shift away from 'imaginationist' claims such as those of Malebranche, that if a woman gives birth to a monstrous child it is a consequence of something she imagined. Anatomists such as Lemery and Winslow try to formulate a strictly mechanical explanation for such events, rejecting moral and metaphysical explanations. Picking up on this work, materialist thinkers like Diderot are compelled to reject the very idea of monsters. We are all material beings produced according to the same mechanisms or laws, some of us are more 'successful' products than others, i.e. some live longer than others. In his late *Éléments de physiologie* he says "L'homme est un effet commun, le monstre un effet rare." Ultimately he arrives at a materialist version of Leibniz's position: there are no monsters, we are all monsters in each other's eyes, at one time or another. This conclusion is a pregnant one in light of twentieth century interest in the problem of 'the normal and the pathological' (Canguilhem), and the broader question of how materialism relates to the biological world.

Tout ce qui est ne peut être ni contre nature ni hors de nature.
Diderot.[1]

... ces noces contre nature qui sont la vraie Nature.
Deleuze & Guattari.[2]

The early modern era or *âge classique* may have been a demystifying or 'naturalizing' era, but it was nonetheless fascinated with monsters. The situation only becomes more extreme as one moves into the eighteenth century and gets to Diderot, whose entire philosophy of nature is a philosophy of monsters – whose entire universe, indeed, is permeated by monsters. The Renaissance fascination gets 'naturalized' without lessening in its intensity: entries like "Centaures" or "Faune" in the *Encyclopédie* reduce fauns to the status of "wild men."[3]   It is only once we reach texts like Albrecht von Haller's "Jeux de la Nature et Monstres" and La Fosse's "Monstres. *Médecine Légale*" (both in the *Supplément à l'Encyclopédie*, dated 1777), that the frenzy of inquiry into 'what is a monster?' seems to have subsided: more sober-minded questions are now being asked, such as 'should the monster be able to inherit from his or her parents?' Of course, the 'legal' problem was not 'discovered' or 'invented' in the late eighteenth century, it did not appear out of thin air: baptism had long been a problem, as we can see in this blunt statement from Guido of Mont Rocher's *Manipulus Curatorum Officia Sacerdotus* of 1480: "but what if there is a single monster which has two bodies joined together: ought it to be baptized as one person or two?"[4] Obviously, the question hinges on whether the monster has one or two souls. The connection between baptism and legal rights is explicitly invoked by La Fosse in his article, which is concerned with "medical jurisprudence" (p. 956a). The Church is willing to baptize certain beings and not others; those who are baptized must thus be entitled to the privileges of the citizen (the full protection of the law, respect of testaments, etc.). It turns out that the criterion of rationality – by which the monster can be

---

[1] *Rêve de D'Alembert* (*D'Alembert's Dream*), in Diderot, *Œuvres*, vol. 1: *Philosophie*, ed. L. Versini (Paris: Laffont, coll. "Bouquins," 1994), p. 673. Unless otherwise indicated all works by Diderot will be quoted in this edition, indicated as V followed by page number.

[2] Gilles Deleuze & Félix Guattari, *Mille plateaux* (Paris: Minuit, 1980), p. 295.

[3] As noted by Patrick Graille, "Portrait scientifique et littéraire de l'hybride au siècle des Lumières," in A. Curran, R.P. Maccubbin & D.F. Morrill, eds., *Faces of Monstrosity in Eighteenth-Century Thought, Eighteenth Century Life* 21:2, special issue (May 1997), pp. 75, 85 n. 26.

[4] *Cit.* in J. Block Friedman, *The Monstrous Races in Medieval Art and Thought* (Cambridge, Mass.: Harvard University Press, 1981), p. 182, and in Arnold Davidson, "The Horror of Monsters," in J.J. Sheehan & M. Sosna, eds., *The Boundaries of Humanity. Humans, Animals, Machines* (Berkeley: University of California Press, 1991), p. 48.

certified to be an *animal rationale* – is the presence of the head. La Fosse thinks this is sufficient, since the seat of the soul should be in the head, and rejects the more severe criterion according to which a malformed body cannot house a soul.

Locke had already commented ironically on these unsettled debates concerning the definition of 'man': some say *animal rationale*, but then, consider the debates on whether or not to baptize an infant *based on its form* ("outward configuration"[5]), along with the case of the Abbot known as the "Abbé Malotru" because of his odd shape (*ibid.*). Locke's own definition is 'formal' in the sense of being non-substantialist: if the being can speak, it has rights.[6] La Fosse in 1777 is already quite comfortable with cultural relativism, declaring that we cannot really judge what a monster is, since we already differ from each other so widely, "from the Laplander to the Eskimo" (p. 956b), but also internally, as "the constitution of our members and our organs varies widely." He concludes that God's will should not be invoked in an ongoing scientific inquiry.

1

I would like to call attention to a peculiar feature of the materialist approach to monsters in this period, which I term the 'denial' of monsters. It amounts to a paradoxical drive towards self-extinction: the materialist philosopher is fascinated with monsters but ends up like the 'professional atheist' or the full-time debunker of the existence of UFOs,[7] devoting her life to the denial of an 'object' that does not exist.[8]

In the earlier understanding of the monster as *prodigium* ('wonder', 'marvel', or literally 'prodigy'), the monstrous birth was an 'omen' or 'portent', like a comet: a theologically or morally grounded sign of something to come – a coming misfortune, to be precise.[9] It has this symbolic status because it is *contra naturam*. Given this status as a being 'contrary to nature', the

---

[5] John Locke, *Essay Concerning Human Understanding*, ed. P. Nidditch (Oxford: Oxford University Press, 1975), III.vi.26, hereafter quoted directly by book, chapter and section number.

[6] *Ibid.*, III.xi.16; cf. Leibniz, *Nouveaux essais sur l'entendement humain* (Paris: Garnier-Flammarion, 1990), II.xxvii.9, p. 182 (on the speaking parrot), which Diderot will later summarize as "Speak and I shall baptize you!"

[7] I thank Bret J. Doyle for this example.

[8] Admittedly, not all early modern materialists were concerned with monsters; conversely, various non-materialist philosophers, such as Aristotle or Augustine, *were* concerned with them. What might be said is that anyone worried about the status of laws of nature – as manifest in the biological realm, in this case – would surely be interested in monsters; and most materialists felt strongly about Nature and its laws.

[9] Ambroise Paré declares this at the very beginning of *Des monstres et des prodiges* (1573; ed. J. Céard [Geneva: Droz, 1971], p. 3).

conceptual trajectory of the monster then branches out into two distinct directions, of which the first will be our primary concern: (i) the biological or physical monster as a challenge for philosophy of nature proper, and (ii) the 'moral monster', as found for instance in the writings of the Marquis de Sade, but already depicted by Diderot with the character of Rameau's Nephew – although of course the Nephew is precisely determined by his "cursed paternal molecules,"[10] that is, by natural causes, since from a materialist standpoint, there are no moral monsters: they are either to be naturalized and thus 'denied', or to be justified: "these creatures are neither good, nor beautiful, nor precious, nor created: they are the surface *foam*, the result of nature's blind laws."[11]   Curiously, even once the monster is 'naturalized' so that it is no longer *contra naturam*, it remains the source of a certain kind of reference. If we reflect on the old French proverb which relies on Latin roots, "le monstre est ce qui montre" ("the monster 'monstrates'," as in 'de*monstrates*', from *monstrare*, to show[12]), we can see that the initial sense of the expression is 'to point out or at something horrific', as in the tragic case of the Elephant Man.[13] And indeed in medieval French the parade of freaks as an attraction at fairs was called "la montre." But then the situation becomes reversed, and, to borrow Annie Ibrahim's phrase, it is the monster which *shows us* something about the order of Nature. In his preface to the *Histoire de l'Académie des Sciences*, in which the 'research results' of the Académie were presented, several decades at a time, Fontenelle discusses the large number of reports (*mémoires*) on mon-

---

[10] "Mon sang est le même que celui de mon père. La molécule paternelle était dure et obtuse; et cette maudite molécule première s'est assimilé tout le reste" (*Le neveu de Rameau*, in *Œuvres complètes*, eds. H. Dieckmann, J. Proust & J. Varloot [Paris: Hermann, 1975-], vol. 12, p. 172 – hereafter DPV followed by volume and page number).

[11] D.A.F. de Sade, *Histoire de Juliette*, in *Œuvres complètes* (Paris: Pauvert, 1967), vol. 9, pp. 170-171.

[12] The Latin verb *monstrare*, to show, derives from the noun *monstrum* (divine portent, prodigy, i.e. something deemed a pre-monition – whence our word 'monster' as well as monitor, admonish, monument, premonition, summon, mind, mania, etc.), which derives from the Latin verb *monere* (to remind, warn, advise), itself deriving from the Indo-European root *'men'* (to think, with derivatives referring to various qualities and states of mind and thought). Hence the idea of the monster as an omen portending the will of the gods, an extraordinary event that served as a divine 'premonition', a supernatural being or object (Professor Stephen Esposito of the Classics Department at Boston University kindly provided this information). For further details on the semantic history of 'monster' I refer to Beate Ochsner's essay in this volume.

[13] In such cases physical monstrosity is taken to be indicative of moral monstrosity, as in the case of Richard III (versus, say, Quasimodo, whose physical appearance is the opposite of his moral goodness); a more complex case is Thomas Middleton's play "The Changeling" (1622), in which the hunchback Deflores is not innately evil, but is instrumentalized by others to commit evil deeds, thanks to his outward appearance, ultimately turning him into an evil person (I thank Roger Savage for this reference).

sters that had been presented (notably on monstrous fetuses), and explains that for the sake of understanding the structure of the human body, not only animals but also monsters "must not be neglected," for "the mechanism that is hidden in one species or ordinary structure might develop in another species, or extraordinary structure"; it seems as if Nature, which is "constantly multiplying and varying its works," "cannot help but betray its secret, sometimes."[14] If the monster is there to show us something which might otherwise remain hidden, then it must exist! This rather Cartesian flourish is not enough, however, to produce a lasting effect; it would seem as if the monster exists 'for a while', in order to reveal an underlying order of Nature, but then vanishes, epochally speaking, after it has performed its function. Jaucourt's article "Prodige" in the *Encyclopédie* says that monsters used to frighten people; now they are there "for the amusement of the physicists" (the natural philosophers).

We might say that there are *three types of 'monstration'*. Fortunio Liceti undertook a first step of naturalization when he explained that it was wrong to proceed etymologically and explain (type 1) that monsters were *signs from God* – that in fact, their name comes from the fact that we *point at them*, we "show" them (type 2). I would suggest a third type, represented for instance by Francis Bacon's idea that "deviations" such as monstrous births are not an omen but rather an event which allows the naturalist to glimpse existing natural structures:

> Errors of nature . . . correct the erroneous impressions suggested to the understanding by ordinary phenomena, and reveal common forms. . . . For he that knows the ways of nature will more easily observe her deviations; and on the other hand, he that knows her deviations will more accurately describe her ways.[15]

Bacon's 'naturalization' culminates with Diderot, for whom monsters *show us* Nature itself. In fact, Jaucourt's comment itself still reflects a certain unique existence of the monster, as found in cabinets of curiosities and their scores of preserved, embalmed, or stuffed creatures; to be consistent, naturalization should entail that monsters fully cease to be a source of amusement.

Why should monsters continue to be interesting, then, if their 'normative' dimension has been 'emptied out', stripped away[16] or de-essentialized?

---

[14] *Histoire de l'Académie des Sciences* for 1699 (1718), Preface. See Anita Guerrini's essay in this volume for more discussion of passages like this one.

[15] *Novum Organum*, II, § 29, in *The Works of Francis Bacon*, ed. J. Spedding *et al.*, vol. 4 (London: Longmans, 1870), p. 169.

[16] As Annie Ibrahim puts it in "The Status of Anomalies in the Philosophy of Diderot"

First, because of the different kinds of reference which are at work. Monstrous births as 'portents' or 'omens' are direct causal reflections of maternal imagination. They are signs the way smoke is a sign of fire. Monstrous births as statistical anomalies,[17] or in more Diderotian fashion, as revelations of an essential monstrosity of Nature, are not signs in this way, since there is no causal connection, no strong signification. But they are not human-made signs either, like the word 'fire'. However, my concern is less with the status of monsters as signs,[18] and more with the materialist denial of any such status, which is closely related to the second reason that monsters remain interesting 'after' or 'within' naturalization: because the path of naturalization does not exactly produce a *science* of monsters.[19] It would be a curious science, after all, that demonstrated the non-existence of its object. To be sure, the stirrings of what will become the science of teratology in the nineteenth century can be detected in Réaumur's and Maupertuis' enthusiasm for 'hybridizations'[20], whether out of an interest in what kind of embryological *Bauplan* best survives, or in the transmission of genetic information. But, as Javier Moscoso points out in his detailed study of the debates on monstrous fetuses in the Académie des Sciences,

---

(this volume). This occurs in the *Letter on the Blind*, in which Diderot puts forth a complex, biologically motivated critique of any universal metaphysics or ethics, using the figure of the blind mathematician Saunderson to stress (a) the determination of our metaphysics and ethics by the 'state of our sense organs', and by extension (b) the ultimate relativity of all such judgments (V 147).

[17] It is only once such events are reduced to statistical anomalies that any 'strong' sense of monstrosity is ruled out, as in Darwin's statement that "monstrosities cannot be separated by any clear line of distinction from mere variations" (*On the Origin of Species*, facsimile of the 1st edition [Cambridge, Mass.: Harvard University Press, 1966], p. 8). Gilles Barroux suggests (personal communication) that it was the mathematician Jean-Jacques Dortous de Mairan who introduced the statistical approach to monstrous births (see the *Histoire de l'Académie des Sciences* [1743]).

[18] This topic is addressed in Beate Ochsner's essay in this volume.

[19] This marks a crucial difference between my perspective and that of Katharine Park and Lorraine Daston's *Wonders and the Order of Nature* (New York: Zone Books, 1998), which, in contrast to their earlier "Unnatural Conceptions: The Study of Monsters in 16th and 17th-Century France and England" (*Past and Present* 92 [1981]), asserts a form of what Max Weber called the "polytheism of values," since they reject any progressive narrative of naturalization as being "teleological" (*Wonders*, p. 176). In their view, the monster as omen and the monster as naturalized entity are 'equal', since scholarship cannot make value judgments about the one at the expense of the other. Religion and science are simply narratives. My concern is not to preserve the integrity of a preexisting history of science, or narrative of a "progrès de la conscience europénne" on a march towards rationality, but to show that the process of naturalization is a crucial component in building the fascinating paradox of monsters as a 'disappearing object' in Diderot's materialism.

[20] René-Antoine Ferchault de Réaumur, *L'art de faire éclore et d'élever en toute saison des oiseaux domestiques de toutes espèces*, 2 vols. (Paris: Imprimerie Royale, 1749); Pierre-Moreau de Maupertuis, *Vénus physique* (1752; Paris: Aubier-Montaigne, 1980).

if we consider the many hundreds of papers presented in the first half of the eighteenth century to such institutions, a strict definition of 'monster', whether intensional or extensional, is never given; thus there was never a 'science of monsters'; even the teratology of the Geoffroy Saint-Hilaire family in the nineteenth century was at most a science of 'major and minor deformities'.[21]

2

Our story, the materialist story, is not caught up in medieval or Renaissance debates on monsters; it can be said to begin with thinkers like Nicolas Malebranche, who are willing to allow for ordinary causal explanations of monstrous births, although the ultimate explanation lies in the 'maternal imagination', through a communication between the mother's brain and the child's brain. If the child bears a birthmark resembling, say, a pear, it is because the mother coveted a pear; if the child resembles a lobster, it is because the mother coveted, and perhaps was frightened by a lobster.[22] The monster is a sign of maternal sin, and thus a sign of divine will itself.[23] The 'fault' or 'flaw' lies in the mother's appetites, but the mechanism of transmission itself is not in question, since it is precisely the channel or instrument of God's will, it allows God's will to be done.[24] The imaginationist

---

[21] Javier Moscoso, "Monsters as Evidence. The Uses of the Abnormal Body During the Early Eighteenth Century," *Journal of the History of Biology* 31:3 (1998). Annie Ibrahim had made a similar point in her "Métaphysique et anatomie au XVIIIe siècle (la théorie des monstres accidentels dans les *Mémoires* de Louis Lémery à l'Académie des sciences)," *Recherches sur le XVIIe siècle* 8 (1986): no experimental solution was ever proposed which might have concluded the *querelle des monstres* (which I shall discuss below).

[22] Park and Daston, in *Wonders and the Order of Nature*, p. 197, quote a description in James Duplessis' *A Short History of Human Prodigious and Monstrous Births* (c. 1680; Sloane ms. 5246, British Museum), of a woman whose "Monstrous Birth was Caused by her Loosing her Longing, for a very Large Lobster which she had seen in Leadenhall Market for which she had been Asked an Exorbitant Price" (her husband later brought the lobster home for her and she fainted).

[23] Park and Daston, in "Unnatural Conceptions: The Study of Monsters in 16th and 17th-Century France and England," p. 25 & n. 13, refer to *De Civitate Dei*, XXI, 8, and the development of the idea in Isidore of Seville, *Etymologiae*, XI, 3.

[24] Nicolas Malebranche, *La Recherche de la Vérité*, II-1, iv and *Traité de la nature et de la grâce*, I, xviii, in *Œuvres*, ed. G. Rodis-Lewis, vols. 1, 2 (Paris: Gallimard-Pléiade, 1979) – actually an attack on Lucretianism. The argument moves from Descartes, following a Biblical tradition (the tale of Jacob and his spotted sheep, *Genesis* 30: 31-42), *via* Augustine (*De Trinitate* III, vii, §15); cf. Jacques Roger, *Les sciences de la vie dans la pensée française au XVIIIe siècle* (3^d edition, Paris: Albin Michel, 1993), pp. 63-88. Leibniz, too, allows for maternal imagination as an explanation (*Nouveaux essais*, III.vi.23, p. 246). The best response to the imaginationist position is Maupertuis' in his *Vénus physique*, pp. 116, 122f. (also found in Buffon's *Histoire des animaux* and the *Encyclopédie* article "Imagination – des femmes enceintes"): accusations based on marks

thesis is indeed an attempt at a causal explanation, since it seeks to improve on earlier claims about, e.g., women having intercourse with succubi,[25] but *it tells us nothing about monsters themselves*: it is precisely an account of maternal imagination.

These questions of origin, crystallizing into causal explanations, give rise to a great debate in the Paris Académie des Sciences, in which anatomical arguments are ultimately metaphysical arguments, or, differently put, in which metaphysics is summoned to the dissection tables (in Annie Ibrahim's vivid formulation): should monstrous births be explained in terms of final causes or accidental causes? The initial position was to reject accidents in favor of the system of "originarily monstrous eggs" ("œufs originairement monstrueux"). The anatomist Jacques-Benignus Winslow explained monstrous births by conditions already present in the egg, so that the monstrosity we experience is simply a sort of sketch which nature merely fills in. His position is consonant with preformationism, even though his 1733 classification of monsters considerably added to available information by its descriptions. The problem is, what about exceptions? Louis Lémery (a practicing physician at the Hôtel-Dieu who was elected to the Académie, first to a chair in botany and later in chemistry) seized on this weakness and attacked the system of 'originarily monstrous eggs' in his *Second mémoire sur les monstres* (1738), which instead invoked accidental causes such as uterine shocks or deformations, as an explanation. His other target was Joseph-Guichard Duverney's providentialist view that when we dissect monstrous fetuses such as Siamese twins, we nevertheless find evidence of *design*, that has simply been 'inverted' (cases of *situs inversus*) or 'doubled' (cases of excessive organs and the like). The empiricist critique of preformationism is also articulated in philosophy, by Locke: the fact that there are "frequent productions of monsters, in all the species of Animals, and of Changelings" (III.iii.18) means that Locke prefers an atomistic / corpuscular explanation of the generation of forms, since it leaves room for accident, as opposed to substantial forms and the like.

Albrecht von Haller discusses the *querelle des monstres* in his article "Jeux de la Nature & Monstres."[26] According to Haller, there are two systems dealing with the formation of monsters. The first and most ancient is also the dominant one. It is the explanation appealing to accidental causes, beginning with Democritus (the vision of 'atoms-and-chance' is the perennial culprit for all finalist, anti-materialist thinkers), and continuing

---

borne by the infant reflect the imagination of the beholder.

[25] Georges Canguilhem, "La monstruosité et le monstrueux," in *La connaissance de la vie* (Paris: Vrin, 2nd revised edition, 1980), p. 175.

[26] In *Supplément à l'Encyclopédie*, vol. III (Amsterdam: M.-M. Rey, 1777), pp. 551a-558b.

with Aristotle. In the contemporary context, Haller identifies this system with Lémery. The other system

> allows for accidental causes in the formation of a great number of monsters, but it recognizes others which appear to be 'above' the power of accidents; these can only stem from a primitive structure, different from the ordinary structure. This system does not go back earlier than M. Regis, but it has on its side Du Verney, Méry, Winslow, M. de Mairan, M. de Haller.[27]

Both Lémery and Duverney believe in the preexistence of germs, but Lémery does not want to hold God responsible for monstrous births: why would He have produced useless beings?[28] Thus he will explain 'fusions' ("soudures") such as Siamese twins, by the *shock* of two 'germs' or 'seeds' in the early stages of embryogenesis. One of the clearest statements of this explanation in terms of 'shock' comes from no less a figure than Shaftesbury:

> Much less let us account it strange, if either by outward shock, or by some interior wound from hostile matter, particular animals are deformed even in their first conception, when the disease invades the seats of generation, and seminal parts are injured and obstructed in their accurate labors. 'Tis then alone that monstrous shapes are seen.[29]

For religious reasons Haller cannot accept the explanation by accidental causes.[30] So he rejects Lémery's appeal to chance and overall 'accidentalism'; if there are indeed 'games of Nature', they are part of God's will. He does not want to decide what actually happens in the "apparent union of two embryos."[31] If something like the jaw is poorly formed, he is happy to allow for some degree of accident, but ultimately, "none of this could have been the effect of chance" (*ibid.*), or, less firmly, "some circumstances do not appear to be the effect of chance" (*ibid.*, p. 557b). La Fosse, in his article "Monstres. *Médecine Légale*," also summarizes the old quarrels, but conveys more of an 'Enlightenment' sensibility when he regrets that confusion as to the causes of monstrous births may have led some unfortunate mothers to being burned at the stake. In "Pyrrhonian" fashion (the article begins by stating "If Pyrrhonianism were ever useful in a question of physics, it would

---

[27] *Ibid.*, p. 556b.
[28] *Mémoires de l'Académie des Sciences* (1740), pp. 269-272.
[29] *The Moralists*, in *Characteristics* (New York: Bobbs-Merrill, 1964), II, p. 23.
[30] On Haller's unspoken convictions, see Jean-Louis Fischer, "L'*Encyclopédie* présente-t-elle une pré-science des monstres ?", *Recherches sur Diderot et l'Encyclopédie* 16 (avril 1994).
[31] Haller, "Jeux de la Nature et Monstres," p. 557a.

undoubtedly be that which treats the existence and origin of monsters"), he prefers not to take sides, between primitively formed, "preexistent monstrous germs," and the accidental explanation (shock). However, he allows that the latter explanation seems to be closer to everyday experience (p. 955b).

Diderot will take up this quarrel, emphasize its metaphysical dimensions, and of course accentuate the hazardous, accidental, random, chaotic dimension of the production of natural forms beyond anything the anatomists ever intended.[32] For the present purposes his 'transformist' vision, in which monsters are one moment among many, of the productions of the universe (some last longer than others, others are quickly "exterminated" by Nature[33]) can be found equally in the *Lettre sur les aveugles* (1749), *Le Rêve de D'Alembert* (circa 1769), and the late, unfinished *Éléments de physiologie* (1780s).[34] Diderot returns the question to its fully 'scandalous' dimensions, but appears to be caught in a dilemma, of simultaneously projecting the figure of monstrosity onto the entire universe and denying that we have any ability to legitimately call something 'monstrous': "If everything is in flux, as we have hardly any reason to doubt, then all beings are monstrous, that is, more or less incompatible with the subsequent order."[35]

3

This *denial* of a certain kind of unique existence of monstrosity first emerges, in two very different strategies, with Locke and Leibniz. Montaigne had indeed declared in the essay "D'un enfant monstrueux" (*Essais* II, 30) that monsters are nothing in the eyes of God,[36] but his intention was primarily to restrict the scope of our judgments about the world, without entering into explicitly 'realist' debates on *what there is* in the universe. The philosophical denial of monsters discussed here is intimately involved with a series of other claims about Nature – its laws, species, kinds and essences – but also humanity itself, considered from a materialist point of view. In order to go as

---

[32] On Diderot and monsters see Geoffrey N. Laidlaw, "Diderot's Teratology," *Diderot Studies* 4 (1963); Emita Hill, "Materialism and Monsters in the *Rêve de D'Alembert*" and David Funt, "On the Conception of the *Vicieux* in Diderot," both in *Diderot Studies* 10 (1968); the work of Annie Ibrahim, including her essay in this volume; most recently, Andrew Curran, *Sublime Disorder: Physical Monstrosity in Diderot's Universe* (Oxford: Voltaire Foundation, 2001).

[33] Diderot, *Éléments de physiologie*, V 1276.

[34] I have discussed the question of Diderot's transformism (or 'proto-evolutionism') in "La querelle du transformisme," presentation to the Groupe de recherches sur le *Rêve de D'Alembert*, École Normale Supérieure, Fontenay Saint-Cloud (April 2000), online at www.cerphi.net/did/seance6.htm

[35] *Observations on Hemsterhuis*, V 768.

[36] See Tristan Dagron's discussion of this text, in this volume.

far as Diderot does, beyond the strictly anatomical questions of the *querelle des monstres*, and also beyond the materialist *and reductionist* positions of thinkers like La Mettrie or d'Holbach, for whom "There can be no monsters, prodigies, marvels or miracles in Nature. What we call monsters are merely combinations with which our eyes are not familiar,"[37] he has to take Lockean and Leibnizian elements and radicalize them. In order to make this clearer, I shall briefly summarize the respective approaches of Locke and Leibniz towards monsters.

For Locke 'monster' can only be a *nominal essence*, not a *real essence*.[38] We have no way of *knowing* if the beings we call 'monsters' really are such. To use the current term of art, monsters are not "natural kinds." The problem comes out of that of *species*: again it is only a nominal essence, 'our way of dividing up the world'. A wolverine or a giant squid is a nominal essence (we decided to individuate them rather than calling them 'animals that live in or near Australia'). Essences are "the workmanship of the understanding" (III.iii.14). They are abstract ideas which rely on the subjective constitution of complexes of ideas (complex ideas). Thus even our own species, which is most familiar to us, still comprises areas of debate, e.g. whether "the foetus born of a woman were a man" (*ibid.*). The "frequent productions of monsters" (*ibid.*, § 18) imply two things for Locke: (i) that we should not speak so confidently about essences (whether monstrous or human), and (ii) that if there are essences, Nature might not successfully 'reach' the essence it 'intends' ("designs") in the "production of things" (*ibid.*, § 16). Essentialism holds Nature to a standard it cannot live up to. The frequency of 'accidents' in development reinforces Locke's preference for the corpuscularian hypothesis – which for present purposes is a modern form of atomism, fully compatible with chance (*ibid.*, § 18).

Monsters are not 'species'; if this seems like unnecessary caution, recall that Locke is reacting against the classificatory fervor of the centuries before him, which sought to distinguish 'good' or 'marvelous' monsters from 'bad' or 'ominous' ones. They are not, since they lack a unique "constitution" (III.vi.17): the viscerae, the skeleton, the organs are *there*, in a different arrangement. Monstrous births, "Changelings," "Drills," beings which are shaped like us but are hairy and "want speech"; beings – the existence of which is only rumoured – which are hairy, *have* speech ... and a hairy tail, are all Men – *or not* – only by virtue of our nominal decisions, that is, by the "workmanship of our understanding." Hairiness or rather the absence

---

[37] Paul-Henri Thiry, Baron d'Holbach, *Système de la nature*, ed. J. Boulad-Ayoub (1781; reprint, Paris: Fayard, 1990), Book I, ch. vi.

[38] *Essay*, III.iii.15-19. Real essences could be defined as: (a) things that necessarily are implied in our nominal essences; (b) what we actually have sensations of; things with powers in them to cause our sensations.

thereof does not make the man.[39] There would be *no debate* about whether a fetus is human or monstrous if these terms were real essences, but they are merely nominal. "Wherein . . . consists the precise and unmovable boundaries of . . . species? 'Tis plain, if we examine, there is *no such thing made by Nature*" (III.vi.27).[40]

For Leibniz, the principle of plenitude prevents us from speaking about monsters, in the strict sense, since monsters, like us, occupy a 'rung' in the great chain of being. All the beings that comprise the universe are, in God's mind, points on a simple curve.[41] Nature leaves no vacuum, and there necessarily are species which have never existed and never will, as they are not compatible with the succession of creatures that God has chosen.[42] Monsters, then, are 'intermediate beings' ("des bêtes qui tiennent le milieu," "des créatures mitoyennes"[43]) which ensure the *continuity* of the chain of beings. For example, the polyp is the being in between plants and insects. Who knows where the monster fits? Leibniz asks the question of baptism, too, and declares that theologians and all the other judges can only judge based on *form*. But when the being is an 'intermediate being', ordinary categories are suspended.

Our understanding of physical species is provisional, and proportionate to our knowledge.[44] As regards the variety of species which we experience, that is, the plurality of forms, precisely the fact that there seems to be an interplay between cats, lynx and the like (and moreover, a 'return' of certain traits after many generations of cross-breeding) implies that there might be an 'essence of cat' which recurs, without having to be present in every generation (*ibid.*). Against Linnaeus, species do not reflect the true order of Nature. Leibniz thus seizes on what one might call Locke's 'agnostic weakness' and asks: how do we know that Nature *does not* have real essences? "If we cannot judge internal resemblances by the external conformation, do they thereby exist any less in nature?"[45] Thinking back to the chain of being, one sees that monstrosity (like evil or suffering) is part of a broader 'canvas' which the human intellect cannot fully make out.

Contrary to Locke, and *against* Locke, Leibniz holds (i) that man is indeed an *animal rationale*, (ii) that there are real essences, and (iii) that

---

[39]Linnaeus will reiterate this in his catalogue of the animals of Sweden, the *Fauna suecica* (Leyden: C. & G.J. Wishoff, 1746).

[40]For more on Locke on species and related questions, see Justin E.H. Smith's essay "Degeneration and Hybridism in the Early Modern Species Debate," in this volume.

[41]Leibniz, letter to Herman, in *Appel au public par M. Koenig* (Leyden: Luzac, 1752), p. 44.

[42]Leibniz, *Nouveaux essais*, III.vi.12, p. 239.

[43]*Ibid.*, pp. 238, 239.

[44]*Ibid.*, § 23, p. 247.

[45]*Ibid.*, III.iii.14, p. 227.

we can know them. The fact that some men are not rational does not refute (i), but is merely evidence of some material obstruction ("empêchement"[46]); precisely, children "who are somehow monstrous" ("qui ont quelque chose de monstrueux") sometimes reach an age where they visibly are rational. Rationality is an essential attribute of man; hairiness or possessing a tail is not.[47] In sum, the existence of real essences and our ability to know them does not entail any validation of the category of 'monster'.

4

Diderot takes the Lockean point that species are merely nominal essences, and moves it one step further: (1) species are *fictions*, (2) boundaries between mineral, vegetable and animal kingdoms are also fictions (*D'Alembert's Dream* proposes in its first pages a thought-experiment involving a marble statue coming to life by progressive "animalisation" of its matter). Species are not essences, but rather temporally bound "tendencies towards a common end which is proper to them,"[48] comprised of whatever happens in between a *terminus a quo* and a *terminus ad quem*, a series of generations. "The monster is born and dies; the individual is exterminated in less than a hundred years. Why shouldn't nature exterminate the species, over a longer course of time?"[49] This is no longer a 'methodological' caution about how we cannot *know* if some being – slightly crustacean-like, or perhaps very hairy, or with an excrescence on its forehead resembling a monk's cowl – is a monster or a human. It is an *assertion* of monstrosity, with a strongly amoral consequence: there is no perfectibility of the universe, there is no progress; there is only a Lucretian chaos of beings produced randomly. As the blind mathematician Saunderson declares, sketching out a brief cosmogony in the *Letter on the Blind*,

> In the beginning, when matter in fermentation gave birth to the universe, my kin [*sc.* monsters – C.W.] were quite common. But why not apply to worlds themselves, what I believe about animals? How many crippled, failed worlds have disintegrated, reintegrated and are perhaps dissipating again at each moment, in distant spaces that I cannot touch, and where you cannot see, but where motion continues and will continue to combine heaps of matter, until they reach an arrangement in which they can persevere? (V 169)

---

[46] *Ibid.*, III.vi.14, p. 241.
[47] *Ibid.*, § 22, pp. 243, 244.
[48] Diderot, *D'Alembert's Dream*, V 637.
[49] *Elements of Physiology*, V 1276.

Order, or rather, the natural regularities which we experience and by means of which we assert the existence of laws of nature, is in fact only the "limits of our understanding," faced with the "infinite multitude of the phenomena of Nature."[50] This is Diderot's Lucretian re-reading of Leibniz's principle of plenitude and the chain of being: "the chain of being is not interrupted by the variety of forms," so that "There is nothing imperfect in nature, not even monsters. Everything is linked together (*tout y est enchaîné*) and the monster is as necessary an effect therein, as the most perfect animal."[51]

The chain of being becomes a conceptual basis for asserting the material unity of all natural beings; in other words, it is open to a monistic interpretation,[52] just as the monad, in Diderot's article "Leibnizianisme," is reinterpreted with reference to Hobbes as a living, sensing unit of matter.[53]

The 'chaosmos' of *D'Alembert's Dream* extends this rather structural and epistemological vision into an atomistic cosmogony (the book was originally entitled *Democritus' Dream*!), in which monsters play a key role. Not only is organic and material unity asserted, via the chain of being, but the dimension of the unknown is added. There is no guarantee that all anomalies have already occurred, so unknown forms can appear at any time. Nature in fact eliminates nothing, it "brings all that is possible, with time," or more strongly, "Time is nothing for Nature."[54] There is a sense here which harks back to Empedocles and Lucretius,[55] of the Earth gradually exhausting its

---

[50] *Thoughts on the Interpretation of Nature*, § 6, V 562.

[51] *Elements of Physiology*, V 1261; article "Imparfait," in *Encyclopédie de Diderot et d'Alembert*, 35 vols. (1751-1780; reprint, Stuttgart/Bad Cannstatt: Frommann-Holzboog, 1966), vol. 8, p. 584a.

[52] On a historical note, this is why Malesherbes, before he became an honorary member of the Académie des sciences in 1750, planned to publish a reaction to the first volumes of Buffon's *Histoire naturelle* (which prominently featured the chain of being), warning Buffon against the notion: the more one emphasized the minute nuances separating each species, the more one facilitated leaps, shifts, transformations, and ultimately the disappearance of boundaries between species. See Chrétien-Guillaume de Malesherbes, *Observations sur l'Histoire naturelle ... de Buffon et Daubenton* (Paris: Pougens, an VII [1798]), pp. 5-37, as quoted by Roger, *Les sciences de la vie*, pp. 687-688. (Voltaire, too, was opposed to the continuity of organic beings for this reason.)

[53] Or rather, as "l'atome réel de la nature" (DPV, vol. 7, p. 692).

[54] Diderot, *D'Alembert's Dream*, V 651, 615; cf. his 1761 text on the calculus of probabilities, in which he declares "Avec le temps, tout ce qui est possible dans la nature, est" (*Sur deux mémoires de D'Alembert*, § 1, observation, DPV, vol. 2, p. 351), itself recalling Buffon's "Tout ce qui peut être, est" (*Histoire naturelle*, "Discours sur la manière d'étudier et de traiter l'histoire naturelle").

[55] And also to a contemporary of Diderot's who was initially unknown to him, the French consul in Cairo, Benoît de Maillet, author of an odd work entitled *Telliamed ou de la diminution de la mer* (1748; trans. A. Carozzi, Urbana: University of Illinois Press, 1968) – a phantasmagoric vision of fish being accidentally stranded on the earth, and learning how to fly over a series of random attempts lasting one million years. The story is often mentioned as an 'anticipation' of evolutionary thought; however, Maillet

fertility, so that the 'normalcy' and stability of species we experience now is simply the result of this diminishment: in its younger years, the Earth produced new – and thus 'monstrous' – beings all the time).

This is why Diderot cannot be a 'Darwinian': not only is there no stability of species, but an additional, metaphysical claim is being made about monsters, as synonymous with the 'innovative', 'transformative' power of Nature, which is beyond the reach of the human intellect[56] – a vision totally at odds with an Aristotelian world in which monsters are just the occasional 'misfirings' of a fully ordered Nature.[57] Indeed, monsters are everywhere: "maybe man is simply the monster of woman, or woman the monster of man" (initially an observation about the symmetry of organs such as the testicles and the ovaries, but extended into a metaphysical posit by Diderot); in the *Letter on the Blind*, Saunderson delicately but firmly reminds the cleric Holmes, who is at his deathbed, that he is one of the "monstrous productions" that still occasionally appear; *D'Alembert's Dream* ends with a query by Mlle de Lespinasse on the origin of "that abominable taste," by which she means homosexuality. Overall, "man is merely a common effect, and the monster a rare effect; both are equally necessary and equally natural."[58]

The monster is used to relativize normalcy, but then there *is* no monster as such – so there can be no normalcy either. How could there be norms, if our morals are dependent on the state or configuration of our organs? In fact, there are still "more or less vigorous natures," or "constitutions," in a typology of characters according to their degree of organic sensitivity. This allows Diderot to maintain a thoroughgoing materialism while at the same

---

does not formulate any idea of species-transformation, because he holds that all species already existed in the sea, and simply generated analogs on earth.

[56] Is the monster something new in relation to norms of organic life? The norm would then be static and unchangeable. Actually, following Canguilhem's suggestion ("La monstruosité et le monstrueux," p. 172), the norm – the species that endures – is only an ephemeral and transitory regularity, a temporary barrier against processes of decomposition and transformation. One might say that only that which is 'teleologically correct', 'on track' can claim to be the actualization of the new. This is roughly Maupertuis' vision of species, and of normalcy: for any novelty ever to occur, a certain 'undercurrent' of monstrosity must be at work; from normalcy alone, no new species could emerge. See his *Dissertation philosophique à l'occasion du nègre blanc* (1744).

[57] Aristotle, *On the Generation of Animals*, IV.4, 770b9 and IV.3, 767b. In his essay "Monstrositäten in gelehrten Raümen" (in P. Lutz, T. Macho et al., eds., *Der [im-]perfekte Mensch* [Cologne/Weimar: Böhlau Verlag, 2003]), Michael Hagner presents Pliny as having a similarly anti-Aristotelian and 'productivist' vision of Nature.

[58] Respectively, *D'Alembert's Dream*, V 645; *Letter on the Blind*, V 168; *D'Alembert's Dream*, V 676, 636. Diderot (through the character of Dr Bordeu) answers Mlle de Lespinasse with a cultural explanation (for ancient Greece) and a natural explanation (the fear of venereal disease in contemporary Paris), effectively deflating once again any normative or substantive definition.

time recognizing the existence of statistically 'abnormal' human types such as "the artist" or "the genius," whose nervous system is literally intensified, more 'powerful' or composed of more numerous interconnexions than ours.[59] The idea of 'vigorous constitutions' is Diderot's concession to 'basement-level' explanations: everything reduces to *faisceaux*, and "the varieties of the *faisceau* in a species produce all possible monstrous varieties within that species."[60] Hence types such as the genius are nothing other than monsters: "it is in the eternal order of things that the monster known as 'the genius' is always infinitely rare."[61]

If, instead of fixed, stable forms with their corresponding norms and value judgments, there is only a universe in constant transformation – such that any species can turn out to be a 'monster' in the sense of a non-viable form with a limited life-span – and more or less 'vigorous' or 'sensitive' constitutions in the midst of these transformations, then normality and abnormality have indeed been reduced to merely statistical regularities or anomalies. The Leibnizian side of Diderot's argument lies in his frequent invocation of the infinite number of possible organic "developments." The Lockean side of his argument would be that our belief in our 'names of substances' implies a belief in the regularity of Nature which is itself unquestioned. Materialism as expressed here is somehow the fusion of these two (traditionally irreconcilable) lines of argument, augmented with a probabilistic, atomistic emphasis on the *aléatoire*.[62] It does not rest on the belief that Nature is fundamentally ordered and lawlike, or that we could ever know any such laws, if they existed. This is why Diderot emphasizes in his late writings on physiology that we only know the "forms" of things, which are merely "masks."[63]

5

If monstrosity has become a feature of Nature itself, then those who are accustomed to finding 'law and order' when they look at Nature will find, like the surgeon Georges Arnaud de Ronsil reacting to the case of hermaphrodites, that "ce n'est qu'à peine que l'on reconnaît la nature dans la nature meme."[64]

---

[59] *D'Alembert's Dream*, V 660.
[60] *Ibid.*, V 645.
[61] *Refutation of Helvétius*, V 788.
[62] On the theme of a 'random' or 'probabilistic' materialism, as presented in contemporary philosophy by Althusser in his late writings, see Jean-Claude Bourdin, "The Uncertain Materialism of Louis Althusser," in C. Wolfe, ed., *The Renewal of Materialism* (*Graduate Faculty Philosophy Journal* 22:1, special issue [2000]).
[63] *Elements of Physiology*, V 1317, 1261.
[64] *Les Hermaphrodites, mémoires de Chirurgie* (London: Nourse / Paris: Dessain, 1768), p. 246, cit. in Andrew Curran & Patrick Graille's introduction to Curran *et al.*, eds., *Faces of Monstrosity*, p. 8.

The nominalist, Lockean side of Diderot's approach to monsters leads him to go beyond the 'secularization' of their theological function as signs – as in Bacon and Fontenelle, for whom monsters, considered as exceptions or deviations, point to the order of Nature itself – and reject the idea of laws of nature itself. However, where Locke's position remained strictly *methodological*, without any 'ontologically realist' claims about the existence or non-existence of monsters, Diderot's Leibnizian, 'metaphysical' side, which is reinforced (or fueled) by biological speculation on generation overall, leads him to make such 'realist' claims; this also distinguishes him from the position of outright materialist denial of monsters in a deflationary sense, as for instance in d'Holbach. The further step Diderot takes is to empty out the concept of monster of any normative content. He does this both in the 'Lucretian' gesture we have seen in the *Letter on the Blind* and *D'Alembert's Dream*, in which empiricism and sensationism are extended into a kind of cosmogony, and, in the third and final dialogue of the latter work, by constructing a thought-experiment involving the *production* of monsters.

In the year of the French Revolution, the prolific commercial pornographer Rétif de la Bretonne published a novel entitled *Dom Bougre aux Etats Généraux*, which contains an extraordinary line that sums up the idea of teratological production, from chicken embryos in the nineteenth century to clones today. A farm boy has been caught committing a bestial act with a cow, and he responds angrily: "eh mais, je faisons un monstre pour la foire Saint-Germain"![65] Rétif's phrase is striking inasmuch it totally abandons any concern with an 'identity' of monsters and asserts their artificiality, equating them with *hybrids*, i.e. 'controlled monsters'. Similarly, in the last dialogue of *D'Alembert's Dream*, Diderot himself moves from Nature's capacity to produce monsters to *our own* capacity to do so: Mlle de Lespinasse imagines the production of a race of *chèvre-pieds*, faun-like men with goat's hooves, who could serve as the ideal 'footmen' and thereby release the lower classes from indentured servitude; Dr Bordeu responds, "je ne vous les garantis pas bien moraux" (V 675): no normativity indeed! This should lead us to ask: if there is no such thing as monsters, what is it that the teratologists – whether Réaumur, the Geoffroy Saint-Hilaires, or Camille Dareste in the later nineteenth century – are producing?

The paradox inherent in the 'materialist denial of monsters' has less to do, I suggest, with a 'primacy of the abnormal over the norm', than with a constitutive tension in materialist thought: if materialism is understood as a 'physicalism', the features of the organic disappear in a fully rational

---

[65] In *Œuvres érotiques de Rétif de la Bretonne* (Paris: Fayard, 1985), p. 554, quoted by P. Graille, *op. cit.*, p. 87, n. 41. The Foire Saint-Germain still exists today but, like Coney Island, has eliminated the 'freak show' component of its exhibitions.

and/or mechanical world, in which monsters could at best be defined in terms of probabilities; if it remains organic (in Diderot's sense, filled with *sensibilité, faisceaux* and the like), the materialist philosopher can retain a "beautiful Nature," in which artists and geniuses continue to exist. Put differently, if there is no such thing as a monstrous machine, to use Canguilhem's image,[66] then it would appear that monsters are so important to early modern materialism *because they reveal something about the biological world*.[67]

Acknowledgements

Some of this material has been presented at conferences at New College, Oxford University (April 2001), Princeton University's Society for 18th Century Studies (May 2001), and the University of Mannheim (May 2003). I am grateful for comments I received on those occasions.

---

[66] "Il n'y a pas de machine monstre" (Canguilhem, "Machine et organisme," in *La connaissance de la vie, op. cit.*, p. 118).

[67] What the specificity of the biological might be (its temporal character? Its type of regularity, perhaps distinct from physical regularity?), cannot be addressed here. I can only emphasize in historical terms, that early modern materialism, at least in the form represented by Diderot (but also Buffon, La Mettrie, Maupertuis, etc.), is a 'biologism'.

Cerebral Assymetry, Monstrosities and Hegel. On the Situation of the Life Sciences in 1800

MICHAEL HAGNER

ABSTRACT. In this paper I will juxtapose three different intellectual approaches found around 1800: (i) debates concerning monstrosity, (ii) theories of cerebral asymmetry, and (iii) the positions of the German idealist philosopher G.W.F. Hegel. The underlying argument for this unusual arrangement is that the understanding of the organism in the life sciences underwent a fundamental shift in the late eighteenth and early nineteenth centuries. Whereas before that period, symmetry in the formation of the body was regarded as a crucial factor in the proper order of nature, and asymmetry was regarded as pathological, after 1800, however, asymmetry at least in some bodily systems was regarded as a normal phenomenon that could be explained in terms of organic development. Teratology and brain anatomy are two fields in which this shift becomes obvious; Hegel, on his part, developed very similar ideas regarding balance and imbalance, in his theory of the development of the human mind.

> Es ist diesem Strome des Lebens gleichgültig,
> welcher Art die Mühlen sind, die er treibt.[1]

How can we best characterize the difference between parts of a house (e.g., stones or wooden beams) and parts of a human body (e.g., a hand or the liver)? According to Hegel, who addressed this question in his *Lectures on Aesthetics*, stones and beams can be characterized as "erratic" entities. Stones "remain the same, regardless of whether or not they form parts of a house; they remain indifferent to any community with other things." Stones are self-sufficient and retain their particular individuality independently of whether they form parts of a whole. It is an entirely different case, however, with the component-parts of an organism; component-parts of an organism

---

[1] Georg Wilhelm Hegel, *Phänomenologie des Geistes*, in *Werke in 20 Bänden*, eds. E. Moldenhauer and K.M. Michel, vol. 3 (Frankfurt: Suhrkamp, 1982), p. 211.

are comparable to social entities, incapable of independent self-definition. Such entities are not indifferent to the whole or "the animated unity." On the contrary, the "animate unity is the substance . . . in and through which they [*parts*] may retain their particular individuality." An isolated body-part does not possess an enduring reality:

> An amputated hand, for example, loses its independent constitution; it no longer remains what it once was in the organism . . .; indeed, an amputated hand quickly decays and loses its entire existence. A hand exists only as part of an organism and has reality only as continually taken back into the ideal unity.[2]

The hand is for itself nothing, even when its function is individual and different from all other parts of the body. Yet, the permanent transformation of its particular functional condition is distinct from its permanent recuperation into a "general ideality" that constitutes the animation of individual body-parts and elevates these parts into "the ideality of a subjective unity." Hegel perceives in this continual "positing and dissolution of the contradiction between ideal unity and real separation of parts" the reality of a "constant process of life." In Hegel's words, "Life is only process."[3]

In the history of science, the claim that Hegel brought into focus a problem that was at the forefront of efforts to establish biological science around 1800 by ascribing priority to the dynamic of life over that of substance is far from novel. Since the classic works of Michel Foucault and Wolf Lepenies, concepts such as "processualization," "temporalization," and "dynamization" have entered into the stock vocabulary for those who seek to understand the momentous changes in the life sciences at the threshold of modernity.[4]

For example, one may consider the concept of biology formulated by the naturalist Gottfried Reinhold Treviranus, whom Hegel often cites. Treviranus opens the first volume of his *Biologie* with a sharp critique of established practice in zoology and botany. Are these disciplines, he asks, anything more than "the dry registers of names, mixed with incoherent experiences and ordered according to systems, which are not, as should be, a means towards something, but an end in itself?"[5] In contrast to the eighteenth century, in which the majority of systematic thinkers assumed that

---

[2] Hegel, *Vorlesungen über die Ästhetik* 1, in *op. cit.*, vol. 13 (Frankfurt: Surhkamp, 1981), pp. 163-164.

[3] *Ibid.*, p. 162.

[4] Michel Foucault, *The Order of Things*, trans. Alan Sheridan (New York: Pantheon, 1994); Wolf Lepenies, *Das Ende der Naturgeschichte* (Munich: C. Hanser, 1976).

[5] Gottfried Reinhold Treviranus, *Biologie oder Philosophie der lebenden Natur für Naturforscher und Ärzte*, vol. 1(Göttingen: J. F. Röwer, 1802), p. 7.

a systematic classification and description of all parts of nature would lead to a general understanding of the natural world, Treviranus argues that in order for the necessity of systems to become apparent, "observation of the behaviors of animals and plants" must be unified into a whole "in which the mind may recognize unity and harmony."[6]

Treviranus is not concerned with a particular species of life, but with life itself: its various manifestations and forms, as well as its conditions and causes are the subject of biology. In a comparable manner to Erasmus Darwin's efforts years earlier, Treviranus attempted to define the dynamic of life in terms of movement. Treviranus did not understand movement as a physical process of attraction and repulsion, but rather as a specific event through which the uniformity or order of appearances is retained. "The uniformity of appearances among non-uniform influences of the external world defines the different characters of life."[7]

Against the backdrop of these preliminary comments, an urgent question emerges, if one does not want to remain at the abstract level of meta-science: What does such a science of life look like? What kinds of techniques and praxis does it possess? Which objects and phenomena become test cases for its novel approach? To what extent are these objects and phenomena infused with new epistemic significance, and in which spaces of knowledge. In which material or symbolic representations, does "life" become transformed into a fruitful field of research? When the "self-activity of force" is established as a reference point, physiological-dynamic investigations attain a priority over static, anatomical-analytic observations.

"Processuality," dynamic, and activity—at first glance, it would appear that the age of physiological experiments had arrived by means of which bodily functional systems could be studied. In France, this occured to a certain extent, for example, if one thinks of François Magendie. In Germany (in contrast to vivisection at the beginning of the nineteenth century) one notices a marked tendency among natural scientists to espouse epistemological prejudices (at times hand in hand with moral arguments) against the cogency of experiments. But other methodological approaches that largely evolved from anatomy were not uncontested. For example, Johann Friedrich Meckel, a major reformer of anatomy, placed great weight on pathological anatomy and the study of anomalies, because from such studies "generally valid laws for the animal form" could be derived.[8] Even if it is clear that pathology as a determination of quantitative deviation from a norm became

---
[6] *Ibid.*, p. 8.
[7] *Ibid.*, p. 38.
[8] Johann Friedrich Meckel, *System der vergleichenden Anatomie*, 5 vols. in 6 (Halle : Renger, 1821), vol. 1, p. IX.

the pivotal point for medical sciences in the nineteenth century, critical objections were nonetheless repeatedly formulated. For example, Treviranus considered it an ideal situation that clinical observations of patients (cases in which a fortuitous death could benefit doctors with a natural scientific bent) could be supplemented through pathological anatomy; but precisely here resides also a problem, since the manifestation of symptoms often did not correlate with post-mortem findings. For the exact arrangement of function, localization and symptom, it was especially troublesome that similar anatomical lesions often revealed entirely different clinical symptoms.

Even this single example demonstrates that biology (or the science of life) was confronted with a dilemma. With experimental physiology and pathological anatomy burdened with such fundamental problems, how could the investigation of dynamic and "processuality" become realized in practical terms of research? If the comparability of different methods of research was so problematic, how could one arrive at a unitary and coherent body of knowledge? Of course, comparative anatomy existed, not to mention the microscopic investigation of the structure and texture of tissue and, most importantly, embryology—yet in this field, only restricted questions could be posed and answered. In addition, it was often the case that the combination of research fields led to unexplainable and hitherto contradictory results.

Was the demand of turning towards life more program than praxis, more philosophy than physiology? If so, one is led to the judgment that has long remained entrenched in the historical assessment of the study of nature around 1800. In the following comments, I would like to sketch two case studies in order to show that the situation was not entirely so and advocate an extrapolation of development and dynamic from an objective perspective. Accordingly, I shall focus on two topics: the asymmetry of the brain and monsters or "monstrosities." I want to demonstrate with both examples how a theoretical concern for "processuality" paved the way for entirely new evaluations and reflections, the relevance of which should not to be repudiated, especially today.

1 Cerebral Asymmetry

Until the early nineteenth century, the asymmetry of form (*Gestalt*) or the pairing of intrinsic body parts or organs was considered a morbid deviation or as *contra naturam*. Regularity and naturalness were expressed in the symmetry of forms (*Bildungen*). Yet, symmetry in animate nature was not always easily established or geometrically determinable, as was the case in inorganic nature. The pleasing appearance of a well-proportioned, symmetrical form (*Form*) sufficed to guarantee the regularity and order of nature.

Such was also the situation with the brain. Since Descartes, both halves of the brain had been widely regarded as identical. As an important consequence of this view, the organ of the soul (as a "medium uniens") could not be found in either half of the brain. Accordingly, one had to argue for "unpaired" inherent structure as the place for the organ of the soul—for Descartes it was the epiphysis, whereas later physiologists looked to the corpus callosum or the brain stem. Even Franz Gall accepted the symmetry of the brain and proposed that 28 or 32 different brain-organs existed in two copies. Gall argued for his view by noting that an injury to one side of the brain was compensated by the activity of a complementary organ on the other side.[9] In this framework, the acceptance of asymmetry between both sides of the brain was theoretically not conceivable.

Around 1800, the dogma of symmetry began to weaken in the life sciences. To be sure, it was not the case that symmetry would now have been seen as atypical; however asymmetry was normalized to a certain extent and accepted as a principle of nature. Xavier Bichat forcefully advocated this view in his *Recherches physiologiques sur la vie et la mort*, especially with his distinction between "animal" and "organic" life. According to Bichat, animal life regulates the relations between an individual and the external world, as mediated through body-limits, sense and muscular systems; in these cases, the principle of symmetry dominated. Both halves of the body were capable of functioning independently, and in cases of illness, one side could compensate for the other.[10]

By contrast, the organic or inner life regulated the cycles of the organism, for example, the intake and expulsion of matter, respiration and excretion. In this system, asymmetry reigned, since organs such as the heart, the liver, and the digestive-system already existed in the body and were not symmetrically formed. Even if organs possessed a double structure (for example, lungs and kidneys), they were not strictly speaking symmetrical; their different, advanced development did not have an influence on the total system. Bichat pushed the comparison between both systems even further: animal functions became fatigued, whereas organic functions did not; animal functions enabled higher forms of development reaching up to culture and civilization among human beings. These functions exist in a rudimentary form in babies; they develop over time, whereas organic systems are fully developed from the beginning.[11]

Bichat's view of the brain as the main organ of animal life and his consid-

---

[9] Franz Joseph Gall, *Sur les fonctions du cerveau et sur celles de chacune de ses parties*, 6 vols. (Paris, 1822-1825), vol. 2, pp. 248-252.

[10] Xavier Bichat, *Recherches physiologiques sur la vie et la mort* [1800] (Geneva/Paris: Alliance Culturelle du Livre, 1962), pp. 49-50.

[11] *Ibid.*, pp. 57-69.

eration of the brain as strictly symmetrical is important for our discussion.[12] However, Bichat was not alone. As we noted above, Gall espoused a similar view, and even Meckel adopted in a large work on asymmetry a remarkably indecisive position concerning the brain. On the one hand, he relied on earlier anatomical observations of Félix Vicq d'Azyr and the Wenzel brothers that emphasized the asymmetry of both sides of the brain in human beings. He stressed in particular, "that the human brain is in this regard [i.e. the convolutions, M.H.] ordered in a more asymmetrical manner than the animal brain."[13] Meckel did not infer, however, any functionally relevant consequences. This lacuna between form and function can be explained given that the compensation thesis (one side of the brain compensating for the other) could not easily be united with the idea of asymmetry. In this instance, we have an example of the methodological dilemma noted above, namely, that an observation from pathology that could not be made coherent with an observation from comparative anatomy. Indeed, only through a flagrant ignorance of this incompatibility was it possible to propose cerebral asymmetry as a criteria for the higher development of human beings vis-à-vis animals.

In this regard, Karl Friedrich Burdach's attempt to connect the structural asymmetry of both sides of the brain with functional differences is especially significant. It was not accidental that asymmetry was the criteria of difference for convolutions, which Burdach considered "in an intimate connection . . . with the understanding and the imagination"[14] – in other words, those qualities that characterized human beings:

> For monkeys and the majority of predatory and clawed animals, they are entirely symmetrical; this symmetry decreases for animals capable of chewing, animals with hoofs, and thick skins, as well as for the bear and the badger, and even more so for the seal and the dolphin; convolutions are mostly asymmetrical with human beings; in this case, the symmetrical main features are rendered unapparent by numerous convolutions.[15]

Burdach did not go as far as other brain scientists during the second half of the nineteenth century, who placed reason, volition, intelligence and humanity on the left side of the brain, and instinct, emotion, hysteria, and

---

[12] *Ibid.*, p. 50.

[13] Johann Friedrich Meckel, *Ueber die seitliche Asymmetrie im thierischen Körper*, in *Anatomisch-physiologische Beobachtungen und Untersuchungen* (Halle: Renger, 1823), pp. 147-334, 243; see also p. 155.

[14] Karl Friedrich Burdach, *Vom Baue und Leben des Gehirns*, 3 vols. (Leipzig: Dyk, 1819-1826), vol. 3, p. 350.

[15] *Ibid.*, p. 363.

insanity on the right side.[16] On the contrary, Burdach thought that "the right side of the brain is more developed than the left."[17] However, it is decisive that in the natural-philosophical milieu around 1800, a parameter such as the asymmetry of the brain was brought into conjunction with representations of mental life; in other words, with psychological and anthropological categories such as reason/emotion, savage/civilized, masculinity/feminity, conscious/unconscious life.[18]

As a consequence of this novel perspective regarding the connection between the brain and mind (*Geist*), coherence, order and the unity of thinking no longer corresponded to structural cerebral simplicity; rather, these features corresponded to greater complexity and differences. In this fashion, for the first time, a novel qualitative parameter was added to the aspect of quantity (the size and weight of the brain), which had been brought into play by physical anthropology in the eighteenth century. Of course, discussions of brain development in terms of size and weight did not become obsolete during the nineteenth century. On the contrary, these quantitative aspects were further developed.[19] Nevertheless, another and equally significant parameter of complexity was introduced, beginning in the early nineteenth century, with the functional interpretation of the asymmetry of both sides of the brain.

The introduction of novel functional or dynamic parameters, closely related to the substance of the organism far exceeded brain and psychophysiology. To a significant extent, this shift allowed for a new coordination of models and manners of explanation in the human sciences. This point is exemplified in Hegel.

In his *Enzyklopädie der philosophischen Wissenschaften*, Hegel attaches to the end of his extensive paraphrase of Bichat's presentation of the distinction between organic and animal life an astonishing reflection that extended "processuality" and asymmetry beyond biological dynamics to human life itself. As if Hegel were himself an experienced observer, he offers the diagnosis that even "the uniform doubled-entity is not perfectly uniform." In the use of hands, eyes and ears, and even with sideburns, subtle differences are manifest that are not natural, but which can be explained through

---

[16]Anne Harrington, *Medicine, Mind, and the Double-Brain* (Princeton: Princeton University Press, 1987), p. 100.

[17]Burdach, *op. cit.*, p. 364.

[18]The difference between front and back is another parameter that I cannot address here. See Michael Hagner, *Homo cerebralis. Der Wandel vom Seelenorgan zum Gehirn* (Berlin: Berlin Verlag, 1997), pp. 217-219.

[19]See Michael Hagner, "Kluge Köpfe und geniale Gehirne. Zur Anthropologie des Wissenschaftlers im 19. Jahrhundert," in J. Schlumbohm, H.E. Bödeker, P. Reill, eds., *Wissenschaft als kulturelle Praxis, 1750-1900* (Göttingen:Vandenhoeck und Ruprecht, 1999), pp. 299-333.

"occupation, habit, activity, and spirituality (*Geistigkeit*)."[20] The point of these considerations is that Hegel takes the small, yet significant step from the principle of asymmetry to a principled "inequality." If asymmetry represents higher biological development, inequality represents higher mental (*geistige*) development. Whereas the "mere bodily exercises, such as physical exercise, gymnastics, running, climbing, moving on a narrow path, jumping and vaulting exercises" are expressions of balance, other higher mental activities such as "writing, music, the fine arts, technical craftsmanship, and fencing" are different, since balance is here not an issue.[21] To be sure, a hierarchy of opposites is thereby assumed, but not, as was commonplace since the eighteenth century, between the hand and the head or between senses and spirit (*Geist*), but rather between dynamic principles, whose formulation and application obtained equally in the life-sciences as well as for the description of human beings.

2 Monstrosities

Hegel's reflections on non-uniformity enter into a neighboring domain that, at first glance, seems far removed: representations of nature and the evolution of monstrosities. It goes without saying that one cannot speak of monstrosities as a higher development of the organism, yet classifying monstrosities within the epigenetic evolutionary process had two consequences. First, the origin of life is made into a less determined event. Second, monstrosities are seen as an explainable phenomenon within biology in contrast to the classification system within natural history into which monstrosities never really found a place.

Whereas the eighteenth century concerned itself with the question of whether monsters were determined by a mechanical lesion in the womb or already formed in the seed, and thus existing in the divine act of creation as imperfect forms, Caspar Friedrich Wolff developed a new perspective with his epigenetic theory of the emergence of life.[22] On the basis of his comparative microscopic investigation of plants and animals, Wolff established certain correlations during development; the individual parts of the body emerged from unorganized matter, from so-called small vesicles; organs developed in succession and to some extent in a separate manner.[23]

---

[20] Hegel, *Enzyklopädie der philosophischen Wissenschaften II*, in *op. cit.*, vol. 9 (1983), p. 458.

[21] *Ibid.*, p. 459.

[22] See Patrick Tort, *L'ordre et les monstres* (Paris: Le Sycomore, 1980); Michael Hagner, "Enlightened Monsters," in W. Clark, J. Golinksi and S. Schaffer, ed.s, *Science in the Age of Enlightenment* (Chicago: University of Chicago Press, 1999), pp. 175-217.

[23] Casper Friedrich Wolff, *Theoria generationis* (Halle: Hendelianis, 1759). See also Shirley A. Roe, *Matter, Life and Generation. Eighteenth-century embryology and the*

The emergence of living beings is no longer seen as a divine act of creation or as the unfolding of a preformed being or entity; instead the emergence of life exhibits succession, and thus temporality. Wolff gave the name of "vis essentialis" to the single principle largely responsible for these structural changes. Only with the introduction of this force, which enabled a transformation into a fully developed form, is a framework established in which it becomes meaningful to speak of life as an effective activity. Whereas previously, in preformation theory, the preformed homunculi were thought to have expanded like a hot air balloon, generation is now conceived as a dynamical process.

It is well known that in the late eighteenth century Johann Friedrich Blumenbach's version of an epigenetic account of the development of life, along with his idea of a "formative drive" (*Bildungstrieb*), triumphed over Wolff's version. Differences existed between both versions, yet Wolff and Blumenbach both agreed that the study of monstrosities through epigenesis did not only offer a new perspective, but could contribute to the establishment of epigenesis. For his part, during the last years of his life, Wolff worked almost exclusively on the issue of monstrosities and hoped that his life's work would end with a *Theoria monstrorum* that would complement his *Theoria generationis*. Wolff never completed his envisioned work, yet he did come to see monstrosities as a definite stage of embryonic development.[24] For Wolff, monstrosities were no longer, as was widely perceived, entirely other and incommensurable with the order of life, but rather could be arranged within the process of development.

This transformation is especially clear in conceptual shifts, which, as far as I can see, was restricted to the German language. In the late eighteenth century people spoke less of freak births (*Mißgeburten*), monsters and monstrosities, but rather of deformation (*Mißbildung*), with a marked emphasis on "formation" (*-bildung*). Thus, Georg Friedrich Jäger considered the word "deformation" (*Miss-Bildung*) an "objective concept" that "flowed from the philosophical spirit of our language. What is thereby meant is deviation from a normal form as an error in the formation of its effective cause, which produced the deformed, appearing organism during its formation."[25] In a footnote, Jäger remarks that Greek and Latin and those languages derived from both do not possess "an expression that refers

---

Haller-Wolff debate (Cambridge: Cambridge University Press, 1981).

[24] An extensive bundle of papers with the title *Obiecta meditationum pro theoria monstrorum*, on which Wolff worked until his death, is available in a Latin-Russian edition, edited by T.A. Lukina (Lennigrad, 1973).

[25] Georg Friedrich Jäger, *Ueber die Missbildungen der Gewächse, ein Beytrag zur Geschichte und Theorie der Missentwicklungen organischer Körper* (Stuttgart: Metzler, 1814), p. 3.

to the essence of the matter." The essence of the matter was however not an entity given a priori but rather "an error in the act of development." By the same token, "processuality," and not the product as such, was the true object of interest; hence, Jäger considered the expression "deformity" (*Miß-Gebilde*) unacceptable.

The compelling force of the word –bildung is also present in Meckel, who made Wolff's principle, namely, that deformations (*Mißbildungen*) represented a certain stage in embryonic development, into a basic principle of teratology. Meckel argued that development was arrested at a determinate stage in the embryo by an "inhibition formation" (*Hemmungsbildung*), which accounted for the majority of deviations; in these cases, either the development of the embryo was arrested or developed in a different direction.[26] These deviations could be explained in terms of a deficiency in the activity of shaping force (*bildenden Kraft*). Friedrich Tiedemann deduced the important and fatal consequence that such deviations "[are] a regression into the animal formation and therefore that every deformed birth is more or less an animal, if not externally, nevertheless internally."[27] With this temporalizing process of individual development and simultaneous misconnection with the developmental trajectory of animals, monstrosities became an effective instrument of the new embryology: they represented the correct manifestations at the incorrect time and therefore represented an in-between stage on the way from animal to human beings that followed a determined regularity. The development of form was subjugated to transformations; yet the diversity of nature was based on a few simple basic forms. Such a view was also accepted by those who were not of the view that a human being in its embryonic development did not really progress through different animal stages, and who were rather of the opinion that different groups of animals (e.g., fish and mammals) but also human beings developed from similar morphological conditions but proceeded according to invariant lawfulness. Accordingly, it was not acceptable to say that a human being progressed through the stages of, for example, amphibians and fish, yet the similarities of development were discernable in cases of arrested development.

Deviations of formation therefore belonged to the canon of the life sciences since its beginning. But there were other aspects in this conception of evolution of great significance from a moral perspective. From the standpoint of anatomy, every type of malformation was regarded as unnatural,

---

[26] Johann Friedrich Meckel, *Beyträge zur vergleichenden Anatomie*, Vol. II-1 (Leipzig: C.H. Reclam, 1809), p. 159.

[27] Friedrich Tiedemann, *Zoologie. Zu seinen Vorlesungen entworfen. Allgemeine Zoologie, Mensch und Säugethiere*, Vol. 1 (Landshut : Weberschen / Heidelberg : Mohr und Zimmer, 1808), p. 178.

and even Tiedemann's talk of "regression into animal forms" led to dangerous generalizations and stigmas in the nineteenth and twentieth-centuries. The polarization of natural and unnatural, normality and abnormality provided a variable and frequently applied parameter for the politics of differences, which played on raw emotions and abused a language of rationality. That history developed in this direction and not in another did not have to be so; in the years around 1800 other options were in play, as demonstrated by Carl Friedrich Kielmeyer and his explicit refutation of the difference between natural and unnatural. For Kielmeyer, what is natural is what "follows from the condition of things themselves. Such is also the case for deformed births; one should not speak of such phenomena as 'unnatural' but rather as exceptional, unfamiliar."[28] What is decisive is that a living animal demonstrates itself to be capable of living under different conditions.

Considered from the standpoint of the dynamic of life, deformation was an exceptional and infrequent phenomenon that could be placed in early stages of evolution, yet a process of adaptation existed between deformed body parts and the organism as a whole. It was precisely this leveling between deformed parts and the organism that was considered as positive or teleological or purposeful or as a self-regulating principle of living force or the formative drive. In other words, even in the unfavorable condition of external deformation, the formative force was present by which to bring about an entire organism. Treviranus illustrated what he termed in 1805 "the pliability of the organism" with the example of the deformed births of two brothers who grew together in the uterus and could move all four of their limbs. "One must admit," Treviranus wrote, "that even misshapen works of nature are more sublime that works of man, much as the highest ideal of art is superior to the wood carvings and paintings of playing children."[29]

The pliability of the organism is nothing other than the ideal unity of the organism and the real separateness of its parts. Hegel failed to mention in his lectures on aesthetics that this idea of unity is nowhere more apparent than in cases of deformation. Treviranus' placement of the work of nature over works of art (one could also say: handcraft and artistically skilled knowledge) may not have entered into the registers of aesthetics. From an ethical perspective, this principle has lost nothing of its force.

translated from the German by Nicolas de Warren

---

[28] Carl Friedrich von Kielmeyer, *Das Wissen von der Natur*, in *Gesammelte Schriften* (Berlin: Keiper, 1938), pp. 211-234; p. 216.

[29] Treviranus, *Biologie oder Philosophie der lebenden Natur*, vol. 3 (Göttingen: Röwer, 1805), p. 454.

The Lady Knight of the Perilous Place
ELFRIEDE JELINEK

ABSTRACT. In this essay I consider the figure of Ripley, the character played by Sigourney Weaver in the "Alien" film series, in a threefold sense: (i) in terms of her status as woman, (ii) as she relates to the monsters against which she struggles, and (iii) as a 'body' under industrial capitalism – in a comparison between "Metropolis," "Alien" and their political subtexts.

In *Harper's Bazaar* I see a woman, 1.80 meters tall, apparently without any make-up on, with a determined face and a marked underbite, whose determination emphasizes, if anything, that she is all but naked under a see-through, ice-blue miniskirt by Versace. The legs are more muscular than we commonly think of a model's as being, but this woman is no such thing. She is a famous film actress named Sigourney Weaver, and one year ago (it is the October 1996 issue) she sold her flesh, which had already had quite a bit of exposure in the "Alien" films, yet again. Her flesh seems to have recuperated since the last time. On the next page she wears a similarly see-through, but full-length dress by Dolce and Gabbana, patterned with tiger stripes. In the interview that is printed with it the woman speaks about sex, on the occasion of a theatre piece that seems to have this as its theme, and in which she plays the leading role. In the "Alien" films sex plays no role. Instead, Sigourney does.

It is amazing in how many places one comes across people and recognizes them *just* from their faces. These are occasionally the faces of people we actually cherish, particularly when they belong to film actors whom we would recognize wherever they might turn up, if not, perhaps, at the local bar, since these are certainly not the sort of people one just bumps into. They are permanently removed from us and yet, in the newspapers, they seem almost as if they could be touched, even if they could never be tamed. Generally speaking, this happens because the imaginary space on the silver screen, even if it shows everyday, genre scenes, is always separated from the space of daily life. It incites the spectators to reach for it, but the invisible, unjust equation has no solution; it is as if one were dipping one's hand into water that perpetually parts itself as the hand approaches. Even though the space in which we live, while it is defined very precisely by natural science, is no firmer or more secure (including the point where we abide), similarly, we cannot attribute a greater density or concentration to the events on a movie screen (which are the only firm and secure thing about a film), as a result of what is happening in the film. It rushes past, leaving us unable to say what is happening. Is film a war of worlds between the real and the unreal, which in turn must be real for us (indeed, the more real the better)? And the more improbable the unreality of the film is (naturally, in sci-fi films, which leave our planet behind and encompass all of outer space, we have the most improbable scenarios of all), the more the directors take pains to make what is shown on the screen appear particularly real. Possibly, they do this so that it will be that much easier to establish relationships between what is shown, on the one hand, and our own reality on the other.

Perhaps the instinctive fear, indeed terror, that we normally feel during scenes in films of battles with sundry monsters (and the "Alien" films follow the ancient schema of man-against-monster, that is, against the non-human), is rooted in the suspicion that behind the space in which these battles are played out (though we know that there in fact is no such space), there could be another one, and behind this another, and so on – spaces that threaten to suck us in, and in which nothing happens that has any relationship to real space. And so we already have the world of the spectator and that of the illuminated screen, on which things 'appear' to us, spaces, which exist in complete separation from one another. And then there is what happens on the screen: that in turn would be another continuum, one that no longer permits of definition, since the characteristics of the space in which we live do not apply to it, even if many things about it appear familiar. That we are being made afraid by what is going on up there on the screen would be the simplest explanation.

But perhaps it is quite different, and what we distinguish as the void or as space are part of one and the same mechanism: the original naturalness of these spaces, and of those spaces that in sci-fi films must be conquered, could long ago have been tamed by means of hard work and industriousness, and the cause of all of this may just have been: a Company that has it all in its hands and that wants to domesticate and dominate the spaces by means of its colonists, its freight and commercial vessels, as well as those it has sent, of various ranks, from the lady commandant down to the androids, who of course were manufactured and programmed by the rulers of The Company. But for what? In the first place, in order to exploit them.

The US-American novelist Thomas Pynchon (*the* author of paranoid global conspiracy, who could have come up with the "Alien" films and may in fact have done so), with a precision like few others before him, spoke of the naturalness of great commercial ventures (everything is connected, any one thing is connected with any other, and the connection is itself the paranoid conspiracy, as well as the one thing that would be worse than being a part of the conspiracy: not to be a part of it). In *Gravity's Rainbow* what is at issue is the creator of the cartellized state, the subsequently murdered German foreign minister and son of the founder of AEG, the first great electric company, Walter Rathenau, who, by connecting the horizontal and vertical structures for which he was the spokesman and architect (in any case, as a social utopian, he was as it were the 'good' father of his employees, while in contrast, at least in the Weimar Republic, Alfred Hugenberg, who himself in the most literal sense of the word owned public opinion, the press, the film studios, and thus the people as well, may perhaps be pegged as the 'evil' ruler), is ultimately at the same time also the one who sets off The Universal Paranoia. In the modern post-war state (by which I mean not just both World Wars, but *all* wars that come after, which, even if they are partially fought, are always diffused by commerce, as the freight shippers in "Alien" for their part show), no political group could emerge any longer as victorious, but instead a rational structure, in which commerce represents the true and appropriate authority – a structure that, not surprisingly, would be based on what Rathenau and (with more far-reaching consequences) Hugenberg established in Germany.

From this it follows, that behind every power there must be another, and to its conquests correspond, in concretized form, all the spaces, behind which other spaces are always already waiting. There is The Company, a faceless kraken, an organization, which knows more than all the rest, because it controls everything, and The Company also knows the horrible structure behind all the conquests, behind all the facades of multisidedness, market economy, colonialization, dread and retribution. And perhaps The Company itself constructed the alien, or alternatively used a genetic culture. Either way it is the same: either to test humans on it or to test it on humans. Perhaps The Company already possesses everything that it purports to test and exploit, and only wishes to dispose of humans and androids economically, like I.G. Farben, the cartel that set up shop in Auschwitz, clearly against common sense and real production interests, for the purpose of destruction as opposed to labor and production, as Hannah Arendt demonstrated. No boundaries are set for paranoia, for otherwise there would be no paranoia. And what people have made and can make becomes ever more like what they cannot make other than in conception and birth: nature, or at least its imitation. From carbon arise organic bonds, from these the benzene ring (an image of our own beauty), and so things begin. In the meantime, the cartel itself becomes organic, it cannot be otherwise but like nature, and the one constant in the "Alien" films is the heroine, Ripley, Sigourney Weaver: she is the one constant, which always stays the same, does not shift but once, for she travels through time in such away that for her it does not pass; all the others change, even the daughter changes and dies eventually as an old woman (cut from the commercial version). Yet, as in an entropic process, one can perceive a paradoxical movement in the opposite direction, namely, the more Sigourney works, the more she plans and directs (now with The Company, now against it. Is she The Company? Is The Company her? Does she know at all about the scheming of the cartel? Is she a part of it?), the more the uninhabitedness grows, the more frequently the participants perish (little Newt, who in part 2 was still alive and who was lovingly put to bed, at the beginning of part 3 is simply dead as the result of a crash-landing. Good riddance!), and the deeper everything seems to sink into the sleep of death, and most of all Sigourney herself who seems to grow ever more resigned, rigid, as if made of stone, even though she is at the center of all of this. And to the cartel, which pulls all the strings (even hers), corresponds a film company, which she herself may perhaps have forgotten, though perhaps not. This film company produces ever more "Alien" films, as if by nature, films that simply cannot come to an end. Why not? Is it because they have long since taken on a life of their own? Because they can still make money? The latter answer seems almost to be too banal.

In the end it is only in sci-fi films that it is possible to show all this, for it is only in these films that the depicted spaces (each for its part itself multidimensional), simultaneously possess the greatest reality as well as the greatest unreality, and no other film genre is able to evoke the spaces, the Conspiracy That Lies Behind, in a manner that is so plastic down to the smallest details. This Behind must of course reveal from itself alone what rules pertain to it: these are rules that some people or other have established, that do not wish to be named even if they may be shown. They bear no similarity to donators who wish to remain anonymous. We spectators, in any case, do not have the privilege of sharing in the experiences that Sigourney Weaver must go through in the "Alien" films. She experiences everything for us, we wouldn't even want to experience what she does in a dream, as they say. But we are happy to watch, even if we do so while hiding our faces behind our hands and peeking between our fingers. What we are actually able to see there, though, the total power that has long enchanted us, is shown to us as possible insofar as, in these films, *everything* is possible, only so that we might forget that death is transformed into more death, so that we might hide this principle under a great deal of technology and special effects. However, so long as we do not try to decipher the rules in their imaginary space behind the screen, we will also be unable to break the code of what this actress is doing on the screen. And yet this is only the beginning. We will never know, even if we penetrate into the innermost depths of her molecules. It is only logical that in part four the heroine Ripley is entirely rebuilt from molecules and DNA, and herself does not know who or what she is, monster or human.

A second, external component is that Ripley often has a hard time doing anything at all amidst all these planetary ruins and all this garbage that entropy has already scattered about, behind all the causes and effects that here at home we call 'history' – though in history it unfolds in the Behind, indeed, behind the spaces that are accessible to us. For in these films the screen is for the most part very full, as if it had had glued to it a wildly patterned – as well as living! – wallpaper from which the heroine and her co-actors, the little Newt, Bishop, the android – who at first is nothing other than a highly developed (highly 'cultivated'!) robot, but in the course of the action of the films becomes ever more human, until he is the most human of all, human and machine at once, a creating creature, for now we see for the first time that the android has had, all along, the face of its master! (here it is already a completely other space in which the master has taken on the face and the interiority of its creation, perhaps since in the process he has perished?) – and the warriors, women and men both (all apparently belonging to the same, androgynous, muscular gender, with the exception of the child, who is the one clearly feminine character and is meant to appear so – a reversal of the legend of the 'sexless' child) are only able to flounder chaotically. They are constrained to run about like savages, to sweat, to throw flames, shoot, toil, in order to somehow liberate the screen and thereby to clear a way for themselves. It is different, by the way, in part 3, "in the penal colony," for there the protagonists have no weapons at all, other than the most primitive ones that were already available in the Stone Age. Very nearly completely nude (stripped to the bone) and sheared of all hair (which naturally pushes androgyny to its limit), they must use their bodies themselves as weapons, thus very literally giving themselves as security deposits.

To make room on the screen means that what is already there, what is already 'put on celluloid', is able to appear in order to show us our place in the In-Front-Of. To clear and to fill up the space on the screen means, from the point of view of the actors, to drive out a many-armed, amorphous monster, a monster that is simply everywhere. And even if the monster does not seem to be home, the tension naturally arises from the fact that it is there. But are they going to find it? (well, the musical score, at least, will be of help here). A tentacled, horrible creature, melting upon itself even before it is in fact burned (the fate of witches of old!), a horrible embryo over which Ripley, still plunged in the inferno with which she will save the world while at the same time annihilating her 'child', bends, almost as if moved by care – the absolute parody of the Virgin Mary and the little child Jesus. The monster, even if it jerks about like lightning and appears cut into pieces – probably so that we will remain unable to examine too closely the made, built, tinkered aspect of the thing; thus we get only a piece of the tail, one, two seconds of a head, etc. – becomes a moving background pattern, since it is able to be 'everywhere' and indeed is everywhere. From this background the star Sigourney, the leader, and her co-actors, must make their way in this 'everywhere' in order to be able in the end to give us some decent movie acting. The art of film, like any other art in which something arises, in which something is 'made', sets a work in motion that displaces everything in its way; sometimes this work can be called truth. In any case it consists in paths and spaces that are carved out from unmoved space.

It is to these tentacles of the monster, of the alien-stranger, that the painted corridors of the worker-city Metropolis correspond, built as models and quickened through the trickery of mirrors, a city in which above and below, ruler and worker, are strictly separated, and the son of the ruler is the connection between the two spheres, the wanderer who bridges the gap. The futuristic lines of transport traverse the frame of the film like living, gripping arms, and at some point the workers (Ernst Jünger first published *Der Arbeiter* in 1932, though it seems to me he must also have been influenced by this film) fill the space entirely, like flowing streams of water; living people fill in, as it were like putty, all of the space between the traffic arteries and the means of transport, into a whole from which nothing more may be removed. Indeed, formally the streets become people who – perhaps out of fear of the void, and out of fear that, behind the void there is another void that is much more comprehensive – are sucked into this vacuum and then become the substance of the film's space, its negative, something other than what any film 'naturally' has and ought to have (no positive without the negative!). Movement arises through an intricate but fundamentally simple choreography of the protagonists, and above all of the actress Brigitte Helm, who in fact appears in a double role: that of (the holy virgin – yet another one!) Maria, and that of the evil robot, created by a human, who bears Maria's traits but who, underneath, consists entirely in shimmering metal, and who drives the masses to revolution, a revolution that consists only in the desire to destroy themselves, their homes, and their children. That is the negative of the revolution that was nonetheless thought as positive. This is not something negative into which the revolution collapses, but a negative that is 'in accord with nature', as in the film. But at any rate in "Metropolis" the ruler and The Company can still be seen, just as one was still able to know the Rathenaus and the demonic Hugenbergs, while in the "Alien" films the Cartel no longer shows itself, only its representatives do. The catastrophe of the Metropolis is prevented at the last minute by the holy virgin and by the sympathizing son of the industrialist, who in the end is someone who poses the Parsifalian "question of compassion" (the connection between hand and body, thus between handwork and headwork, 'the heart', and without this nothing can succeed, as Fritz Lang says – least of all breathing, as I say): is revolt, should it occur, 'natural'? In any case, as we have in the meantime learned from real space, it ended badly. Well then.

The enemy either comes from without, which is the harmless variant, or from within, in which case things get interesting (soon we will see that "Metropolis," like "Alien," is a hybrid, and draws its fascination not least from this), for this inside is not simply the inside of a human, not simply his evil or good drives and plans. Rather, to this inside there corresponds a wholly different space than the one that can be seen. In the "Alien" films the monster comes simultaneously from without as well as from within, for it is almost always perceived first as a monster when, slavering, spitting, snarling, triumphing, it emerges from the host body that it has inhabited like an evil spirit, popping out like a jack-in-the-box. Yet it also has to get in there first. How does Fritz Lang solve the problem of showing his artificial person, who comes from without as well as from within, who is something made as well as something that "lives unbeknownst among others" and is perceived as a foreign species, his robot, who bears the traits of the girl Maria, now as a human and now as a demon that entices into ruin? The witch Maria, the personification of evil itself, thus (it is important to mention that Maria and Maria-as-demoness are not only identical and of course played by one and the same actress, but that they are also in fact interchangeable, one *is* the other, since evil – and here this may also be proved – in the end always comes from within, and only the other Maria, the evil one, can suggest to us this second space, a place that has left the predetermined place and created one of its own in order to unfold itself there, without any barriers; for evil tolerates no limitations, in contrast to the good, which 'means something' in the sense of signifying, which is to say it acts towards ends), sits on the shoulder of a revolting worker, the masses push their way along behind her, filling up the surface of projection, as if they had been sprayed on there just like water. And Maria-the-Devil, waving her hands with a mad and at the same time transported smile upon her face (Brigitte Helm, who has more of an oval-shaped, or, perhaps better, a heart-shaped face, was made up for this scene, in the fashion of the time, with artificial rings under the eyes, the sign of decadence and of nights spent drinking, which does not cease to produce an uncanny effect, like a living skull, straightforwardly duplicated forty years later, though with a somewhat darker colour, in Herk Harvey's "carnival of souls"!), turns, and with her of course her "Untermann," on whose shoulders she sits with legs spread and who in fact makes her spin at break-neck speed, 'over-revved' in the truest sense of the word, in a circle. (When she sacrifices herself, Ripley/Weaver sinks into the flames along with her monster/child, slowly rotating around her axis in a resigned giving of herself, hovering in a single skeptical gesture of her entire body.)

Beyond the space of the film, by means of an aggressive gyroscopic motion, a segment is as it were formally bored out, a hole emerges amidst the crowd, and through this hole, which was produced by a person, by means of motion, this other space, the one behind, is able to push forward, setting loose the viewer's true horror. This space behind bores into the viewer and formally tears him out of the seat in the movie theatre. And the more the screen fills with human material (the workers, as is characteristic for them, almost always appear *en masse*, threatening, faceless, amorphous. In this sense, they are the source of such a danger. At the same time, however, they are a raw material, one cannot distinguish between them, they are actually garbage, rubbish, there are just too many of them) and is again cleared out, the more the masses seem to have been sent onto the screen only in order that they might be wiped out once and for all so that we might have more space to live and breath. The screen was thus filled to the brim, but the water is then drained so that we might remain (Metropolis indeed really does threaten to be flooded! But the real flood is that of the people themselves).

Are we thus the true lords of the screen? Did we liberate it so that we might, as in a sacral act, have a place to live rendered to us, a place that is intact, where one might live undisturbed by foreign elements (even though these elements are among us... no, they *are* us! Not in the romantic sense, that we are all foreigners on this earth or something like that, but much more comprehensively: that ultimately everyone must believe in the totality, even if originally destruction only pertained to isolated groups). A few years after "Metropolis" they would all be shouting "Heil!".

Considered more superficially, we witness in the "Alien" films on the contrary a regression back to a state short of Fritz Lang's aesthetic possibilities (naturally this does not concern his technical possibilities): the abstraction of the cinematic artist Lang is, in the "Alien" films, as in a children's film, re-concretized and appears... as what then? Of course! it appears as a many-armed monster, as a sort of hydra, as material and at the same time as materialized. In "Metropolis," the people bear a proletarian character, which is to say no character at all, on their evidently unchanging mass-faces, faces that say nothing. And those to whom individuality is allowed, above all the son of the ruler and of course the ruler himself, rise far above this, not just by means of their clothing and the close-ups of their faces. At any rate, these are rulers who can still be depicted, and who lead us to suspect no others pulling the strings behind them. At the dawn of the cartellized state, power had as yet no need to cover its tracks, since 'under normal conditions' none think to rival it. The proletarian character of the figures in "Metropolis" is so strong that it must hide itself behind these non-faces (the faces probably emerged only at the moment when labor was inserted into their features, as books onto shelves), and the faces blur and vanish, and, in contrast to the rulers and to Maria, who is elevated among the women, they are no longer perceptible as individual and individualized. It is first in the 'Revolution', which in fact is not one at all, that individual workers' faces, by means of close-ups, first emerge from the mass. May we conclude from this that the worker becomes human only in the revolution, since blind will grabs hold of the individual? (It exists in order to revolt. It is not permitted to revolt.) No, we may not.

This process has its parallel in the "Alien" films. Here, the 'workers' (in this case, the colonists and the space warriors), standing in opposition to the alien and to its ever-expanding brood (!) (the individuals in "Metropolis" exhibit a similar naturalness, as if they were there for the culling and thus also destined for extinction, and indeed in Germany people would soon be culled as a consequence of their Jewish nature!), disappear before the background of their terrible 'work', the many-armed hydra, the kraken that they cannot annihilate, that they *must* not annihilate, lest the sequels come to a halt, though this is still only *one* reason (and what are the interests of The Company here?). The conversion of the 'proletarian character' of the masses, or of the warrior class – in the third part we see that the 'primitive' members of the penal colony, mostly rapists, flesh that has pounced on flesh, but that, through battle against the beast is now manifestly that of a warrior, may be ennobled – in the "Alien" films into a purely martial character continues to bear in both films an artisanal character, when we consider how silently and relentlessly annihilation has long since been able to occur, and indeed has occurred. Do the "Alien" films indicate a sort of artistic regression in comparison with "Metropolis"? Can the interpretation be sustained according to which a transition has taken place, from the purely human construction, 'The City', to a complex that is recognized as something made and that signals the uninterrupted power of a technology that involves, on the other hand, no concept of making, but rather one of knowing? And indeed, is this a transition to an organic construction that may be called 'The Monster'? And at the same time a spiritual, dynamic abstraction, a planning of the life-space taken over by humans – a space that on the one hand attempts to seize them but which on the other hand first enables them to appear as they are, paradoxically, precisely because it seems to eliminate the humans who live there and thereby first frees up the space! – is carried over into nature, into a being, half animal, half plant, that first comes from a sort of pod (a beloved image in science fiction) so to speak into nature of the fist degree. Naturalness of the second degree, in turn, that of the inhabitants of the Metropolis, emphasized to such an extent that they are able to disappear, would be a nature that is attained through human labour, literally carved out of them. And their product, the gigantic machine in the megacity-machine (thus a machine within a machine), Moloch in the film, may be seen, pushes its way into our attention as that which towers above everything else. Technology, ordinarily the most important thing in science-fiction films, in the "Alien" films retreats behind the evidently 'pure nature' of the monster and willingly makes room for it, until, as I said, this nature has overgrown and covered the screen. I attempted to show at the beginning of this text how deceptive naturalness is, that it is probably even a more refined form of that which is made, since we do not even know whether the alien was produced by The Company or whether The Company is not *itself* in fact the alien. Put another way: while "Metropolis" emphasizes the tension between nature and civilisation, to the extent that humans must ultimately take hold of that which they have made and thereby triumph (all the sentimental stuff that accompanies this need not concern us here), in the "Alien" films naturalness becomes the very pinnacle of that which is made, produced, which can only mean that something was inserted into the world, previously not appearing as present, as shown, and this is perhaps because these films by now have all technology at their disposal, and thus are able to depict visions of the future in which the actors have access to technologies that have not even been invented. Nature is depicted as triumphing, over technology too.

Superficially, this is how things look. I have tried to show that this is not in fact how they are. A being, extraterrestrial but still clearly living, certainly still seems to triumph over sophisticated weaponry and thus over men, for it is immanent to these films that they must go ever farther, since otherwise that would be the end of them. But this being is itself probably only technology (and in the film this is technology in the truest sense of the word), and the rulers of technology, who 'know what's what' in the sense that they are conscious of what there is to be conscious of, and know what there is to know, have their reasons for not trusting indomitable nature, and for preferring to make nature themselves, and indeed from and with what is available today, from and with what they are capable of today, and from and with what they, in consequence, will be ever more capable of in the future.

In one of her best scenes in "Alien 2," Sigourney Weaver, in order to save the little girl Newt, must as it were expand herself, as a living person, by means of a machine. She climbs into a sort of enormous steel excavator in order to enlarge her person, to construct a machine around herself that on the one hand will protect her, and that on the other hand will drive the monster away from her. When she puts her body in the machine and projects her robotic arms toward the monster, she is untouchable. The hydra cannot come near her, while the claws of steel are able to grip and crush the hydra. But at bottom Ripley's attempt to literally take technology into hand and to seize nature through recourse to the uncritical affirmation of technology as something inevitable, corresponds to a current conception of technology as instrumentality, and it thus gives the impression of a step backwards in comparison with that space that is dominated by the rulers in "Metropolis" (and by their 'instruments', the workers), and that in its own way has even planetary dimensions, encompassing everything outside of it that we detect within it: the outer space of outer space! The planets themselves must send their people to the alien, into the 'colonies', an almost rural idyll, for toward this end, even if horrible and attractive things happen there, small and manageable branches must be constructed, doubles of the earth, in order to concretely accommodate the events. Metropolis, in contrast, is everywhere. In leaving it behind, one can conquer the planets and enable any construction to become a reality, including the woman as robot, the woman as indistinguishable from the robot. (Only the voice of love, the son of the ruler, can distinguish between them. Amidst all this technology, they experience a regression into archaic times and archaic beliefs, a regression that drives the masses to burn the 'witch'. But she only laughs, for she is not human and thus cannot die, which of course she knows. In an interesting parallel to the witch-burning in "Metropolis," in which in truth it is an artificial construct that is burnt, Sigourney Weaver, who embodies what is positive in a witch, who is thus the good – white – woman who is to save the world from the horror that 'is growing within her body', plunges into the fire, but for a fraction of a second is herself the mother of this horror!). And with the help of this same technology modern man, mass man, whose revolutions will be thwarted again and again but who will nevertheless never be killed off, since there are just too many of him, will take over the world. A film such as "Metropolis" brings this technology clearly into view, in that the creation of the robot is a quasi-medical act of creation, and not a technical one, when Brigitte Helm's face is projected onto the robot, as in a Mickey Mouse cartoon the soul of an angry pig is projected over that of a happy one, and vice versa, by the ingenious Daniel Düsentrieb, and in this way helmet and wires are shared by the two, nothing is soldered, welded, or cut. If we look first with innocent eyes, eyes that The Company has not yet caught, that, as said, nobody has yet seen, the situation may appear on the other hand perfectly simple, just as it is from the point of view of the worker: simply, he must work in order to live. By contrast, the fighters against strange beings, against aliens (and for the 'aliens' the strange colonists are of course in turn aliens), have set up their medical station here, and there they've placed their android, who has been sent by the Cartel and grows ever more human (also a hint that nature can be the ultimate transformation of technology and that, through nature, The Company leads the people to believe that they are only dealing with something very refined: the android as the very most human human), and over there the sleeping cabins; and behind all this, without anyone having pasted it up (or did someone?) there is again this wallpaper, this original but also ultimately somewhat plain background effect, this extraterrestrial continuation, that is in fact the essence of the film. But of course the heroine must be even more essential, Sigourney, who, almost resignedly, fights against the monster at the end in an act of colonization that goes well every time but that suggests that next time it's probably not going to work out (the third sequel, we really believe, will finally be it). And thus we are led to believe anew every time that these colonisable spaces are only there so that people possessed of decisiveness, an upright chin (un-made-up women in film!) love for children, and a nice, thankfully slim and long-legged figure in sensible wool underwear, wearing them just like I do (here, quite simply, the plain little cotton dress worn by Maria in "Metropolis" is overcoded), in order to settle in this new and beautiful colony ripe for exploitation (for in the end, make-up or no, the goal of all of this is exploitation), to insert themselves in the place of those who were there before. And this whole bric-a-brac, all of these constructions of monsters in the manner of a Swiss clockmaker and all of these simulations of life have as their result that a terror that is more dense and profound does not arise in the spectator, since demise is always also triumph (of the heroine). The organicity of technology (a monster that is put together by means of technology) and the mechanicity of men (the robotic workers), this opposition still arises, and signifies that men remain a cut below their spaces, below all space. Thus they must first liberate themselves from these spaces with their organic and technological constructions ("Raum im Osten schaffen,"[1] this was already once the terrible consequence, that an inhabited area was cleared out so that other inhabitants, who nonetheless apparently inhabit differently, and of course more nobly, might move in and replace them). The clearing of spaces does not however mean that there could not be other, more dangerous ones behind them, with which we are threatened, and which, since they can no longer be cleared, since they cannot be entered, and ultimately in consequence cannot be named, cannot even be shown. And that is where The Cartel itself resides. We must stay outside (inside?). The colonists, like the penal colonists in part 3, struggle to destroy the monster. They are covered with sweat, they are pure effort personified, as if they themselves were things that, again through struggle, have been brought forth by others. Yet struggle on its own does not suffice, it is in itself no achievement. It seems to me that all the efforts in these films only serve to re-conceive individual beings from an amorphous, flailing mass of people. But woe unto them if they are then set loose! At the end of "Metropolis," Frieder and Maria fall into each other's arms and yield an instance of coupledom. Sigourney too gets out alive even if, at the end of part 3, she is quite crushed, or indeed burnt though at this point we see nothing. She can however evidently be reconstructed, though what will come of her would seem to be a new genus, a new species, half person, half function, or indeed the function will have literally passed through her into flesh and blood. Is this a step backwards to part 3, in which flesh and flesh were made to stand over against one another, as it were naked and sexless, and even little Newt is now but a clump of flesh dissected under the gaze of a Ripley touched to the marrow? Who or what awaits this completely new species in part 4, this freshly arrived species? Again, as always: domination. For what is empty may also be taken over, for what is chaotic may also come to know the severity of law. But this law will then hold for all, since what is not yet present may yet come someday. It may even be the eternal that will come upon the temporal. When this happens, things will have to be worthy of the eternal, and they will issue from us, even if no one has entrusted them to us, and even if it were the case that we simply dwelled here and could not put up with it.

As if intuiting this, the director reconstitutes Sigourney Weaver with the help of her DNA formula in what is for now the final part, the fourth (I haven't seen it yet), since he has slowly used up all the technological possibilities and ideas (and in part 3 already is forced to reach back to 'natural' ones). This is similar to the evil Maria, to the robot in "Metropolis," since Sigourney/Ripley is burnt, and is thus dead without a trace, and now seems uncertain whether the DNA-mass of the alien that she, Ripley, has killed,

---

[1] ["To create some space in the East."—Trans.]

or that she has killed in and with herself, has not also insinuated itself into her genes. That will be interesting, since now the enemy is explicitly, without any doubt, without any ambivalence, within oneself, but again we don't know this with precision. Or perhaps one is one's own enemy. Why yes, of course! The fact that the heroine no longer knows herself whether she is human or not is in any case a new twist, in that she is now negative as well as positive, she must remain 'outside', like all heroes, ultimately. Yet another symptom speaks to this: the actress complains in an interview that in part 3 a short sequence, some three minutes, was cut from the film, a sequence that shows what it is that really makes Sigourney Weaver/Ripley tick: to wit, her daughter, and that this sequence, left out in order to stay within the prescribed length of time (the sequence is there in the director's cut on video), would have toppled everything, would have changed the whole story ("If you bust your gut trying to play a character and they take away your *raison d'être*, it's such a slap in the face." In the same interview Weaver also relates that she herself became pregnant, that she wanted to have a child because she got on so well with the actress who played little Newt! If that is not a case of art and life becoming one...!). The question is: was this biographical detail cut from Ripley's life perhaps in order to dodge her humanity? In order to make her into something-other-than-human, which she will manifestly be in the final episode? It would probably be paranoia to believe this. We will learn of Sigourney Weaver that she will again wear transparent clothing and stiletto heels and will look as if she did this every day, indeed because she in fact does do this quite often. I do not know how Brigitte Helm dressed in private. Both are spaces behind spaces, but spaces that we are permitted gently to see.

Translated from the German by Justin E.H. Smith and Michael M. Seifried

Acknowledgements

This piece originally appeared in *Meteor* 11 (Vienna, 1997). It can be seen (in the original German) with illustrations at: http://www.a-e-m-gmbh.com/wessely/falien.htm

Monster: More than a Word. From Portent to Anomaly, the Extraordinary Career of Monsters

BEATE OCHSNER

ABSTRACT. This essay tries to retrace the discursive history of the term 'monster' from ancient times to the invention of teratology at the beginning of the nineteenth century. Even though most of the meanings of the word 'monster' still exist in today's modern languages, a merely etymological approach would not be able to show the different discursive implications, semantic derivations or, in a more 'monstrous' sense, deviations. In order to draw a more efficient and distinctive tableau of these varied applications, I propose to retrace the astonishing career of the monster by turning the spotlight on selected exemplary (pre-scientific and scientific) periods and texts — one might also say interfaces — in which the monster and the 'monstrous discourses' bear witness to religious, scientific and / or cultural change.

Monstrare — to show; *monere* — to warn; *miraculum* — miracle; p*ortentum* — portent; *ostentum* — marvel; *prodigium* — prodigy; *lusus naturæ* — freak of nature; *monstrum* – symbol of the gods; *Monstrositäten* – monstrosities; . . . *teras* — sign, portent, horror; congenital anomalies; abnormality.[1]

As the above epigraph shows, etymological studies, which are generally assumed to shed light on the historical derivation and development of words, may in fact present a manifold and rather disorganized variety of lexemes as well as different syntactic and semantic uses. Starting with the Greek word TERATOLOGIA meaning an extraordinary story of untrue, fantastic and fictitious content, recounted by a TERATOLOGOS, narrator of unreliable

---

[1] Volker Oldenburg, *Der Mensch und das Monströse. Zu Vorstellungsbildern in Anthropologie und Medizin in Darwins Umfeld* (Essen: Blaue Eule, 1996), p. 7.

fictions, we get to know TERATOPOÏOS, somebody who performs miracles or TERATOMORPHOS which refers to the monstrosity of the form and TERATOSCOPOS describing someone able to explain bizarre things observed by him or other people. The most undefined and semantically broad word in this series, however, is TERAS which — according to its contextual distribution — means monster, portent, bad omen, phantom and sorcerer as well as congenital anomalies or abnormality.[2] Further research on the meanings of the Latin words MONSTRO, MONSTROSITAS or MONSTRUM[3] reveals a rather widely diversified field, stemming either from the reference to different etymological origins (MONSTRO from MONERE) or from semantic change. While MONSTRO means "to indicate or demonstrate something by gestures or words," MONERE means "to warn," "to announce" or to "give a signal indicating that something is on its way." Both, however, emphasize the functions of indication, warning, exposition or demonstration. As to MONSTRUM, the semantic spectrum ranges from un- or super-natural phenomena to miracles in a weaker sense. Even though most of these meanings still exist in today's modern languages, this short (and moreover, incomplete) word-history of the term 'monster' cannot treat the various discursive implications, semantic derivations or, in a more 'monstrous' sense, deviations. In order to draw a more efficient and distinctive tableau of these varied applications, I propose to retrace the astonishing career of the monster by turning the spotlight on selected exemplary periods —one might also say interfaces — in which the monster, the 'monstrous discourses' bear witness to religious, scientific and / or cultural change.

1 In ancient times . . .

Aristotle begins with the idea that monsters on the one hand express the *world-constituting* contingency while, on the other hand, they are a constant reminder of nature's failing in getting closer to God's creative potential.[4] Assuming that nature follows certain laws and purposes, Aristotle concludes that except for man all creatures are unsuccessful — a conception in which women are no more than 'mutilated men'.[5] But unlike monsters which,

---

[2] Cf. among others, J. B. Hofmann, *Etymologisches Wörterbuch des Griechischen* (München: Oldenburg, 1966).

[3] Cf. Karl-Ernst Georgess, ed., *Ausführliches Lateinisch-Deutsches Handwörterbuch* (Darmstadt: WBG, 1992), vol. 2, p. 9977f.

[4] While most researchers locate the beginning of naturalization at the end of the seventeenth and beginning of the eighteenth century, this reading, suggested by Michaël Hagner, seems to be rather interesting (see Hagner, ed., *Der falsche Körper. Beiträge zu einer Geschichte der Monstrositäten* [Göttingen: Wallstein Verlag, 1995]).

[5] Cf. Aristotle, *De generatione animalium*, IV.3, 767 b 5ff. Some centuries later another philosopher, Diderot, comes back to the same idea by adding the possibility of reversal: "L'homme n'est peut-être que le monstre de la femme ou la femme le monstre

although natural, are only accidents of nature, women at least represent one of its necessities. The difference, however, is not always quite clear.

The notion of 'monster' thus is reserved for failures of nature which violate the basic law that the same can only create the same. Meanwhile, 'monster' in the Aristotelian sense means an animal "that does not violate nature as such but that exceeds normality."[6] Even if monsters mark a deviation from normality, they do not go beyond nature's limits. By rationalizing or — in modern language — 'naturalizing' the existence of monsters, Aristotle thus excludes any kind of superstition. Monsters are merely a kind of modification, deformation or anomaly. This definition, however, implies the existence of a definite scale of what is or is not 'normal' and Aristotle surely does not ignore the problem of the observer's perspective in this context.[7] But, since "deformity is a kind of dissimilarity,"[8] he skillfully eludes the above-mentioned complication and, in the following, he concentrates largely on the problem of resemblance. Hence the decision, whether an animal is or is not a monster, mainly seems to be a question of physically marked genealogical deviation.

In Book II of the *Physics*, Aristotle specifies the double structure of nature, that of matter and form. Mistakes in nature's production certainly do not result from a lack of purpose, but only reveal a necessity of matter — as in the case of women's existence — that prevents nature from obtaining its aim. If a monster, that is a descendant which does not resemble its parents, is born, it is most often due to the fact that the male seed failed to put up against the resistance of the female matter.[9] With reference to the different pregnancy durations, Aristotle excludes sexual intercourse between animals of different species and, once again, focuses purely on physical resemblance. Due to limited space, I cannot dwell further on Aristotelian monster theory, but I'd like to emphasize the complete absence of arguments for either the role of God or the semiotic function of monsters, topics which emerged later on in scientific discourse.

In the following centuries, the majority of works about monsters and

---

de l'homme" (*Le Rêve de D'Alembert*, DPV XVII, 152).

[6] Aristotle, *op. cit.*, 769b11-25.

[7] On the concept of 'normality', see Jürgen Link, *Versuch über den Normalismus. Wie Normalität produziert wird* (Opladen: Westdeutscher Verlag, 1996); Georges Canguilhem, *The Normal and the Pathological*, trans. C. Fawcett & R.S. Cohen (New York: Zone Books, 1989); Carol Donley & Sheryl Buckley, eds., *The Tyranny of the Normal* (Kent: Kent State University Press, 1996); Leslie Fiedler, *Tyranny of the Normal. Essays on Bioethics, Theology & Myths* (Boston: Godine, 1996).

[8] Cf. Aristotle, *op. cit.*, IV.3, 769 b 30.

[9] Aristotle divides monsters into three categories: (i) individuals with incomplete or superfluous members (defective monsters and monsters by excess), (ii) individuals with hermaphroditism or polydactyly and (iii), individuals with anomalies, i.e. minor defects.

monstrosities influenced by Plutarch (*Pericles*, *Coriolanus*) or, mostly, Cicero's *De divinatione* focus on the above-mentioned two elements, that is the divine provenance and the semiotic character of monsters. The successors take over the notions of monster, miracle or portent used in *De divinatione* and try to exemplify and differentiate their particular meanings. But as Cicero was not quite consistent regarding the contextual distribution or semantic scope of the different lexemes, we are faced with a rather undefined field of meanings. However, no matter which notion is used, all of them seem nevertheless to serve as means of communication between god and man:[10]

> Again, prophecies and premonitions of future events cannot but be taken as proofs that the future may appear or be foretold as a warning or portended or predicted to mankind — hence the very words 'apparition' [*ostenta*], 'warning' [*monstra*], 'portent' [*portenta*], prodigy [*prodigia*]. Even if we think that the stories of Mopsus, Tiresias, Amphiaraus, Calchas and Helenus are mere baseless fictions . . . ., shall not even the instances from our own native history teach us to acknowledge the divine power?[11]

These lines are almost literally repeated in *De divinatione*.

Beside Cicero, another outstanding precursor is Pliny. I restrict myself to a brief but exemplary quotation from the *Historia naturalis*:

> Also one section has the mouth closed up and has no nostrils, but only a single orifice through which it breathes and sucks in drink by means of oat straws, as well as grains of oat, which grows wild there, for food. Some of the tribes communicate by means of nods and gestures instead of speech . . . . Some writers have actually reported a race of Pygmies living among the marshes in which the Nile rises.[12]

---

[10] Cicero distinguishes two forms of prophecy: 'natural prophecy' means that God talks directly and immediately (without any mediation) to a man's soul, whereas 'artificial prophecy' means the communication is being conveyed by (e.g. monstrous) signs, which are to be interpreted by specialists. In contrast to the traditional divine ambassadors, i.e. angels, monsters, however, do only speak through their physical appearance, as a phenomenon.

[11] "Praedictiones vero et praesensiones rerum futurarum quid aliud declarant nisi hominibus ea, quae sint, ostendi, monstrari, portendi, praedici, ex quo illa ostenta, monstra, portenta, prodigia dicuntur. Quod si ea ficta credimus licentia fabularum, Mopsum, Tiresiam, Amphiaraum, Calchantem, Helenum . . ., ne domesticis quidem exemplis docti numen deorum conprobabimus?" (Cicero, *De natura deorum*, ed. H. Rackam [Cambridge, Mass.: Harvard University Press, 1979], II, 7).

[12] Pliny, *Natural History*, Book VI, § 188.

Referring to Ktesias, Isigonos, Megasthenes and others, Pliny, in his volume concerning *Anthropology*, gives detailed reports about different people while concentrating, lastly, on individual deviations which, because they happened accidentally, cannot be proved by resemblance or dissimilarity.[13] In addition, we notice a focus on *semiotization* that reflects the historically prevailing scientific knowledge of its time: "Persons are also born of both sexes combined — what we call Hermaphrodites, formerly called androgyni and considered as portents, but now as entertainments" (*ibid.*). Compared to the astonishing abundance of the represented forms and figures, Pliny's explanation as to the origin of monsters and monstrous races seems to be rather terse: "These and similar varieties of the human race have been made by the ingenuity of Nature as toys for herself and marvels for us" (*ibid.*, § 32): monstrous variety as nature's own amusement, a symbol of its power and, at the same time, an enchantment for men. In a modern context, Pliny's reasoning strategy — monster as merely *lusus naturae*, nature's playground — thus anachronistically falls behind Aristotle's thesis based on natural history and genealogy. Concerning the 'biodiversity' of Ethiopia, however, Pliny condemns those assuming ignorant violation of rules or nature's whim by making an exception, that is only one part of nature's variety, to the rule. This estimation already refers to more recent theories concerning the observer's role in drawing a border between normality and abnormality. In spite of the geographical, climactic and ethnic diversity, all of the settings mentioned share one quality: they are all far away, *in ultima quadam terra, ad ultimas orientis terras*.

After Aristotle, Cicero and Pliny, the works of Augustine reveal another variation concerning the function of monsters. First of all, we notice that, in contrast to the authors quoted above, the notion of 'miracle' plays an important role. The etymological connection between *miraculum* and *mirari* leads Augustine to *curiositas*, i.e. a phenomenon based on forms of rather critically judged bookish or iconic knowledge: ". . . it is not necessary to believe in all of the races of men, which are said to exist."[14]

Thus Augustine does not contest the existence of monstrous phenomena, but assumes that these facts go beyond human understanding. Therefore he condemns the presumptuous scientists who destroy the initial awe (*mirari*) without being able to categorize it: "But He who cannot see the whole is offended by the deformity of the part, because he is blind to that which balances it, and to which it belongs."[15] Every human being, as strange as

---

[13] *Ibid.*, § 34.

[14] Augustine, *The City of God*, vol. V (London: Heinemann, 1965), book XVI, chapter 8. The original passage is as follows: "Sed omnia genera hominum, quae dicuntur esse, credere non est necesse."

[15] *Ibid.* The original passage is as follows: "Sed qui totum inspicere non potest,

s/he may be, was undoubtedly born as a rational, moral creature.[16] Like Cicero, Augustine admits a certain autonomy of production, but instead of Cicero's creating nature, Augustine places God as the creator of the progenitor Adam. In contrast to Pliny's idea of nature, God does not play with monsters but he uses their mediatory capacity to communicate with man.

One last example of the ancient concept of monsters is Isidore of Seville's *Etymologiae*, a work which Pierre Duhem considered to be a kind of inventory, less focused on defining the appropriate *termini technici* than on presenting the doctrines of different sciences.[17] Indeed, Isidore discusses Augustine's thesis about monsters as god-given and therefore not unnatural creatures.[18] In contrast to Augustine, who by means of etymological research wished to show that God himself realizes his prophecies, Isidore's analysis of *portenta, ostenta, monstra* or *prodigia* refers to the ancient notion of *portenta* being signs sent by God. But, and in this point his reflection differs from classical thought, Isidore's *portenta* 'visualize' the message physically, thus we speak of an iconic (and sometimes also indexical) relationship between the signified and the signifier. The death of Alexander the Great is announced by a stillborn monster with a human torso and a lower body composed of elements of different animals. Its message is to be decoded by analogy or similarity: the sovereign will die and his empire will collapse. Isidore also differs from classical thought in his morphological classification which, in contrast to the ancient signs of social and geographical provenance or genesis, gives priority to significant corporal deviations, while classification is organized by the degree of metamorphosis. His aim lies in the visualization of the divine order, hinting already at medieval conceptions of *ordo*.

---

tamquam deformitate partis offenditur, quoniam cui congruat et quo referatur ignorat."

[16] Even Leibniz hesitates in his decision regarding the rationality of monstrous beings: "on dira que cet innocent vient de parents raisonnables et que par conséquent il faut qu'il ait une âme raisonnable. Je ne sais par quelle règle de Logique on peut établir une telle conséquence et comment après cela on oserait détruire des productions mal formées et contraintes. . . . Un défaut dans le corps fera-t-il un Monstre, et non un défaut dans l'Esprit? C'est retourner à la première supposition déjà réfutée, que l'extérieur suffit. . . . . Je vous demande maintenant, où trouver la juste mesure et les dernières bornes qui emportent avec elles une âme raisonnable" (*Nouveaux essais concernant l'entendement humain*, IV.iv.16 [G V, 375]).

[17] Pierre Duhem, *Le système du monde: histoire des doctrines cosmologiques de Platon à Copernic* (Paris: Hermann, 1954), vol. 3, p. 5.

[18] While Isidore recognizes the functional character of monsters, monstrous races don't play any role in his conception. So he reduces Augustine' argumentation and draws a parallel between the existence of monstrous individuals and people, thereby taking their existence for granted.

2 Medieval monsters

> Monsters exist because they are part of the divine plan, and even the most horrible mugs reveal the greatness of God.
>
> Umberto Eco, *The Name of the Rose*

Quite often, the architecture of medieval cathedrals exposes monstrous or demonic figures in hierarchically predominant places; one finds them underneath the representation of Christ and his apostles. These figures frequently appear in the likes of *cynocyphalidae*, flat-nosed people, or, as in the tympanum of Vézelay, panotians and pigmies. The same is the case in books, where monstrous figures appear according to normative rules in the margins of the initial canonical framework. The same hierarchy can be found on pillars decorated with beasts or encyclopedias of the early Middle Ages.[19] Monsters are marginalized, they are beyond the limits of human perception: "As agents of the impossible, monsters have always been sensitive to the strange things which are not located beyond the borders of the known world, but rather come straight from the heart of producing, self-producing man."[20] The taxonomy of monstrous figures, classified between man and animal, repeats the same marginal position: "Writers of medieval travel guides let their imagination and fantasy run wild . . . to explain unknown phenomena. Draughtsmen and authors, taking them at their word, thus created grotesque beings, bizarre animals, strange men, hybrids made of both."[21] Due to a certain caution, in medieval travel guides — and not only there — monsters were placed at the farthest borders of the world or rather of humanity, where they mark the transitional zone to the unknown, to the new, to the inhuman, or, to put it in a nutshell, to all factual knowledge. Thus the authors changed the formerly *contra naturam* origin of monsters into an origin *extra naturam*. Supernatural beings are always located in extraordinary geographical places: "The India-Ethiopia complex is an ex-

---

[19] Cf. Jurgis Baltrušaitis, *Le Moyen Âge fantastique. Antiquité et l'exotisme dans l'art gothique* (Paris: Flammarion, 1981); id., *Réveils et prodiges* (Paris: Flammarion, 1988); id., *Aberration. Essai sur la légende des formes* (Paris: Flammarion, 1995); Friedrich von Bezold, *Das Fortleben der antiken Götter im mittelalterlichen Humanismus* (Bonn: K. Schroeder, 1922); Fritz Saxl & Erwin Panofsky, "Classical Mythology in Medieval Art," in *Metropolitan Museum Studies* 6:2 (1933); Erwin Panofsky, *Hercules am Scheidewege und andere antike Bildstoffe in der neueren Kunst* (Leipzig-Berlin: Teubner, 1930); Jean Seznec, *La survivance des dieux antiques. Essai sur le rôle de la tradition mythologique dans l'humanisme et dans l'art de la Renaissance* (London: Warburg Institute, 1940).

[20] Dietmar Kamper, *Unmögliche Gegenwart* (München: Fink, 1995), p. 149 (cf. especially chapter 4: "Language and body: the perception of monsters," pp. 149-185).

[21] Werner Wunderlich, "Dämonen, Monster, Fabelwesen. Eine kleine Einführung in Mythen und Typen phantastischer Geschöpfe," in Ulrich Müller & Werner Wunderlich, eds., *Dämonen, Monster, Fabelwesen* (St. Gallen: UVK Facherlag für Wissenschaft und Studium, 1999), p. 12.

ample of medieval signmaking at work in the field of teratological geography, where spatial semiotics express the idea of the monster as simultaneously participating in the material and spiritual world and thus forming a bridge between the two."[22] Once the physical reality of the monster is displaced, its real existence can be accepted, whereas its empirical authentification remains problematic: "The monster both affirms the discourses that describe the physical world by grounding the teratological phenomenon in geography, history, and science, and then negates these discourses by transcending their limitations in order to raise the signifying power of the deformed to an anagogical level, raising nature from the physical to the divine, as Isidore stated."[23]

In her fundamental study *Monstres, démons et merveilles à la fin du Moyen Âge* Claude Kappler also deals with the problem of the monster's borderline situation and comes to a rather terse conclusion: "The marvelous rarely exists at the edge of our horizon: mostly, it arises in areas no one ever looked at. That is why the 'extremities' of the world are fertile, be they polar regions, the world's periphery or simply mysterious, unexplored areas. . . ."[24] This geographical marginalization, however, is not unique to the 'Occidental' imagination, as many Asian people locate monstrous races preferably in the Western world.[25]

In general, the Middle Ages judged monsters from a purely theological point of view and in all the works concerning this topic — even with different interpretations — God takes the place that creative nature occupied in ancient times.[26] Nearly all shared the idea that monsters transgress natural laws and, as signs of divine punishment, assume a moral function. The danger of visual and spiritual distraction caused by the growing number of *mirabili* is averted through increasing distance: "The kind of strangeness which is co-substantial to them [to monsters, B.O.] is perhaps expressed by the fact that their number is increasing to the same extent as the distance

---

[22] David Williams, *Deformed Discourse. The Function of the Monster in Mediaeval Thought and Literature* (Montreal: McGill-Queen's University Press, 1996), p. 13; see also Justin E.H. Smith's essay in this volume.

[23] Williams, *op. cit.*, p. 14.

[24] Claude Kappler, *Monstres, démons et merveilles à la fin du Moyen Âge* (Paris: Payot, 1980), p. 36.

[25] "Pour n'en donner qu'un exemple: comme nous imaginions à l'Est un peuple de monoculi . . . ils plaçaient dans nos régions les mêmes créatures: et que ce fût à l'Est ou à l'Ouest, ces êtres avaient bien sûr la vue extrêmement courte!" (*ibid.*, p. 37.)

[26] On monstrous beings in medieval times, cf. Claude Lecouteux, *Les Monstres dans la pensée médiévale européenne* (Paris: Presses universitaires de l'Université Paris-Sorbonne, 1993); Baltrušaitis, *Le Moyen âge fantastique*; Kappler, *op. cit.*; Herbert Schade, *Dämonen und Monstren. Gestaltungen des Bösen in der Kunst des frühen Mittelalters* (Regensburg: Friedrich Pustet, 1962); Müller & Wunderlich, *Dämonen, Monster, Fabelwesen, op. cit.*

that separates us grows . . ."²⁷

Unlike Augustine, who radically rejected the semiotic character of monsters, the medieval authors, although they do not treat monsters as signs of divine communication, at least accept their indexical or iconic function: to symbolize failures of nature or demonic influences. Thunder in the east, according to Beda Venerabilis' prophetic meteorology, announces a bloodbath, namely, the imminent death of sinners. Natural, or rather, unnatural signs and marks become carefully arranged bookmarks in the great book of nature.²⁸

The *ordo* of the medieval universe is determined by a symbolic geometry and a scale of values according to which every element finds its spiritual and material place. So, "while preserving its self, [each element] is a part of the whole of which it contains the qualities and the secret. Affinities and correspondences exist between each element and the world. That is why, as soon as a particular field of creation is concerned, the whole universe is affected." ²⁹ In Vincent de Beauvais' three volumes, *Speculum Majus*, *Speculum Historiale* and *Speculum Naturale*, the author takes up the idea of nature as a mirror of physical and moral reality. The medieval monsters thus become metaphors, arranged in a kind of *physiognomic* tableau which assigns a characteristic feature to each phenomenon: pigmies stand for humility, giants for pride, long-lipped people for justice and so on. Céard does not neglect to emphasize both the uncanny proximity and the distance of monsters compared to other animals of medieval bestiaries: "Similar to animals which, in the medieval bestiaries are a kind of moral mirror of man, the monsters, closer to us than the animals, bear a funny and, at the same time, uncanny caricatural resemblance: by approaching us they threaten our identity." ³⁰

In his *Secreta Mulierum* (1580) Albertus Magnus presents his opinion of human monsters, with regard to human responsibility. In his view, the birth of monsters often results from violating certain laws, such as practicing coitus in an 'unnatural' position, or reproduction during menstruation (which means that the child has been nourished with dirty blood). Other reasons for the birth of monsters are exemplified by the theory of monstrous imagination³¹ as well as cases of sodomistic procreation. Obviously, these monsters do not announce future disasters, miracles or other forms of di-

---

[27] Céard, *La nature et les prodiges. L'insolite au XVIᵉ siècle en France* (Geneva: Droz, 1977), p. 42.
[28] *Ibid.*, p. 32.
[29] Kappler, *Monstres, op. cit.*, p. 20.
[30] Céard, *La nature et les prodiges*, p. 45 (emphasis mine).
[31] Cf. Marie-Hélène Huet, *Monstrous Imagination* (Cambridge, Mass.: Harvard University Press, 1993).

vine intervention but they come as punishment for committed sins which are mimetically represented by the deformed bodies. St. Thomas Aquinas also leaves the assumption of the 'first cause' untouched and even if, according to him, the existence of monstrous beings is contradictory to the nature of the individual, it is cosmologically comprehensible and can be traced back to natural reasons: "Monstra, licet fiant contra naturam particularem, non tamen fiunt contra naturam universalem."[32] According to Cazenave, Thomas de Cantimprés' *Liber de natura rerum* (between 1225-1241), with its emphasis on natural history, can be understood as a preparation of the future naturalization of monsters, "because his book, instead of beginning with a chapter about God and the angels, first deals with anatomy, then with the human soul. He thus presents a panorama of the visible universe where the abnormal follows the normal."[33] Similarly, Konrad von Megenberg, author of the first German natural history at the end of the fifteenth century, defends the Augustinian thesis of the descent of monsters from Adam, and concentrates on the problem of the human soul:

> There are two kinds of human prodigies: the soulful and the soulless. Among the first, I count those who have a soul but who are fraught with disability. By their physical appearance, the soulless may remind us of human beings, but they don't have a soul. The soulful prodigies can be classified into two groups, those with physical and those with mental defects. Both derive from Adam and his sins, because I think, if the first man hadn't sinned, mankind would have been born without disabilities.[34]

Megenburg maintains the importance and representation of God's will, while his work contains early approaches of natural history.

In his excellent study *Deformed Discourse* David Williams calls attention to another element; referring to the neo-Platonic approach of Pseudo-Dionysus, he shows to what extent the valorization of the grotesque and the monstrous *functionalizes* the monster as a representation of what in fact does not exist: "Whereas the rational concept of time insists upon the separate and discrete realities of past, present, and future, the monstrous Cerberus with his three heads, each representing one of the modes of time, united in the body of a single being, transcends these exclusionary categories imposed by logic."[35] Transcending both *ratio* and cataphatic theology, Mathias Grünewald, one of the most famous religious painters,

---

[32] Aquinas, *Quæstiones disputatæ de potentia Dei*, q. 6, art. 2, ad 8m.
[33] Cazenave, "Monstres et merveilles," *Ethnologie française* 9 (1979), p. 245.
[34] Konrad von Megenberg, *Buch der Natur (Augsburg 1478)* (Stuttgart: Karl Aue, 1861), p. 418.
[35] Williams, *Deformed Discourse*, pp. 4-5.

represents the holy trinity as a three-headed being.[36] God, who is actually unrepresentable, can only be represented as a human-corporal being by means of a rhetorical figure that refers neither to a predecessor nor to a pre-existing meaning: pure 'monstration' in the sense of "show forth"[37] (*monstrare*) or, rhetorically speaking, a catachresis. Since tropological speaking means figurative speaking, tropes can be considered as notions of difference characterizing the distinction between literal and figurative speaking.[38] If the literal expression does not exist, we cannot speak of representation, but must deal with what Williams calls "apophatic monstration," a 'monstration' of the non-existing, a meta-reflection on 'one's own' function and that of language as such. This kind of semiological interpretation requires the (geographically marginalized) physical existence of the monster to start the symbolic machinery: "[M]onstrous semiology is authorized by the physical existence of the monsters, despite the fact that this existence is invented. The fiction of a historical existence authorizes a symbolic program that in turn produces signs which can be applied metaphorically to other 'things' so as to reveal their grotesque absurdity."[39]

Luther's purely symbolic reading of the monstrous hieroglyphs testifies to the above-mentioned prerequisite that the sign must not refer to a real, previously existing element. He understands the monk calf which was seen in Saxony in 1522 as an allegory on the status of the monk.[40] Basing himself on a non-existing natural relation between sign and referent, he thus creates the only possible form of a relation of simultaneous difference and connection.[41] As divine communicators monsters, positive signs of a negative existence, bring to bear their creative potential: "[T]he monster's proper function is to negate the very order of which the monster is a part, and to critique the philosophical principles that sustain order itself."[42]

---

[36] Baltrušaitis, *Le Moyen Âge fantastique*, p. 50.
[37] Williams, *Deformed Discourse*, p. 4.
[38] Wolfram Groddeck, *Reden über Rhetorik. Zu einer Stilistik des Lesens* (Basel / Frankfurt a.M.: Stroemfeld, 1995 [Nexus 7]), p. 209.
[39] Williams, *Deformed Discourse*, p. 11.
[40] Regarding the symbol of the monk calf, cf. Konrad von Lange, *Der Papstesel: ein Beitrag zur Kultur- und Kunstgeschichte des Reformationszeitalters* (Göttingen: Vandenhoeck & Ruprecht, 1891); Hartmann Grisar, Franz Heege, *Luthers Kampfbilder* (Freiburg: Herder, 1921).
[41] "The deformed simultanesously exposes the gap between sign and signified and bridges it. In this way grotesque language not only eschews the epistemological problems of conventional language, it functions as a point outside language from which we may observe the very form of language itself" (Williams, *op. cit.*, p. 12).
[42] *Ibid.*, p. 14.

3 The 'renaissance' of the monstrous

[A] compilation, or particular natural history, must be made of all monsters and prodigious births of nature; of every thing, in short, which is new, rare, and unusual in nature. This should be done with a rigorous selection, so as to be worthy of credit (Francis Bacon).[43]

The Renaissance widely celebrates the rebirth of the monster and the valorization of the monstrous founded on a mostly secular, aesthetic fascination for the strange Other. This change is essentially indebted to a growing skepticism that tries to find support in the initial 'flowering' of the natural sciences. Deprived of his religious certainty, man comes to know himself as a strange being in a likewise strange and challenging world.[44] In order to reveal the last remaining secrets, numerous explorers, travel with a growing joy of discovery to places still unknown, hoping to encounter monstrous races: "Who has not seen monsters, has not traveled."[45] Under certain conditions, however, it seems to be quite sufficient to know somebody who *pro certo* describes his experiences with monsters ... In fact, a large number of books in the sixteenth century are populated by strange and wild people, monsters and prodigies. Knowledge thus equals a certain semiotic capacity; placed in the interstices of the mental and the material world, the interpretation of the sign allows for an approach to the world of material objects. At the same time, however, it seems to be quite clear that this sign-based mediation won't pave a direct way to it but is merely founded on images or reflections.

As mentioned above, the knowledge of monstrous races and individuals is mainly based on reports of travelers who, for lack of experience or for their own fame, populate foreign areas with imaginary beings. Besides Empedocles' 'theory of evolution' as well as Herodotus', Ktesias' or Megasthenes' reports, Pliny's *Historia naturalis* (which ran to seven editions between 1504 and 1534!) is still an inventory of miracles. The last edition — astonishing coincidence! — is published at the same time as Rabelais' *Gargantua* with

---

[43] Bacon, *Novum Organum* (1620), ii, 29, in *The Works of Francis Bacon*, ed. B. Montagu (London: W. Pickering, 1831), vol. 14, p. 138.

[44] In her excellent article "Wunder, Naturgesetze und die wissenschaftliche Revolution des 17. Jahrhunderts," *Jahrbuch der Akademie der Wissenschaften in Göttingen für das Jahr 1991* (Göttingen: Vandenhoeck & Ruprecht, 1992), Lorraine Daston draws attention to the fact that many developments in the field of natural philosophy of the seventeenth century didn't influence the campaign against miracles but, on the contrary, scientific observations and the stress on evidence serve as arguments in favour of the existence of wonders, something that Francis Bacon called "the new, rare, and unusual in nature."

[45] Kappler, *Monstres*, p. 115: "[Q]ui n'a pas vu de monstres, n'a pas voyagé."

its prologue listing a series of mythological monsters. Without extending the problem, the striking difference between the ugliness and the intelligence of Socrates confirms the assumption of a semiotic conception founded on the differentiation between signified and signifier.[46] Behind the rhetorical strategies of Rabelais, the fundamental mechanism of a cultural battle appears which, according to Gérard Defaux, presents an "internal Western version of the drama of 'ethnocentricity' such as it is for example so eloquently presented to us by Claude Lévi-Strauss at the end of the second book of his *Structural Anthropology*."[47] In the works of the above-mentioned French anthropologist, cultural diversification is always related to a kind of monstrosity or scandal. The first reaction when encountering the Other implies repulse and denial: ". . . the other, *l'autre*, is exactly what he already was for the Greek in ancient times, a Barbarian, a Goth, a Magot, a Cannibal, somebody, or rather something . . . that 'hates' and 'flees the company of men', has the 'face of a dog', and 'barks instead of laughing'."[48] For the humanists, the scholastic — like Lévi-Strauss' barbarian — firmly believes that manhood, culture and civilization end at the border of his own tribe.[49] Rabelais' dialectical argumentation, his anti-physical monster, refers to the fact that rejection of the other gives free reign to narcissism.[50]

---

[46] "Silenes estoient jadis petites boites, telle que voyons de present es bouticques des apothecaires, pinctes au dessus de figures joyeuses et frivoles, comme de harpies, satuyres, oysons bridez, lievres cornuz, canes bastées, boucqs volans, cerfz limonniers et aultres telle pinctures contrefaictes à plaisir pour exciter le monde à rire . . . ;Tel disoit Socrates parce que, le voyans au dehors et l'estimans par l'exterior apparence, . . . , tousjours dissimulant son divin sçavoir; mais, ouvrans ceste boyte, eussiez au dedans trouvé une celeste et impreciable drogue: entendement plus que humain, vertus merveilleuse, couraige invincible, sobresse non pareille . . ."(François Rabelais, *Gargantua, Prologue de l'auteur* [Paris: Gallimard, 1992], pp. 55-57). Cf. also Stéphane Charitos, "Un monstre du rire et un rire monstrueux: Directions pour une étude sur François Rabelais et Georges Bataille," *Romance Notes* 28:3 (1988), and Gérard Defaux, "'Hoc est porcus meus': Rabelais et les monstres du Quart Livre," in *Travaux de Littérature* 9 (1996).

[47] Gérard Defaux, "Rabelais and the Monsters of Antiphysis," *MLN* 110 (1995), p. 1029.

[48] *Ibid.*, p. 1030. Defaux quotes Rabelais: "Cannibales, peuple monstrueux en Africque, ayant la face comme chiens, et abbayant en lieu de rire" (Rabelais, "Briefve Declaration," in *Le Quart Livre* [Paris: Librairie Générale Française, 1994], p. 629).

[49] Cf. Lévi-Strauss, quoted from Defaux, "Rabelais," p. 1031.

[50] "Jue vous en diray, respondit Pantagruel, ce que j'en ay leu parmy les apologues antiques. Physis (c'est nature) en sa premiere portée enfanta Beaulté et Harmonie sans copulation charnelle: comme de soy mesmes est grandement feconde et fertile. Antiphysie, laquelle de tout temps est partie adverse de Nature, incontinent eut envie sus cestuy tant beau et honorable enfantement: et au rebours enfanta Amodunt et Discordance par copulation de Tellumon. Ils avoient la teste sphaerique et ronde entierement, comme un ballon: non doulcement comprimée des deux coustez, comme est la forme humaine. Les aureilles avoient hault enlevées, grandes comme aureilles d'asne; les oeilz hors la teste, fichez sus des os semblables aux talons, sans soucilles, durs comme sont ceulx des Cancres:

Neither *physis* nor *antiphysis*, neither the normal nor the monster possess a pre-existent, absolute identity; both of them need the Other to build up their Selves. All of the opponents, the monstrous Physeter as well as the diabolic creatures of Calvin are monstrous children of Antiphysis, "monstres difformes et contrefaictz en despit de Nature," which, nevertheless, show an astonishing resemblance to the humanists.[51] Rabelais provides an excellent illustration of agonistic structures, i.e. culturally determined gestures of aggression and dialectical processes with all their polemical and ideological elements; a discussion which gives us revealing insights into the function and the role of monsters in cultural history.

Many of the early cosmographies are less committed to Pliny than to the arguments of Augustine. In *Rudimentum Novitiorum* (published 1475 in Lübeck) or Antonius' of Florence's world chronicle, but especially in Hartmann Schedel's *Liber cronicarum* (1493), the emergence of monstrous races coincides with the Babelic confusion of tongues (*post linguarum varietatem*). Like Philippe de Bergamo in his *Supplementum Cronicarum* (1483 and 1503), Schedel, however, does not understand them as part of the divine punishment for the tower-building hubris of men, but rather as a sign of beauty of a diversified universe. Each normal evolution entails similarities and differences which allow a classification according to species and, at the same time, ensure the individuality of each single element. A little morphological deviation, however, is enough to radically change our ideas.[52]

Even if the Renaissance does not classify differences on an evolutionary scale and thus does not speak of biological failures, a certain feeling of unease finds its expressions in astonishment, fascination and fear. In the context of a pre-scientific understanding, Paracelsus first excludes demonic influences, but skillfully eludes the question whether or not god is responsible for the deformed beings. His contemporary Jean-Baptiste van Helmont also refuses to acknowledge that demons do cause monstrous births, yet he won't exclude the cooperation of witches or magicians.[53] More success-

---

les pieds ronds comme pelottes, les braz et mains tournez en arriere vers les espaules. Et cheminoient sus leurs testes, continuellement faisant la roue, cul sus teste" (Rabelais, *Le Quart Livre, op. cit.*, chapter XXXII, p. 391.)

[51] Cf. Defaux, "Rabelais," p. 1033ff.

[52] "Un échec de la vie nous concerne deux fois, car un échec aurait pu nous atteindre et un échec pourrait venir par nous. C'est seulement parce que, homme, nous sommes des vivants qu'un raté morphologique est, à nos yeux vivants, un monstre. . . . le monstre ce serait seulement l'autre que le même, un ordre autre que l'ordre le plus probable" (G. Canguilhem, "La monstruosité et le monstrueux," in *Diogène* 40 [Oct.-Dec. 1962], p. 29). [This essay was collected in Canguilhem's *La connaissance de la vie* (Paris: Vrin, 2nd expanded edition 1975).]

[53] Cf. Ernest Martin, *Histoire des monstres depuis l'antiquité jusqu'à nos jours* (Paris:

ful than medicine or anatomy in this context, zoology, according to explorers' reports, reconstructs the monstrous races and beings to catalogue them in multifarious inventories. In addition to that, zoology makes use of these stores of knowledge to extrapolate further forms in order to satisfy and stimulate the public's desire for 'natural' oddities. Ambroise Paré's *Des Monstres et prodiges*, Ulisse Aldrovandi's *Historia monstrorum*, Pierre Boaistuau's *Histoires prodigieuses*, Werner Rolevinck's *Fasciculus Temporum* (1474),[54] Julius Obsequens' famous *Prodigiorum liber* (1552)[55] and, last but not least, Fortunio Liceti's *De monstris* are impressive examples of the Renaissance relation to monsters, but it is more than obvious, however, that all these authors have explored the same sources or simply copied each other. The large number of definitions and functions correspond to a richness of lexical attributions that, admittedly, varies from one author to another but ultimately lead to a rather common representation of monsters as divine or demonic communicators, warning signs or punishments for committed sins.

According to Céard, however, the Renaissance was not of one mind on the topic, so we are actually faced with at least two contradictory interpretations of the status and meaning of the signs, as divine signs or stigmata. Briefly, authors like Luther, Melanchton, Arnauld Sorbin or Cornelius Gemma support the argument of divine provenance while others vote instead for the stigma thesis. The latter, founded on a system of rules and varieties, especially demonstrates the relativity of the formerly unreflective parameters of monstrosity and normality. In contrast to the argument of divine provenance, this position largely contributes to the 'modern' or 'en-

---

Reinwald & Cie, 1880), chapter III.

[54] Werner Rolevinck (1425-1502), *Ein Chronica von anfung der Welt byss uff die jar Christi MCCCLXXXII: Benant fasciculus temporum* (Strasbourg: Johann Pruss, nach dem 27. Oktober 1492). Although the interest in these phenomena isn't new, the increasing publication number of bestiaries, however, is striking. Especially the genre of illustrated 'broadsheets' seems to prefer monstrous beings, thus promoting curiosity. (Cf. Irene Ewinkel, *De monstris: Deutung und Funktion von Wundergeburten auf Flugblättern im Deutschland des 16. Jahrhunderts* [Tübingen: Niemeyer, 1995]; Elfriede Hagmann, *Studien zur Flugblattliteratur des 16. Jahrhunderts mit besonderer Berücksichtigung Dürers*, Dissertation, University of Vienna, 1955; Wolfgang Harms, *Deutsche illustrierte Flugblätter des 16. und 17. Jahrhunderts* (München: Kraus, n.d.). Cf. also Joseph Grünpeck, *Prodigiorum, ostentorum et monstrorum quae in saeculum Mxaimilianeum inciderunt, interpretatio* (1502), Jakob Mennel, *Tractatus de Signis, Prodigiis et Portentis antiquis et novis* (1503), Johannes Nauclerus, *Chronica* (Köln: Calenius & Quentel, 1579).

[55] Conrad Lycosthenes, ed., *Julii Osequentis Prodigiorum liber, ab urbe condita usque ad Augustum Caesarem, cuius tantum extabat fragmentum, nunc demun historiarum beneficio, per Konradum Lycosthenem Rubeaquensem, integritati suae restitutus. Polydori Vergilij Urbinatis de prodigiis libri III. Joachimi Camerarij Paberg de ostentis libri II* (Basel, 1552).

lightened' movement of naturalization. One of its most famous representatives is Montaigne, according to whom we only talk about monsters as long as we haven't encountered one. His so-called "theatre of difference" even seems to convert them: "As he writes, and his thoughts are free to wander, the so-called human monsters metamorphosize and rise high in the skies, so as to reveal their true identity to others — that which society inculcates with its customs, habits and opinions."[56] At a time when monsters are largely viewed as deviations from a fundamental order, Montaigne suspects that they indicate the inner instability and disorder of nature, signs which escape from the control of *ratio*, "creux du discours où vibre la voix d'un Autre indomptable."[57] Montaigne's occasionally strange examples demonstrate the force of habit — "violonte et traitresse maistresse d'escole" — which, in time, ends by building up rules: "Nous luy voyons forcer tous les coups les règles de nature."[58] Some cannibal habits thus only seem barbarian to those whom

> appelle barbarie ce qui n'est pas de son usage. . . . Ces nations me semblent donc ainsi barbares, pour avoir receu fort peu de façon de l'esprit humain, et estre encore fort voisines de leur naifveté originelle. Les loix naturelles leur commandent encores, fort peu abastardies par les nostres; mais c'est en telle pureté, qu'il me prend quelque fois desplaisir dequoy la cognoissance n'en soit venuë plustost, du temps qu'il y avoit des hommes qui en eussent sceu mieux juger que nous.[59]

Later this concept will be used to substantiate the theory of the so-called missing links, reflecting our own origin as well as the possibility of inferring the original natural laws by studying customs and ways of life. One of Montaigne's particularities is his epistemological method which, in contrast to the predominant resemblance-based approaches, is founded on differences: "Le monde n'est que variété et dissemblance."[60] At a time when authors like Tesserant feel uneasy about the possible variety of the world, Fumée vehemently pursues the expulsion of monstrous races and even Thevet "conteste leur existence au nom d'une sorte de dignité de la nature qui lui interdit de créer des êtres si ridicules,"[61] Montaigne asserts the existence of diversified

---

[56] William J. Beck, "Montaigne et Paré: leurs idées sur les monstres," in *Rinascimento*, Rivista dell'Istituto Nazionale di studi sul rinascimento (1990), p. 319.

[57] Fausta Garavini, *Monstres et chimères. Montaigne, le texte et le fantasme* (Paris: Champion, 1993), p. 10.

[58] Montaigne, *Essais* (Paris: Garnier-Flammarion, 1969), I, 23: "De la coustume et de ne changer aisément une loy receüe," p. 155.

[59] *Ibid.*, I, 31: "Des Cannibales" (*op. cit.*, pp. 254-255).

[60] *Ibid.*, II, 1: "De l'yvrongnerie" (*op. cit.*, p. 12).

[61] Céard, *La nature et les prodiges*, *op. cit.*, p. 395.

worlds — "La ressemblance ne fait pas tant un comme la différence fait autre"[62] — an attitude which will not be theoretically reflected until the end of the seventeenth and beginning of the eighteenth century. So it is not the dream of reason but habit which brings forth monsters: "La coutume, en les masquant, enfante des monstres."[63] Like Augustine, Montaigne is convinced of the fact that monsters are not unnatural beings but merely the results of human ignorance and imagination.[64] The power of visual imagination keeps us caught in representations and simulations of the monstrous: "the monstrous stems from the perception of deviation from the normative; difference, portrayed as a visual 'effect', attests to the rarity attributed to the object of the gaze."[65] At the same time the visualization of difference might contribute to a neutralization of horror: "Faced with the monstrosity of difference, one reduces the perceived aberration of otherness through a process of recuperation that has a neutralizing effect" (*ibid.*). We thus create imaginary monsters which by different visualizations disappear into thin air. "Notre vue représente ainsi souvent de loin des images étranges, qui s'évanouissent en s'approchant."[66] Or, as Jacques Derrida concludes: "A monstrosity never presents itself; or else, if you prefer, it only presents itself, that is, lets itself be recognized, by allowing itself to be reduced to what is recognizable; that is, to a normality, a legitimacy which it is not, hence by not letting itself be recognized as what it is — a monstrosity. A monstrosity can only be 'mis-known' [*méconnue*], that is, unrecognized and misunderstood. It can only be recognized afterwards, when it has become normal or the norm."[67] To denounce the influence of habit, Montaigne in fact praises variety while, at the same time, he displaces the problem of monstrosity towards man's inner being, thus preceding the philosophy of evil, under which the phenomenon will be mostly subsumed, by almost three centuries.[68] In the face of the one and only true monster, one's own ego, all the other specimens created by our deformed thinking, discourses

---

[62] Montaigne, "De l'expérience," *op. cit.*, p. 354.
[63] Céard, *La nature et les prodiges*, *op. cit.*, p. 390.
[64] Montaigne, *Essais*, I, 21, "De la force de l'imagination" (*op. cit.*, p. 145).
[65] Lawrence D. Kritzman, "Representing the Monster: Cognition, Cripples, and Other Limp Parts in Montaigne's 'Des Boyteux'," in Jeffrey Jerome Cohen ed., *Monster Theory: Reading Culture* (Minneapolis: University of Minnesota Press, 1996), p. 175.
[66] Montaigne, "Des Boyteux," *op. cit.*, p. 310.
[67] Jacques Derrida, "Some Statements and Truisms," in David Carroll, ed., *The States of 'Theory': History, Art, and Critical Discourse* (New York: Columbia University Press, 1990), p. 79.
[68] Cf. Christoph Schulte, *radikal böse. Die Karriere des Bösen von Kant bis Nietzsche* (München: Fink, 1988). While moral monstrosity exists since the beginning, Montaigne is one of the first to discuss the monstrosity of the self, emphasizing the idea of the Self as the Other.

or habits fade into insignificance: "Jusqu'à cette heure, tous ces miracles et événements étranges se cachent devant moi. Je n'ai vu monstre et miracle au monde plus exprès que moi-même. On s'apprivoise à toute étrangeté par l'usage et le temps; mais plus je me hante et me connais, plus ma difformité m'étonne, moins je m'entends en moi."[69] The variety of miracles, portents and monsters populating our world originates from a feeling of strangeness with respect to oneself:

> The chimæra and monsters that the mind produces make the essayist a narcissistic observer of his mind's monstrous progeny. . . . Montaigne's acceptance of self-deficiency, represented by the rambling and inconstant motion of his mind, enables him to acquire strength through the power of a scriptural gait that proceeds at an uneven pace: 'à saut et à gambades', as it stumbles along the circuitous path to self-knowledge. The assumption of the Socratic *docta ignorantia* enables the essayist to be seen as he is, and in this exhibitionist pose of self-portraiture (from the Latin *protrahere*, to draw out, disclose, or reveal), he is able to get into much closer contact with the monstrous deformities that might otherwise have escaped him. The desire to write is concomitant with the monstrous externalization of his inner phantasms.[70]

The continuous creating of new monsters thus guarantees a reassuring feeling of having them under control. The innovative potential of his theory does not reveal revolutionary knowledge concerning the science of monsters but demonstrates how we keep in check the inner monster by domesticating and (at least visually) fixing the monsters on the outside: "Montaigne remains — for ever anchored in a kind of strangeness that he perceives as slightly external, and which turns out to be less the 'bookshop' of the tower than the very presence of his name."[71]

While Montaigne counts as an epistemological predecessor in monstrous thinking, the role of Ambroise Paré's *Des monstres et prodiges* (1573) as a scientific, i.e. medical pendant may be questioned. Jean-François Malgaigne, editor of his *Œuvres complètes* (1840-41),[72] calls him a predecessor of modern teratology; Edouard Calixte first agreed but later revised this

---

[69] Montaigne, "Des Boyteux," *op. cit.*, p. 310; and see Tristan Dagron's essay in this volume.

[70] Kritzman, "Representing the Monster," *op. cit.*, p. 175.

[71] Julia Kristeva, *Étrangers à nous-mêmes* (Paris: Fayard, 1988), p. 172.

[72] Edouard Calixte, *Les Monstres d'Ambroise Paré et la tératologie moderne* (Paris: Imprimerie Foulon, 1946), p. 3.

opinion.[73] Within the scope of his 'history of the irrational' Céard raises the question whether it is historically correct or not to attribute the scientific results of Renaissance to modern teratology. In order to avoid an inventory of curiosities, monsters should be defined in their own historicity and, therefore, in the *imaginaire scientifique* of the Renaissance. Unfortunately, he does not pursue this theme. Even if he criticizes the missing theoretical impact of Paré's work,[74] Céard nevertheless emphasizes the idea of naturalization embedded in Paré's description of a purposeful evolution of nature which – in contrast to other supporters of nature's variety — integrates potential varieties not as signs of disorder but as particularities. With regard to Paré's basic theological attitude, an anti-finalistic movement of naturalization should instead be understood, according to Mathieu-Castellani and Kors, in the context of the Enlightenment, with respect to the emergence of teratology: "Only with the century of the Enlightenment, and Diderot's decisive intervention, will finality and causality be distinguished... Only with Isidore Geoffroy Saint-Hilaire..."[75] Where do these different assessments concerning Paré's role come from? Let's briefly consider Paré's treatise.

First of all, Paré distinguishes between monsters and prodigies:[76] "Il y a d'autres causes qui nous estonnent doublement, parce qu'ils ne procedent des causes susdites, mais une confusion d'estranges especes, qui rendent la creature non seulement monstrueuse, mais prodigieuse, c'est-à-dire qui est

---

[73] "Si par la classification étiologique des monstres et des prodiges, et par l'importance qu'il donne aux causes naturelles et pathologiques, par la méthode et la précision qu'il apporte dans l'étude des monstres qu'il lui a été donné d'observer, il a fait œuvre vraiment personnelle et s'il mérite d'être compris parmi ces indépendants de la Renaissance soucieux de laisser s'épanouir leur talent hors de toute docile imitation, il n'en a pas moins cru aux causes surnaturelles, donné son adhésion à la théorie des incubes et des succubes et accepté les divagations de la sorcellerie" (*ibid.*, p. 67).

[74] Cf. Céard, *Pour une histoire de l'irrationnel: l'imaginaire scientifique au XVIe siècle* (Liège: Section d'Histoire, 1983).

[75] Mathieu-Castellani, "Préface," in A. Paré, *Des monstres et prodiges* (reprint, Geneva: Slatkine, 1996), pp. 18-19. Regarding the philosophy of finality in France, cf. Alan Charles Kors, "Monsters and the Problem of Naturalism in French Thought," in A. Curran & P. Graille, eds., *Faces of Monstrosity in Eighteenth-Century Thought* (*Eighteenth-Century Life* 21 [1997], special issue). Kors shows that this philosophy which seems to fail because of the monsters, in fact refers to these phenomena in order to prove the existence of God: "What was a monster, after all, if not precisely a gross deviation from the recognized standard: the known, obvious, intended model of what God purposefully had designed for the creation? Monsters struck humankind so forcefully because they violated the known natural order, adapted design, regularity, and purposeful causes of nature. They were, in fact, exemplars of those exceptions that demonstratively proved the existence of the rule" (p. 30).

[76] Regarding the research on prodigies, see Céard, *La nature et les prodiges, op. cit.*; Raymond Bloch, *Les prodiges dans l'antiquité classique, Grèce, Etrurie, Rome* (Paris: PUF, 1973).

du *tout abhorrente et contre nature.*"⁷⁷ In 1579, he replaces "contre le cours de nature" by "outre le cours de nature."⁷⁸ His famous definition – "Monstres sont choses qui apparaissent outre le cours de Nature . . . . Prodiges, ce sont choses qui viennent du tout / entièrement / contre nature . . ."⁷⁹ — has been described as opposing "a hyperbolic figure of the norm" to "a subversion which distorts and thwarts all laws."⁸⁰ We thus call a child with only one arm or two heads a monster while a snake born by a human mother counts as a prodigy. The different meaning of the signs corresponds to their triple discursive function: (i) the rationalistic discourse of the Aristotelian tradition which parts from the idea that man with his limited understanding cannot read the divine signs, (ii) the hermeneutic-theological argumentation of Augustine and (iii) a kind of scientific or medical approach like Paré's, whose interdisciplinary knowledge lies somewhere in between myth and scientific observation.⁸¹ For Mathieu-Castellani, Paré, between his desire to interpret monstrous signs as divine indications and the will to build up an etiological classification, ends up in a rather jumbled combination of the three discourses.

Like Céard, Georges Hoffmann confronts the question concerning the historicity of the monster. Like the former, he faces serious historical problems in accepting that the Renaissance gave rise to rational and empirical science.⁸² Scientists like Pico della Mirandola or Jean Bodin certainly do not deny their inclination towards the occult and the irrational. Paré's systematics is more reminiscent of medieval bestiary than of scientific taxonomy. On closer examination his classification in fact does not reveal real innovation but simply recalls Aristotle's three fundamental characters of being (*differentia, propria* and *accidens*). We thus have to ask whether it really makes sense to insist on this alleged turning point. Trying to develop Céard's thesis of the faithful scientist, Hoffmann concentrates on Boethius' notion of *contingens* which interprets the Aristotelian definition as an identification between what is and is possible. Scientists like Paré, Rondelet

---

⁷⁷Paré, *Monstres et prodiges, op. cit.*, p. 39.

⁷⁸Cf. Céard, "Tératologie et tératomancie au XVIᵉ siècle," in Marie-Thérèse Jones-Davies, ed., *Monstres et prodiges au temps de la Renaissance* (Paris: J. Touzot, 1980), p. 5.

⁷⁹"Quaecunque contra communem naturae legem et ordinem siunt, Monstra nominamus. . . . Prodigia vero definimus, eaque contra omnem naturae normam eveniunt, a natura nempe plane aliene et abhorrentia: quemadmodum si ex muliere Anguis aut Canis nascatur" (Paré, *Des Monstres, op. cit.*, p. 9).

⁸⁰Mathieu-Castellani, *op. cit.*, p. 9.

⁸¹Paré, *Monstres et prodiges*, ch. XXXII: "milliace de surperstitieuses sornettes."

⁸²Cf. Hoffmann, "Monsters and Modal Logic among French Naturalists of the Renaissance," in *South Central Review: The Journal of the South Central Modern Language Association* 10:2 (Summer 1993).

or Belon thus demonstrate that there is no causal determination, whereas modern research just concentrates on causality in order to predict contingent events. The difference between the chimæra and Paré's half-woman-half-bird monster may illustrate the problem: according to the principle that different objects cannot exist at the same time in the same place, the complete unified essences of all the different elements makes the chimæra impossible. Paré's hybrid, however, is an amalgam of different parts of the body and, therefore, is possible.

Numerous treatises and novels prove that at the end of the Renaissance, the golden age of the monsters, the interest in strange or miraculous beings has not died out. The triumph of rational thinking, however, can no longer be denied, although the intention of one of the above-mentioned works, Aldrovandi's *Monstrorum historia*, quoted by the founder of modern teratology, Isidore Geoffroy Saint-Hilaire, as well as by that expert on monsters, Gustave Flaubert, is the one which is farthest from the seventeenth century's principles of scientificity as represented by the "nouveaux tératologues."[83] The so-called "crisis of monsters" (*ibid.*) is thus announced halfway between Aldrovandi and Alessandro Vecchi:[84] while the 'history of monsters' of the former stagnates between the old belief in miracles and modern teratology, the latter obviously couldn't decide between mythical creatures and an anthropological-ethnological work in a more modern sense.

4 The "nouveaux tératologues"

Even in view of the increasing demand for a scientific approach the authors of the Renaissance did not forget that the notion of the monster derived from divine prophecy. Most of the treatises simply consider them as part of nature's wonders. Different attempts to find an etymological explanation lead — as we have already seen — to a dead-end-street and the idea that monsters probably not always threaten nature's *ordo* but could also be understood as signs of the beauty and variety of God's creation. God's creative potential meanwhile passes over to nature without, however, completely denying him. The 'Conseiller du Roy, Lieutenant particulier, Assesseur Criminel au siège Presidial de Condom' Scipion Du Pleix, thus defines the monster as "effet naturel, lequel dégènere de la droite et ordinaire disposition de son espèce: de sorte que les monstres sont bien outre

---

[83] Cf. Céard, "The Crisis of the Science of Monsters," in Philippe Desan, ed., *Humanism in Crisis. The Decline of the French Renaissance* (Ann Arbor: University of Michigan Press, 1991).

[84] Alessandro Vecchi, *Alla Quarta parte dell'Indie del Signor Giovanni Botero Benese. Di Mostri, & usanze di quelle parti, e di quei Ré con le sue figure al naturale. Raccolte novamente da Alessandro de Vecchi* (Venice, 1643).

nature, mais non pas pourtant contre nature, *praeter non contra* . . ."[85] As nature moves towards perfection it is, nevertheless, impossible to call monsters natural. The explanation that follows is rather half-hearted: "Bref, la nature, le but et la fin de laquelle est la génération, aime mieux produire quelque chose quoy qu'imparfaicte, que rien du tout. Mais tout aussi qu'un Peintre ne représente pas toujours naïvement la chose qu'il s'est imaginée ou proposée à peindre: de mesme la nature ne produit pas toujours son semblable" (*ibid.*, p. 494). Within the context of a growing autonomy of nature, a systematic diversity seems to be impossible, a change in thinking which is largely taken into consideration by the *nouveaux tératologues* like Johann Schenck, Martin Weinrich, Jean Riolan or Fortunio Liceti. Along with a growing uncertainty as to the origin of monsters, the number of fictions about miracles is increasing: "What remains then is the pleasure of relating some enjoyable stories and of counting on readers who will sample them. This pleasure is substituted for the desire for edification, or at least changes its meaning in a profound way: one will perhaps want to inspire a sense of the limits of knowledge, but one will no longer seek to make the signs legible."[86]

The development of the first scientific approaches to monsters is largely dependent on the movement of secularization at the end of the sixteenth and the beginning of the seventeenth century. As Kaspar Bauhin shows in his bibliography *De hermaphroditorum monstrosorumque*,[87] the *nouveaux tératologues* undertake a fundamental revision of the problem. Bauhin takes a closer look at the criterion *contra naturam* and, like Du Pleix, replaces it by *praeter* or actually *secundum naturam*, because in fact it is only the form that changes while the matter remains the same. Unfortunately Bauhin's argumentation displays several weak spots that probably hinder his aim. An examination of the notions *monstrum*, *portentum* and *prodigium* convinces Weinrich (*De ortu monstrorum*) to define monsters – like Aristotle did — as beings who do not resemble their parents. In his interpretation of the monster born in Paris (*De monstro nato Lutetiae A. D. 1605*) Jean Riolan strips the term 'monster' of all figurative meanings and, like Weinrich, differentiates between *monstrum in specie* (different species) and

---

[85] Scipion Du Pleix, *La physique ou science des choses naturelles* (1603; Rouen: Louys du Mesnil, 1640), p. 494.

[86] Céard, "The Crisis," *op. cit.*, p. 197.

[87] Kaspar Bauhin, *Caspari Bauhini ... De hermaphroditorum monstrosorumque partuum natura extheologorum, iureconsultorum, medicorum, philosophorum et rabbinorumsententia libri duo hactenus non editi ... : ex theologorum, iureconsultorum, medicorum, philosophorum et rabbinorumsententia ; libri duo hactenus non editi plane philologici infinitisexemplis illustrati omnium facultatum studiosis, lectu ut iucundissimi, sic & utilissimi* (Oppenheim: typis Hieronymi Galleri, aere Johan-Theodori de Bry, 1614).

monstrum in individuo (malformation). This should be regarded as an innovation preparing the ground for a new way of thinking, even if monsters as malformations can't be systematized and Riolan denies every possibility of classification: "L'irrégularité et le désordre n'ont pas de loi."[88] Fortunio Liceti's appeal to scientific exactness leads to the elimination of minor malformations whereas he fully recognizes the monster as an object of scientific research: "Monsters, like any other effect in nature, fall under four main causes: matter and form, the efficient cause and the final cause. . . . Hence the study of monstrosity belongs to the science of nature."[89] Johann Schenck (*Observationum medicarum, raraum, novarum, admirabilium et monstrosarum*, 1596), another representative of Céard's so-called *nouveaux tératologues*, concentrates mainly on refuting the thesis concerning the divine provenance of monsters. According to him, monsters are to be considered as medical objects. In his *Monstrorum historia memorabilis* (1609), his son, Johann-Georg Schenck, also qualifies monstrosity by telling the story of the armless but happy Thomas Schweicker. In fact, the *nouveaux tératologues* Weinrich, Riolan, Liceti and Schenck reserve the term 'monster' for beings which do not resemble to the specie of their parents or show striking malformations. The problem of prophecy thus seems to be resolved: "divination is futile, because the purported signs are not signs."[90] It is Liceti who throws light on the matter:

> Les monstres sont proprement ainsi nommés, non pas parce qu'ils soient, comme l'a cru Ciceron avec le Vulgaire, des presages des choses à venir; . . . Les monstres ne s'appellent donc pas ainsi, parce que ce sont des Signes qui presagent en quelque manière les choses qui doivent arriver: mais c'est parce qu'ils sont tels en eux-même, que leur nouveauté, et leur énormité les faisant considérer avec autant d'admiration que de surprise et d'étonnement, chacun se les montre réciproquement.[91]

Weinrich confirms:

> Si les monstres signifient, ils sont des signes. Ceux-ci seront ou naturels, ou artificiels. Car il n'y a que deux manières de signifier. S'ils sont artificiels, ils sont nécessairement ou divins ou humains. Que s'ils ne sont ni divins, ni humains, ni naturels, ils ne seront pas des signes. Dans les choses naturelles, il y a

---

[88] Riolan, quoted from Céard, *La nature et les prodiges, op. cit.*, p. 489 (cf. *De monstro nato Lutetiae* A. D. 1605, p. 6b).
[89] Liceti, quoted from *ibid.*, p. 446.
[90] Céard, *La nature et les prodiges*, p. 446.
[91] Liceti, quoted from *ibid.*, p. 453.

nécessairement entre le signe et le signifié une liaison (*connexio*), de sorte que l'un dépende de l'autre, comme le froid et le feu. Or, les guerres, les morts princières, les changement religieux . . . n'ont rien à voir avec les monstres et leurs causes. . . . On ne peut donc pas dire que les monstres sont des signes naturels. . . . Mais ils ne sont pas non plus des signes artificiels, car ce n'est pas décision humaine qu'ils naissent puisque personne ne voudrait ou ne pourrait engendrer un monstre à cette fin qu'il annonce quelque malheur . . .[92]

By this time at the latest the 'monster' has been freed from the chains of teratomancy. The new concepts of the above-mentioned scientists mark the beginning of a new scientific era in which monsters are no longer otherworldly phenomena or divine messengers. Instead, after being naturalized, they can be classified according to anatomic and etiological criteria and thus have found their place in the scientific system of nature.

5 The "quarrel of the monsters"

In the context of institutionalizing the new scientific thinking the art of anatomy with its public dissections is especially at the center of public interest.[93] At that point only entomology was able to keep up with the ongoing changes. Thanks to the discovery of the microscope at the beginning of the century, entomology provided a realm of endless marvels and imagination: "An entire world was revealed to the astonished observer. . . ."[94] In the emerging scientific approach, traditional legends and fantastic stories are gradually replaced by facts, reports on dissections or medical studies. But instead of vanishing, those stories reappear in different papers and reviews that do certainly not count among the most popular! Even serious journals like the *Journal des Savants, Recueil des Mémoires, Philosophical Transactions* or the *Giornale dei Letterati* publish these kind of stories. The alleged theory of imagination seems to return when the *Histoire de l'Académie Royale des Sciences* tells the story of a child that has been born with an ox kidney in place of the head because his mother couldn't satisfy her craving for innards. Not only do reviews and journals try to answer the

---

[92] Weinrich, quoted from *ibid.*, p. 449.
[93] Regarding the history of the life sciences, cf. Jacques Roger, *Les sciences de la vie dans la pensée française du XVIIe siècle* (1963; 3^d edition, Paris: Albin Michel, 1993 — translated as *The Life Sciences in Eighteenth-Century French Thought* by K. Benson [Stanford: Stanford University Press, 1997]). On the Theatrum Anatomicum, cf. Jo Brunnenberg & Emmanuel Cooper, *Theatrum anatomicum* (London: Aubrey Walter, 1993); Peter Gilles & Rainer Speck, eds., *Theatrum anatomicum* (Köln: Salon-Verlag, 1997).
[94] Roger, *Les sciences de la vie*, p. 185.

question "D'où viennent les monstres?"[95]; the Académie des Sciences vehemently discusses the same problem without coming to a solution.[96] The increasing number of public exhibitions of monsters emphasizes the enormous heterogeneity of different individual cases, but this tends to produce mere 'inventories' of curiosities.[97]

Most of the debates concentrate on the relation between the existence of monstrous beings and the theologically based theory of preformation, defended, e.g., by Fontenelle, the secretary of the Académie des Sciences, or Leibniz, who confirms the regularity of monsters but points out that it can't be grasped by human understanding.[98] In the anti-Cartesian philosophy of Malebranche this approach finds its most concise expression. Referring to the opposing position of the accidentalists, he skillfully eludes the question: "[N]éanmoins, il est certain qu'ils [sc. living beings, B.O.] ne reçoivent [leur] accroissement que par les lois générales de la nature, selon lesquelles tous les autres corps sont formés, ce qui fait que leur accroissement n'est pas toujours régulier et qu'ils s'en engendrent de monstrueux."[99] With the emergence of embryology, the scientific discussion intensifies and in 1724 Louis Lémery presents a bicephalous fetus which, according to him, is a product of accidental malformation of two originally 'normal' germs.[100] The subsequent famous academic quarrel about the "logic of the deviation" between Benignus Winslow on the preformationists' side and Lémery on the accidentalists' side starts in 1733 when Winslow, in a stirring speech against

---

[95] See Jean Saury, *Précis d'histoire naturelle, extrait des meilleurs auteurs français et étrangers; servant de suite et de supplément au "Cours de physique" de l'auteur, et à son "Histoire naturelle du globe," et formant la cinquième partie des opuscules de M. l'abbé Saury* (Paris: chez L'Auteur, 1778).

[96] To Fontenelle, the story of a Dutch princess who simultaneously gave birth to 265 children seemed to be purely fictitious; however, his own reports (e. g. on a child with a head formed like a kidney of a cow (1713) or a fetus who ressembled a bush of redcurrant (1715), etc.) published in the *Mémoires de l'Académie des Sciences*, do not really sound more trustworthy.

[97] See Anita Guerrini's essay in this volume.

[98] Gottfried Wilhelm Leibniz, *Essais de Théodicée*, III, § 241 (G VI, 261).

[99] Nicolas de Malebranche, "Eclaircissement sur le 6e livre de la Recherche de la Vérité," in *La Recherche de la Vérité* (Paris: M. David, 1700), vol. III, p. 325.

[100] "[L]e désordre, la confusion, le dérangement, la dépravation et l'abolition de différentes fonctions . . . une infinité de singularités d'autant plus insensées qu'elles attaquent formellement ou la vie, ou la santé, ou les usages des différentes parties . . .; dira-t-on que c'est un dessein qui a donné lieu à de pareils ouvrages? Mais, si c'en est un, on peut le regarder comme très mauvais, puisque ces procutions sont si folles, si défectueuses. . . . Mais lorsque abandonnant l'idée de dessein pour des ouvrages qui n'en méritent, ni n'en supposent, on se retourne du côté des causes accidentelles, on y aperçoit . . . tout le rapport et toute la production possible avec les défauts et l'extravagance des constructions monstrueuses. Ces causes sont aveugles; elles ne ménagent rien" (Louis Lémery, "Second mémoire sur les monstres," in *Mémoires de l'Académie des Sciences* [1738], pp. 323-324).

accidentalism, refers to Duverney's thesis.[101] His argumentation, founded on the existence of originally malformed germs, carefully eludes the notion of irregularity: "The monstrous arrangement is the trace of the workings of *another rule* — or an identical rule that has been misapplied, without losing its force or purpose – the manifest indication of *another order*, a *heterotaxia* in the Greek sense."[102] For his opponent Lémery, however, each monstrosity is the product of mechanically deformed, originally normal seeds. This approach supports both the secularization of anatomic discourse and, regarding his etiological orientation, the process of scientification. Lémery bases his arguments on the dissection of a monster by Duverney. He refuses Winslow's explanation of the malformation of the testicles, arguing that this kind of monstrosity can only be the result of a accidental mechanical pressure:[103] "Mais ce désordre devient moralement impossible dans le cas des œufs originairement monstrueux, où rien n'aurait dû se faire qu'en conséquence d'un dessein régulier," implying the notions of *regularity* and *irregularity* carefully avoided by Winslow. Those who do not — like Leibniz — accept the theory of the limited human understanding, can hardly integrate the "alliages bizarres et déraisonnables" or "constructions folles et extravagantes" in a divine conception. As an answer to that, Winslow in 1740 presents a monster without upper torso that does not show any signs of malformation. To Lémery's rather weak argument concerning the restriction of God's will and wisdom, Winslow responds with two other examinations based on rather old ideas of Goiffon and Haller. Meanwhile Lémery had fallen ill, couldn't answer and the quarrel seemed to be settled. As Tort's excellent study shows, Lémery's strategy undermines the preformationist theory without attacking orthodox metaphysics. He thus integrates the monsters as scientific objects within the field of pathological anatomy, and thereby paves the way for a new scientific thinking, in which Étienne and Isidore Geoffroy Saint-Hilaire play a key role, in their elaboration of an anti-preformationism reinforced by the successes of embryology.[104] Without denying his originality, Annie Ibrahim, however, refuses to consider Lémery as a predecessor of modern teratology. According to her, the accidental theory leads rather to an unsorted inventory of curious individual cases which,

---

[101] Cf. Tort, "La logiqe du déviant (Isidore Geoffroy Saint-Hilaire et la classification des monstres)," in *Revue des Sciences humaines* 4:188 (1982): special issue, *Le Monstre*.

[102] *Ibid.*, p. 7-8. In one of his reports published in the *Histoire de l'Académie* (1703, p. 28) Fontenelle even claims that the monstrous creations do not transgress the law: "Il peut y en avoir d'extraordinaires, mais non pas d'irréguliers."

[103] Lémery, "Sur les monstres. Premier Mémoire. Dans lequel on examine quelle est la cause immédiate des Monstres," in *Mémoires de l'Académie des Sciences* (1738), pp. 260-272.

[104] Tort, "La logique du déviant," p. 8.

in contrast to modern teratological thinking, does not obey any regularities.[105] So Lémery actually does not offer pioneer ideas but looks back on a world where nature acts blindly and where monsters refer to the borders of representation, "a limit-case in the theory of representation, which both threatens it and restores it."[106]

Obviously neither theory seems to have found an argument against the logical problems of anatomical and etiological classification. The old differentiation between monsters of excess und defective monsters finally becomes obsolete when anatomy raises the question: which kind of 'normality' do the notions of 'excess' and 'defect' refer to? The lack of a teratogenic base thus undermines every classification; as to the preformationists, they still believe in the divine character of the monster and save themselves the trouble of taxonomy. At first sight, the thesis of mechanical influences seems to pave the way to a systematic classification of anatomical deviations, but, in fact, the individuality of each case makes a homogeneous classification impossible. So we have to wait for Buffon to introduce a new way of thinking in natural history that theoretically confirms the classification system.

6   Buffon's principle of continuity

The first three volumes of Buffon's *Histoire Naturelle* represent not only a collection of different monstrous phenomena but, in the best pre-positivist sense, try to combine and generalize single facts by analogy.[107] Besides the three classical categories (*monstres par excès, monstres par défaut, monstres par transposition*) discussed in Jean-Henri Samuel Formey's article "MONSTRE,"[108] Buffon further innovates in teratology by explicitly making it a part of anatomy. The most relevant difference with the above-

---

[105] Cf. Isidore Geoffroy Saint-Hilaire: "Il [Lémery, B.O.] était conduit à ne voir dans les êtres anormaux que les produits aveugles et désordonnés du hasard" (*Histoire générale et particulière des anomalies de l'organisation chez l'homme et les animaux: ouvrage comprenant des recherches sur les caractères, la classification, l'influence physiologique et pathologique, les rapports généraux, les lois et les causes des monstruosités, des variétés et vices de conformation, ou traité de tératologie*, 3 vols. [Paris: J.-B. Baillière, 1832-1837], vol. 3, p. 491).

[106] Annie Ibrahim, "Métaphysique et anatomie au XVIIIe siècle. La théorie des monstres accidentels dans les Mémoires de Louis Lémery," in *Recherches sur le XVIIe siècle* 8 (1986), p. 31.

[107] Georges-Louis Leclerc de Buffon, *Histoire naturelle générale et particulière; servant de suite à la Théorie de la Terre & d'introduction à l'Histoire des minérau*, 44 vols. (Paris: Imprimerie Royale, 1749-1804). Cf. also J. Roger, *Buffon. Un philosophe au Jardin du Roi* (Paris: Fayard, 1989); Amor Cherni, *Buffon, la nature et son histoire* (Paris: PUF, 1997).

[108] Formey, "MONSTRE," in Diderot & D'Alembert, eds., *Encyclopédie ou dictionnaire raisonné des Sciences, des arts et des métiers* (Bern/Lausanne: chez les Sociétés Typographiques, 1753). Hereafter all articles from the *Encylopédie* are quoted in that form.

mentioned approaches in natural history or philosophy is what Foucault calls the 'principle of continuity':[109] "Pourquoi les ouvrages de la Nature sont-ils si parfaits? c'est que chaque ouvrage est un tout, et qu'elle travaille sur un plan éternel dont elle ne s'écarte jamais; elle prépare en silence les germes de ses productions, elle ébauche, par un acte unique, la forme primitive de tout être vivant: elle la développe, elle la perfectionne par un mouvement continu et dans un temps prescrit."[110] His work *Addition à l'article qui a pour titre: Variétés dans l'espèce humaine* marks one of the problems:

> [L]es hommes qui prennent la peine d'aller voir des choses au loin, croyent se dédommager de leurs travaux pénibles en rendant ces choses plus merveilleuses; à quoi bon sortir de son pays si l'on n'a rien d'extraordinaire à présenter ou à dire à son retour? Les récits bizarres dont tant de Voyageurs on souillé leurs écrits en croyant les orner. Un esprit attentif, un Philosophe instruit reconnaît aisément les faits purement controuvés qui choquent la vraisemblance ou l'ordre de la Nature.[111]

According to Greenblatt, those anecdotal, strange narrations might, however, give insights by representing the unexpected, the encounter with difference.[112] Besides Buffon's interest in individual cases such as Geneviève, the 'white negro',[113] his definition of monsters is based on a notion of continuous evolution, which excludes all individual and accidental cases. He concludes his chapter on monsters by ironically criticizing the theory of preformation: "Mais n'est-ce pas ajouter une absurdité ridicule et indigne du Créateur, à un système mal conçu que nous avons assez réfuté, volume IV, et qui ne peut être adopté ni soutenu dès qu'on prend la peine de l'examiner?" (*ibid.*, p. 416).

7 Maupertuis and the evolutionary transformations

Inspired by the public exhibition of a 'white negro' in Paris, the French philosopher Maupertuis starts to write a *Dissertation sur le nègre blanc*,

---

[109] Cf. Foucault, *Les mots et les choses* (Paris: Gallimard, 1966), translation, *The Order of Things*, trans. A. Sheridan (New York: Pantheon, 1994), chapter 5: "Classifying."
[110] Buffon, *Histoire naturelle, op. cit.*, supplement to vol. VII, p. 8.
[111] *Ibid.*, supplement to vol. VIII, pp. 207-208.
[112] Cf. Stephen Greenblatt, *Marvelous Possessions. The Wonders of the World* (Chicago: University of Chicago Press, 1991).
[113] Cf. Buffon, *Histoire naturelle*, supplement to vol. VIII, pp. 389-390. He reports his examinations of the eighteen-year-old Geneviève meticulously, but even more interesting than his descriptions are the illustrations, depicting her in the iconographically well-known pose of the "good savage" — quite a contrast to the alleged 'objectivity' of the scientific description.

followed only one year later (in 1745) by his famous work, *Vénus physique*. Whilst the *Dissertation* concentrates on the question of generation, the *Vénus physique* emphasizes the genealogical principles. The phenomenon of the 'white negro', already classified as non-monstrous by Liceti[114] and Buffon, takes up a large part of the discussion.[115] In fact, the eighteenthcentury seems to be highly interested in this phenomenon, so it is not surprising that even Diderot and D'Alembert's *Encyclopédie* contributes to the debate:

> Quelques-uns ont cru que cette bizarrerie de la nature était due à l'imagination frappée des femmes grosses. D'autres se sont imaginés que la couleur de ces nègres venait d'une espèce de lèpre dont eux et leurs parens étaient infectés. . . . Quelques-uns ont cru que les nègres blancs venaient du commerce monstrueux des gros singes du pays avec des négresses; mais ce sentiment ne paroît pas probable, vû qu'on assure que ces nègres blancs sont capables de se propager. Quoi qu'il en soit, il paroît que l'on ne connoît pas toutes les *variétés et les bizarreries de la nature*; peut-être que l'intérieur de l'Afrique, si peu connu des Européens, renferme des peuples nombreux d'une espèce entièrement ignorée de nous.

Referring to the problem of these *variétés* and *bizarreries de la nature*, Maupertuis tries to articulate his position on evolutionary continuity by assuming the existence of a perfect instinct, a kind of Aristotelian entelechy or, in more modern terms, a *vis essentialis*.[116] At the same time he brings together the physical laws of attraction, described by Newton, the theories of generation and the works of Étienne Geoffroy Saint-Hilaire on the laws of chemical affinity. The principle of epigenesis, that is the development of an organism by continuous evolutionary process, constitutes another pillar of his approach. His attitude towards preformationist theory is perfectly clear:

---

[114]Liceti, *Traité des monstres, op. cit.*, p. 163.

[115]More than a century later, the German scientist Rudolf Virchow refers to the phenomenon that seems to 'thwart' Maupertuis' atavistic theory: "Denn obwohl es sich gelegentlich ereignet, daß ein Neger weiß und ein Weißer schwarz wird, so geschieht dies doch nur auf dem Wege der Abnormität, wie bei den Mißbildungen. Ein weißer Neger hat trotz seiner hellen Haut alle sonstigen Eigenschaften eines Negers; er ist und bleibt ein weißer Neger" (*Menschen- und Affenschädel* [Berlin: Lüderitz, 1870], p. 35).

[116]*Dissertation inauguraris metaphysica, de universalis naturae systemate* (1751), which will be translated and republished later as the *Essai sur les corps organisés* or *Système de la nature*. Cf. also Caspar Friedrich Wolff, *Theoria generationis* (1759; Halle: J.-C. Hendel, 1774). On the notion of development cf. J. Roger, "La notion du développement chez les naturalistes du XVIIIe siècle," in O. Bloch *et al.*, eds., *Entre forme et histoire. La formation de la notion de développement à l'âge classique* (Paris: Klincksieck, 1988), pp. 119-125.

> Cependant si l'on examine avec plus d'attention ce système, on voit qu'au fond il n'explique rien; que supposer tous les individus formés par la volonté du créateur dans un même jour de la création, est plutôt *raconter un miracle* que donner une explication physique; qu'on ne gagne même rien par cette simultanéité, puisque ce qui nous paraît successif est toujours pour Dieu simultané. Enfin les expériences les plus exactes et les phénomènes les plus décisifs font voir qu'on ne peut supposer cette suite infinie d'individus, ni dans un sexe ni dans l'autre, et renversent le système de fond en comble.[117]

Although Maupertuis does not elucidate the latter argument, he summarizes all provisos as to the preformationist theory, which in the scientific context, however, has to be regarded as the most successful approach during the first half of the eighteenth century, even in light of Harvey's revolutionary experiments. In order to analyze the system of evolutionary continuity, Maupertuis works on the possible sources of error. First of all he brackets off hybrids, because of their inability to reproduce. His evolutionary-transformist thinking is primarily founded on the so-called 'memory' of the elements, or in other words, "the recognition that *matter posses its own 'thought'*, presiding over physical order as a whole."[118] Combined with the tendency of the elements to return to their original state, Maupertuis explains the onto- and phylogenesis of normal and monstrous phenomena: ". . . chaque degré d'erreur aurait fait une nouvelle espèce; et à force d'écarts répétés serait venue la diversité infinie des animaux que nous voyons aujourd'hui . . ."[119] Failures and breaks, that is monsters, thus do not only ensure differentiation and diversification, but build up the norm. As Tort puts it, "the anomaly can become, through hereditary transmission, the *norm* of a species. This leads in turn to the multiplication of species *by accidental variation* carried on by heredity, which then serves as a stabilizer; but this does not rule out a new accident, the basis for a new variety, which the 'white negro' of the *Vénus physique* might be the prototype of."[120]

---

[117] Maupertuis, *Essai sur la formation des corps organisés* (Berlin, 1754), pp. 10-11.

[118] Tort, *L'Ordre et les monstres. Le débat sur l'origine des déviations anatomiques au XVIIIe siécle* (Paris: Le Sycomore, 1980; 2nd ed., Paris: Editions Syllepse, 1998), p. 46. The mnemonic capacity could relate to Lucretius who, in the second book of his natural history, parts from the idea that all elements are capable of retaining their specific characters. According to Bénabou this capacity proves that monsters are a mere product of our imagination, a merging of different simulacra (Marcel Bénabou, "Monstres et hybrides chez Lucrèce et Pline l'Ancien," in Leon Poliakov, ed., *Hommes et bêtes: Entretiens sur le racisme* [Paris: Mouton, 1975], p. 144).

[119] Cf. Maupertuis, *Système de la nature*, in *Œuvres* (Lyon: J.-M. Bruyset, 1756), § XLIV, emphasis mine.

[120] Tort, *L'Ordre et les monstres*, op. cit., p. 48.

If, at the beginning, the innovative 'breaks' still count as a discontinuous disorder, the principle of evolutionary continuity at last becomes effective by integrating this 'temporary weakness' of memory in the economy of the process. Without further discussing Maupertuis' theory of generation, let's retain that his basic aim is to abolish preformationist theory in favour of a more economical approach based on continuity. Despite different argumentations Maupertuis and Buffon both come to the conclusion that monsters have to be considered as breaks or failures in the process of a continuous evolution. As valuable sources of synchronous and diachronous reconstruction, monsters thus contribute to the history of science.

8 The science of monsters

René-Antoine Ferchault de Réaumur, Albrecht von Haller, Lazzaro Spallanzani, Charles Bonnet and Chrétien Guillaume Lamoignon de Malesherbes turn out to be hostile towards Buffon's method of reason and combination. Defending the predominance of 'pure' observation, theses theories, in fact, mainly serve to falsify the thesis of epigenesis and spontaneous generation. Only a speculative atheist may accept epigenesis, because his "sobre imagination ne pèse pas les vraisemblances." Each non-divine creation, however, is a matter of chance which, according to Bonnet, "ne peut former que des bâtards."[121]

In the course of consolidation of the modern sciences, the Enlightenment promotes the process of naturalization of monsters. This epistemological shift, however, is far too often simplified and reduced to a logical consequence of the rationalizing explanations of a universal Cartesianism.[122] Having awoken from Descartes' dream of universal mathematics, his successors distrusted all kind of universal systems. Of course, the early eighteenth century proceeds much more systematically, but Voltaire's fondness for unexplained curiosities and rarities has not lost its fascination: "Vous cherchez en vain comment un enfant se forme, et vous voulez que je sache comment il se déforme."[123] If natural laws can't be entirely understood, scientists rather hold onto descriptive and numerical success and, once again, science seems to become a mere inventory. In the mid-eighteenth century, the *Encyclopédie* reflects a much more rational understanding of monstrosity. Even if malformations still violate the *ordo* of nature, their demystification

---

[121] Charles Bonnet, quoted from Roger, *Les Sciences de la vie, op. cit.*, p. 732.

[122] "For, in truth, when painters try to create sirens and satyrs by the most fantastic and extraordinary forms, they cannot give them natures which are new in all respects; they simply make a medley of the limbs of different animals" (Descartes, *First Meditation*, in *Œuvres*, eds. Adam-Tannery [Paris: Vrin/CNRS, 1964-1976], VII, 20).

[123] Voltaire, "Influence," in *Questions sur l'Encyclopédie*, in *Œuvres Complètes*, ed. L. Moland (Paris: Garnier, 1879), vol. 19, p. 466.

is already largely accepted. Jean-Henri Samuel Formey defines the monster as follows in the article "MONSTRE": "[A]nimal . . . avec une structure de parties très différentes de celles qui caractérisent l'espèce des animaux dont il sort."[124] If, according to Louis de Jaucourt, who wrote the article "PRODIGE," in former times, monsters could terrify entire nations, nowadays they only serve as pure amusement for scientists.[125] La Fosse, writer of the second article on monsters in 1777, completely agrees with that interpretation. Contemporaneous to observations, dissections and analysis of monstrous forms, new scientific discourses came up drawing attention on two basic notions, that is *ordo* and chaos: "Far from serving as a benign reference point within a rational nature . . ., the monster was, in many ways, the anatomical corroboration of the breakdown of objective truth."[126]

In recent years, many researchers have tried to reconstruct a kind of Foucauldian *archéologie de l'imaginaire scientifique et littéraire* concerning monsters and monstrosity in the eighteenth century. Consider in particular the revolutionary works of Jean Ehrard and Jacques Roger, Patrick Tort or Jean-Louis Fischer, not to mention the excellent texts of Thomas Macho, Michaël Hagner or Volker Oldenburg.[127] Further, Barbara Stafford has carefully analyzed the metaphoric meaning of the monster during the Age of Enlightenment, and Antoine de Baecque has dealt with the role of monsters

---

[124]Formey, "MONSTRE," *Encyclopédie*, vol. XXII, pp. 162-166.

[125]Louis de Jaucourt, "PRODIGE," in *ibid.*, vol. XXVII, p. 2.

[126]Andrew Curran & Patrick Graille, "The Faces of Eighteenth-Century Monstrosity," in *idem*, eds., *Faces of Monstrosity in Eighteenth-Century Thought, op. cit.* p. 3.

[127]Jean Ehrard, *L'idée de nature en France dans la première moitié du XVIIIe siècle* (Paris: Albin Michel, 1994); *id.*, *L'invention littéraire au XVIIIe siècle: fiction, idées, société* (Paris: PUF, 1997); Jean-Louis Fischer, "L'hybridologie et la zootaxie au siècles des Lumières," *Revue de synthèse* 101-102 (1981), and "Sens, contre-sens et synonymie dans l'emploi des termes "mulet," "métis" et "hybride" en zoologie de 1749 à 1860," in *Documents pour l'Histoire du vocabulaire scientifique* 2 (1981); *idem*, "De la genèse fabuleuse à la morphogenèse des monstres," *Cahiers d'histoire et philosophie des sciences* (SFHST) 13 (1986); *idem*, "Des mots et des monstres: réflexions sur le vocabulaire de la tératologie," *Documents pour l'Histoire du vocabulaire scientifique* 8, CNRS, INALF (1986); *idem*, *Monstres: histoire du corps et de ses défauts* (Paris: Syros, 1991); *idem*, *Leben und Werk von Camille Dareste, 1822-1899. Schöpfer der experimentellen Teratologie* (Leipzig: Barth, 1994); *idem*, "L'Encyclopédie présente-t-elle une pré-science des monstres?," in *Recherches sur Didérot et sur l'Encyclopédie* 16 (1994); *idem*, "Monstre," in Michel Delon, ed., *Dictionnaire européen des Lumières* (Paris: PUF, 1997); J. Roger, "La notion de développement," *op. cit.* and *Les Sciences de la vie, op. cit.*; P. Tort, *L'ordre et les monstres, op. cit.*, and "La logique du déviant," *op. cit.*; Thomas Macho, "'Der Traum der Vernunft gebiert Ungeheuer'. Spekulationen über Geschichte und Topik der Grusselliteratur," in *Unter dem Pflaster liegt der Strand* 15 (1984); *id.*, "Ursprünge des Monströsen. Zur Wahrnehmung verunstalteter Menschen," in Kirsten Breitenfellner & Charlotte Kohn-Ley, eds., *Wie ein Monster entsteht* (Bodenheim: Philo Verlagsgesellschaft, 1998); Hagner, ed., *Der falsche Körper, op. cit.*; Oldenburg, *Der Mensch und das Monströse, op. cit.*

in caricatural representations of the same era. Many literary monsters are, amongst others, examined by Marie-Isoline Françoise Marsaud or Jean-Luc Steinmetz who gave us new insights into Sade's monstrous writing, Alberto Beretta Anguissola who discussed the same subject in the works of Foigny, Casanova and Rétif de la Bretonne. Several articles of Annie Ibrahim (including one in this volume), as well as a dissertation by Andrew Curran focus on Diderot's interpretation of monstrosity. The imagination theory also does not come off badly, and following from Marie-Hélène Huet's excellent, interdisciplinary work, Denis Todd examines the recurrent theme of feminine imagination as a source of monstrosity.[128]

Within the scope of different methods and models, the eighteenth-century monster seems to be a formless, fluctuating and hybrid being, occupying an ambiguous position between empiricism, fantasy and metaphoric speaking.: "[L]e monstre est une forme informe qui n'appartient pas (encore) à un genre déjà connu, recensé, affublé de nom."[129] Even if we accept that the eighteenth century has delivered rich material and theoretical approaches to the process of naturalization, some authors can't free themselves from their deeply rooted superstition or monstrous fantasies, as for example Maupertuis and his fantastic Patagonia or Voltaire's satyrs. Undoubtedly, Delisle de Sales' question "What is a monster?" opens onto one of the most important notions of alterity in eighteenth century thinking, but, in fact, initially, the rationalization of the monster was obviously less urgent than the representation of the moral and / or physical anomalies of man: "[I]f not on a dissection table, in a *cabinet d'histoire naturelle*, or at a fair, then within the monster's other eighteenth-century venue — the learned journal."[130] Some researchers thus rather seem to provoke the process of naturalization. More modestly, we should state that during the Enlightenment, most of the monsters have been moved to the world of fantasy while physical anomalies

---

[128] Annie Ibrahim, "The Status of Anomalies in the Philosophy of Diderot" (this volume); *id.*, "Métaphysique et anatomie au XVIIIe siècle," *op. cit.*, and her "Diderot ou le paradoxe du développement aléatoire," in O. Bloch *et al.*, eds., *Entre forme et histoire*, *op. cit.*; A. Curran & P. Graille, "The Faces of Eighteenth-Century Monstrosity," *op. cit.*, *id.*, P. Graille, "Exhibiting the Monster: Nicolas-François and Geneviève Regnault's Les Écarts de la Nature," in *Faces of Monstrosity*, *op. cit.*; *id.*, *Sublime Disorder: Physical Monstrosity in Diderot's Universe* (PhD, New York University, 1996; revised version, Oxford: Voltaire Foundation, 2001); *id.*, "Monsters and the Self in the "Rêve d'Alembert," in *Faces of Monstrosity*, *op. cit.*; Huet, "Living Images: Monstrosity and Representation," in *Representations* 4 (1987); *id.*, *Monstrous Imagination*, *op. cit.*; *id.*, "Deadly Fears: Dom Augustin Calmet's Vampires and the Rule Over Death," in *Faces of Monstrosity*, *op. cit.*; Denis Todd, *Imagining Monsters: Miscreations of the Self in Eighteenth-Century England* (Chicag: University of Chicago Press, 1995).
[129] Christian Jaedicke, *Nietzsche: figures de la monstruosité. Tératographies* (Paris: L'Harmattan, 1998), p. 8.
[130] Curran & Graille, "The Faces of Eigtheenth-Century Monstrosity," p. 12.

were classified within the largely unexplored field of biogenesis, where they "emerge both as threat for order and epistemic signs."[131] At the end of the century, the rather different epigenetic approaches were lumped together to form the central argument against preformationist theory and thus the 'old monsters' become highly interesting objects of scientific study. In the epigenetic perspective, deviations mostly represent malformation during different phases of onto- or phylogenetic development. Of course, this is not an actual explanation, but nevertheless it allows insights into normal development.[132] The central notions of that era's scientific restructuring thus are, according to Wolf Lepenies, "breakthrough of evolutionary thinking," "processualization and denaturalization of notions of time," and "trivialization of the extraordinary."[133] The wave of naturalization thus sweeps away the monster and makes it disappear in order to let it reemerge in different variations and contexts: medicine now treats it as a pathological deviation or anomaly, ethnological or anthropological discourses call it either *bon sauvage*, stranger or strange being, whereas aesthetic contexts mostly functionalize it as the evil, the grotesque or, simply, the Other. The different approaches are located, as Lepenies argues, in different representational forms of knowledge and deviations, such as the cabinet of curiosities, natural history or rarities, fairs and sideshows as well as laboratories and anatomical, ethnological or anthropological research.

9 Diderot and the aesthetic or metaphoric question of the monster

> L'homme n'est qu'un effet commun, le monstre qu'un effet rare, tous les deux également naturels, également nécessaires, également das l'ordre universel (Denis Diderot).[134]

While Voltaire's answer to Delisle de Sales' question *What is a monster?* — "Donnerons-nous ce nom [monstre] à un animal énorme, à un poisson, à un serpent de quinze pieds de long? mais il y en a de vingt, de trente pieds, auprès desquels les premiers seraient peu de chose"[135] — obviously proves

---

[131] Hagner, "Vom Naturalienkabinett zur Embryologie," in Hagner, ed., *Der falsche Körper*, op. cit., p. 74.

[132] It was the conviction of the English anatomist John Hunter that monstrous deviation could enlighten normal evolution which paved the way for the monster's naturalization in the eighteenth century. So the notion of 'monster' disappears, to be replaced soon by 'anomaly'.

[133] "Durchbruch des Entwicklungsgedankens," "Prozessualisierung und Denaturalisierung der Zeitvorstellungen," "Veralltäglichung des Außerordentlichen" (Lepenies, *Das Ende der Naturgeschichte* [München: C. Hanser, 1976], p. 203).

[134] Diderot, *Le Rêve de D'Alembert*, DPV XVII, 138.

[135] Voltaire, "Questions sur l'Encyclopédie," in op. cit., vol. 20, p. 273.

the need for further discussion, Diderot, confronted with the same problem, comes to another conclusion and thus defines the monster as "[u]n être, dont la durée [est] incompatible avec l'ordre subsistant."[136] The existing order, however, shows "fluctuating figures of uncertainty,"[137] and cannot bear comparison. D'Holbach falls behind both authors by restricting himself to the argument of the limited human understanding: "Il ne peut y avoir de monstres, ni prodiges, ni merveilles, ni miracles dans la nature. Ce que nous appelons des monstres sont des combinaisons avec lesquelles nos yeux ne sont pas familiarisés."[138] In *Exposition des variations de la nature dans l'espèce humaine* (1771), Toussaint Guindant tries to put the epistemological shift into words: "Nous trouvons dans l'ordre de la nature tout ce qui s'en écarte: qu'aucun de ces phénomènes ne lui est contraire..."[139] Diderot's admiration for nature's disorder thus refers less to scientific innovation than to an aesthetic surplus: "L'ordre d'un cabinet ne peut être celui de la nature; la nature affecte partout un désordre sublime."[140]

In the course of a growing general interest in monsters which finds its expression in numerous articles in journals like the *Mémoires* of the Académie des Sciences or the Académie de chirurgie as well as in magazines like the *Gazette* or the *Mercure de France,* Diderot — whose career actually began with his translation of Robert James' *Dictionary of Medicine* — seems to be more and more enthusiastic about teratological research.[141] The figure of

---

[136] Diderot, *Éléments de physiologie*, DPV XVII, 444.

[137] Curran, *Sublime Disorder, op. cit.*, p. 4. For Curran, the Diderotian monster is to be understood in a logic of similarity, a "mirror-image reflecting the endemic pathology of the human race" (*ibid.*)

[138] Baron d'Holbach, *Système de la nature, ou des Loix du Monde Physique et du Monde Moral* ('London', 2nd edition, 1781; reprint, Paris: Fayard, coll. "Corpus," 1990), i.e. *Système de la nature* (...) I, vi.

[139] Guindant, *Exposition des variations de la nature dans l'espèce humaine, où l'on demande si, posées les lois naturelles et les plus générales sur lesquelles portent l'ordre et l'harmonie du corps humain, la nature peut quelquefois s'en écarter* (Paris: Debure Père, 1771), pp. 171–172.

[140] Diderot, "Cabinet d'histoire naturelle," DPV VI, 240. In the same text, however, Diderot marks the incompatibility between the conception of a *cabinet d'histoire naturelle*, a *Kunstkammer* and the principles of enlightenment: "Pour former un cabinet d'histoire naturelle, il ne suffit pas de rassembler sans choix, & d'entasser sans ordre & sans goût, tous les objets d'histoire naturelle que l'on rencontre; il faut savoir distinguer ce qui mérite d'être gardé de ce qu'il faut rejeter, & donner à chaque chose un arrangement convenable. ... un cabinet d'histoire naturelle est fait pour instruire; c'est là que nous devons trouver en détail & par ordre, ce que l'univers nous présente en bloc" (*ibid.*).

[141] For further information on Diderot and monsters cf. Anne-Marie Chouillet & Jacques Chouillet, eds., *Colloque International Diderot (1713-1784)* (Paris: Aux Amateurs de Livres, 1985); Curran, *Sublime Disorder, op. cit., id.*, "Monsters and the Self in the *Rêve de D'Alembert," op. cit.*; Fischer, "L'Encyclopédie présente-t-elle une pré-science des monstres?", *op. cit.*; Emita B. Hill, "Materialism and Monsters in *Le Rêve de D'Alembert,*" in *Diderot Studies* 10 (1968); *id.*, "The Role of *le monstre* in Diderot's

the monster captivates his interest and he dedicates a central part of his philosophy to it. The *Lettre sur les aveugles* (1749),[142] *Entretien entre Diderot et D'Alembert, Suite de l'Entretien* and, especially, *Le Rêve de D'Alembert* (1769) prove his increasing, extraordinary interest in monsters. For Diderot, monsters without noses, ears, feet, hand or even headless beings, monsters with two heads, four eyes, four ears, three testicles, four arms or six fingers, Siamese twins, a *situs inversus* and even hermaphrodites are no mere *lusus naturæ* or nature's failures but natural deviations which are produced in the context of evolutionary, that is natural, selection. Numerous monsters, however, are created either by man's lacking knowledge, as Diderot shows with his example of the cyclops in the *Rêve de D'Alembert*,[143] or they are results of the human need for wonders: "Docteur, racontez-le-moi. Je suis comme les enfants, j'aime les faits merveilleux, et quand ils font honneur à l'espèce humaine, il m'arrive rarement d'en disputer la vérité."[144]

As the eighteenth century can be considered as a golden age of research on generation, Diderot's treatment of monsters as peripheral phenomena of evolution confirms his scientific interest, which at the same time seems to be metaphorically transformed to reflect both his political and his aesthetic ideas:

Thought," in *Studies on Voltaire and the Eighteenth Century* 97 (1972); Ibrahim, "The Status of Anomalies in Diderot's Thought," this volume, and "Diderot ou le paradoxe du développement aléatoire," *op. cit.*; Norman G. Laidlaw, "Diderot's Teratology," in *Diderot Studies* 4 (1963); Jean Mayer, "Les Êtres et les monstres dans la philosophie de Diderot," in Chouillet & Chouillet, eds., *Colloque International Diderot*, *op. cit.*; Marc Regaldo, *Lumières et tératologie* (Bordeaux: Université de Gascogne, Bordeaux-III, 1980).

[142] The blind Saunderson calls himself a monster; according to Hill he is "a throwback, anomalous to the present order" ("The role of *le monstre*," p. 178). And like the continuous noise of Foucault's monsters (*Les mots et les choses*, p. 169), Diderot / Saunderson part from the idea of original monstrosity: "Imaginez donc, si vous voulez, que l'ordre qui vous frappé a toujours subsisté; mais laissez-moi croire qu'il n'en est rien, et que, si nous remontions à la naissance des choses et des temps, et que nous sentissions la matière se mouvoir et le chaos se débrouiller, nous rencontrerions une multitude d'êtres informes, pour quelques êtres bien organisés. . . . que les monstres se sont anéantis successivement; que toutes les combinaisons vicieuses de la matière ont disparu, et qu'il n'est resté que celles où le mécanisme n'impliquait aucune contradiction importante et qui pouvaient subsister par elles-mêmes et se perpétuer" (Diderot, *Lettre sur les aveugles*, DPV IV, 50). Only a few years later, Diderot develops a kind of evolutionary theory.

[143] If Bordeu concludes that cyclops are the result of a mutation, Mademoiselle de l'Epinasse parts from the conviction that "[l]e Cyclope ne pourrait donc bien ne pas être un être fabuleux" (Diderot, *Rêve*, DPV XVII, 149). The monster becomes a "diversité" and, in fact, the annotation refers to the wax figure of a Cyclops, made by Mlle Biheron, future Mme Tussaud. An illustration of the same figure was published in the *Mercure de France* (1766) and reappears in Supplément IV (1777) of Buffon's *Histoire Naturelle*.

[144] Diderot, *Rêve*, *op. cit.*, p. 166.

> Tout change, tout passe, il n'y a que le tout qui reste. Le monde commence et finit sans cesse; il est à chaque instant à son commencement et à sa fin. ... Dans cet immense océan de matière, pas une molécule qui ressemble à une molécule, pas une molécule qui se ressemble à elle-même un instant. *Rerum novus nascitur ordo*, voilà son inscription éternelle. ... *Naître, vivre et passer, c'est changer de formes*. Et qu'importe une forme ou une autre? Chaque forme a le bonheur et le malheur qui lui est propre.[145]

Discoveries like the parthogenetic reproduction of the greenfly by Charles Bonnet as well as the regenerative ability of the freshwater polyp by Abraham Trembley largely influence Diderot's 'neo-Epicurean' system of natural transformations.[146] The center of this system, which is ruled by chance and necessity, is the embryonic structure of the *faisceau*, running through various metamorphoses: "Le faisceau de fils constitue la différence originelle et première de toutes les espèces d'animaux. Les variétés du faisceau d'une espèce font toutes les variétés monstrueuses de cette espèce."[147] Species thus only represent tendencies of an always fluctuant universe, in which "everything acts and reacts continually."[148] Accidental breakdowns and rare mutations thus produce new species which stabilize by continuous repetition: "L'homme n'est qu'un effet commun, le monstre un effet rare."[149]

Of course, and I already mentioned this, Diderot — according to Annie Ibrahim — does not put forth a biological, embryonic or teratological theory. Curran shares this opinion: "It is the conviction that the deformed become 'monstrous' against a variety of conceptual criteria and shifting epistemological backgrounds."[150] As Hill points out, Diderot's theory on monsters thus has to be understood both in interaction with the shifting epistemological background of his own era and with his own reflections on his translation of Shaftesbury's *An Enquiry Concerning Merit and Virtue* (originally published 1699). His works offer a gallery of monstrosities located on discursive and situative levels which recall contemporary aesthetics:

> Indeed, Diderot's presentation of monstrosity might be better linked to the aesthetic of exhibition at the Foire Saint Germain and Foire Saint Laurent (where monsters were shown to a paying public) than to the academic debates concerning the origin of monstrous formations. Thrust before the reader's eyes,

---

[145] *Ibid.*, pp. 128, 139.
[146] Cf. Regaldo, *Lumières et tératologie, op. cit.*
[147] Diderot, *Rêve*, DPV XVII, 150.
[148] Hill, "The Role of *le monstre*," *op. cit.*, p. 184.
[149] Diderot, *Rêve*, DPV XVII, 138.
[150] Curran, *Sublime Disorder, op. cit.*, p. 16.

> Diderot's monsters signal an epistemological uncertainty; their very form is designed to corrupt contexts, question a universal morality based on a normative view of the human body.[151]

Diderot's eccentric and, at the same time, seductive position does not scientifically differentiate between the notions of *monstre, bizarrerie, vice, désordre* or *écart*, but creates a lot of metaphors reflecting both the awkward semantics and the fragile epistemological basis of such notions. The abundance of material supposed to prove teratological knowledge turns out to be useless for positive teratology because of the originality of the individual cases. The model of an originally chaotic and, therefore, deviant world proposed in the *Lettre sur les aveugles*, both gives up the dream of homology between the rational and the real world, and transgresses the borders of teratological science.[152] In order to establish a theory of difference as variety of borders, Diderot refers to Lucretian and Spinozist models as Bordeu indicates several times in the *Rêve*. As Ibrahim states, Diderot's intention was less directed to teratology, and more "towards the materialist fiction of the uneasiness of the molecule, an unpredictable uneasiness that produces the new and combines unexpected variations, through grafts and spontaneous hybridizations." In aesthetic theory, the monster does not represent the negative standard but a gradual alterity in a continuum of forms.[153]

In a detailed comment on his translation of Shaftesbury's *Enquiry Concerning Merit and Virtue*, Diderot places the problem of the monster in the context of aesthetic representation:

> Si l'on désigne par ce terme un composé de parties rassemblées au hasard, sans liaison, sans ordre, sans harmonie, sans proportion, j'ose assurer que la représentation de cet être ne sera pas moins choquante que l'être lui-même. . . . Qu'entendez-vous donc par un monstre? Un être qui ressemble à quelque chose, tel que la sirène, l'hippogriffe, le faune, le sphinx, la chimère et les dragons ailés? Mais n'apercevez-vous pas que ces enfants de l'imagination des peintres et des poètes n'ont rien d'absurde dans leur conformation; que, quoiqu'ils n'existent pas dans la nature, il n'ont rien de contradictoire aux idées de liaison, d'harmonie, d'ordre et de proportion?[154]

---

[151] Curran & Graille, "Faces of monstrosity," *op. cit.*, p. 9.

[152] "The current state of the universe ('ordered') was preceded by an original chaotic state ('disordered'). Order came after the fact" (Ibrahim, "The Status of Anomalies").

[153] The above-mentioned suggestion, to consider man as an "effet commun" and the monster as an "effet rare" already makes the irreducible difference of the monstrous other disappear in order to bring both varieties closer to each other.

[154] Shaftesbury, *Essai sur le mérite et la vertu*, trans. Diderot, DPV I, 323 (translator's

Moral, physical, real and fictitious monsters play an important role by reflection the beauty of the ugly as an autonomous aesthetic category: "Il n'est point de monstre odieux qui, par l'art imité, ne puisse plaire aux yeux[155]; quelque difforme que soit un être (si toutefois il y a difformité réelle), il plaira pourvu qu'il soit bien représenté" (*ibid.*, p. 323). This approach inevitably contradicts contemporary aesthetics with its aim to create eternal values: "Even when Diderot is persuaded of the existence of monsters in nature, their appropriateness to artistic representation seems questionable. The artist attempts to create works with eternal validity. If monsters are ephemeral creatures, doomed, as Diderot claims, to be destroyed by nature herself, why should the artist risk offending his public by representing ugly misfits and immoralizing nature's mistakes?"[156] Charles Batteux, a contemporary of Diderot, also states that the mere existence of monsters should not be a reason to eternalize these "êtres contradictoires" instead of the notions of "belle nature" and "beau absolu":

> Que dirait-on d'un Peintre qui représenterait les hommes petits, maigres, bossus, boiteux, etc. comme ils le sont souvent dans la nature? . . . L'esprit humain ne peut créer qu'improprement: toutes ses productions portent l'empreinte d'un modèle. Les monstres mêmes, qu'une imagination déréglée se figure dans ses délires, ne peuvent être composés que de parties prises dans la Nature. Et si le Génie, par caprice, fait de ces parties un assemblage contraire aux lois naturelles, en dégradant la Nature, il se dégrade lui-même, et se change en une espèce de folie. Les limites sont marquées, dès qu'on les passe on se perd. On fait un chaos plutôt qu'un monde, et on cause de l'horreur plutôt que du plaisir.[157]

Batteux thus simply excludes monsters as objects of artistic creation, whereas Lessing's aesthetic assigns them an aesthetic role, however insignificant. Diderot's position is quite different. On the one hand he fully agrees with Bordeu, on the other hand the "emotive or evocative power"[158] of individual deviations counts as an essential criterion for beauty: "Voulez-vous que je vous dise une idée vraie, c'est que ces visages réguliers, nobles et grands, font aussi mal dans une composition historique qu'un bel et grand arbre, bien arrondi, dont le tronc s'élève sans fléchir, dont l'écorce n'offre

---

annotation).
[155] Boileau, quoted by Diderot, in *ibid.*, p. 323.
[156] Hill, "The role of *le monstre*," *op. cit.*, p. 245.
[157] Batteux, *Les beaux-arts réduits à un même principe* (Paris: Durand, 1746), p. 162.
[158] Hill, "The role of *le monstre*," *op. cit.*, p. 248.

ni rides, ni crevasses, ni gerçures . . . . Cela est trop monotone, trop symmétrique."[159]

Considering the brevity of this comment on a highly impressive theoretical approach, I nevertheless come to the conclusion that, in fact, Diderot's teratology mainly serves his aesthetic discourse which, even if I can't further examine this question here, seems to be closely intertwined with his political and philosophical thinking. Diderot thus is in fact less interested in the biological or teratological particularity of the monsters but he uses them metaphorically — or, actually, metaphorologically in the sense of "rudiments on the way from mythos to logos"[160] — in order to nourish his aesthetic and political discourses.

10 Teratology or the 'scientification' of monsters

Nous appellerons donc malformation tout caractère anormal que l'on peut rattacher à une aberration du développement embryonnaire. L'objet de la Tératologie est de définir la nature et la genèse de cette erreur. La plupart des malformations connues rentrent dans ce cadre
Étienne Wolff.[161]

At the beginning of the nineteenth century, teratology, endowed with a rich inventory of descriptions, classifications and definitions, seems to be accepted as a new life science between comparative anatomy, embryology or epigenesis.[162] In the course of development, the formerly 'deviant' monster becomes a key figure for the scientific description of normality.[163] By different experiments the existence of a factual basis for the *imaginaire* of the monster has been proved and scientific theory replaced belief and imagination. At the same time, positivist anthropology dismantled religious myths and their representations. Canguilhem expresses this development as the separation of the notions of 'monstrosity' as biological malformation and the 'monstrous' as the imaginary: "The transparent character of monstrosity from the standpoint of scientific thought, severs any relation it might

---

[159] Diderot, *Salon de 1965*, DPV X, 249.

[160] Hans Blumenberg, *Paradigmen zu einer Metaphorologie* (Frankfurt a.M.: Suhrkamp, 1999), p. 10.

[161] Wolff, *La science des monstres* (Paris: Gallimard, 1948), p. 16.

[162] The experimental approach is represented by Camille Dareste who boasted about having used a chicken embryo on which he had reproduced almost all simple monstrosities described by Saint-Hilaire. In her article "Living Images," Huet draws a line between Dareste's works and the imagination theory: "The genetic accident became a scientific phenomenon, and the researcher assumed the double role played earlier by the desired image and the mother's desiring imagination" (*op. cit.*, p. 74).

[163] Darwin, for one, welcomed Dareste's experiments, calling them "full of promise for the future" (quoted from Canguilhem, "La monstruosité et le monstrueux," *op. cit.*, p. 180).

have had to the monstrous. Realism systematically condemns the monstrous in art to being nothing other than the transfer or copy [*décalque*] of monstrosity."[164]

In order to obtain new results concerning the determination of embryonic anomalies, Étienne Geoffroy Saint-Hilaire in 1826 revives old, Egyptian experiments on artificial incubation: "Je cherchais à entraîner l'organisation dans des voies insolites."[165] According to the *Robert* "insolite" means *abnormal, bizarre, astonishing, extraordinary, exceptional, rare*. A rather unusual description of scientific research which reveals its fantastic aim: "what will we say when, one day, we learn that teratogenic experiments have been carried out on humans?"[166] While pre-scientific discourses of the past centuries treat monsters as *lusus naturae*, they reappear as a kind of scientific contest in the teratological discourse of the nineteenth century which also makes the border between imaginary and real monsters disappear: "If we weren't already familiar with the author, the expression 'chercher à entraîner l'organisation dans des voies insolites' ['seeking to carry *organization* onto unknown paths'] might sound like the announcement of a diabolical project. In this case, the monstrous would indeed be the origin of monstrosities — real ones. What the Middle Ages dreamed of, the century of posivitism carried out, while thinking it was abolishing it" (*ibid.*). In tandem with the superficial disappearance of monsters during the process of naturalization, the experimentally created monstrous returns to (re-)conquer its place in scientific as well as literary and aesthetic discourses: "But how could one resist the temptation to discover the monstrous located at the very heart of the scientific universe, from which it was supposed to have been expelled? How could one not catch the biologist in the act of Surrealism? . . . Could the submission of the scientific mind to the reality of laws be nothing other than a ruse of the Will to Power?"[167]

11 From father ...

Un peu d'histoire naturelle pour terminer.
(Victor Hugo)

Taking into consideration the fundamental studies of Olivier de Serres, Réaumur and Gabriel Jouard, Étienne Geoffroy Saint-Hilaire (1772–1844) publishes a basic work in 1821 treating the observation and classification of

---

[164] *Ibid.*, p. 181.

[165] Quoted from Dareste, *Recherches sur la production artificielle des monstruosités, ou, Essais de tératogénie expérimentale par Camille Dareste* (Paris: Reinwald, 1877), p. 35.

[166] Canguilhem, "La monstruosité et le monstreux," p. 182.

[167] *Ibid.*, p. 181.

monsters in order to scientifically describe the borders between monstrosity and anomaly.[168] Despite his numerous failures, he counts as the 'teratogenetic' predecessor of Camille Dareste, Paul Ancel or Étienne Wolff.

The first volume of his *Philosophie anatomique* (1818) paves the way to evolutionism by firstly refuting the theory of preformationism and, secondly, explicitly naturalizing monsters:

> Par conséquent, si j'ai recueilli quelques documents concernant les monstres, ce ne sont que de seconds fruits dans mes recherches. J'avais voulu d'avantage, et c'était en effet viser plus haut que d'aller chercher dans ce labyrinthe alors inextricable, des preuves aussi nombreuses que décisives du principe de l'unité de composition organique... Les Monstres ne sont plus des jeux de la nature; leur organisation est soumise à la loi commune; *les Monstres sont d'autres êtres normaux; ou plutôt il n'y a pas de Monstres et la Nature est une.*[169]

Monsters thus are completely absorbed by the system of 'normal' nature, for whose integrity they guarantee in return.

According to Étienne Geoffroy Saint-Hilaire, all scientific analyses have to be governed by five principles: first of all, the theory of analogy has to be applied, then the principle of relation has to be established in order to identify one species by defining its relations to others. He thus already considers the monster as the product of an 'arrested' or 'delayed' development, that is, a being that was 'frozen' in an embryonic state. This thesis, however, clearly contradicts the position of Georges Cuvier, as Geoffroy Saint-Hilaire announces in a letter to Georges Sans (July 13th, 1838). Once again, an academic quarrel like the one between Lémery and Winslow begins; the implications of this quarrel concerning the theory of continuity or discontinuity have been extensively discussed by Foucault, for whom Cuvier's view is that God's great miracle, the creation of species, was undertaken once and for all, never to be repeated.[170] As Cuvier puts it,

> C'était tout simplement la plus lourde bêtise qu'il fut possible de proposer à la crédulité humaine... Dieu n'avait point créé des germes ... pour l'éternité ... emboîtés les uns dans les autres

---

[168] Gabriel Jouard's *Des monstruosités et bizarreries de la Nature, principalement de celles qui ont rapport à la génération; de leurs causes; de la manière dont elles s'opèrent, etc., avec des réflexions philosophiques sur les monstrueux et dangereux empiètemens des sciences accessoires ...* 2 vols. (Paris: Allut, 1806-1807) is held up as an example.

[169] E. Geoffroy Saint-Hilaire, quoted from A. Morin, "La tératologie 'De Geoffroy Saint-Hilaire à nos jours'," in *Bulletin de l'Association des Anatomistes* 248 (1996), p. 23 (emphasis mine).

[170] Cf. Foucault, *op. cit.*, chapter 8: "Work, Life and Language."

> ...absurdité révoltante (comme) je l'ai voulu démontrer... J'ai donc adopté cette thèse: Dieu a créé les matières prédisposées à l'organisation, en leur attribuant des conditions virtuelles pour passer par toutes les transformations possibles selon les prescriptions des milieux ambian(t)s incessamment variables. Les formes animales sont donc variables incessamment.[171]

For Étienne Geoffroy Saint-Hilaire, deviations can always be explained by the underlying norm; he justifies his method by referring to the rhetorical principles of Du Marsais (1730): "the monster is the figurative expression of the rule."[172] The metaphorical relation between the monster and the development of norms is thus compared to the relation between the tropes and the grammatical development of language: "but this nature of the trope actually expresses its slow development in comparison to the grammatical evolution of language — just as the monster conveys the sense of slower development than the 'complete' development of a being."[173] The monster (the trope) thus may be understood both as a fixing of origin and proof of a regular evolutionary process.[174]

12 ... To son

> [I]l y a exception aux lois des naturalistes, et non aux lois de la nature; et toutes les espèces sont ce qu'elles doivent être dans ce grand ensemble où règnent partout la variété dans l'unité et l'unité dans la variété (Isidore Geoffroy Saint-Hilaire).[175]

In the context of his article "De la nécessité et des moyens de créer pour les Monstres doubles, une nomenclature rationnelle et méthodique," the "father of teratology"[176] — and son of Étienne — Isidore Geoffroy Saint-Hilaire proposes to integrate all research concerning monsters which, until then had been part of pathological zoology, into the new scientific field of "teratology."[177] The new designation seems to cut off the reference to the curious, the rare and the unbelievable but, in fact, the term *teras*, known

---

[171] E. Geoffroy Saint-Hilaire, quoted from Morin, "La tératologie," *op. cit.*, p. 23 (emphasis mine).

[172] Tort, "La logique du déviant," *op. cit.*, p. 24.

[173] *Ibid.* (in the sense that the trope is a remnant of an archaic phrase of the grammatical development of the language).

[174] Cf. Tort, *La constellation de Thot* (Paris: Aubier, 1981), chapter "Taxinomie et transfiguralité."

[175] *Histoire des anomalies, op. cit.*, p. 37.

[176] In fact, he calls himself the "father of teratology": see "De la nécessité et des moyens de créer pour les Monstres doubles, une nomenclature rationnelle et méthodique," in *Annales des Sciences Naturelles* (juillet 1830).

[177] At the age of 19, Isidore became "aide naturaliste" in his father's laboratory in the

since antiquity as an ambiguous word, causes the same uncertainty: on the one hand it is a monstrous being, on the other hand it possesses all the qualities of a sign.[178] The first meaning locates the term within the realm of natural history, whereas the second meaning obviously refers to the context of prophecy. In fact, the latter sense was older, so that it was prophecy which supplied natural history with the term describing its malformations.

In his most important work, *Histoire générale et particulière des anomalies . . . ou traité de tératologie*,[179] Isidore Geoffroy Saint-Hilaire divides the history of teratology into three different phases: the childhood of science, the so-called *période fabuleuse* before the eighteenth century, still relies on medieval superstition. During this period monstrous births were often quite simply killed, a barbarian habit which Jean Riolan, about whom we heard earlier, does not seem to disapprove of: "On peut se dispenser de faire périr sexdigitaires, les macrocéphales, les géants et les nains, et il suffit de les reléguer loin de tous les regards."[180] The *période positive* during the first half of the eighteenth century obviously emphasizes the importance of scientific observation, but most of the examinations are still based less on scientific interest than on pure sensation. The third and last phase, the *période scientifique* began with the publication of the revolutionary works of Haller in the middle of the century.[181] It is interesting that the second representative of this era is Montaigne with his fundamental text "D'un enfant monstrueux,"[182] which, according to Isidore Geoffroy Saint-Hilaire largely confirms his own definition of anomaly in the sense of "insolite" or "inaccoutumé."[183] Including different pieces of scientific knowledge, Isidore

---

Musée d'Histoire Naturelle. In 1829 his dissertation *Propositions sur la monstruosité considérée chez l'homme et les animaux* appeared, followed by the *Histoire générale et particulière des anomalies de l'organisation chez l'homme et les animaux ou Traité de Tératologie* (1832-1837), a monograph on a "nouveau genre de monstres parasitaires" (1851), an article about "un nouveau genre de monstres doubles" as well as the *Histoire générale des règnes organiques* (1854).

[178] He rejects the etymological root 'monere' for the notions of "monstre" and "monstruosité," but for his new science he returns to the root 'tera' which, in fact, has the same meaning.

[179] *Histoire générale et particulière des anomalies de l'organisation chez l'homme et les animaux . . ., ou traité de tératologie, op. cit.*, vol. 1, p. 5.

[180] Quoted from I. Geoffroy Saint-Hilaire, *Histoire des anomalies, op. cit.*, p. 6.

[181] Albrecht Haller, *De monstris dissertatio 2., qua trium monstrorum anatome etad contraria D. Lemeryi argumenta responsiones continentur*, Göttingen [c. 1738]; *id., Ad disputationem inauguralem docitissimi viri Henrici Christiani Zencker Clausthaliensis de opii partibus constitutivis ... invitat suamque et Winslowi de monstris sententiam contra D. Lemery N. F. novis argumentis defendit* (Göttingen, 1745); *id., Opuscula sua anatomica de respiratione de monstris aliaque minora recensuit* (Göttingen: Schmidt, 1751).

[182] *Essais* II, 30.

[183] I. Geoffroy Saint-Hilaire, *Histoire des anomalies*, p. 40.

Geoffroy Saint-Hilaire follows his plan to establish a methodical classification in order to integrate the monsters in the natural system of general rules of organization:

> The monster gradually ceases to be identified with an impure disorder of anatomical elements, and then brings about order in classification. This is apparently a fairly straightforward process — a consequence of the connection between the progress in anatomical observation of teratological cases, the accumulation of cases, the first experiments in artificial teratogenesis (with Étienne Geoffroy Saint-Hilaire), the development of embryology, the decline of the dogma of preformationism, the rise of comparative anatomy, the widespread use in natural history of Linnean nomenclature, Cuvier's introduction of the natural method in zoology, and lastly, the increasing influence of the theory of the unity of the organic compositional schema. Isidore Geoffroy Saint-Hilaire's teratology indeed benefits from the convergence of various discourses and practices of organization and reorganization of positive knowledge and inquiry in the natural sciences.[184]

Like Linnaeus, Isidore Geoffroy Saint-Hilaire focuses on significant characteristics in order to trace back their development: "Les variations normales et anormales des organes et des appareils ne sont que des modifications d'un fond commun et identique soumises à l'empire des lois communes."[185] The specific type, determined by an average development and structure of the specie, derives from normal and abnormal variation. Each deviation from this type thus counts as anomaly.

According to the model of embryology, the relationship between different anomalies has to be examined and proved: "the descriptive teratology of the 'scientific period' implies a teratogenesis, which obviously could only take place after normal embryogenesis, and based on it."[186] The particularity of teratology thus lies – according to Isidore Geoffroy Saint-Hilaire — in this so-called "effet en retour," "after normal embryogenesis." Hence the new scientific field is not simply an annex of natural history, zoology or — as was the case with the classification established by Étienne Geoffroy Saint-Hilaire — pathological anatomy: "teratology can only be presented methodically because it has been re-ordered, in its descriptive and classificatory dimensions, by a science of 'anomal' formations, a teratogenesis which has found

---

[184]Tort, "La logique du déviant," p. 12.
[185]I. Geoffroy Saint-Hilaire, quoted from Morin, "La tératologie," *op. cit.*
[186]Tort, "La logique du déviant," p. 13.

its status at last."[187]

The modern concept of anomaly thus has to be understood as a product of an abnormal evolution, a chain of relations set off by a particular cause.[188] This approach integrates both the individual case (the particular cause) and the subsequent abnormal development. Only by constantly representing genetic development can teratology define and classify the various deviations. As Foucault has demonstrated, the taxonomic nomenclature does not refer to similarities between words and things, but merely establishes relations between words. Monstrosity and normality thus are not essentially different, but their difference is produced by misguided rules and defective mechanics which interrupt or delay normal development. This approach finds its expressions both in a simplified denomination of individual deviations and in their classification in the 'normal' system.

> La théorie de l'arrêt de développement montre enfin le vide caché sous de telles explications. Elle fait voir que jusqu'alors on s'était payé de mots, et qu'on avait délaissé les faits. À l'idée d'êtres bizarres, irreguliers, elle [sc. teratology, B.O.] substitue celle, plus vraie et plus philosophique, d'êtres entravés dans leurs développements, et où des organes de l'âge embryonnaire, conservés jusqu'à la naissance, sont venus s'associer à ceux de l'âge foetal. La monstruosité n'est plus un désordre aveugle, mais un autre ordre également régulier, également soumis à des lois; ou, si l'on veut, c'est le mélange d'un ordre ancien et d'un ordre nouveau, la présence simultanée de deux états, qui, ordinairement, se succèdent l'un à l'autre.[189]

What was once a *lusus naturæ* thus 'artificially' represents individual continuous phases of evolution: "Monstrosity is the fixing of the development of

---

[187] *Ibid.*

[188] The double monster examined by Étienne Geoffroy Saint-Hilaire might serve as an example: "Ils nous conduisent à cette considération très curieuse et très propre à simplifier au plus haut degré l'étude de la monstruosité double, que deux sujets réunis sont entre eux ce que sont l'une à l'autre la moitié droite et la moitié gauche d'un individu normal; en sorte qu'un monstre double n'est, si l'on peut s'exprimer ainsi, qu'un être composé de quatre moitiés plus ou moins complètes, au lieu de deux" (Tort, "La logique du deviant," p. 17). Étienne Geoffroy Saint-Hilaire calls this law "loi de l'affinité de soi pour soi," later on he'll describe it as teratogenetic processes of growing together and fusion. This law confirms the supposed analogy between the laws of teratological and normal organisation. Isidore Geoffroy Saint-Hilaire will call it a "corollaire de la théorie générale de l'unité de composition organique" (*Histoire des anomalies, op. cit.*, p. 466).

[189] *Ibid.*, "Introduction," p. 18. In fact, the genealogical theory of the *arrêts de développement* dates back to the eighteenth century and its anthropological concepts of cultural difference. Later on, in the nineteenth century, it will be reflected in the approaches of comparative linguistics and history of language.

an organ at an earlier stage than others. It is the endurance of a transitional embryonic form. For an organism in any given species, today's monstrosity is yesterday's normal state. And in the comparative series of species, it might be that the monstrous form in one is the normal form in another."[190]

By connecting different fetal states, the new theory establishes a logic of monstrous forms in the scope of an embryo-genetic determinism. Thus a correct lecture of the deviant structures directly reveals the rule of the 'normal':[191] "the anatomical disorder of the monstrous *organisation* is simply the spatial translation of the order of genesis of normal *organisation*, but stuck in one of its moments. . . Normal embryogenesis can now serve as a stable, unified and coherent foundation for a teratology, which by this means can be methodical."[192] As for the *monstres par excès*, there the theory of 'excentric development' can be applied. Here, as in the above-mentioned theory of 'arrest in development',[193] different phases of monstrous development are compared to normal development in order to reveal the active rules: "Les monstres, d'après la nouvelle théorie, sont, à quelques égards, des embryons permanents, ils nous montrent à leur naissances des organes simples comme aux premiers jours de formation, comme si la nature se fût arrêtée en chemin, pour donner à notre observation trop lente, le temps et les moyens de l'atteindre."[194]

Frozen in an eternal embryonic state, monsters — a series of snapshots to assist the insufficient human capacity for scientific observation — help the scientists reach and understand nature. Geoffroy Saint-Hilaire's model firstly postulates a kind of reflexive relation between normal and abnormal development and, secondly, it understands monsters as the origin of man,[195] a thesis which later ethnological studies about the savage will refer to. Regarding this universal classification system, a certain 'vertigo' of taxonomic efforts seems to be justified:[196] "Each part of the table . . ., each entry,

---

[190]Canguilhem, "La monstruosité et le monstrueux," p. 38.

[191]Beneke considers Meckel to be the founder of scientific teratology, because Meckel understands the "Ergebnisse der normalen und abnormen Entwicklungsvorgänge als gleichwertige und unentbehrliche Grundlagen der Formenwelt" (Rudolf Beneke, *Johann Friedrich Meckel der Jüngere* [Halle: Niemeyer, 1934], p. 68). The difference between monstrosities and varieties is only a question of their degree of deviation.

[192]Tort, "La logique du déviant," p. 19.

[193]As to the theory of "arrest of developpement, leading to the diminution or suppressions of parts" see Darwin, *The Descent of Man, and Selection in Relation to Sex*, in P.H. Barrett & R.B. Freeman, eds., *The Works of Charles Darwin*, vols. 21 and 22 (New York: New York University Press, 1987), p. 34.

[194]I. Geoffroy Saint-Hilaire, *Histoire des anomalies, op. cit.*, p. 19.

[195]". . . les êtres inférieurs sont comme des embryons permanents des êtres supérieurs; et réciproquement, les êtres supérieurs, avant de présenter les formes définitives qui les caractérisent, ont offert transitoirement celles des êtres inférieurs" (*ibid.*, p. 436).

[196]Étienne Geoffroy Saint-Hilaire already parts from the idea of a common natural

each jetty is not both a part and the whole, a part for the whole, synecdoche and metonymy, indeed a part larger than the whole, but a jetty whose momentum, movement, and structure, both internal and internalizing, takes it beyond the whole and folds it back on the whole to comprehend it and speak before it."[197] Bringing up the classification of anatomical anomalies, the epistemological condition reveals a complex network concerning the representations of the different relations between rules and deviations as well as science and metaphysics. In order to elude the aesthetic-metaphysical argument of the single image, the deviation, in a first step, has to be elucidated in order to disappear in the serialization of individual images in a second step:

> Rather than insisting on the absolute idiosyncrasy of the deviant structure, accidentalist pathology was the only logical way to turn monstrosity — removed from providentialism — into an object of science. But the concept of order then also has to undergo a shift so it can include the very 'fact' of these gaps (the typology of which can be arranged parallel to the series of stages in normal development), and reflect the theory of embryo development, thus becoming an 'evolutionary' order.[198]

The teratological structures absorb the monster until it finally seems to vanish.[199] At the same time, however, different monstrous figures reappear in ethnological, sociological, anthropological discourses or are reanimated by literature, photography and film, thus paving a new way for the theory of difference. The monster is dead, long live the monster or, probably each medium creates its own monsters? In fact,

> it was in the nineteenth century . . . that teratology normalized the representation of the monster. But at the same time — and thanks to the same schemas — the logic of deviance, in the service of a very old ideology, reintroduces the theory of *arrêts*

'plan', a kind of homogeneous typus who underlies all different individual forms. This method, however, leads straightaway to the positivist construction of normality according to Auguste Comte or the physiognomical-phrenological appraoches of Cesare Lombroso. The teratological exception has to be reduced to the underlying rule, and "le triomphe complet de l'ordre s'inscrit dans la réduction du désordre à une simple apparence" (Tort, "La logique du déviant," *op. cit.*, p. 19) even if this "simple apparence," the all-organizing order is not visible.

[197] Derrida, "Some Statements and Truisms," p. 67.
[198] Tort, "La logique du déviant," p. 22.
[199] Bataille compares this striking disappearance of all interferences and faults to the "accursed share" of Hegel's systems, i.e. poetry, laughter or ecstasy and their (re-)functionalization in other contexts. (See Charitos, "Un monstre du rire et un rire monstrueux," *op. cit.*).

or delays in evolution in the combined field of sociology and anthropology, and thereby naturalizes inequality and 'anomalizes' difference.[200]

---

[200]Tort, "La logique du déviant," p. 25.

INDEX

abnormal, abnormality, 170n., 176, 201–203, 215, 230, 232, 235, 240, 275, 277
Académie des Sciences, 62, 84–86, 88–91, 94–95, 97–99, 103, 106, 155, 174, 255, 265
accidental, 19n., 45, 52, 58, 72, 92, 96–98, 149n., 183, 194–196, 255–256
   (accidentalism), 260, 267
   accidental cause, 58, 92, 96–98, 194–195
Aeschylus, 16
aesthetic(s), 38, 52, 55, 59, 215, 242, 264–271, 278
Albertus Magnus, 17n., 124, 239
Aldrovandi, U., 71, 74, 80, 106, 245, 251
analogy, analogies, 5–6, 9, 13–14, 163, 165, 182–184, 236, 257, 272, 276n.
anatomy, anatomists, 37, 63, 72, 75, 82, 86–101, 103–104, 106, 116–117, 120–124, 126, 150, 153–168, 170, 173–174, 178, 183–184, 194, 196, 207–208, 210, 214, 240, 245, 254, 256–257, 262, 270, 275, 277–278
Anaxagoras, 8, 13, 15n.
androgyny, 221, 235
animal(s), 1–3, 5–19, 56, 65, 69, 71, 79, 84–85, 91–92, 94, 98, 105, 110, 114–129, 140, 142–143, 146–149, 154–156, 159, 164, 183, 194, 197, 210, 214, 226, 233, 237, 239, 264
anomaly, anomalies, 38, 106, 153, 156, 158–159, 161, 165, 168, 170, 172, 174, 176, 178, 185, 192, 200, 202, 207, 233, 260, 263–264, 271, 274–276
apes, 110–111, 116, 118–124, 126–128
Aquinas, T., 19n., 39n., 52n., 240
Ariew, R., 131
Aristotle, 1–19, 39, 44–45, 53, 57, 67, 69, 71–72, 75–77, 83, 103, 111, 194, 201, 232–233, 250
ataraxia, 22–23, 25, 27, 31–34
atomism, 22, 30–31, 174, 180
Augustine, 40–42, 44, 47, 52, 54–55, 58, 68–69, 73, 74, 79, 100–103, 235, 236, 239, 247
Averroes, Averroism, 42, 48, 50, 52

Bacon, F., 83, 113, 114, 158, 177, 191, 203, 242
Baltrusaïtis, J., 37
baptism, 77–78, 85, 188–189, 198
Bauhin, C., 65, 68, 71, 75, 87, 91, 252
beauty, 40, 52, 74, 105, 219, 244, 251, 269
Bichat, X., 209

INDEX

biology, biological, 1, 4–13
   (Aristotelian), 29, 44, 47, 58, 110–112, 115, 124, 135, 177n., 179, 203–204, 206–208, 211–212, 268
Bitbol-Hespériès, A., 61
Blumenbach, J.F., 213
Blumenberg, H., 26, 30–31, 34
Boaistuau, P., 63–68, 73, 78–79, 245
body, bodies, 3, 5–6, 9n., 18, 48, 63, 66, 70, 72–73, 77, 81–82, 87–88, 94, 121, 124, 158–161, 164, 175n., 205–206, 209, 227
Bonnet, C., 261, 267
Bordeu, T. de, 178, 180, 184–185, 203, 268
boundaries, 32–33, 111, 114, 116, 118, 124, 126, 173, 198–199
brain, 85, 89, 122, 160, 165, 193, 208–211
breeding, 113, 116, 127, 198
Bretonne, R. de la, 203, 263
Buffon, G.-L.-L. de, 200n., 257–258
Buissière, P., 159–160, 165
Bulwer, J., 110, 119, 122–124
Burdach, K. F., 210–211

Canguilhem, G., 37–38, 44, 55, 173, 204, 270
Cardano, 45–46, 48–51, 56–58, 64
Cartesian, 83, 85, 91, 93, 112, 124, 175, 255, 261
cause(s), causality, 2, 4, 10–11, 13–14, 22, 41, 53–54, 56–57, 69, 75, 96, 113, 148, 154–157, 162, 167, 192–195, 249, 251, 255n. (see also 'efficient cause', 'final cause')

Céard, J., 239, 245, 249–251
chain of being, 51, 164, 198, 200
chance, 14, 85–86, 88, 102, 112–113, 170–172, 175–176, 178–181, 195, 261
Charleton, W., 112–113, 117
chimæras, 29, 248, 251, 268
Cicero, 39n., 70n., 79, 234, 236
conjoined twins, 61–67, 69–73, 76–78, 85–86, 90–92, 94–96, 99–100, 105–106, 154, 158–159, 161, 166–167
contra naturam, 39n., 75–76, 177, 189–190, 208, 237, 240, 252 (see also nature, against)
cosmos, 7, 16–17, 31
curiosity, 30–31, 33–34, 39, 105, 131, 151, 168, 169
curiosities, 131, 134, 136, 151, 168, 191, 255, 261, 264
Cuvier, G., 272

Dagron, T., 37
Dapper, O., 117–119, 124, 126
Dareste, C., 183, 203, 270n.
Darwin, C., 112, 192n.
Darwinian, 15, 116, 201
Daston, L., 155, 162, 168, 192n., 242n.
Davidson, A., 162
death, 86, 185, 220
Democritus, 21, 194
Descartes, R., 62, 74, 80–84, 90–91, 104, 106, 110, 113, 123n., 151, 209, 261
design, 13–14, 68, 87, 91, 97–102, 105, 113, 128, 161, 176, 182, 194,
Diderot, D., 169–186, 188, 190–191, 196, 199–204, 265–270

disorder, 172–174, 176, 261, 265, 275, 277
dissection, 76–77, 84, 86, 92–93, 95, 99, 121, 157–161, 166, 174, 229,
Douglas, J., 161
Duhem, P., 236
Duverney, J.-G., 86–93, 95–97, 101, 103, 105, 159, 161, 167, 174, 194, 195, 256
dwarf, 164

efficient cause, 4, 46, 148
embryo, 56, 69, 72, 82, 84, 100, 125, 167, 173, 214
embryogenesis, 110–113, 195, 213, 270, 275–277
embryology, 37, 72, 82, 111–112, 127, 129, 170, 208, 214, 255–256, 270, 275
Empedocles, 1, 13–18, 24, 176, 242
Enlightenment, 35, 169, 195, 249, 261, 263
Epicurus, Epicureanism, 21–23, 26–28, 30–31, 34, 88, 176
epigenesis, epigenetic, 167, 174, 212–214, 259, 261, 264
epistemology, epistemological, 39, 42, 54–55, 200, 207, 246
essence, 2–3, 38, 42–43, 47, 52–53, 110–111, 114, 129, 165, 196–198, 251
ethics, 22, 34–35, 47
evolution, evolutionism, 15, 115, 121, 128, 171, 176, 196n., 214–215, 244, 249, 258–261, 266, 272–273, 276
explanation(s), 2, 29, 40, 64, 69, 74–75, 80, 82, 86, 93, 98–99, 112, 134, 149, 155, 162, 177, 180, 193–196, 201n., 202, 211, 235, 252, 256, 261, 264

fear, 7, 21, 30, 218
female, 3, 11–12, 45, 125, 233 (see also 'woman')
fetus, 53, 68–70, 85, 86, 90–92, 94, 97–98, 104, 111, 125, 174, 192, 194, 198, 255,
final cause, 41, 45, 52–53, 72, 83, 91, 177, 180, 194
Fontenelle, B. de, 84, 85, 88–89, 92, 99, 103, 132, 155–156, 175, 190, 203, 255
form, 3–8, 10–13, 18, 38, 42–45, 52n., 53, 59, 76, 110, 127, 148, 155, 208, 214, 232–233, 252–253
Formey, J.-H.-S., 257, 262
forms, 7, 10, 39, 42, 47, 53–54, 112, 173, 177–178, 198, 200, 202, 208, 214, 262, 268, 277,
fossils, 142, 144–149
Foucault, M., 54n., 107, 158, 206, 258, 262, 272, 276
Freind, J., 157
Fritsche, J., 1
functionalism, 3, 5, 13, 16–17
function, 3, 5–9, 81–82, 182, 206–207, 209–211, 229, 240–241

Galen, 68–69, 72, 83, 87
Gall, F., 209–210
games of nature (*lusus naturæ*), 84–85, 146–147, 149n., 152, 175, 195, 231, 235, 266, 271, 276
Gassendi, P., 118, 126
generation, 44–45, 67, 68–71, 82,

96, 110, 114, 154–155, 166–167, 174, 213, 259,
genetics, 179, 192, 219
genus, 6, 11, 43–46, 50, 53, 124, 229,
giants, 147n., 154, 159, 163–164, 167
Geoffroy Saint-Hilaire, E., 105–106, 193, 256, 259, 271–273, 275–276n.
Geoffroy Saint-Hilaire, I., 63, 105–107, 170–173, 193, 249, 251, 256, 273–277
goats, monstrous, 117, 137–138
goat–men, 184, 186, 203
goat–stag, 2–3, 7, 17, 19n.
Guerrini, A., 153
Guido of Mont Rocher, 188

Hagner, M., 157n., 201n., 205, 232n.
Haller, A. von, 99–101, 104–106, 180, 188, 194–195, 256, 261, 274
harmony, 41–42, 52, 55, 59, 139, 174, 207, 268
Hegel, G.W.F., 205, 211–212, 215
Heidegger, M., 4
hermaphrodite(s), 65, 72, 75, 166–167, 179, 180, 202, 235, 266
Herodotus, 116
Hesiod, 1, 16
d'Holbach, Baron, 197, 203, 265
human, humanity, 4, 11–13, 25, 30–31, 40, 45–46, 71, 86, 110–112, 116, 119–126, 154, 159, 165, 196, 205, 210, 218, 221, 228, 239–240
hybrid, 111, 116–117, 124–129, 182–183, 186, 192, 203, 237, 251, 268

Ibrahim, A., 169, 190, 256
identity, 12, 54n., 55, 165, 203, 239, 244
imagination, 2, 61, 67, 90, 104, 125, 193, 194
  maternal, 174, 175n.
irrational, 7, 19, 22, 98, 249–250
Isidore of Seville, 236, 238

Jäger, G.F., 213
Jaucourt, L. de, 184, 191, 262
Jelinek, E., 217

Kant, I., 184
Kielmeyer, C. F., 215
kind(s), 18, 43, 110, 112–113, 129 (see also 'genus', 'natural kinds')

La Fosse, 188–189, 195, 262
La Mettrie, J.O. de, 175n., 197
laws of nature, 2, 13n., 41n., 62, 65, 74, 80, 82–84, 91, 93, 101–103, 175, 189n., 199, 203, 238, 246, 261
Le Comte, L., 118
Leibniz, G., 105, 131–152, 193n., 196, 198–200, 236n., 255
Lémery, L., 90–100, 102, 154, 167, 174, 180–183, 194–195, 255–257, 272
Liceti, F., 66, 71, 76n., 78–81, 126n., 191, 245, 252–253, 259
life, 69, 77, 81, 185, 201n., 206–208, 213
Locke, J., 110–112, 114, 124, 127, 129, 189, 194, 197–198, 203
Lucretius, Lucretian, 23–35, 71, 170, 176–177, 200, 260n., 268

Malebranche, N., 90, 93, 111–112, 174–175, 193, 255
Malesherbes, C. de, 200n., 261
man, 4, 8, 45, 49, 110, 112, 114, 125, 189, 201, 232
marvels, marvelous, 39, 68, 80, 88, 146, 197, 231, 238
material cause, 58, 148 (see also 'accidental cause', 'efficient cause')
materialist, materialism, 22, 31, 34–35, 49n., 169, 172, 176, 178, 186, 189, 192–193, 196, 201–204
matter, 3, 5, 8, 12, 25, 45–46, 52, 57–58, 62, 75–76, 80, 110, 122, 148, 169, 176–177, 181, 199–200, 212, 233, 252–253, 260
Maupertuis, P.-L. M. de, 179, 183–185, 192, 201n., 258–261
mechanism, mechanistic, 81–82, 87–88, 110–112, 149, 155–157, 169, 172, 176, 182, 193
Meckel, J. F., 207, 210, 214, 277n.
medical, medicine, 65, 68–70, 72, 74, 77, 79–82, 85, 87, 91, 144, 150, 178, 185–186, 208, 253, 264
Megenberg, K. von, 240
Meis, M., 21
Melissus, 3
Mersenne, M., 81n., 151–152
metaphysics, 15n., 75, 91, 99, 112, 123–124, 132–136, 149, 167, 169, 173–174, 181, 194, 196, 201, 203, 256, 278
miracle, 39n., 41, 47, 54, 151, 197, 231–232, 234–235, 239, 242, 248, 251–252, 260, 265,

272
molecule, 178–181, 184–186, 190, 268
Molyneux, T., 154–155, 162–165, 167
monstration, 173, 190–191, 241
monstrous births, 40, 45, 53, 62–63, 67, 70, 73, 75, 78, 83n., 89–90, 106, 112, 125, 158–161, 165–167, 189, 191–195, 213–215, 239, 242, 244, 274
Montaigne, M. de, 38–40, 42–44, 47, 53–55, 59, 67, 196, 246–248, 275
Monti, M.T., 155
morals, morality, 48–49, 58, 116, 123n., 190, 199, 239, 268–269
morphology, 72, 155, 165–166, 214, 236, 244,

natural kinds, 115–116, 128, 197
natural laws, see 'laws of nature'
natural selection, 112, 129, 266
naturalism, naturalist, 22, 42, 48, 49n., 51n., 54, 58, 147, 178, 191
naturalization, 31, 83n., 153, 188, 190–193, 232n., 233, 240, 246, 254, 261, 263–265, 271–272, 279
nature, 2, 7, 19, 24, 27, 29, 39–44, 48, 50, 62, 73, 80–81, 104, 156, 183–184, 201–202, 226, 232–233, 243n., 265
    against, 12, 39n., 41, 44, 54, 104, 188, 250, 252
Nizami al Arudi, 117
nominal essence, 114, 197, 199

nominalist, nominalism, 47, 114–116, 129, 202
norm(s), 16, 38–41, 45, 47, 51–52, 55, 59, 79, 158, 164, 172–173, 201–202, 207, 247, 260, 273
normal, normality, 38, 41, 47, 87, 154–155, 158–159, 165, 168, 170n., 176, 201–202, 209, 213, 215, 233, 240, 244, 247, 257, 270. 275–277
Nussbaum, M., 26–27, 31

Ochsner, B., 231
ontology, 17, 52, 110–112, 115–116, 127, 203
orang-outang, 116–117, 121, 127
order, 38, 40–46, 52, 57–58, 93–94, 129, 165, 168, 169, 173, 176–178, 199, 202, 208, 236, 246, 256, 265, 268n., 278
organs, 5–6, 13, 50, 62, 72, 76, 81, 98, 100, 122, 158–161, 179–180, 183–184, 194, 197, 201, 208–209

Paré, A., 63–68, 71–74, 78–81, 83, 86–87, 93, 156, 245, 249
Paracelsus, 124–126, 244
Park, K., 83n., 155, 168, 192n.
Parmenides, 3, 24
Parsons, J., 154, 166–167
passions, 29–31, 34–35, 77
Peter the Great, 150–151
philosophy, 2, 7, 26, 73, 83, 132, 134–135, 196, 208
physics, 23, 30, 35, 80–83, 103, 132, 135, 149
Plato, 2–3, 8
Pliny, 71, 117, 201n., 234–236, 242, 244

Plutarch, 76, 234
Pomponazzi, 42n., 48, 51n., 57–58
precursor, 171, 179
preformation, preformationism, 167, 180, 194, 213, 255–261, 264, 272, 275
probability, 102, 177, 180–181, 204
prodigies, 29, 41, 47, 51, 53, 56, 65, 68, 70n., 73, 78, 83, 89–90, 105, 189, 197, 231, 234, 236, 240, 242, 249, 252
providence, providentialism, 41–43, 47, 50, 52–53, 56–58, 70, 88, 91, 93, 99, 101, 155, 167, 194, 278
pygmies, 117, 121–122, 234

Rabelais, F., 242–244
race, 40, 43, 203, 234–235, 238, 242, 244–246
rational, rationality, 19, 24, 29, 38, 45, 53, 155, 173, 176, 188, 199, 236, 250, 261, 268
real essence, 110–111, 114, 197–199 (see also 'essence')
Réaumur, R.-A. de, 192, 203, 261, 271
Riolan, J., 64, 76–78, 80–81, 87–88, 91, 95, 252–253, 274
Rüff, J., 69–71, 75, 77, 79
Ruysch, F., 157, 159

Sade, D.A.F. de, 190
Schenck, J.G., 64, 71, 78, 79, 252–253
science, 2–3, 6n., 22, 31, 34, 38, 110, 131–135, 171–172, 192–193, 206–209, 261, 270
Scipion Du Pleix, 135n., 151, 251–252

signs, 56–57, 70n., 74, 78–79, 189, 191–193, 203, 231–232, 236, 238–239, 241–246, 250–253, 274
sin, 43, 48–49, 80, 102, 124, 193
slaves, 7–10, 17
Smith, J E.H., 109
soul, 18–19, 48–49, 61–62, 69, 77, 81, 110, 122–124, 188–189, 209, 240
species, 7, 10, 12, 15–18, 33, 39–40, 43–47, 51–53, 58–59, 71, 76, 97–98, 110–116, 121, 124, 126–128, 149n., 156, 162, 164, 177, 184–186, 191, 194, 197–202, 229, 233, 260, 267, 272, 277
spectacle, 47, 62, 64–67, 73, 79, 81, 157
Sphinx, 10–11, 14, 17
Spinoza, Spinozist, 40, 177, 268

taxonomy, 54, 111, 117, 124, 127, 129, 250, 257, 276
teleology, teleological, 13–14, 72, 76, 82–84, 86–91, 95, 97–98, 101, 103, 111, 129, 154–155, 171, 215
teleonomy, 179
teratology, 37, 58, 63, 79, 105–106, 170–173, 192–193, 203, 214, 231, 238, 249, 256–257, 267–268, 270–278
theology, theological, 44, 52–53, 55, 62, 68–70, 74–75, 79, 86–87, 89, 91, 95, 99–103, 112–113, 132, 135, 156, 165, 198, 238, 250, 255
Tiedemann, F., 214–215
transformism, 170, 196, 260
Trembley, A., 182, 267
Treviranus, G. R., 206, 208

Tulpius, N., 117, 126
twins, 61–66, 68–70, 72–74, 76–78, 84–90, 92, 94, 99, 100, 103, 105–106, 166, 194, 195
Tyson, E., 116, 119–124, 126–129, 159, 162, 167

unicorn(s), 140–146, 149, 151

Vanini, G.C., 48–53, 55, 57–59
viability, 29, 33, 64, 155,165, 179, 202
Voltaire, F.–M.–A., 30–31, 33–35, 103, 175n., 261, 264

Williams, D., 240–241
Winslow, J.–B., 91, 94–102, 104, 154, 167, 174, 182, 194–195, 255
Wolfe, C.T., 187
Wolff, C.F., 212
woman, 67, 89, 125–127, 201, 218, 232–233 (see also 'female')
wonder, 41, 44, 68, 73, 82, 154, 161–162, 168, 189, 242n., 251, 266

zoology, 129, 150, 206, 245, 275

www.ingramcontent.com/pod-product-compliance
Lightning Source LLC
Chambersburg PA
CBHW031707230426
43668CB00006B/135